CULTURAL
ANTHROPOLOGY

RANDOM HOUSE · NEW YORK

CULTURAL ANTHROPOLOGY

University of Michigan **Conrad Phillip Kottak**

Copyright © 1974, 1975 by Random House, Inc.

All rights reserved under International and Pan-American Copyright Conventions. No part of this book may be reproduced in any form or by any means, electronic or mechanical, including photocopying, without permission in writing from the publisher. All inquiries should be addressed to Random House, Inc., 201 East 50th Street, New York, N.Y. 10022. Published in the United States by Random House, Inc., and simultaneously in Canada by Random House of Canada Limited, Toronto.

Library of Congress Cataloging in Publication Data

Kottak, Conrad Phillip, 1942–
  Cultural anthropology.
    Abridged ed. of the author's Anthropology: the exploration of
    human diversity.
    1. Ethnology. I. Kottak, Conrad Phillip. Anthropology: the
    exploration of human diversity. II. Title.
GN315.   K64   301.2   74–19179
ISBN 0–394–31905–2

Designed by James M. Wall

Cover Credits:
Francisco Hidago/Woodfin Camp
Lynn Millar/Rapho Guillumette

First Edition
9 8 7 6 5 4 3 2 1

Manufactured in the United States of America. Composed by Cherry Hill Composition, Pennsauken, N.J. Printed and bound by Halliday Lithograph Corp., West Hanover, Mass.

Dedicated to my mother,
MARIANA KOTTAK ROBERTS

PREFACE

Over the dozen or so semesters that I have taught Anthropology 101, a one-trimester introduction to anthropology, at the University of Michigan, I have considered adopting one of the various textbooks in the field. For various reasons, however, I never did. I have found most to be anthropology cookbooks, attempts to provide encyclopedias of anthropology more oriented toward anthropologists' data than toward the interests and organizing principles that hold anthropology together. Others, while less eclectic, seemed to forget the interests of contemporary college students, to supply an overabundance of detail, or to be written on a more advanced level than most beginners in anthropology appreciate.

This book *Cultural Anthropology* is a brief and slightly revised version of my *Anthropology: The Exploration of Human Diversity* (Random House, 1974). The original book was written for introductory general anthropology courses and for semester-long cultural anthropology courses whose instructors wished to provide a broad background in anthropology as a field. The present brief edition is designed for use in quarter, trimester, and semester courses that deal exclusively with the field of cultural anthropology.

I do not intend this book to be a bible or sole source for any anthropology course. In order that case studies and other paperbacks presenting contrasting views about some issues in anthropology can be assigned along with this book, I have tried to eliminate some details which I have found only confuse beginning students.

I confess that in some ways the extraction of *Cultural Anthropology* offends my sense of the unity of anthropology as a discipline. Unlike any other discipline, anthropology as a general field draws its data from different times and different places, imparting a comparative and historical dimension to the study of human life. *Anthropology: The Exploration of Human Diversity* integrates the four subdisciplines—biological, archeological, linguistic, and sociocultural anthropology—through a common set of evolutionary and adaptive principles. The present brief edition, in excluding chapters on biological and archeological anthropology, inevitably eliminates some of the studies and data that most convincingly demonstrate evolution through sociocultural means and the import of ecological relationships for understanding human behavior.

Nevertheless, *Cultural Anthropology* retains

the ecological and evolutionary interpretations of its parent text, though its time span is more limited. The changes documented and discussed herein are relatively recent and involve colonialism and the spread of international political and economic relationships. Chapters 13 and 14 are especially significant for the understanding of recent change.

In *Cultural Anthropology* I have tried to present a readable, integrated account of some major interests of contemporary cultural anthropologists and their students. I believe that this book is unique among presently available texts in cultural anthropology by virtue of its discussions of evolutionary and ecological theory, including theories of the origin of the state; ethical problems facing contemporary anthropologists; culture and poverty; and underdevelopment in Third World nations. I have tried also to provide readable discussions of the major topical interests of cultural anthropology, including varieties of kinship and descent groups, marriage patterns, kinship terminology, and the comparative study of political organization, economics, religion, personality, and language. The result, I hope, will help students appreciate the anthropologist's fascination with, and respect for, contemporary human diversity.

While I accept full responsibility for presentation and interpretation, several colleagues, including my former teachers, fellow faculty members, and students, will recognize their influence on my ideas and exposition.

Marvin Harris has been a source of intellectual stimulation since my undergraduate days at Columbia University. Lambros Comitas, Georges Condominas, Morton Fried, Daniel Gross, Robert Murphy, Elliott Skinner, and Charles Wagley guided me to many of the interests discussed in this book.

I have profited from my exposure to the varieties of evolutionary and comparative thought exemplified by such men as Marshall Sahlins, Elman Service, Julian Steward, Leslie White, and Eric Wolf. My interest in ecological interpretations of anthropological phenomena was developed with Harris, Fried, and Murphy at Columbia, and has been increased by con-

tact with Roy Rappaport, Kent Flannery, and Richard Ford at Michigan. For several semesters we have jointly taught a course on ecological approaches in anthropology.

Among my colleagues in cultural anthropology, I am especially indebted to Joseph Jorgensen for teaching me what I know about quantitative techniques; to Nan Pendrell for sharing with me her massive knowledge of the literature on culture and poverty, urban studies, and other areas of anthropology; and to Aram Yengoyan, who commented thoughtfully on some chapters of this book and who is a source of constant intellectual stimulation. Norma Diamond provided me with long bibliographies on culture and personality and applied anthropology.

I especially want to thank Robbins Burling, not only for his detailed criticisms of several chapters of this book, but also for enlightening me about certain recent developments in linguistics. As prepublication readers, Peter Miller and Ralph Faulkingham also provided useful criticisms. Of course, I absolve all three from any deficiencies in the final product.

Several of the teaching fellows who have helped me with Anthropology 101 have contributed to my ability to organize and present ideas in a form that most undergraduates at Michigan seem to appreciate, and thus indirectly to this book. I want to thank especially Catherine Cross, who originated most of the characters named in the discussion of segmentary lineage organization in Chapter 8, and Rohn Eloul, who has helped me tremendously with kinship charts. John Omohundro, Verena Haas, Cary Meister, Bea Bigony, Donald Callaway, Susan Stokes, Timothy Earle, Susan Kus, and Marjorie Wiener also deserve my thanks. Paul Doughty, Napoleon Chagnon, and Cecilia and Charles Wagley spent considerable time helping me choose illustrations for this book.

Several people at Random House deserve my thanks. Susan Rothstein, as project editor of *Anthropology: The Exploration of Human Diversity*, motivated me to work constantly to meet the book's schedule and assumed some of the author's last-minute responsibilities, thus enabling me to devote a summer to fieldwork in Brazil. I also thank Kristiina Anttila for her work in helping me prepare *Cultural Anthro-*

pology. Whatever faults it may still have, the book's style has profited tremendously from the copyediting labors of Ilene Haimowitz, who managed to retain most of my meanings while compressing and clarifying them. An able Random House staff illustrated this book, and V. Susan Fox made several of the line drawings.

I would not have started a textbook without the encouragement of publishers, and I am especially indebted to Hugh Treadwell and Mark Sexton, formerly of Random House, and to Raleigh Wilson and Walter Lippincott for their interest and confidence. I also thank Barry Fetterolf for his ideas which, I believe, have improved the book.

My children, Juliet and Nicholas, and especially my wife, Betty, bore the brunt of my irritability and occasional irresponsibility as the pressure of meeting deadlines mounted, and I thank them for their patience. I am indebted to Betty Wagley Kottak, not only for discussing with me many of the topics treated in this book, but also for her assistance in ethnographic fieldwork in Brazil and Madagascar since 1962. Many of the cases and examples presented herein depend as much on her fieldwork as on mine.

This book is dedicated to my mother Mariana Kottak Roberts, who kindled my interest in the human condition and made my conversion to social science inevitable.

Ann Arbor, Michigan
May 31, 1974

CONTENTS

10. Religious and Ritual Behavior 183

11. Diversity in Language 209

The End of the Primitive World and the Contemporary Relevance of Anthropology 235

12. Culture and Personality 237

13. The Anthropology of Complex Societies 261

14. Uses and Abuses of Anthropology 287

The Exploration
of Human Diversity

1. Introduction to Anthropology

Anthropology is a science of man which is concerned with widely ranging aspects of the human condition. Questions of interest to the anthropologist encompass the origin and development of man as a biological organism and a social animal with distinctive means of adapting to his environment, the nature and explanation of human diversity in the past and present, and differences and similarities in the ways in which specific human populations have adapted to their immediate environments and to contacts with other human groups.

Anthropology is uniquely a *holistic* science of humanity: its aim is the study of the whole of the human condition. It deals with human biology as well as human society, organized life in groups, and culture—learned behavior patterns. Its subject matter is bound in time only by the limitations which the fossil and prehistoric records impose.

In the United States, anthropology is a relatively recent addition to the curricula in many colleges and universities. It is a discipline which brings together four interrelated areas of specialization: social,

cultural, or sociocultural anthropology; archeological anthropology; biological, or physical, anthropology; and anthropological linguistics.

Anthropology has a different meaning in Europe and Latin America. Europeans use the term for only one of the four subdisciplines of American anthropology—biological, or physical, anthropology—rather than as a general term for the study of man. The study of the social life of human populations is called *social anthropology* (*comparative sociology* in Britain), while the study of the customs of men in different societies is termed *ethnology*. European archeology, the study of the works and life-ways of men of the past, is still another separate discipline, as is linguistics.

The Subdisciplines of Anthropology

The four subdisciplines of American anthropology are united by a common concern with human populations of the past and present. University departments of anthropology usually include at least one representative of each subdiscipline. Most

American anthropologists, the author included, specialize in social or cultural anthropology. However, in order to complete your requirements for a degree in most programs of study involving concentration in anthropology on either the undergraduate or graduate level, you must take courses in, and be familiar with, the basics of all the subdisciplines.

There are several historical reasons for the incorporation of four subdisciplines into a single science of man in the United States. American anthropology grew up in the late nineteenth and early twentieth centuries, out of a concern with natural history and with the native populations of North America. Over time, related interests in the origins and diversity of American Indians brought together the study of customs, social life, language, and physical traits. A historical concern with the origins of, and relationships among, the native populations of the New World was combined with an interest in describing, reconstructing, and cataloging the variety of Indian life-ways and customs.

There are also logical reasons for this unity. Each of the four subdisciplines is concerned with variations in time as well as in space, that is, in different geographic areas. Cultural anthropologists and anthropological archeologists alike are interested in historical problems—changes in social life and customs of specific groups of people. Biological anthropologists have provided data about the major changes in man's physical form and means of adaptation to his environment over long periods. Anthropological linguists have reconstructed languages and events of the past from the study of contemporary languages.

This common concern with variation in time may be stated differently: the study of *evolution* unifies the four subdisciplines of anthropology. Defined simply, evolution is change in form over generations. According to Charles Darwin, it is descent with modification. An evolutionary approach, supplemented by an interest in

ecology, orients this book. In Chapters 2 and 3, the terms "evolution" and "ecology" are clarified.

Sociocultural anthropology

The sociocultural anthropologist is concerned with the social life of man, that is, with the relationships of individuals to other individuals, of individuals to groups, and of groups to other groups. Basic to anthropology is the concept of *culture*, the notion that man adapts to his environment primarily through learned behavior patterns rather than through biological means. Human populations are equipped with "cultural adaptive kits" which enable them to wrest a living from the specific environment that surrounds them. Along with customary tasks and activities, these kits contain tools used in the exploitation of the environment. The cultural adaptive apparatus of a human population also consists of its ideology, typical ideas about how things should be done and what things should be done in everyday life.

A simple illustration of the fact that men adapt to their environment principally through sociocultural rather than biological means is provided by the Eskimos, who span the extreme Arctic region of the Western Hemisphere. Various mammals which are hunted by the Eskimo have, over centuries of biological evolution, developed fur coats which enable them to survive in the extreme climate. On the other hand, the technology of the Eskimo includes a range of techniques which enable him to hunt, kill, skin, and use these animal skins as his own. Contemporary human populations adapt to their environment principally through sociocultural means, but, as will be seen in this book, there has been an increasing reliance on sociocultural means of adaptation in man's evolution. Biological means of adaptation were much more important to early man—for example, to the protohuman populations that lived some 5 million years ago—than to any contemporary human group.

The sociocultural anthropologist is concerned with the nature of society in gen-

eral and with the distinctive features of specific societies. He is interested in changes in form which have taken place in human society since man first evolved, and also in changes in specific human societies of the past and present. He seeks to describe, analyze, and explain these changes. His interest indicates that the anthropologist believes there are some things which are shared by all men and some things which are distinctive in a given society. The general nature of society is the broad domain of sociocultural universals; the nature of specific societies is the domain of sociocultural divergence, diversity, and uniqueness.

There is also a middle ground in anthropology, certain sociocultural phenomena which occur in some but not all societies. An example is the nuclear family, a basic kinship unit made up of parents and children. The nuclear family is important in extremely primitive human societies which live by hunting and collecting wild plant foods. It is also the characteristic kinship unit among contemporary, middle-class Americans and Western Europeans. Anthropologists have concerned themselves with explaining why this kinship group exists in such different societies. An explanation of the nuclear family as a basic kinship unit in specific *types* of society will be given later in this book.

Sociocultural anthropology is traditionally divided into two phases: *ethnography* and *ethnology*. These two phases are usually combined by any sociocultural anthropologist in his work. Ethnography is the primary, data-gathering phase of sociocultural anthropology, that is, field work in a given society. My own field experience has been in two different parts of the world: among ocean-going fishermen of northeastern Brazil and among rice farmers of central Madagascar, a large island off the southeast coast of Africa. My approach to field work was typically ethnographic. I lived in small communities of peasants. I studied their everyday behavior, their normal social life, their economic activities, their relationships with their kinsmen and relatives by marriage, their relationship to the nation-state in which they live, their rituals and ceremonial behavior, their notions about appropriate social behavior. The ethnographer is in a position to recognize, and is himself often caught up in, the web of personal relations and problems encountered by those he studies. Perhaps this is the reason why most sociocultural anthropologists tend to be humanists. The people they study are, in many cases, nonliterate, that is, they have not developed a writing system for the language they speak; or in nation-states, they

Archeologists at work on a dig in Ife, Nigeria.
(Dr. Georg Gerster/Rapho Guillumette)

programs which nations develop; the former see how these programs work on the local level. Both are probably necessary to an understanding of human life in the twentieth century.

Ethnology, the other phase of sociocultural anthropology, is akin to what British social scientists call comparative sociology. Data not from a single society but from several are considered and compared. The ethnologist attempts to make generalizations, to explain differences and similarities in human behavior in different societies. It is in this phase of the anthropological endeavor that the distinction between universal behavior patterns, generalized behavior patterns such as the nuclear family, and distinctive behavior patterns is relevant. The ethnologist is interested in ascertaining what things occur in all human societies and why; what things occur only in a limited number of societies and why; and what things occur only in a single society. Data which enter ethnological formulations come from monographs, books published by ethnographers about their field work. Data of relevance to ethnology also come from the other subdisciplines of anthropology, particularly from archeology.

may be illiterate, that is, they cannot write the national language.

Like the people studied by many anthropologists, those I worked with were relatively poor and powerless in the context of their total society, the nation which enclosed them. The ethnographer is in a position to see the kinds of discriminatory practices that are directed toward such people in many contemporary nations. He is able to see poverty in terms of dietary deficiencies. His perspective sometimes differs radically from those of economists and political scientists, who have traditionally been concerned with organizations at the national level, and who have been forced by the nature of their inquiries to work with political and economic elites. On the other hand, the anthropological perspective is not necessarily better. Anthropologists and political scientists merely see different aspects of the same problem. The latter see

Archeological anthropology

Archeological anthropology might be called *paleoethnography*. It is concerned with the analysis, description, and interpretation of the ways of life of peoples who no longer exist. Archeologists attempt to infer as much as possible about these people from the remains they have left. Study of material things which have endured over several centuries or even millenniums enables the archeologist, familiar with ethnological theory, to make inferences about the nature of life in the community that existed on the archeological site he is excavating.

Several kinds of material remains are of interest to archeologists. Garbage dumps often reveal a great deal about diet; analysis of corprolites (fossilized human feces) also gives information about diet. Examination of animal bones lets the archeologist know such things as the average age of animals for slaughter. From such mundane data, the archeologist can reconstruct an amazing amount about the economy of the people he is studying. He can tell whether they were primarily hunters or whether they domesticated and stockbred animals, killing for food only those animals of a certain age and sex. He can tell if most of their vegetable food came from collecting wild plants or from sowing, tending, and harvesting crops, that is, plant cultivation. At the site of long-abandoned settlements, he finds *artifacts*, manufactured items. He examines the materials that were used to make these things and discovers whether these materials were available locally. If they were not, he can attempt to determine where they were available. From such information, he may reconstruct trade routes of the past.

Archeologists have spent a great deal of time studying *potsherds*, seemingly mundane fragments of earthenware which may provide a great deal of information about the archeological population. The range of pottery types, for example, may be a diagnostic of technological complexity. Furthermore, the quantity of pottery fragments in a given area may permit inferences about population size and density. Discovery that materials not locally available were employed by potters may point to systems of interregional trade. Archeological interest in pottery also reflects the fact that potsherds are more durable than many other artifacts—textiles and wooden objects, for example. For many years archeologists have used pottery as a diagnostic of sedentary populations with food-producing economies, those of cultivators, for example, rather than of people who subsisted on hunting and collecting. Finally, many archeologists have been especially interested in pottery styles, arguing that similarities in potsherd manufacturing techniques and decoration encountered at different sites can be taken as evidence for cultural connections. Peoples with similar inventories of pots and similar decorative techniques have been assumed either to be historically related—for example, offshoots of a common ancestral population—or to

have been in contact, perhaps through trade networks.

The inferences that archeologists have made and can make are not limited to the local economy or even to regional trade patterns. By dating sites and through regional surveys and aerial photographs, the archeologist can plot the range of variation in village sizes and distances between villages at a given point in time. From this, he may estimate population of local and regional units for the society he is studying. From examination of certain types of structures and buildings, he may say a great deal about the political organization of the people. There are certain societies called chiefdoms and states which are capable of mobilizing large groups of people to work together on public works projects. Where temples and pyramids endure, one can infer that the society in question was probably an archaic state with a central authority and an administrative structure whose edicts, backed by the threat of force, convoked corvée, or slave labor.

Archeology has contributed a tremendous amount to ethnology and promises to contribute even more. Many young archeologists are interested in *paleoecology*. Ecology is the study of the interrelationships among living things in a given environment. The living organisms and their environment together constitute an *ecosystem*, a patterned arrangement of energy flows and exchanges. Human ecology studies the ecosystems of which human populations are part. Paleoecology is concerned with ecosystems of the past. Thus, archeologists with this interest can expand considerably our knowledge of the kinds of relationships human populations have established with their environments at different times and in different places.

In addition to this, archeologists often chart changes in a society by excavating the same site at two or more levels, revealing information about two or more points in time. Anthropological archeology is therefore also vital to ethnology because it tells us a great deal about evolution or change of form, in this case, change of settlement form; change in the interrelationships between settlements; and, in a larger sense, change in forms of basic economic, social, and political activities. Do not forget that ethnographers have traditionally done their field research among nonliterate people. In order to know accurately about the past of populations who have no written records of that past, archeology is essential. Comparison of different historical sequences in different parts of the world has enabled anthropologists to formulate certain laws and generalizations, for example, concerning influences of environment and economy on social and political organization. In fact, one might reasonably argue that archeology and ethnography have contributed equally to the comparative science of ethnology.

A primatologist at work: Jane Goodall gives a wild chimpanzee a handout of bananas near her camp in Gombe Stream Game Reserve in Tanganyika. (Wide World Photos)

Biological, or physical, anthropology

Biological, or physical, anthropologists, as the names suggest, are principally, though not exclusively, interested in man as a biological organism. Three areas of study are traditionally covered by biological anthropology: human biological evolution, human genetics, and the study of subhuman primates, that is, monkeys and apes, man's nearest zoological relatives.

Biological anthropologists study changes in the morphology, or form, of man as a biological organism. They are interested in reconstructing the major biological stages of human evolution, and in identifying man's remote ancestors and making inferences about their ways of life. Thus, often, they are also archeologists, but they are generally concerned with a more remote time period than the paleoethnographer. In short, they are interested in the different physical stages that man has gone through since his emergence from subhuman primate stock, and the reasons for these changes. Finding explanations often requires considerable familiarity with ethnological theory.

To explain human biological evolution, it is necessary to understand human genetics, and this is the second area studied by biological anthropologists. Human populations, like members of other species, are affected by natural selection, leading over generations to evolution, or change of form. Raw materials on which natural selection may operate are provided by genetic differences among individuals, insofar as these genetic differences are revealed in the outward physical appearance or behavior of the organism. Evolution through natural selection is an interplay between the outward appearance and behavior of an organism and immediate environmental forces. Some individuals are able to pass on more of their genetic material to descendants than others because their traits are favored by their environment. Thus, the gene pool of future generations is affected by natural selection. The study of human genetics is also intrinsic to the science of man because it provides explanations for physical variations among contemporary

A physical anthropologist at work: Dr. L. S. B. Leakey examining fossils at an excavation site in Kenya. *(Mohamed Amin/Keystone Press Agency)*

groups of humans living in different parts of the world. The study of genetics is, of course, not limited to human subjects. Geneticists study other species and genera, which allies them with other scientists who are basically zoologists or botanists. Often, universities maintain separate departments of human genetics. There is, however, much exchange (sharing) of ideas between disciplines.

Finally, biological anthropologists have traditionally been interested in *primatology*, the study of man's closest nonhuman relatives, members, like man himself, of the zoological order Primates. In the past, studies of primates concentrated on morphology, genetics, and evolution. More recently, however, primatologists have undertaken studies of primates in the wild, their natural environment. Students of primate behavior undertaking field work among baboons, gorillas, or chimpanzees, for example, perform a task which is similar to the ethnographer's study of specific human populations and their behavior. Both stress environmental adaptation. The study of primate behavior may shed some light on the behavior of our own remote ancestors.

Anthropological linguistics

Finally, there is anthropological linguistics. Although we do not know—perhaps cannot know—when the genus *Homo* or the species *sapiens* began to speak, all contemporary humans do speak languages. Anthropological linguists study languages of the present and make inferences about languages of the past. Linguistics, like other subdisciplines of anthropology, has both a contemporary and a historical interest. Linguistic techniques are traditionally taught to anthropologists, and they are especially useful to the ethnographer, for they enable him to learn rapidly while in the field, languages which, in some cases, have never been written.

Traditionally there have been three basic approaches in linguistics. *Descriptive linguistics* is the analysis of systems of sound, grammar, and meaning in language. *Historical linguistics* studies a language that has existed at two or more points in time. Historical linguistics can, for example, chart the changes in sound system, grammar, and vocabulary between Middle English and modern English. Some of its findings enable anthropologists to demonstrate contacts between the English-speaking population and groups speaking other languages. Finally, there is *comparative linguistics*, which is not as simple as its name implies. It is not merely the comparison of features of different languages. Rather, it examines a group of languages which have developed over time out of a common ancestral language, called the protolanguage. The example most familiar to you is probably the Indo-European language family. Several languages exist today after a long period of differentiation from proto–Indo-European. Examination of the contemporary languages enables the comparative linguist to reconstruct a great deal about the parent language. Comparative linguistics is useful to cultural anthropologists interested in the past because it provides historical information. Some of its specific uses will be indicated in subsequent chapters.

Anthropological linguists have recently become interested in a more general linguistic approach which attempts to determine linguistic universals, features common to all languages. Cultural anthropologists, particularly those with primarily ethnographic concerns, have also begun to devote a great deal of attention to the relationship between language and culture. They have examined the different ways in which people in various parts of the world conceive of and divide up their world. Some have argued that study of such native category systems tells a great deal about the psychological make-up of the people being investigated. Certainly, the study of language and culture offers promise of contributing to the understanding of human behavior.

Anthropology and Other Disciplines which Study Man

The basic distinction between anthropology and other academic disciplines which study man has to do with anthropology's holism, its study of man from a biological, sociocultural, and linguistic point of view. But there are also important distinctions between the anthropologist who considers himself to be primarily a social scientist and members of other disciplines.

Sociocultural anthropology and sociology

The question most often asked anthropologists by people who know a little about the discipline concerns the distinction between sociocultural anthropology and sociology. The anthropologist (throughout this discussion I will be referring to the sociocultural anthropologist) and the sociologist share a common interest in human society, in the behavior of humans in groups, and in networks of social relations. However, there are differences between the practice of sociology and the practice of anthropology which result from the different kinds of societies which each discipline has traditionally selected for study. Thus, sociologists are best known for their studies of only one kind of society, the industrial West, and in the United States, principally studies of American life. Anthropologists, on the other hand, have tended to concentrate on primitive and peasant societies. Following from the different kinds of society which the two disciplines have studied are differences in the techniques of data collection and analysis employed. Sociologists have extensively used questionnaires and other means of gathering quantifiable, or countable, data. Accordingly, expertise in statistical techniques and formal methods of analysis has been more widely valued in sociology than in anthropology. Sociologists have concentrated on societies in which their informants or respondents—the people who answer their questions and are their objects of study—are often literate. Thus, sociologists can mail out questionnaires which the respondent will fill out and mail back. Anthropologists, on the other hand, have worked most often with informants who are members of nonliterate societies or who, as peasants within a nation-state, are illiterate. In addition, the anthropologist traditionally has worked in small, simple societies, while the sociologist has been concerned with analyzing nation-states, which are usually much more complex. The anthropologist living in a small community has developed different techniques of data collection. He lives with local people, observes their everyday behavior and the ongoing process of social life. He gathers data by getting to know people personally and becoming their friend, by getting to know the things they do, the people they see, and the web of relationships that unite them. One of the traditional techniques of ethnographic field work is participant observation: the anthropologist takes part in the events he is observing and analyzing.

This is a somewhat oversimplified description of the difference between disciplines. Often it has not been so clear-cut. Today there is increasing convergence between anthropology and sociology, both in subject matter and in techniques. Sociologists are now carrying out research in areas of the world that were once almost exclusively within the anthropological orbit, and anthropologists are undertaking studies in areas of industrial society, for example, in urban ghettos in the United States. As anthropologists extend the scope of their studies, they are adopting many of the techniques of data collection used by sociologists. In my own ethnographic work in Madagascar, for example, I used questionnaires which provided a basis for formal interviews. By asking a large sample of people the same questions, I was able to determine how widespread certain behavior patterns and social relationships are. My knowledge of the people that I studied in Madagascar is not based on my own impressions and unstructured observations alone. Rather, I have enough information to say definitely what is typical or atypical and to measure the range of variation. Similarly, sociologists have found that there is something of value in anthropological techniques and are increasing their use of informal interviews.

Anthropology, economics, and political science

As their names suggest, the social sciences of economics and political science concentrate on particular areas of human behavior. Furthermore, economists and political scientists alike have tended to limit their studies to modern nations. In the primitive and peasant societies which the anthropologist has traditionally studied, politics and economics often do not stand out as distinct areas of human activity amenable to separate analysis, as they do in modern nations. In fact, in primitive societies the political and economic orders are usually submerged in the social order. In many of the societies studied by anthropologists, there is nothing comparable to the political structure of nation-states. There is no government or central authority to regulate interrelationships between individuals, between individuals and groups, and between groups. Authority is vested in kinship statuses. Fathers and grandfathers may be the only individuals who can exercise au-

thority over their children and grandchildren, or authority may be a function of age and sex, so that all men can hope to exercise similar authority when they have reached a certain age.

Often in technologically primitive societies, people conceive of a social world which contains only two broad categories of people: friends and enemies. One's friends are those people with whom one has a personal relationship. They include one's actual blood kinsmen and those who are regarded as kinsmen because of some ceremonial, such as blood brotherhood; they also include one's in-laws and potential in-laws and those of other members of the group. Anyone related neither by kinship nor marriage is considered to be an enemy until, through an alliance between two groups that is often accomplished by marriage, enemies are converted into friends.

Statements about the economy—the system of production, distribution, and consumption of material resources—are usually included within the monographs which result from ethnographic field work. In his holistic approach, the anthropologist tries to deal with as many aspects of human behavior as possible in the society he is studying. Anthropological studies have contributed to the comparative study of economics by revealing differences between societies in the principles which regulate the distribution of resources. They have added to the comparative study of political systems by analyzing means of preserving order and preventing or resolving conflict in stateless societies. As a result, the findings of economists and political scientists who have confined their studies to Western nations may be placed in a broader perspective.

Anthropology and the humanities

Like political science and economics, the humanities tend to be interested in single aspects of human behavior. They are concerned with such things as art, literature, and music. Anthropologists are also interested in these matters in the societies that they describe, but they differ from people in the humanities disciplines in that they draw a distinction between great and little traditions. In the art history courses I took in college, we studied works of art that were part of the great cultural traditions of complex societies like Italy and France. These works of art were often done by artists who were commissioned by members of that society's elite. The ethnographer, on the other hand, is often interested in the little traditions, in the art, music, and oral literature of the people he is studying. In other words, he is interested in folk art and music.

Anthropology and psychology

There is an overlap between the subject matters of anthropology and psychology—as there was with sociology. All are concerned with human behavior. Although there are several areas of psychology, anthropology has most relevance for those psychologists interested in motivation, personality structure, and the tenor of social relationships. Like the other social scientists I have mentioned, psychologists have a tendency to gather their data and make their observations in the society of which they are themselves members. Anthropologists have placed on a comparative basis psychological statements founded on the observation of behavior in a single society or a single type of society.

Most important in this regard is the subdivision of sociocultural anthropology known as the study of personality in culture. Anthropologists, psychologists, and psychiatrists have collaborated in studies of child rearing and the formation of personality types in non-Western societies. Anthropologist Margaret Mead, in her books *Coming of Age in Samoa, Growing up in New Guinea,* and others, has shown that as cultures differ in what they regard

as normal and appropriate, so too do the personality types which are produced by those cultures. Thus, those anthropologists studying personality in culture have shown that different cultures interested in inculcating different values train their children differently and that the personalities of adults in a culture reflect its child-rearing practices. More recently, anthropologists have tried to ascertain the economic factors which are important in producing different personality types in different cultures. Barry, Child, and Bacon (1959), for example, have attempted to demonstrate statistically an association between the extent to which food resources are accumulated in a given society and the typical personality of members of that society. They have argued that among populations with a low accumulation of food resources—for example, those with economies based on hunting or fishing, where people procure food on a daily basis—adult personalities tend to be individualistic, assertive, and daring. On the other hand, in food-producing societies, particularly among cultivators who rely on a harvest, conscientious, compliant, and conservative personalities are encountered. In their intriguing article, the authors discuss reasons for such an association between type of economy and type of personality.

One of the most famous contributions by an anthropologist to the cross-cultural study of human psychology was made by Bronislaw Malinowski, well known among anthropologists for the many books and articles he wrote on the population of the Trobriand Islands of the South Pacific. Like many other people, the Trobrianders reckon kinship and descent matrilineally. The individual is considered to be related to his mother and her kinsmen, but not to his father. At birth the individual is incorporated into his mother's, rather than his father's, group. As Malinowski pointed out for the Trobrianders, in a matrilineal society the relative who exercises authority over an individual is not his father, who is, after all, not even a relative, but his mother's brother, his maternal uncle. The uncle rather than the father is the disciplinarian.

Furthermore, it is from the mother's brother rather than from the father that one inherits resources basic to livelihood. No wonder one shows marked respect toward one's uncle, and no wonder the relationship is often cool and distant. In contrast, the father-son relationship among the Trobrianders typically involved free and easy, friendly behavior and considerable affection.

Malinowski used his knowledge of the Trobrianders to dispute Sigmund Freud's famous theory of the universality of the Oedipus complex. Malinowski suggested that Freud had been ethnocentric in basing a generalization about human psychology on data gathered from only one society or, at best, one kind of society. Freud had lived in patriarchal Austria of the late nineteenth and early twentieth centuries, a social milieu in which the father was a strongly authoritarian figure. Malinowski pointed out that in Freud's society the father played a dual role. He was both primary authority figure to the individual and the mother's sexual partner. In the Trobriand Islands, on the other hand, the two roles were separated: the father was only the mother's sexual partner. If the Oedipus complex were universal, based on jealousy toward the mother's sexual partner, it would have shown up in the son-father relationship among the Trobrianders. It did not. Therefore, Malinowski argued, the nature of the authority structure is a more important determinant in producing a cool and distant relationship between father and child in Freud's society than is sexual jealousy.

Malinowski's dispute with Freud illustrates that individual behavior exists in, and depends on, a sociocultural context. Cross-cultural contrasts in personality types and social relationships are determined by the same factors which produce cultural differences. The continuous inculcation of the behavior patterns that lead to the formation of these personality types through a process known as *enculturation*, or *socialization*, is necessary to maintain that culture.

A final contrast between anthropology and psychology involves attitudes toward the individual in the two disciplines. Psychologists are interested in the individual as an individual but anthropologists often are not. Rather, many anthropologists study individual behavior in order to determine behavior typical of certain positions and relationships in that society. Ethnographers observe several cases of interaction between fathers and sons, husbands and wives, old men and young men, and so forth, to build up a picture of how the total social system operates and of the social divisions and contrasts that are essential parts of that social system.

Anthropology and history

I have saved the subject of anthropology and history for last, as it leads logically into Chapter 2. A broad statement about history would define it as the study of the past, of changes through time. However, like many historians, anthropologists recognize that there are two approaches to temporal change. The first approach concentrates on individuals as individuals. Imagine, for example, a stable society such as have existed in certain parts of the world for time periods of various lengths. Individuals enter this social system by birth and leave it by death. It is to refer to such changes in personnel that I use the word "history." The second approach studies individuals as representative of something larger. A stable social system, perhaps because of changes in its physical environment, perhaps because of some invention, perhaps because of a change in its relationships with neighboring societies, can become unstable. *A social system can change its form.* This temporal process involving change of form I refer to as "evolution." Many anthropologists, when approaching the past, are interested in evolution rather than history, in change in form rather than change in personnel.

For those who have studied history in high school and primary school the contrast should be easy to understand. I remember that I memorized names and dates. The emphasis was on individuals as individuals. Of course, some major changes in social form were also mentioned—the French and the American revolutions, for example. It is obvious that archeologists studying prehistoric societies cannot be interested in changes in personnel, for it is usually impossible to identify specific individuals who lived at a given site. Similarly, the biological anthropologists who study human evolution through the bones of our remote ancestors cannot concern themselves with changes in personnel, even if they want to. For the so-called South African ape-man *Australopithecus*, we can never know about the life of Sam Australopithecus or Joe Australopithecus or even Australopithecus the Great. We can only

SUMMARY

The four subdisciplines of anthropology—sociocultural anthropology, archeological anthropology, biological anthropology, and anthropological linguistics—are united by their common interest in human behavior of the present and past. Sociocultural anthropology examines diversity of the present and very recent past. Archeological anthropology approaches diversity of the past by reconstructing social, economic, religious, and political patterns of prehistoric populations. Biological anthropology examines diversity, in genetic make-up and outward expression, of human populations of the present and past. Anthropological linguistics documents diversity among contemporary languages and studies ways in which speech habits change in different social situations and over time spans of various lengths.

Anthropologists share a common interest in origins of and changes in aspects of the human condition. Their concern may be with the origin of humankind from subhuman primate ancestry and the major changes in biology and culture glimpsed through the fossil record; or the origin and evolution of food production out of foraging economies; or the origin and evolution of complex societies in different parts of the world; or the origin and differentiation of groups of related languages; or variations in speech patterns over short time spans; or the origin and evolution of distinctive cultures and the impact on them of changes in world power relationships.

Anthropology is united as well in its attempt not only to describe, but also to explain, differences and similarities in patterns of human behavior in time and space. In addition, the subdisciplines share a humanist approach, expressed in the pri-

Sources and Suggested Readings

BARRY, H., III, CHILD, I. L., and BACON, M. K.
    1959   Relation of Child Training to Subsistence Economy. *American Anthropologist* 61: 51–63. Using quantitative data on a variety of world cultures, demonstrates a relationship between subsistence economy, child training techniques, and adult personality types.

BEATTIE, J.
    1964   *Other Cultures: Aims, Methods and Achievements in Social Anthropol-*

ogy. New York: The Free Press. Introduction to social anthropology as practiced in Great Britain.

FRIED, M. H.
    1972   *The Study of Anthropology.* New York: Crowell. Anthropology as a field, and anthropologists as teachers and researchers; intended for college students.

FREUD, S.
    1950   (orig. 1918). *Totem and Taboo,* trans-

know what the physical form of *Australo-pithecus* was, and how it differed from the contours of later fossil men. Of course, we can also attempt to give reasons for such formal changes.

My distinction between history and evolution is not necessarily a distinction between university professors of history and university professors of anthropology. There are many historians who are principally interested in changes in social

form. Often they call themselves macro-historians. Likewise, there are anthropologists who attempt to reconstruct the genealogies of rulers in some society they are studying, but, more typically, they are interested in the events associated with each reign and the changes in social form through time.

---

mary objectives of inculcating respect and appreciation for other ways of life, of demonstrating the falsity of popular notions about relationships between genetics and learning ability.

Concern with the past and present—with biology, society, culture, and language—links anthropology to other social sciences. Sociocultural anthropology is closely related to sociology, and the principal difference has been that sociologists have studied urban and industrial populations while anthropologists have studied rural, non-Western peoples. Economics and politics are also of interest to anthropologists, who bring a comparative perspective to these domains of Western society. Anthropologists often study art, music, and oral literature, but their concern is with the esthetic expressions of common people rather than with art commissioned and appreciated

mainly by elites. In the study of culture and personality, which attempts to relate personality structure to social and cultural variables, anthropology and psychology have a common interest. By introducing a comparative dimension, anthropology is able to broaden understanding of this field. Like historians, anthropologists study the past, although they often deal with a more remote past, and they are less concerned with individuals and individual events than with major changes in forms of human adaptations and in the institutions of social life.

The study of anthropology was originally limited to isolated, rural populations, but as the field expands, anthropologists study cultural modifications and do research in cities and other parts of complex societies. Human diversity of the past and present is the subject of this book.

---

lated by J. Strachey. New York: W. W. Norton. Speculative account of the origin of the Oedipus complex, which Freud wrongly believed to be a human universal.

MALINOWSKI, B.
1927   *Sex and Repression in Savage Society.* London and New York: International Library of Psychology, Philosophy and Scientific Method. Examination of a society with no Oedipus complex.

MEAD, M.
1928   *Coming of Age in Samoa.* New York: Morrow. Field study of Samoan adolescence.

1930   *Growing up in New Guinea.* New York: Blue Ribbon. Enculturation in the South Pacific.

1935   *Sex and Temperament in Three Primitive Societies.* New York: Morrow. Sex role differences in three New Guinea societies.

2. Change: Historical

genes. The concept of culture
been basic to anthropology.
so basic, there are perhaps
tions of culture as the
gists. Let me give
learned behavior.
habits acquired
society. We
specific hu
in time.
lation
tur

Most anthropologists study evolutionary change rather than history. In examining the human fossil record and attempting to reconstruct the stages of human biological evolution, physical anthropologists are interested in changes in man's biology and physical form through time. Individual fossils merely exemplify these changes. The same applies to the sociocultural changes studied by the archeologist. This anthropological prehistorian is not usually interested in individuals as individuals. His concern is with encompassing changes, those involving the milieu in which individuals live and die.

The changes examined here are sociocultural. In the early stages of human evolution, at least through Neanderthal man, who came into existence some 100,000 years ago, the biological changes that led to modern *Homo sapiens* are the most obvious. The interrelationship between biology and culture is of major concern in the study of human evolution. In the remainder of the book, sociocultural changes will be emphasized as most important in explaining differences in the adaptations of human groups.

The ethnographer's study of specific populations in a given environment emphasizes the dependence of humans on the means of adaptation which they have evolved culturally. The ethnographer or cultural anthropologist pursues the evolutionary development of human groups and views their adaptive changes socioculturally, without losing sight of the genetic contributions to evolution. Therefore, the anthropologist concerned with human evolution focuses on the specific—a population existing at a particular point in time, directly influenced by the environment—in order to comprehend the total interaction of biology, environment, and culture.

Culture and Society

Contemporary human populations adapt to their immediate environments principally through sociocultural means. Although genetically determined means of adaptation were more important in the early stages of human evolution, never have the adaptive means of even historically remote populations of the genus *Homo* been totally programmed by their

has long
Because it is
as many defini-
are anthropolo-
my own: *culture is*
consists of skills and
by humans as members of
ay speak of the culture of a
an population at a given point
The individual born in that popu-
begins immediately to learn its cul-
. This process is known as *encultura-*
tion. He learns through experience and
through his observation of the behavior of
other members of his group. He also learns
because he is consciously taught by his
parents, his peers, and other members of
his group who wish to mold him. And he
is taught through language. He receives
through language an accumulated tradition
built up over the years by his group. His
behavior and responses to environmental
stimuli depend on what he has learned
rather than on a rigid program dictated by
his genes.

Culture rests on man's biology, but it is
not biological. Among species and genera,
it is *Homo sapiens* whose ability to learn,
to communicate with their fellows, to store
and use knowledge, is greatest. Genetics,
the biology of man, apparently made it
possible for him to develop these cultural
capacities early in his evolution. Cultural
abilities are certainly responsible for the
tremendous variety of different environments occupied today by *Homo sapiens*
compared to most other species.

Unlike some anthropologists, I shall not
rigidly separate culture, conceived as
learned behavior, from society, conceived
as group behavior. Throughout the book,
I use the words "society" and "culture"
more or less interchangeably in the com-
pound "sociocultural" to refer to the phenomena studied by the social or cultural
anthropologist. I do this because both
learned behavior and group organization
are basic to man's adaptation to his total
environment.

Culture is man's major means of 'adapting to his environment. No other species
places so great a burden on adaptation
through learning. For *Homo sapiens*, culture is analogous to the species-specific behavior and means of adaptation of other
animal species. Although human populations have cultural means of adaptation,
they nonetheless remain animals—superior
animals perhaps, but never completely
freed from problems of survival.

Environment and Culture

If we are to understand the adaptation of
any human population, it is essential that
environment not be defined simplistically.
Accordingly, we will assign it several components. There is a physical environment,
which includes such variables as rainfall,
temperature, soil types, and topography.
There is also a biotal environment, consisting of plants and animals consumed by the
population or profitably exploited in various ways and those which are pests and
which the human population strives to
control or to eliminate. Finally, there is a
social environment, which involves both
intergroup and intragroup relationships.

Imagine a population, P_1, living in a
given physical and biotal environment.
There are likely to be neighboring populations of the same species which have different relationships with P_1. Some of them
make war on P_1 or raid it. Others may provide raw materials or finished goods, that
is, have an exchange relationship with P_1.
Its relationship to other populations is
therefore relevant to understanding the
adaptation of P_1. The people in P_1 also
have to adapt to one another. P_1 is subdivided into different social groups to
which its members belong. Relevant to the
adaptation of P_1 are interrelationships between individuals and individuals, between
individuals and groups, and between internal groups and other internal groups.

My definition of culture, or of man's
sociocultural adaptive kit, is in terms of its
attributes. Different adaptations of contemporary human populations do not inhere primarily in biomorphological or ge-

netic characteristics of the population, but are extrasomatic, that is, not bodily. Man .adapts to his environment through technology and language, through patterns of group organization, and through ideology. This global concept of man's adaptive means includes the phenomena normally included under the terms "culture" and "society." For this reason much of the traditional subject matter of sociocultural anthropology appears in this book.

The Adaptive Means of Human Populations Compared with Those of Other Genera

Means of Adaptation

Homo	Other Genera
culture, learned behavior	greater adaptive burden placed on instinctive behavior
extrasomatic	somatic
nonbiological	biological
nongenetic	genetic

Evolutionary Change: How It Works

Most people think of Charles Darwin as discovering evolution. However, Darwin's major contribution was not the model of evolution, defined as change in form, but the postulation of a mechanism, natural selection, which is responsible for evolution. To understand Darwin's contribution, some discussion of the body of evolutionary thought which preceded his publication of *On the Origin of Species* in 1859 is necessary.

During the eighteenth and nineteenth centuries, natural scientists were concerned with classifying the array of plant and animal species found on earth and explaining the origins of the diverse genera and species. The commonly accepted explanation for the origin of species was the one outlined in Genesis, that God created the species during the original six days of creation. During the seventeenth and eighteenth centuries, biblical scholars James Ussher and John Lightfoot, through calculations based on genealogies included in

the Bible, purported to trace creation to the year 4004 B.C., specifically to October twenty-third of that year, at nine o'clock in the morning. The belief was that God had created the animals and plants found on earth in a series of individual acts. The acceptance of this doctrine was placed in some doubt as the volume of fossil discoveries increased during the eighteenth and nineteenth centuries. The fossil evidence demonstrated that forms of plant and animal life no longer found on earth had existed in the past. How were the absence of past species on earth now and the absence of contemporary species from the fossil record to be explained?

A modified explanatory framework combining creationism with catastrophism soon arose to replace the original doctrine. The catastrophists interpreted the fossil record by arguing that many of the species which had once lived had been obliterated from the face of the earth as a result of major catastrophes—fires and floods, for example. The French natural scientist Georges Cuvier (1769–1832), the principal proponent of catastrophism, argued that the biblical flood involving Noah's ark was merely the last of these major cataclysms. Following such destructive events, God embarked on new creative enterprises, bringing into existence the species of plants and animals now found on earth. However, to explain similarities between fossil and modern animals, Cuvier and other catastrophists recognized that some species had managed to survive the major catastrophes. Noah's two of a kind, for example, later spread out, migrating to other parts of the world from the isolated areas where they had been able to avoid extinction.

The alternative to creationism was transformism, which has come to be called evolution. Transformists held that over the course of time species had arisen gradually from others through a process of transformation or descent with modification. Charles Darwin has become the best known of the transformists, but he was influenced by earlier scholars, including his own grandfather, Erasmus Darwin, who, in a book called *Zoonomia* published in 1794, had argued for an ultimate relationship of common descent among all animal species. Charles Darwin was also influenced by James Lyell, generally considered to be the father of geology. During his famous voyage to South America aboard the *Beagle*, Darwin read Lyell's controversial book *Principles of Geology* and was thereby exposed to Lyell's principle of uniformitarianism. According to uniformitarianism, the present is the key to the past: the explanations for past events should be sought in factors that continue to work today. In his book Lyell argued that geological formations such as mountain ranges had been caused by the same natural forces which work in the modern world—rainfall, soil deposition, and earthquakes, for example. Lyell asserted that features of the earth's physical structure were gradually transformed through the operation of natural forces. Darwin applied transformism through natural forces to living things.

Like other transformists, Darwin argued that all life forms currently found on earth were ultimately related. Differences between contemporary species, said Darwin, have arisen gradually over time as a result of modification and branching out of ancestral forms. In contrast to proponents of divine creation, Darwin argued that the number of species on earth is not immutable; in fact, the number of species has increased over time. To explain this process of descent with modification, Darwin developed the doctrine of natural selection as a single principle capable of explaining the origin of species, biological diversity, and similarities encountered among related life forms. Charles Darwin's major contribution was not, therefore, transformism or the theory of evolution. Rather, it was his postulation of natural selection to explain evolutionary change in life forms.

Essential to the doctrine of evolution through natural selection is the assumption that nature, the sum of natural forces associated with a given environment, selects the forms most fit to survive and reproduce in that environment. Darwin postulated that in order for natural selection to operate on a given population, there must be variety within that population. As Darwin observed, there are differences between individuals in any population. Today we are aware that natural selection may operate not only on differences in physical appearance but also on differences in behavior. Natural selection would operate, argued Darwin, in situations where competition for resources strategic to life, such as food or space, existed among members of a population. Such competition, the struggle for existence, would always be present. Darwin was acquainted with the work of Thomas Malthus, an English economist and social theorist who in his famous piece "An Essay on the Principles of Population" had argued that competition was the natural result of a universal tendency for populations to increase faster than their food supply. Malthus intended his essay to apply principally to human populations. He saw war, disease, and other means of limiting or reducing population as fundamental to human life. Darwin applied this struggle for existence to the biological realm. In a situation of competition, in the struggle for existence, the fittest members of a varied population would survive and reproduce in greatest numbers. Those individuals whose attributes rendered them most fit to survive and reproduce in their environment would, in fact, survive and reproduce in greater numbers than those individuals whose characteristics rendered them less fit. Over the years, the less fit individuals would be eliminated from the population, while the favored ones would survive.

While natural selection remains the most powerful and the most satisfactory explanation for evolution, it is necessary to place Darwin's contribution within the context of more recent observations and discoveries which relate to evolution. Essential to the modern theory of evolution through natural selection is the distinction between *phenotype* and *genotype*. Phenotype refers to the outward appearance of an individual and to his behavior; genotype to his internal composition as programmed by genes and chromosomes, the hereditary units he has received from his parents. However, individuals with different genotypes may be identical in certain features of their phenotype, and it is important to realize that natural selection operates only on the latter. In a given environment certain phenotypes will have a better chance of surviving and reproducing than others. In general, this will mean that their genetic compositions will have a greater chance of being passed on to subsequent generations than those of other individuals who do not manifest traits which are adaptive, or favored, by that en-

vironment. Thus, selection operating on phenotypes will have genetic implications. Natural selection will ultimately change the composition of the population's *gene pool*—the sum total of the genetic make-up of all interbreeding organisms in that population. However, because favored phenotypes may be produced by different genotypes, this process of perfecting the fit between the attributes of the organisms and the environment is gradual. Natural selection decides on types which are most adaptive in a new environment. Less fit individuals are eliminated during each generation. Eventually, a point is reached where the population is optimally adapted to its environment. We say that an equilibrium or ecological *homeostasis* has been reached. Disadvantageous traits that arise for various reasons are eliminated almost immedi-

Variety in a nonhuman population. *(Ylla/Rapho Guillumette)*

ately from the population; the range of phenotypes encountered gradually narrows as the typical phenotype comes to represent an ever better, ever more adaptive fit with its environment.

Such a situation will prevail for as long as the relationship between the population and its environment remains the same. However, given some change in the immediate environment, or given a subpopulation which splits off from the original pop-

ulation and migrates to a new environment, natural selection will begin to select new phenotypes which are favored in the new environment. This selection will continue in the changed or newly colonized environment until ecological homeostasis is reached. The environment then may change again, or subpopulations may emigrate and interplay with natural selective forces in still other environments. It is through such a gradual process of adapting to different environments that natural selection, through modification and branching, has produced the tremendous array of

SUMMARY

Of two varieties of change, evolution and history, anthropologists more characteristically study the former. History refers to changes in personnel: individual organisms living and dying, migrating in and out of populations or social systems; evolution refers to changes in form over generations. Anthropologists concern themselves with several types of evolutionary problems involving humans: changes in physical and other biological aspects of the genus *Homo*; changes in the form of human society in general and in man's cultural means of adaptation over long periods; and changes in biological and sociocultural form of specific human populations and their means of adaptation over time.

Human populations, especially those of the present and recent past, adapt to their specific environments principally through extrasomatic means. Variations in their patterns of behavior reflect different learning experiences rather than genetic differences. Environmental factors affecting adaptation include not only aspects of the physical environment such as temperature and rainfall, but also the biotal and the social environment. Aspects of the sociocultural adaptive kit of any human population include its technology, its social organization, and its ideology.

During the eighteenth and nineteenth centuries, evolutionary or transformist doctrines of natural scientists were opposed by creationist and catastrophist doctrines. Charles Darwin was a leading exponent of evolution and of natural selection, the doctrine that the sum total of natural forces associated with a specific environment selects those forms whose physical make-up and behavior will render members of the population fittest to survive and reproduce in that environment. Selection of such phenotypes will eventually have genetic results since the fittest forms, insofar as they reflect hereditary differences, will make greater contributions to the gene pools of ensuing generations. Eventually, a stable relationship, homeostasis, is established between a population and its environment. Homeostasis will be maintained until one of the components of the environment changes or part of the population occupies a new environment.

Since natural selection operates on phenotype and since humans, more than any other species, rely on learned behavior in adaptation, differences in behavior of human groups of the present and recent past may also be partially explained by natural selection operating within specific environments.

plant and animal forms found in the world today.

Essential to the understanding of natural selection as it works on any population is the fact that it operates in terms of *specific environments.* As I have already stated, the environment to which a given population adapts involves physical, biotal, interpopulational, and intrapopulational components. A change in any one of these components can mean that new selective forces come into play. A model of natural selection can therefore be used to explain different adaptations of human groups to their immediate environments as well as changes in a population over time. In recent history, however, natural selection has operated principally on behavior, and specifically on cultural or learned behavior, in humans rather than on physical appearance and biology. Thus, as subsequent examples will demonstrate, natural selective forces associated with specific environments may explain differences in social life and cultural ways in human populations.

Sources and Suggested Readings

ALLAND, A.
1967 *Evolution and Human Behavior.* Garden City, N.Y.: The Natural History Press. Interesting brief introduction to natural selection and genetics, with discussion of ecological approaches in cultural anthropology.

BRACE, C. L.
1967 *The Stages of Human Evolution.* Englewood Cliffs, N.J.: Prentice-Hall. Although in need of updating, and although Brace argues for a linear interpretation of the fossil record which many anthropologists reject, this remains the most entertaining general introduction to the human fossil record available.

COHEN, Y., ed.
1968 *Man in Adaptation: The Biosocial Background.* Chicago: Aldine. Organizing essays, in which articles are used as footnotes to major points. More valuable than the average reader in biological anthropology and archeology.

CUVIER, G.
1811 *Recherches sur les Ossements Fossiles.* Paris: G. Dufour and E. d'Ocagne. Original statement of catastrophism.

DARWIN, C.
1958 (orig. 1859). *Origin of Species.* New York: New American Library. Foundation stone of biology and anthropology.

DARWIN, E.
1796 (orig. 1794). *Zoonomia, Or the Laws of Organic Life.* 2nd ed. London: J. Johnson. Nature discussed and classified by an early transformist.

GREENBERG, J. H.
1968 (orig. 1959). Language and Evolution. In *Man in Adaptation: The Cultural Present,* ed. Y. Cohen, pp. 29–40. Chicago: Aldine. Transformism, catastrophism, and other early approaches to change, as well as linguistic change.

LYELL, C.
1850 (orig. 1830). *Principles of Geology.* 8th ed. London: J. Murray. Influential application of natural principles to land forms; early statement of uniformitarianism.

MALTHUS, T.
1803 (orig. 1798). *An Essay on the Principle of Population.* London: J. Johnson. Classic demographic essay. Asserts that while human population increases geometrically, its food supply increases only arithmetically.

MOORE, R.
1964 *Evolution.* New York: Time-Life Books. Well-illustrated introduction to natural selection and genetics.

Sociocultural Diversity and Adaptive Means

3. Evolution in Sociocultural Phenomena

The preceding chapters have provided a basic introduction to the subdisciplines of anthropology and to the role of change in the evolution of man. With the advent of *Homo sapiens Sapiens*, the burden of adaptation shifted noticeably from biological to sociocultural means. These, embodied in the notion of culture, are unique to the human species. It is this unique concentration and combination of evolutionary traits that makes man distinct. Throughout the rest of the book sociocultural changes will be emphasized. My concentration will be on sociocultural diversity, and I shall also try to explain, drawing on my own knowledge and interpretations as well as on the works of several other scholars, differences and similarities in social life and cultural traits among human populations of the present and past.

The present chapter provides a framework for the application of evolutionary principles to human populations, particularly those of the present and the recent past. The reader is reminded of the Darwinian model of evolution through natural selection set forth in Chapter 2. The unit of study is the population. Like other animal populations, humans have developed adaptive means whose function is to maintain them in their immediate environments. Natural forces select phenotypes, including behavior patterns, which are adaptive in terms of specific environments. Once a viable and stable relationship with the immediate environment has been established, natural selection operates to maintain that relationship.

If the environment changes, different selective forces come into play. Remember that I have defined the environment very broadly, as including physical, biotal, and conspecific components. The environmental change does not have to be major. It may involve a seemingly minute difference, for example, one or more mutations in a plant or animal species important to the population's subsistence or a gradual change in the pattern of alliances between a human group and one of its neighbors. When an environmental factor changes, selection may favor new adaptive means. It is also important to remember that possessing sociocultural means of adaptation does not free human populations from nature. Extensive reliance on extrasomatic adaptive means merely allows *Homo sapiens* to adjust to changed circumstances more quickly and more flexibly than other species. It is always possible, however, for the environmental change to be so severe, or for the adaptive apparatus of the group to be so limited or so inflexible, that extinction rather than evolution results. Many of the human populations which existed when Europeans began their voyages of discovery have perished because their adaptive means did not enable them to compete successfully with European invaders and conquerors. Note here that I am thinking of populations like the Tasmanians, hunters and gatherers who used to be the exclusive human inhabitants of Tasmania, a large island located off the southern coast of eastern Australia. The Tasmanians were wiped out as a human population in the nineteenth century. They have left no descendants.

The matter of cultural extinction is different but more common. To the extent that the human populations whose cultures changed have left descendants, one can speak of evolution rather than extinction. These populations have left descendants, that is, survived in a genetic sense, because they have modified their adaptive means to deal with even very major changes in the environment.

Evolution: Various Approaches

It is important to understand the difference between general evolutionary statements and specific evolutionary statements about humans. General evolutionary statements, as opposed to specific evolutionary statements, concern the genus *Homo* as a whole. They designate long-term evolutionary trends—broad changes in the adaptive means employed by members of the genus without regard for special adaptive prob-

lems associated with particular environments. Such generalizations abstract certain broad changes by considering populations of that genus period from several different periods and several different geographical areas. Specific evolutionary statements, on the other hand, refer to particular human populations living in specific environments of various sizes—for example, the upper Nile region of Africa, Australia, the valley of Mexico, the northwestern shores of Lake Victoria. A study in specific evolution involves documentation of changes in adaptive relationships between particular environments and the human populations within them over an extended time period.

General evolutionary statements

Consider some general evolutionary statements regarding the evolution of stone technology: through the successive stages in the evolution of *Homo*, the reliance on tools has increased. Tools have become more numerous; tools have become functionally differentiated and have been designed for ever more specialized tasks; and tool types have diversified. Other general evolutionary observations note that during the evolution of *Homo* there has been a shift from biological to sociocultural means of adaptation; that populations representing later stages of human evolution have been more successful in a reproductive sense than earlier populations; and that the range of environments occupied by members of the genus *Homo* has expanded through time.

Means of harnessing nonhuman energy sources for human use have improved. Muscle power is human energy. Fire, on the other hand, is an indirect energy source which was brought under human control during the *Homo erectus* stage of human evolution and which conferred on *Homo* adaptive advantages: the ability to adapt to a wider variety of environments and, because of cooking, the ability to consume a wider variety of foods. Plants and animals are indirect sources of energy. Through photosynthesis plants capture and transform solar energy to manufacture carbohydrates. Some animals eat plants. Some animals eat other animals. When humans gather plants or hunt animals they exploit, directly or indirectly, some of this solar energy to keep themselves alive. However, when humans grow plants or supervise the mating and survival of their animal herds, they are able to concentrate and control the stores of nonhuman energy at their disposal. So, too, do they concentrate and control when they harness a steer to a plow or to a cart, when they tap the wind to sail boats or rivers to run industrial plants; or—the present culmination of man's nonhuman energy-capturing abilities—when they put the atom to use.

Enlarging our frame of reference from the evolution of *Homo* to the evolution of all life, certain general trends are also apparent. There has been, for example, a proliferation of parts and subparts. Multicelled plants and animals have evolved out of single-celled antecedents. One observes a similar trend in the evolution of *Homo* and of his adaptive means. *Australopithecus* probably lived in small bands which, like baboon troops, were part of no larger social unit. Each band was probably like any other, in the same way that one amoeba resembles another. By the time of *Homo erectus*, however, larger units were forming seasonally as subparts —microbands congregated for the purpose of communal hunting. Then, with the appearance of *Homo sapiens Sapiens*, the number of human populations increased. The size of such populations also increased, as did their degree of association with others.

Obviously, food production accelerated the general evolutionary trend toward proliferation of parts and subparts, subpopulations of the species *Homo sapiens*. Control over the reproduction of plants and animals eventually enabled people to live together throughout the year in permanent villages. Throughout the world, food production sustained an increase in population and an expansion in range of the genus *Homo*.

In addition to the proliferation of parts and subparts, other trends observable in the general evolution of life also apply to the evolution of *Homo*. As parts and subparts have proliferated, they have also become functionally specialized. From unicellular plants and animals in which a single structure performs a variety of functions have evolved more generally advanced organisms with specialized systems and subsystems—alimentary, reproductive, circulatory and excretory, for example. And, as Chapter 4 will document, among many food-producing populations, functionally specialized systems and subsystems—military, judicial, administrative or, in broader terms, economic, political, and ritual—have arisen out of less differentiated forms.

Another trend in the general evolution of life which may be extended to *Homo* is the development of more effective means of integrating the functionally specialized parts and subparts, systems and subsystems. Central governments play integrative roles comparable to that of the central nervous system in the coordination of bodily parts and systems.

Several anthropologists have suggested that general evolutionary trends—the proliferation of parts and subparts, their functional differentiation, the development of more effective means of integration, reproductive success as revealed by numbers and biomass, and adaptability as revealed by environmental and geographic range—may be used as bases for comparative statements about human populations present and past. Stated in terms of trends, the comparison has temporal implications. On the basis of the five criteria just listed, early populations of *Homo* must be adjudged less *advanced* than later ones. Furthermore, one or more of the five criteria may be used as a basis for comparing, for assessing, the general evolutionary status of human populations of the present and recent past. As we shall see, according to all these criteria, most human

Stage	Characteristics
1. Lower Status of Savagery	Infancy of the human race
2. Middle Status of Savagery	Subsistence on fish; a knowledge of the use of fire
3. Upper Status of Savagery	Invention of the bow and arrow
4. Lower Status of Barbarism	Invention of pottery
5. Middle Status of Barbarism	In the Eastern Hemisphere, domestication of animals; in the Western Hemisphere, cultivation of maize and plants by irrigation
6. Upper Status of Barbarism	Invention of the process of smelting iron ore
7. Status of Civilization	Invention of a phonetic alphabet, with the use of writing

FIGURE 1 Morgan's stages in the evolution of human society.

populations whose subsistence is based on hunting and gathering may be adjudged less advanced—that is, characterized by more rudimentary development of each of the general evolutionary trends—than most food-producing populations.

Specific evolutionary approaches

Specific evolutionary statements describe changes in adaptive means employed by a human population in a specific area of the world. It is possible, for example, to focus study on the French or on the Ganda, a population living on the shores of Lake Victoria in East Africa, rather than on the genus *Homo*. We may describe changes in means of adaptation and other traits and behavior over an extended time period. Comparison of the specific evolutionary sequences in different human populations, once the reasons for these changes have been understood, informs us about the reasons for evolution in human populations of the present and recent past. By examining many specific evolutionary sequences, we can see whether there are some broadly similar trends in development—in other words, whether analogous selective forces operating in broadly similar environments have produced conver-

gent or parallel evolutionary sequences among human populations in different parts of the world. And by delineating the kinds of conditions and stimuli that produce specific change, we may attempt to make generalizations about the evolution of these human populations.

Unilinear evolution

Anthropologists and other students of human groups have used the term *evolution* to refer to still other developmental trends. For example, in Britain and the United States during the latter half of the nineteenth century, social scientists were making *unilinear* statements about the evolution of human groups. A unilinear evolutionary viewpoint assumes that certain stages will occur in the evolution of any human society. Lewis Henry Morgan, one of the earliest American anthropologists and author in 1877 of the anthropological classic *Ancient Society*, named three broad stages: savagery, barbarism, and civilization. Savagery and barbarism were each subdivided into three parts, called lower, middle, and upper. (See Figure 1.) According to Morgan, civilization came with the advent of writing.

Other scholars with a unilinear evolutionary bias described different stages. What makes their viewpoints unilinear is the fact that all human societies were thought to have evolved in the same order through a set series of stages, and any society which had attained one of the higher stages was assumed to have passed through the lower stages. It is ironic that none of the so-called unilinear evolutionists were consistently unilinear. Some of them at times admitted that stages could be skipped, that is, that society X might reach stage 6 directly from stage 4 without passing through stage 5.

Twentieth-century ethnographic and archeological work has demonstrated the limitations of a unilinear evolutionary framework. It is indeed possible for societies to skip stages. It is also possible for them to develop the same traits but in different order and for developments consisting of different stages to lead to broadly similar results. Human groups may even undergo *devolution*; that is, because of changes in natural selective pressures, evolve from a more to a less generally advanced condition. In the terminology of the unilinear evolutionists, this would be reverting from a "later," or more complex, to an "earlier," or simpler, stage.

Leslie White and the evolution of culture

In the present century, two sociocultural anthropologists, Leslie White and Julian Steward, have used evolution to refer to still other concepts. Neither has been principally concerned with either the evolution of the genus *Homo* (general evolution) or the changes in adaptive relationships between single human populations and their environments over time (specific evolution). White's understanding of the term "evolution" is similar to general evolution as defined above, but for him the evolving unit is not the genus *Homo* but the most basic adaptive apparatus of that genus, namely culture. According to White, the evolution of culture, or cultural advance, is directly proportional to, and therefore may be measured by, the amount of energy harnessed per capita per year or by improvements in the means of controlling energy. White's views on cultural evolution are most completely developed in his book *The Evolution of Culture* (1959). In this modern anthropological classic, White discusses major developments in culture from Paleolithic hunters and gatherers through the fall of Rome. The panoramic movement he describes involves a transition from primitive society, which relied almost exclusively on human energy, to the complex societies which emerged following what White calls the "Agricultural Revolution," encompassing the domestication of plants and animals. Out of food-producing economies came civilization. White applies his grand movement view of evolution not only to development over time from Paleolithic foragers through food producers to civilization, but also to contemporary sociocultural systems. In White's evolutionary scheme, those populations of foragers and primitive food producers that have survived into the twentieth century can serve as present-day representatives, living fossils, of early sociocultural systems because of their relatively simple or inefficient means of harnessing energy. A kind of technological or economic determinism seems to inhere in White's work. Culture advances as improvements in technology or economy permit greater energy capture by humans. White recognizes, however, that technological, economic, and social developments are associated and interrelated. For example, social, political, and legal changes followed the Agricultural Revolution. Private property, distinctions involving wealth and class, and other social relations unknown in the sociocultural systems of the Paleolithic arose in food-producing societies. It is therefore to technological, to economic, and to associated sociopolitical forms that White's observations on the evolution of culture apply most directly. His comparison of sociocultural systems, his use of the terms "primitive" or "simple" versus "complex" or "civilized," do not contain moral judgments. Nor do they denote increase in happiness. In fact, White is explicit in arguing that the simpler type of social system based on non–food-producing economies represents the most satisfying kind of social environment that humans have ever experienced. While, therefore, it may be possible to speak of evolutionary advance, measured according to certain trends of criteria, "progress" is too value-laden a term to apply either to the evolution of culture, which has been White's concern, or to the long-term evolution of the genus *Homo*.

Julian Steward and convergent evolution

Julian Steward has used the term *multilinear evolution* to refer to the sociocultural phenomena he has studied. *Multi* means "many," and multilinear evolution refers to the fact that many different lines of development have taken place in human populations in different parts of the world. The reader will recognize that the study of any one of these lines brings us back to specific evolution. Steward has, however, chosen a middle ground between general and specific evolutionary studies. He has concentrated on examples of convergent evolution involving historically, genetically, and geographically unrelated populations in different parts of the world. One of Steward's best-known articles, "Cultural Causality and Law: A Trial Formulation of the Development of Early Civilizations" (1949), compared the specific evolutionary sequences leading from hunting and gathering band organization to nation-state organization in five separate world areas—Peru, highland Mexico, Egypt, Mesopotamia, and China. Steward found that not only did the human populations in each of these regions complete an analogous evolution from foraging to agricultural economies, with convergent social forms and other adaptive means throughout the sequence, but they also passed through roughly similar stages and generally in the same order. He attributed the five examples of convergent evolution to analogous long-term interactions between the human populations and to broadly similar natural selective forces associated with the five geographically distant but ecologically similar environments.

Steward wrote his 1949 article in order to demonstrate noteworthy similarities in five specific transitions from foraging to civilization or nation-state organization. According to Steward, the convergent sequences did not occur by chance. In fact, given long-term adaptations to similar environments and analogous selective forces, there was a certain amount of inevitability in the order and development of sociocultural forms in these five areas. It seemed to Steward, therefore, that natural law determines human behavior and evolution as surely as it does other organic and inorganic forms and phenomena.

Along with other sociocultural anthropologists, Steward has been interested in constructing sociocultural typologies. A typology is a system of classification which takes similar units and subdivides them, assigning some to category or type A, others to B, and so on. In 1949 Steward proposed that the five areas of the world examined in his article belonged to a single *developmental type*. This type involved convergent evolution over long time periods, but was limited to arid areas. Thus, unlike unilinear and other formulations, it was not composed of universal stages. Steward believed that different developmental types, involving different long-term interactions between human populations and their environments, would have prevailed in nonarid areas—regions of tropical rain forest, for example.

Steward has, then, contributed to our understanding of evolution in relatively recent human populations by calling attention to parallel changes in sociocultural forms and other adaptive means that have taken place repeatedly and independently of one another in different parts of the world. These are *parallels through time*. In numerous articles, he has also directed the attention of anthropologists to examples of sociocultural *parallels in space*, observed at a single point in time. Compare several of the human populations which have been studied by ethnographers during the twentieth century, and you will be struck by certain similarities—certain parallel sociocultural forms. Steward explains such parallels in space the way he explains parallel evolutionary sequences. He points out that many sociocultural similarities may be shown to reflect convergent evolution. If, in the case of a developmental typology, parallel selective pressures associated with analogous environments have interacted with human populations over thousands of years to produce a similar sequence of sociocultural forms, evolutionary convergence involving only a single time level should be even more obvious. For example, in examining a large *sample*, or study group, of foraging societies from all over the world, Steward was able to show that similar sociocultural forms represented convergent adaptation to similar environmental variables such as rainfall patterns, distribution of wild plants, habits of game animals, and others. But Steward did not find that there was a single type of foraging society. Rather, differences in ecological relationships involving particular groups of foragers and their specific environments produced a variety of types, which he called "patrilineal bands," "composite bands," "multi-family predatory bands," and "the family level of sociocultural integration." Since the stages leading to them may have been different, the types which are abstracted from observations on a single time level are obviously not developmental types, although they are the convergent end results of specific evolutionary sequences. These might be called *ecological types.*

Steward never developed an extensive typology based on the examples of cross-cultural convergence he studied and described, but another anthropologist, Yehudi Cohen (1968), has. Like Steward, Cohen is interested in cross-cultural similarities observable at a single point in time. These represent analogous sociocultural forms which have developed independently in nonrelated and nonneighboring groups. Cohen argues that the most important determinant of these similarities is a human group's strategy of adaptation to its environment. For example, he points to striking similarities between most contemporary populations that have what he calls a *foraging* (hunting and gathering) strategy of adaptation. Like Steward, Cohen emphasizes broad similarities in certain features of subsistence and technology, and in ecological relationships. From these similarities, other sociocultural features are shown to flow. Cohen's types are, however, much broader than Steward's and pay less attention to contrasts associated with particular environments. Steward and Cohen have been interested primarily in similarities which are observable cross-culturally. However, simply because sociocultural similarities exist that can be related to analogous

adaptative problems, it does not mean there are not also differences between the units included within a type. In fact, ecological and evolutionary principles may be used to explain sociocultural divergence and differentiation as well as convergence and parallelism, as subsequent chapters will document.

Strategies of Adaptation

Yehudi Cohen identifies six strategies of adaptation: foraging, horticulture, pastoralism, agriculture, mercantilism, and industrialism. Confining our attention to the first four, which are most characteristic of the groups anthropologists have studied, let us examine some of the social and cultural traits and patterns associated with each. (Trade and industrialism are considered in later parts of the book.) Do not forget that there are differences between populations placed within each type. In the following discussion, however, emphasis is on the similarities.

Foraging

Until men and women began to cultivate plants and to domesticate animals, some 10,000 to 12,000 years ago, human populations throughout the world relied on foraging for subsistence. Of course, the particular resources associated with specific environmental niches dictated differences in foraging strategies. Compare, for example, the big game hunters of the Upper Paleolithic and the more generalized foragers of the European Mesolithic. But a basic feature was shared: people relied on natural reserves for their food and for other materials essential to their lives. In both the Old World and the New World, food production, once begun, spread rapidly, and most hunting and gathering populations eventually came to orient their economies around plant cultivation, animal domestication, or a combination of the two. Foraging economies held on, however, in certain parts of the world. Today there remain two broad zones of foraging adaptations in Africa. They are the Kalahari Desert of southern Africa, home of the Bushmen, and the equatorial forest of central and eastern Africa, where the Pygmies survive. In Southeast Asia, Malaya, and on certain islands off the Indian coast live other foragers. They survive generally in forests or on isolated islands. Some of the most famous contemporary hunters and gatherers are the aborigines of Australia, who, during the more than 20,000 years they have lived on their island continent, have never cultivated plants or domesticated animals. To the south, the island Tasmanians were also hunters and gatherers.

In the New World, the Eskimos are probably the hunters and gatherers most familiar to you. The Indians of California, the Northwest Coast of North America, interior Canada, and the northern Midwest were still foragers at the time when Europeans began to colonize North America. Near the southern tip of South America lived three hunting and gathering populations: the Ona, the Yahgan, and the Alacaluf; and on the *pampas* of Argentina, southern Brazil, Uruguay, and Paraguay lived others.

Why did populations with foraging strategies persist in certain areas while food production was spreading throughout most of the world? There are several reasons. Certain environments pose major obstacles to food production and, in fact, to any economic base other than foraging. It is only in the twentieth century that technological means which enable human populations to irrigate extremely arid lands like the Kalahari and the central desert of Australia have been invented. The environmental obstacles to plant cultivation in the Arctic are obvious. Yet the combination of environmental limitations with rudimentary technologies is not the only reason for the survival of ways of life based on foraging.

Though their range of specific environments is large, the niches of contemporary hunters and gatherers share one feature in common: their marginality. This means that they are not of immediate interest to other strategies of adaptation. The Kalahari, for example, offers few attractions to food producers. Rather, should modern technology be applied to the Kalahari, it probably would not be to irrigate it for agriculture but to extract mineral wealth from the subsoil.

Another observation on the survival of hunters and gatherers is in order. In some cases, human populations with foraging

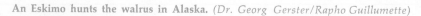

An Eskimo hunts the walrus in Alaska. *(Dr. Georg Gerster/Rapho Guillumette)*

Plains Indians of the Delaware hunt Buffalo. *(Brown Brothers)*

economies have lived in areas which could be cultivated and have had contact with cultivators but have not become food producers. A good example is aboriginal California, where plant cultivation never arose as a strategy of adaptation. Because of the variety and productivity of the California environment under a foraging regime, aboriginal populations simply never turned to plant cultivation. A stable relationship based on foraging yielded enough to support human populations and, in fact, supported population densities higher than in some neighboring areas of plant cultivation. So productive and satisfactory was the relationship between the California population and its environment that the people never cultivated anything but tobacco. The point is that the availability of a potentially more productive economy may not serve as sufficient motivation for people to give up what is a stable and already productive economy and gamble on a future adaptation which might enable them to produce more. People do not necessarily turn into cultivators simply because the knowledge of plant cultivation is available.

THE CORRELATES OF A FORAGING ECONOMY
Typologies are useful because they suggest

correlations, that is, associations, covariations. A specific constellation of other sociocultural features is generally characteristic of each of Yehudi Cohen's strategies of adaptation. Populations with adaptive strategies based on foraging have often been characterized as *band-organized* populations or societies, because, for many of them, the basic unit of social organization is the band. A band is a small group of people—fewer than one hundred—related by ties of actual or believed kinship and/or marriage. The typical band size varies from one foraging population to another, and often from one season to another in any one population. Band size reflects the specific environment which the population exploits and the seasonal appearance of resources used by the band's members. Thus, in some hunting and gathering societies, band size stays about the same all year long. In others, however, during part of the year the band disintegrates as smaller units, often family groups, leave to take advantage of seasonally available resources which are better exploited by only a few individuals. During one season of the year, the band fragments will recongregate to engage in cooperative economic or ceremonial activity. Among some foraging populations, annual congregations may even involve several bands. Among late *Homo erectus* populations, for example, there is the possibility that bands may have congregated in autumn to prey on large mammals migrating south for the winter. As a unit the band amplified its resources. These larger units are called *macrobands*, composed of several *microbands*.

Of interest in the discussion of band organization are the Bushmen and the Pygmies, among whom band size does not appear to vary significantly during the year. Although bands of Bushmen do not fragment seasonally into family groups, there is great variation in their composition. A Bushmen or a Pygmy may shift his band membership many times during his life. He may be born, for example, in a band where his mother has kin. Later, his father, mother, and siblings may move to a band where his father has relatives. Bushman bands tend to be exogamous units. As a result, a father and mother will come from two different bands, and grandparents may have come from four different bands. Hunters and gatherers apparently enjoy the possibility of affiliating with any of these grandparental bands

or, in fact, with any band where they can show a personal connection. Personal connections may be based on kinship. They may also be based on marriage. When a Bushman couple marries, they have the option of residing in either the husband's or the wife's band. Later they may decide to move and join the band of the other spouse for a while.

Finally, one may affiliate with a band through fictive kinship. Bushmen have a limited set of personal names, and they believe that there is a special relationship between any two individuals who share the same personal name. Such individuals treat each other like siblings. Furthermore, each has the same right to hospitality in a band where he has a namesake that he does in the band where his real sibling is living. By virtue of their common name, each assumes some of the sociological identity of his namesake. Thus, he will call everyone in his namesake's band by the kin terms that his namesake uses, and band members will use the same terms to refer to him that they use for his namesake. Thus through kinship, marriage, and fictive kinship ties, the Bushman has, throughout his life, the opportunity to join many bands, and individuals change band membership many times before they die. If one looks

Bushmen headmen. *(Marvin E. Newman/Woodfin Camp Inc.)*

at the same band from year to year, he will find that its membership varies tremendously.

All human societies have established some sort of a division of labor on the basis of sex. The pattern in many foraging societies is for men to hunt and women to collect, but the specific economic tasks allotted to each sex depend on the environment and the traditions which, over time, the human population has developed for dealing with it. Thus, among some hunters and gatherers, women are the major collectors, and their labor provides more than two-thirds of the calories consumed by band members. Among other foraging populations, men do some collecting as well as hunting, and their contribution to the diet is greater. In still others, women gather vegetation, insects, slow-moving game, and some marine and fresh-water fauna, while men hunt, collect, and fish for different types of food.

As there are differences in the activities expected of an individual because of his sex, so, too, are there differences related to his age. In many band-organized societies, old people receive great respect as guardians of myths, legends, stories, and traditions of the band. Because of their contributions during their active years, old people may be the objects of considerable affection and admiration. Their knowledge of ritual as well as of practical matters is highly regarded.

All human societies allocate varying degrees of respect to different people. In foraging societies, the amount of respect attached to any individual depends on his age, sex, and personality. Good hunters receive more respect than mediocre hunters. Many kinds of individual bent may serve as reasons for respect—a man can sing or dance well, he is an especially good storyteller, or he has the ability to go into a trance and communicate with supernatural forces. There is, however, an important difference between band organization and other forms of social organization. Among foragers there is very little differential authority, and no differential power, that is not based on the relationship be-

tween parent and immature child. There are band headmen in many foraging societies, but they are headmen in name only. They serve as focal points for the bands which they head; they are usually more permanent band members than the others. Their position in band life makes them first among equals, and they are sometimes asked for advice or information, which they give. Sometimes they make decisions. However, they have no means of enforcing their decisions.

Food-producing strategies of adaptation

Yehudi Cohen has distinguished between three major strategies of adaptation based on food production which are encountered in nonindustrial populations. They are horticulture, pastoralism, and agriculture. In the following discussion, some trends of general evolutionary significance will be indicated.

Horticulture

Horticulture refers to nonmechanized systems of plant cultivation which make intensive use of neither land nor human labor. Characteristic cultivating tools of horticulturalists are hoes or digging sticks. Horticulture is sometimes called *swidden*, or slash-and-burn, cultivation. Horticulturalists customarily clear a tract of land which they wish to cultivate by cutting down primary or secondary forest or bush or by setting fire to the grass which covers the plot. The felled vegetation is burned, and the ashes remain to fertilize the soil. The crops are then sown, tended, and harvested. Often, a plot is cultivated for only one year. This depends, however, on specific environmental factors, including soil fertility and rapidity of invasion of plots by weeds and grasses which compete with cultivated plants for vital nutrients.

Cultivation of horticultural crops varies tremendously in duration from society to society. In the tropical forest of South America, the Kuikuru Indians grow two or three crops of the edible root manioc before abandoning the plot. In some areas of New Guinea, where dense populations compel more intensive use of the land, horticultural plots are planted for two or three years in succession, allowed to rest for three to five years, and then recultivated. The plot is abandoned for a longer time only after several of these plant-fallow cycles. The anthropologist Eric Wolf (1966) calls such horticultural systems *sectorial fallowing systems* and points out that, in addition to New Guinea, they have been found in both the Old World and the New World—in West Africa and highland Mexico, for example. In all cases, they are associated with denser populations than the extensive horticultural systems often found in tropical forests.

Whether the reason for abandoning a plot is declining yields or difficulty in cultivation because of thick stands of weeds and grasses, once the plot is withdrawn from cultivation, the cultivator clears another stretch of land. The original plot is allowed to revert to forest. Normally, after a fallow period of several years, and with the duration varying for different horticultural populations, the cultivator returns to the same land and cultivates it again.

Because the relationship between man and plot is not permanent, anthropologists also use the term *shifting cultivation* to refer to horticultural systems. Formerly it was thought that shifting cultivation meant also that whole villages of horticulturalists shifted sites because of declining yields. Yet the anthropologist Robert Carneiro (1956) has demonstrated that large and permanent villages may exist with horticultural strategies. Among the Kuikuru Indians whom he studied, for example, a village of 150 people had remained in the same spot for ninety years. In fact, he calculates that there was sufficient arable land located within walking distance of the village to maintain a permanent population of some 2,000 people.

Carneiro found that permanent village sites seemed to be the rule rather than the exception for South American horticulturalists.

A situation of true shifting cultivation might occur if the amount of cultivable land controlled by a village were insufficient to support a permanent settlement. After a few harvests, it would be necessary for the village to move in order to seek new lands to clear and farm. Eventually, the population might return to the original site after having occupied one or more in between. It appears rare, however, that shifts in village sites are prompted by exhaustion of soil fertility. Rather, one must examine the interaction, mediated by specific sociocultural means of adaptation, between the human population and its immediate environment. For example, the houses in a Kuikuru village are large and well made, and, since the toil involved in rebuilding them is great, the Kuikuru would rather walk further to their plots than construct a new village. On the other hand, Carneiro (1961) describes horticultural populations of the *montaña* of Peru, who live in small villages of about thirty people. In contrast to the Kuikuru's, their houses are small and simply constructed. After a few years' residence at a site, these horticulturalists typically construct new villages near virgin land. Because their houses are so simple, they prefer this alternative to walking even a half-mile to their fields.

Horticultural strategies of adaptation prevail among a large number of human populations throughout the world. The first food-producing populations in Europe were horticulturalists. Horticultural systems were until recently the predominant form of plant cultivation in most of Africa; in large areas of Southeast Asia and Indonesia, especially highland and tropical forest regions; in many parts of the Philippines; in Oceania, including most of Polynesia and Melanesia and Micronesia; among many Indian groups in Middle and Central America; and in the South American tropical forest.

The suggestion by Cohen that there are differences in the sociocultural correlates of horticultural strategies of adaptation has definite historical implications. Prehistoric transitions from foraging to horticultural and other food-producing adaptive strategies were gradual. Both in Mexico and in the Near East, the transition, the increase in the proportion of domesticates included in the diet, was also gradual. Populations were not hunters and gatherers one year and horticulturalists the next. Rather, the transition spanned several millennia. Plant cultivation began as only part of a broad spectrum of activities in prehistoric economies. Gradually, plant cultivation contributed more and more to the diet.

According to Cohen, when horticulture contributes only about one-tenth of a group's diet, as was the situation when food production first began in prehistoric populations, it may be impossible to maintain sedentary, permanent villages. After all, it is not attributes of the soil, but the distribution and seasonal appearance of wild plants and animals which remain critical in determining the movement and settlement patterns of the human population. People may assemble, plant, and disperse soon after, then forage and come together

again for the harvest. Depending on the environment and the specific human adaptation to it, they may spend a few months together after the harvest, consuming the plant foods they have harvested. Foraging resumes for the remainder of the year.

When horticulture makes a larger contribution to the diet, sedentary village life is possible, especially if the local ecosystem includes sufficient quantities of other resources for a balanced diet. Among many populations of the Old World, domesticated animals supplement a diet of cultivated plants. Since animal protein is essential to a balanced diet, hunting, fishing, and collecting may still go on. When less than half of the diet comes from cultivated plants, unless natural food resources are particularly concentrated and abundant, population densities are low, and village populations do not exceed 200 people. Often there will be only 100 or even fewer inhabitants.

In each horticultural society, there is a characteristic division of labor on the basis of sex. Among the Kuikuru, men do virtually all the horticultural work—clearing, burning, planting, weeding, and fencing in

The straw hut of the Amahuaca. *(Cornell Capa/Magnum)*

the plots. Women harvest the tubers, carry them back to the village, and undertake the time-consuming task of converting poisonous raw manioc into edible flour. The Kuikuru, however, appear to assign more work in cultivation to males than is true in most horticultural societies. Generally, men clear, burn, and build fences. They also may assist at harvest time, and they will usually do the hunting and fishing. Women may also do some of the fishing and collecting. However, female horticulturalists typically dig holes and plant the seeds, tubers, or roots. In many horticultural societies, they also weed and harvest. Preparation of the harvested crop for cooking, by pounding, mashing, grinding, or roasting, is also a female task. If there are large domesticated animals, men will tend them. Women, on the other hand, will care for pigs and fowls.

DESCENT GROUPS   There is such tremendous variation among horticultural societies of the past and present in terms of the relative importance of horticulture in the group's diet and the plant species cultivated that it is difficult to generalize about other sociocultural correlates of horticultural strategies of adaptation. Let me, however, attempt a few generalizations concerning the social organization of horticultural peoples.

The band is the basic unit of social life in most hunting and gathering societies, and the *descent group* is a basic social group in many horticultural, pastoral, and agricultural societies. Descent groups are composed of people who are all descended —or believe they are descended—from a common ancestor. There are normally several descent groups in a given society. Any one of them may be confined to a single village, but usually they will span more than one village. Any branch of the descent group which resides together is called a *localized descent group*. One of the things that keeps one descent group distinct from others in that society is its *estate*. This refers to possession and control over land

and herds or, more generally, to a variety of rights that have been inherited from the ancestral members of that descent group.

If we consider a large sample of societies with descent group organization, we see that there are several ways in which individuals may affiliate with descent groups. Probably the two most common ways are through *matrilineal* and *patrilineal descent*. In a society with matrilineal descent groups, individuals of both sexes belong to their mother's group automatically at birth, and they usually remain members of that group throughout their lives. The descent group is composed, therefore, of individuals who have been recruited through the group's female members.

When the descent rule is patrilineal, males and females belong automatically at birth to their father's descent group, and they normally remain members of this group throughout their lives. The children of all male members of the descent group become members, too, and the children of female members are excluded.

Matrilineal descent is far less common than patrilineal descent. In a sample of 564 societies, anthropologist G. P. Murdock (1957) found that there were about three times as many societies with patrilineal descent (247 to 84). Why should this be? To answer this question we must first discuss *postmarital residence rules*.

In most societies there is some prevailing opinion about where it is proper for a couple to live after their marriage. When a practice is sanctified by tradition and is considered right and appropriate in that society, we call it a *cultural rule*. In the United States, for example, people generally feel that the best arrangement after marriage is one in which the couple finds a home of its own rather than reside with the parents of either spouse. Anthropologists refer to residence of this sort as *neolocality*, which literally means "new place." When a neolocal residence rule prevails, couples will establish their own residence after marriage.

Neolocality is not very common outside of the United States, western Europe, and European-derived cultures of contemporary

Latin America. Far more common is *virilo-cality* (*vir* in Latin is "husband"), whereby the couple is expected to reside with the husband's relatives after marriage. Virilo-cality is often associated with patrilineal descent. This makes sense. If only children of male members of the group are to be descent group members and to have rights in the descent group's estate, then it is well to bring them up on that estate. This can be done if males bring their wives to, and raise their children on, the man's estate rather than the woman's.

A less common postmarital residence rule, but one often associated with matri-lineal descent groups, is *uxorilocality* (*uxor* is the Latin word for "wife"). This means that the couple is expected to live with the wife's group after marriage. However, there is a problem involved with uxorilocal residence and matrilineal descent which is not so pressing in patrilineal societies. It relates to the role of men and women in either society. In patrilineal societies, once a female member of the group marries out of her own and into her husband's group and bears children who will be members of that group, she usually has little say in the administration of her own descent group estate. Its affairs are the concern of the men who have remained at home. In most matri-lineal societies, too, men make major deci-sions and are expected to concern them-selves with the affairs of their own descent groups.

How is this reconciled with a uxorilocal residence rule which tells men to leave their descent group estate when they marry? A common way of solving the problem is to maintain descent group exog-amy and village endogamy. Endogamy re-fers to marriage within a specified social group, in this case the village of one's birth. Imagine a matrilineal society in the tropical forest of South America. There are two descent groups living in its village. The village is a circular settlement, with an open central area and houses along the periphery. Each of the two descent groups is associated with its own side of the vil-lage. When a man marries, he moves to his wife's place, but this merely involves pick-

ing up his things and walking across the village. He is residing uxorilocally, but he is close enough to home to take an active part in the affairs of his own descent group.

In societies with patrilineal descent, on the other hand, there is no major obstacle to a woman's leaving her own village en-tirely, and she normally does. The kind of village endogamy I have just mentioned may place a strait jacket on the human populations who follow the custom. If peo-ple always marry in, how does the group expand its population beyond a single vil-lage? A branch of descent group A cannot leave to found a new village unless it takes along a branch of descent group B. This is a possible explanation for the greater fre-quency of patrilineal over matrilineal socie-ties throughout the world.

While matrilineal societies are not nu-merous, they are proportionately more common among horticulturalists than among other groups. Don't misunderstand me, most horticultural societies are still patrilineal. However, the higher incidence of matrilineality among horticultural pop-ulations indicates an association between horticultural adaptation and matrilineal descent.

It has long been argued that the relating factor is the subsistence role of women in horticultural societies. The argument typi-cally runs as follows: since they have an important role in plant cultivation and since they often engage in cooperative eco-nomic activities, it is advantageous for women to be able to work together smoothly. Therefore, kinswomen should be kept together. A good way to keep them together permanently is through uxorilocal residence and matrilineal descent. Further-more, men are less important in the econ-omy; thus it does not matter so much if they move. Note, however, that this argu-ment does not explain why more than half of the world's horticultural societies are not matrilineal. Nor does it face the fact that raiding and other forms of primitive

Cooperative work among women in China. *(Mark Riboud/Magnum)*

warfare are not uncommon in horticultural societies. One could just as well argue that since cooperation among males is advantageous for warfare, patrilineal descent should be favored. The problem deserves further study, and I can offer no solution here.

HEADMEN AND BIG MEN We have seen that the authority structure of foraging societies compared with that of most other human societies is relatively *egalitarian*. The same is true of many horticultural societies. Egalitarianism generally wanes as village size and population density increase. When less than half the diet comes from horticulture, and when foraging activities are still important, villages are usually small, population density is generally low, and everyone has unimpeded access to strategic resources. Age, sex, and personality determine the respect a person will receive and the amount of support he will be able to obtain from others if he makes plans or

decisions. Although men tend to be the most important political figures in most horticultural societies, women do not hesitate to give their advice.

In horticultural villages there is usually a village *headman*, sometimes erroneously called a chief. His authority, like that of the band headman, is severely limited. If he wants something to be done, he must lead by example and persuasion. In his book *Yanomamo: The Fierce People* (1968), anthropologist Napoleon Chagnon describes the manner in which the headman gets his covillagers to prepare for a feast which will bring outsiders to their village. The headman lacks the right to issue orders. He can only persuade, harangue, and try to get public opinion on his side. If he wishes people to clean up the central plaza, he must get out and begin sweeping himself, hoping that his covillagers will take the hint and relieve him so he can turn his attention to other preparations. When conflict erupts, the Yanomamo headman may be called on to listen to both sides of a dispute. He will render his opinion and offer his advice. If one of the parties is unsatisfied, however, the headman can do nothing. He has no power to back his decisions; he has no way to impose punishments or other kinds of physical sanction. Like the band headman, he, too, is first among equals.

Horticultural populations in many areas of the Melanesian Islands and in New Guinea have a particular type of political leader that anthropologists call the *big man*. The big man is an elaborate version of the Yanomamo headman, with some of his same characteristic personality attributes and limitations. Consider the Kapauku Papuans of western New Guinea, who have been described ethnographically by Leopold Pospisil (1963). Like most other New Guineans and Melanesians, the Kapauku cultivate plants (the sweet potato is their staple) and raise pigs. The varied horticultural practices of the Kapauku are far too complex, however, to be described as simple slash and burn. Beyond the household, the only political figure encountered among the Kapauku is known as a *tonowi*. Like the Yanomamo headman, he achieves his status because he works hard—in this case, to amass wealth in pigs and other native riches. Pospisil states that the attributes which separate the Kapauku headman from his fellows include wealth, generosity, eloquence, verbal daring, and physical fitness, and, in some cases, bravery in war and supernatural powers.

Among horticultural peoples, political prominence is generally achieved by virtue of personality attributes. In this, the similarity to foragers is clear. Among the Kapauku, wealth depends on successful pig breeding and trading of wealth. But anyone who is determined enough can become a big man, since a man creates his own wealth through hard work and good judgment rather than by inheriting it. His wealth and his charisma attract supporters to the big man, make his reputation, and give him influence. He extends interest-free loans; he sponsors pig feasts in which

pigs are slaughtered ceremonially and their meat distributed to his guests.

The big man enjoys one advantage not characteristic of the Yanomamo headman. His wealth, created by his own hard work, is superior to that of his fellows. His supporters, in recognition of past favors and anticipation of future rewards, recognize him as a leader and accept his decisions as binding. The adaptation of 45,000 Kapauku to their environment involves more regulation than is the case with 10,000 Yanomamo. The big man is an important regulator of events in Kapauku life. He helps determine proper dates for feasts and markets. He persuades people to sponsor feasts, which distribute meat and other wealth. He regulates intervillage contacts by sponsoring dance expeditions to other villages. He initiates large projects which require the cooperation of the entire community.

From the example of the Kapauku big man a generalization can be made about big men and relatively egalitarian societies: if a man does manage to achieve wealth and prestige, to command respect and support beyond that of his fellows, he is expected to be generous. The big man characteristically works hard to be able to give away the fruits of his labor, to convert wealth into prestige and gratitude from his fellow tribesmen. Should an individual who aspires to become a big man renege on his obligations to be generous, he is soon deserted by his supporters and his reputation plummets. The Kapauku, in fact, take even more definite measures against big men who hoard. Pospisil reports that in some areas of Kapauku country, selfish and greedy rich men are frequently executed by their fellows, often including their own close kinsmen.

There are also differences in the decision-making authority and influence over other tribesmen between the Yanomamo and Kapauku headmen. One can generalize that the authority of political figures is a function of the complexity of regulatory problems encountered in the population's adaptation to its environment. The horticultural economy of the Kapauku Papuans is much more complex than either the Yanomamo's or the Kuikuru's, involving more varied techniques and specialized cultivation practices for specific tracts of land. In addition to two types of shifting cultivation, called by Pospisil *extensive* and *intensive*, the Kapauku practice labor-intensive cultivation of the valley floors. This involves mutual aid of individual cultivators in turning the soil prior to planting. An even more complex regulatory problem is the joint effort of the entire community to construct long drainage ditches in the valley fields.

Although it requires more regulation, Kapauku horticulture is not more productive than that of the Yanomamo or Kuikuru. Productivity may be assessed in several ways: yield per person supported per unit of land; yield per labor invested; yield per unit of land per year; yield per unit of land over several years; or, in the case of sedentary agriculture, yield on a permanent basis.

Considering a large sample of horticultural populations, one could generalize that as village population increases, distance between settlements decreases, in short, that population density increases as reliance on horticulture increases or as more productive horticultural techniques are elaborated. For example, an increase in population density in a given area will occur when multiple crops are grown around the village throughout the year. Whatever the reasons promoting increased population density and larger villages in the area, these demographic changes represent environmental modifications that pose new regulatory problems and require new adaptive means. As villages grow, as the number of people regularly living together increases, interpersonal conflicts also increase. In Nigeria, in western Africa, there are villages of sectorial-fallowing horticulturalists whose populations exceed 1,000 people lo-

cated in areas where population densities exceed 200 people per square mile. In Amazonia, Carneiro (1968) found documentation for a village of 1,400 inhabitants in 1824, supported by extensive slash-and-burn cultivation. When village size exceeds 1,000, there may be several, and perhaps ten or more, descent groups in the same village instead of one or two. Not only are there myriad interpersonal relationships to worry about, there are intergroup relationships as well. In societies with a well-developed descent group structure, a man's allegiance is principally to his descent group, only secondarily to village and tribe. He is expected to take the side of his own group in any dispute with another group that resides in the same village.

If disorder is not to be a day-to-day characteristic of these large-scale horticultural societies, it is necessary to have someone to regulate conflict, to arbitrate disputes among individuals and groups. The functions of the headman and his manner of selection vary among larger-scale horticultural societies, but the task of this political figure as regulator is fairly demanding. He may have to direct military actions or hunting expeditions. He arbitrates disputes between villagers. He may have to reallocate land used by villagers if, because of different rates of population increase, some descent groups have grown too big for their ancestral estates while others are still too small to exploit their own. He and other elders in the community may resolve conflicts over land or other matters from time to time.

Note another difference. In the smaller-scale societies a man's position rests on age, sex, and personality characteristics. When human populations are organized into descent groups, another basis for status develops—descent group leadership. Localized descent groups normally have their own leaders. In some cases, villages are so small that there is only one man, the oldest male member of the descent group, who is appropriate for the job. But what happens if by chance there are two of the same age who want it? Personality may still determine whom most people regard as the head, or the position may be assigned according to some order of birth. Generally, however, there will be consultation among all the older males, and sometimes the females, over descent group affairs.

In villages with multiple descent groups, each of these has a head. All heads together may form a council of advisers or, normally, a council of elders, to assist the headman. Cooperating, they represent the local power structure: the authority of the headman is supported by his council of elders, and it is up to them to make sure that decisions reached through their deliberations are carried out by the members of their individual descent groups. You can understand that the headman must obtain agreement by all council members on decisions which apply to the village population. Sometimes, however, it is difficult to reach agreement, since decisions good for the community at large may adversely affect the interests of one or more of the descent groups—and descent groups are still important. Societies that rely heavily on horticulture are rarely nation-states; they are, instead, *tribal societies*. This means that there is no centralized rule and that decisions made by such political bodies as headmen and councils of elders cannot be enforced through any constituted physical means. If the head of one descent group is recalcitrant, the only means of coercion that the other heads and the headman can employ are persuasion and public opinion. And if individuals do not wish to follow the advice of their descent group elders, they may be asked to leave the village; but, again, community opinion and persuasion are usually brought to bear.

Despite their enlarged powers, the descent group leaders and the headman are still expected to be generous. The wealth and life styles of these political figures are normally not very far above those of their fellow villagers. They take part in subsistence activity. They are only part-time political specialists. If they control more land and larger and more productive households, they are expected, like Kapauku big

men and other headmen, to give more feasts and support more dependents than ordinary cultivators. Social classes do not exist in most large-scale horticultural societies. However, when horticultural populations are also involved in long-distance trade networks, significant wealth and class differences may exist.

The manner of choosing the illage headman varies with horticultural strategies of adaptation. In some cases, in villages where there are several descent groups, the headmanship rotates among them. In other societies, there are elections among descent group leaders. In still other cases, the office of headman is confined to one of the several descent groups, perhaps the largest, but the incumbent relies on the support and approval of representatives of the other descent groups. Finally, choice of the headman may be associated with ritual. He may be chosen because of supernatural powers that he is believed to possess. His abilities may be the result of training in ritual matters; or people may believe that they are inherited or have come through divine revelation. In some horticultural societies, the headman's supernatural associations support his general authority. Among the Kapauku, shamanistic expertise, although not essential to headmanship, does enhance its power.

Pastoral strategies of adaptation

In the Near East and North Africa, in several eastern European and Asiatic regions, and in Africa south of the Sahara live human populations who orient their activities around the care of domesticated animals. They are called *pastoralists*. There are differences between stockbreeding populations in their use of herd animals. In the adaptive strategies of some, animals are a means rather than an end of production. Among the Indians of the Great Plains, for example, the horse was not consumed as food but was used to pursue the large bison herds, which were major subsistence resources. Later, you will see that in many agricultural economies, too, animals have been used as a means rather than an end of production.

East African pastoralists may be considered typical of human populations who live symbiotically with herd animals and who derive food and other necessary items from their herds. Herds supply East Africans with milk and other dairy products. In addition, cattle blood is regularly consumed, and the meat is eaten. Meat is often available in East Africa only for ceremonial purposes. Cattle are slaughtered at funerals and when there are other ceremonies. Since these occur throughout the year, beef is available on a fairly constant basis. Cattle also provide leather, used by East Africans in making sandals and other items of adornment and also for containers.

Like horticulture, pastoralism as an adaptive strategy is an ideal type. Some human populations rely on their herd animals more completely than others. It is impos-

sible, however, for people to base subsistence exclusively on a single animal species, and most pastoral populations supplement their diet by hunting, gathering, fishing, horticulture, or trade. As is true in all nonindustrial human populations, there is a sex-based division of labor in pastoral societies. In East Africa, women usually look after the children and collect and cultivate crops, using horticultural techniques, while men care for the herds.

There are two characteristic patterns of life associated with pastoral strategies of adaptation: *transhumance* and *pastoral nomadism*. Transhumance involves a characteristic movement of herd animals throughout the year as pastures in different areas and at different elevations become available. There is a distinction between grazing lands of the summer and winter or between those used in the dry and rainy seasons. When the pastoral strategy is transhumance, only a part of the population accompanies the herds. Generally, certain men and boys supervise the seasonal grazing of the herds while other men, and women and children, remain at a vil-

Cattle slaughter to provide meat for the village in Tanzania. *(Ray E. Ellis/Rapho Guillumette)*

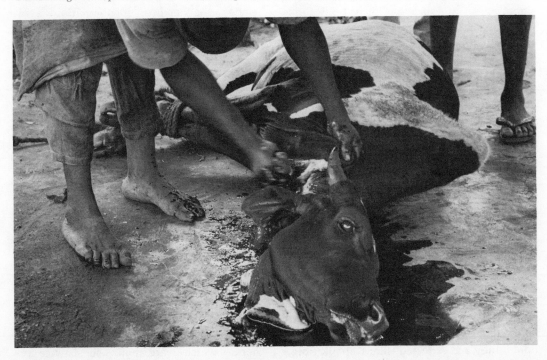

The pastoral strategy of adaptation. A Masai boy herds cattle. *(John & Bini Moss/Black Star)*

lage site located close to horticultural plots, other subsistence sources, and the pasture land where herds graze longest during the year.

When the pastoral strategy is nomadic, on the other hand, the entire population—men, women, and children—moves along with the herds throughout the year, following grazing lands as they become available seasonally. There is no permanent home camp or village site. Since no pas-

toral population can subsist on its herds alone and crops are needed to supplement the diet, all pastoralists have developed ways of getting plant foods. Normally, transhumants also cultivate. Nomads typically maintain trade relations with plant-cultivating groups that they meet in their annual movements. Transhumants may have trade relationships with plant cultivators, too. Often the relationships between pastoral and plant-cultivating popu-

Camp Fulani nomads in Chad. *(Jacques Jangoux)*

lations are symbiotic in an ecological sense. Each supplies resources needed by the other. In nonindustrial societies where herd animals are important, they are the equivalents of the contemporary bank. Plant cultivators, when they have a surplus, can trade this surplus for herd animals. Later, if their crops fail or their harvests are meager, they may convert their animals into vegetable food by trading them to other plant cultivators who fared better that year.

It is possible to observe some trends in the social organization of pastoral societies. For example, very few are matrilineal. In most, there is fairly strict virilocal residence after marriage. When a woman marries, she generally leaves her home to join her husband's group. Herds are usually transmitted patrilineally from father to son. Yet pastoralists are often not strictly patrilineal. As with hunting and gathering, individual mobility is possible with a pastoral adaptive strategy. Herds, representing the basic pastoral resource, are mobile. Individuals are not tied inextricably to any one plot of land. If a man is unhappy with his father's group, he usually has the option of residing with his mother's group or in the group of some other kinsman instead. Fictive kinship is also important to many pastoralists, and it can be used to gain entrance to a group. The composition of pastoral villages and camps, like that of the foraging band, varies considerably from year to year.

Agriculture

Agriculture refers to systems of plant cultivation which require greater labor input and use land more intensively and more continuously than horticultural systems. As the discussion of horticulture suggested, the differences between horticulture and agriculture are quantitative rather than qualitative; they are contrasts of degree rather than of kind. Examination of a large sample of horticultural societies indicates that some use land much more intensively than others. Even when we limit our attention to a sample of populations representing only one area of the world, we see a continuum in intensity of land use and human labor invested in cultiva-

"Trampling" among the Betsileo of south central Madagascar. *(Conrad P. Kottak)*

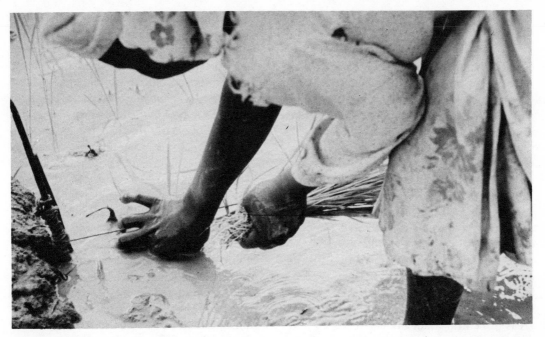

A Betsileo woman transplants rice seedlings. (*Conrad P. Kottak*)

tion. For example, Jacques Barrau (1958) demonstrated continuous variation in cultivation techniques among seventeen Melanesian populations—from rudimentary, extensive slash and burn through sectorial fallowing to long-term use of the same plot requiring soil turning, drainage techniques, terracing, composting, and crop rotation. Such advanced horticulture supports population densities in excess of 100 individuals per square mile, comparable to many agricultural systems. Indeed, in a few areas of the New Guinea highlands, population density rises to over 400 people per square mile. Understanding then that horticulture and agriculture are only *ideal types*, let us adopt the following rule of thumb to distinguish them. If plant cultivation involves use of domesticated animals, irrigation, or well-developed terracing systems, then we are dealing with an agricultural rather than a horticultural economy.

Animals may be used as a means of production in several ways. They may be harnessed to plows and harrows for field preparation. They may be attached to carts for transport. Agriculturalists find other uses for their livestock, for example, as cultivating machines. Among the Betsileo, rice

cultivators of central Madagascar, rice is sown in nursery beds. When seedlings are big enough, they are transplanted to flooded rice fields. The Betsileo keep humped zebu cattle. When the rice fields have been flooded and tilled, they let the cattle into them. By yelling at them and switching them, young men drive the cattle into a frenzy so that they will trample the fields, breaking up the clumps of earth and thoroughly mixing the water with the earth to form a smooth mud in which women can transplant the rice seedlings. Like many other agriculturalists, too, the Betsileo collect the manure of their domesticated animals and use it to fertilize their plots, thereby increasing yields.

The Betsileo also irrigate their rice fields with water which they bring in canals from rivers, streams, springs, and ponds. To an extent, irrigation frees the farmer from the vagaries of nature. He does not have to wait for rainfall before he can plant his crops, for he controls sources of water. Furthermore, irrigation makes it possible for a given plot of land to be cultivated year after year. It is a means of soil enrichment. The irrigated field is a unique ecosystem in which several species of plants and animals, many of them minute organisms, live. Their organic wastes, the products of metabolism and decomposition, fertilize the land. The Betsileo, like other agriculturalists throughout the world, have been farming the same fields for generations, and yields do not appear to have fallen off since the days of their ancestors. In fact, it takes an irrigated field some time to get going. It reaches full productivity only after having been cultivated for several years.

Terracing is another agricultural technique which the Betsileo have mastered. Many agriculturalists wrest their livelihoods out of rugged countryside. Some areas of central Madagascar are very hilly, with small valleys separated by steep hillsides. If cultivation is to proceed in densely populated areas, it is necessary to farm these hills. If one simply plants on the steep hillsides, however, crops and good soil will be washed down during the rainy season. So the Betsileo cut into the hillside and construct stage after stage of cultivable field rising from the valley floor. These terraced fields are irrigated from springs above them, and the same advantages associated with irrigation in any field accrue

to them. The amount of labor involved in building and maintaining a terrace system is great. The walls of the terraces crumble every year and must be partially rebuilt. The canals and outlets which convey water from terraces above to those below also demand attention.

Given any of these cultivation techniques, there are some important differences between agriculture and horticulture. More human labor is involved in constructing and maintaining irrigation and terrace systems than in slashing and burning. Domesticated animals must be fed and cared for by populations that use them as part of the technology of cultivation. In return for intensive labor investment, the same land can produce one or more crops a year for several years and even across generations. Sedentary populations are always characteristic of agriculture, growing up around the permanent fields. Agricultural techniques do not necessarily increase annual crop yields over those produced horticulturally. The first crop cultivated by horticulturalists after clearing new or long idle forest land may have a higher yield than a crop cultivated agriculturally from a plot of the same size. With regard to the amount of labor invested, too, the yield of the horticulturalist is usually higher. Actually, in terms of crop production, the major

SUMMARY

Two different kinds of evolutionary statements may be made about humans: general evolutionary, which apply to the genus *Homo*, and specific evolutionary, which apply to particular human populations adapting to changing environments. The doctrine of unilineal evolution, a general evolutionary doctrine, was proposed by nineteenth-century scientists. More recently, anthropologist Leslie White has written of the evolution of culture, an approach similar to general evolution but concentrating on changes in *Homo*'s basic adaptive apparatus, culture. Anthropolo-

gist Julian Steward has advocated studies of multilinear evolution, examination of cases involving convergent evolution, comparison of specific evolutionary sequences among widespread unrelated populations.

Anthropologist Yehudi Cohen has proposed six strategies of adaptation to the environment: foraging, horticulture, pastoralism, agriculture, mercantilism, and industrialism. The first four are examined in detail in this chapter. Foraging was the only strategy of adaptation pursued by humans until the advent of food production 10,000 years ago. Food production replaced

In the foreground, a Betsileo woman tends pigs. Terraced fields cut into the hillside beyond. *(Conrad P. Kottak)*

difference between horticultural and agricultural strategies is that the *long-term yield per unit area* is far greater under agricultural systems. A single area continuously supports the population that cultivates it. Thus, it is understandable that populations of agriculturalists are usually denser than populations of horticulturalists.

As humans learn new ways of dealing with some of the inhospitable aspects of nature, the range of environments open to human utilization and settlement becomes greater. There are agricultural populations in many areas of the world that would be too arid for horticultural strategies of

adaptation. We shall see in the following chapter that many of the world's ancient civilizations in arid lands arose on an agricultural base.

There are tremendous differences in the social and political organization of typical agricultural populations on the one hand, and those employing foraging, horticultural, and pastoral strategies, on the other. Some of these differences, including significant contrasts in wealth and power within agricultural populations, will also be discussed in the following pages, which deal with the emergence of civilization and the state.

foraging throughout most of the world, but foragers survive today in marginal areas. Correlates of a foraging strategy reflect the nature of specific environments. The band is often the basic social unit among foragers. Sometimes band members remain together throughout the year; other times they fragment seasonally into foraging microbands or elementary or extended families. Ties of kinship and marriage, trade, and other arrangements link members of bands. In most foraging societies, tasks are assigned on the basis of sex and age; men generally hunt and females

gather. Old people often retire partially from subsistence activities and care for children. Foragers characteristically form the most egalitarian of all human societies; there is little differential authority and no differential power among band members; prestige reflects age, sex, and individual achievements.

Like other strategies of adaptation described, horticulture and agriculture are ideal types. Horticulture refers to nonindustrial systems of plant cultivation which do not use either land or human labor intensively. Horticulturalists generally cultivate a plot of land for one or two years, then abandon it. More intensive variants exist in horticulture, but there is always a fallowing period. This represents the major contrast with agricultural systems, where the same plot of land is used on a permanent basis. Horticulturalists may shift their plots while remaining in the same village. The first plant-cultivating economies were horticultural, and this strategy of adaptation still occurs in many areas of both Old and New Worlds.

The social and economic correlates of horticultural strategies reflect the amount of food that horticulture contributes to the diet and the intensity and yields of produc-

tive labor. Since horticulture is only an ideal type, it is often combined with other strategies of adaptation—for example, pastoralism or foraging. Horticulturalists normally live in villages and often belong to descent groups. Horticultural societies span a large range in terms of village size and population density, reflecting the differential productivity in their economies.

Egalitarianism generally wanes as village size and population density increase, since there are now more interpersonal relationships to be regulated. Horticultural villages generally have a headman; however, his authority is very limited. He must lead by example and persuasion and has no sure means of enforcing his decisions. Authority associated with political figures in horticultural societies generally increases

Sources and Suggested Readings

BARRAU, J.
1958   *Subsistence Agriculture in Melanesia.* Bulletin 219. Honolulu: Bernice P. Bishop Museum. French ethnobotanist examines variations in cultivation techniques in Melanesia.

CARNEIRO, R.
1956   Slash-and Burn Agriculture: A Closer Look at Its Implications for Settlement Patterns. In *Men and Cultures,* Selected Papers of the Fifth International Congress of Anthropological and Ethnological Sciences, pp. 229–234. Philadelphia: University of Pennsylvania Press. Influential article which suggests that shifting cultivation may be compatible with permanent villages.

1968   (orig. 1961). Slash-and-Burn Cultivation among the Kuikuru and Its Implications for Cultural Development in the Amazon Basin. In *Man in Adaptation: The Cultural Present*, ed. Y. Cohen, pp. 131–145. Chicago: Aldine. Intriguing comparison of different slash-and-burn adaptations in South America, with implications for understanding the origin of the state.

CHAGNON, N.
1968   *Yanomamo: The Fierce People.* New York: Holt, Rinehart and Winston. Fascinating account of South American Indians; very popular among introductory anthropology students.

COHEN, Y.
1968   Culture as Adaptation. In *Man in Adaptation: The Cultural Present*, ed. Y. Cohen, pp. 40–60. Chicago: Aldine. Sets forth his typology of strategies of adaptation and uses it to organize the uniformly interesting essays in this reader in cultural anthropology.

GEERTZ, C.
1963   *Agricultural Involution: The Process of Ecological Change in Indonesia.* Berkeley: University of California Press. Includes often-cited chapter contrasting horticultural and agricultural adaptations in Java.

HARRIS, M.
1968   *The Rise of Anthropological Theory.* New York: Crowell. Provocative and controversial account of the history of anthropology.

MORGAN, L. H.
1967   (orig. 1877). *Ancient Society.* Cleveland: World Publishing. An anthropological classic; the transition from savagery through barbarism to civilization. Although many specific arguments are now discounted, Morgan has influenced generations of anthropologists.

MURDOCK, G. P.
1957   World Ethnographic Sample. *American Anthropologist* 59: 664–687. Coded quantitative data on 565 cultures for fifteen variables, including aspects of social, political, and economic organization.

as population size and density and the scale of regulatory problems increase.

Pastoral strategies of adaptation involve domesticated animals, usually cattle, sheep, or goats. Pastoralists occupy large areas of the Near East, North Africa, sub-Saharan Africa, and eastern Europe. There are two basic variants of pastoralism—transhumance and nomadism. Transhumants often maintain permanent village communities, and part of the population leaves the village seasonally to travel with herds to pasture lands. Among pastoral nomads, the entire population moves seasonally with the herds. Since humans cannot subsist on herds alone, nomads usually trade with cultivators, and transhumants cultivate various crops. Pastoralists usually belong to descent groups.

Agriculture describes nonindustrial systems of plant cultivation in which the same land is used continuously. Agricultural systems also characteristically demand intensive use of human labor. Agricultural systems are often associated with one or more of the following practices: irrigation, terracing, use of domesticated animals for labor, and manuring. Because the same land is used permanently, agricultural populations are commonly denser than those supported by other strategies of adaptation. While there are some tribal agriculturalists, agriculture is often associated with state organization. Descent groups exist here, too.

POSPISIL, L.

1963   *The Kapauku Papuans of West New Guinea.* New York: Holt, Rinehart and Winston. Interesting case study; includes a discussion of the Kapauku *tonowi* or "headman."

SAHLINS, M. D.

1963   Poor Man, Rich Man, Big-Man, Chief: Political Types in Melanesia and Polynesia. *Comparative Studies in Society and History* 5: 285–303. Compares political and authority figures in Polynesian chiefdoms and Melanesian tribes.

SAHLINS, M. D., and SERVICE, E. R.

1960   *Evolution and Culture.* Ann Arbor: University of Michigan Press. Application of evolutionary principles to cultural anthropological data a century after Darwin.

SCHNEIDER, D. M., and GOUGH, E. K., eds.

1961   *Matrilineal Kinship.* Berkeley: University of California Press. Everything you always wanted to know about matrilineal descent; includes case studies and comparative essays.

SCHNEIDER, H. K.

1957   The Subsistence Role of Cattle among the Pakot and in East Africa. *American Anthropologist* 59: 278–300. The role of cattle in the ritual and economic life of an East African people.

STEWARD, J.

1949   Cultural Causality and Law: A Trial Formulation of the Development of Early Civilizations. *American Anthropologist* 51: 1–27. Brilliant essay synthesizing archeological and cultural data to show convergent evolution, through analogous stages, of the state in five areas of the world.

1955   *Theory of Culture Change.* Urbana: University of Illinois Press. Modern anthropological classic; Steward argues for studies of convergent sociocultural evolution, suggests ecological approaches to sociocultural data, and offers techniques for the anthropological study of complex societies.

WHITE, L. A.

1959   *The Evolution of Culture: The Development of Civilization to the Fall of Rome.* New York: McGraw-Hill. Modern classic; major statement of general evolution and its application to culture.

WOLF, E. R.

1966   *Peasants.* Englewood Cliffs, N.J.: Prentice-Hall. Best introduction to the cross-cultural studies of peasants.

YENGOYAN, A. A.

1968   Demographic and Ecological Influences on Aboriginal Australian Marriage Sections. In *Man the Hunter,* ed. R. B. Lee and I. DeVore, pp. 185–199. Chicago: Aldine. In this anthology about foragers, Yengoyan explains some puzzling features of Australian section (marriage) systems in terms of demographic and other ecological factors.

4. Chiefs, States, Cities, and Civilization

Anthropologist Elman Service (1971) has suggested that there are five broadly different types or levels of sociocultural organization or integration: _band, tribe, chiefdom, archaic state,_ and _industrial state._ Band organization is characteristic of most foragers. Tribes, on the other hand, pursue strategies of adaptation based on food production that is extensive rather than intensive in its use of land and labor. Thus the economy of most tribal societies involves horticulture or pastoralism or a mixture of the two. Rarely, one encounters tribal agriculturalists. The human populations of the Paleolithic and Mesolithic periods—foragers and early food producers —were organized according to band and tribal principles, which are based on ties of kinship and marriage.

Differential Access

We are ready to turn now to forms of sociopolitical organization which appeared later in the evolution of _Homo_—the chiefdom and the archaic state. Both in chiefdoms and in states one encounters _differ-_ _ential access_ to strategic and socially valued resources. This means that some members of the population included within any chiefdom or state enjoy privileged access to power, prestige, and wealth; others do not. Privileged members commonly control access even to strategic resources—food, water, and other items necessary to sustain life. There are also similarities in the economic underpinnings of chiefdoms and states. In many chiefdoms and most archaic states, the economy is agricultural. Furthermore, both chiefdoms and states are usually forms of sociopolitical organization which administer populations occupying a variety of ecologically diverse niches. Associated with this diversity are systems of exchange.

There are also certain significant differences between chiefdoms and archaic states. The most basic is that in chiefdoms social relations and individual membership in sociopolitical groups are regulated as in band or tribal society, by principles of kinship, marriage, fictive kinship, descent, age, generation, and sex; whereas, in states they are also regulated by common residence and relationship to a government. Because the chiefdom retains the kinship emphasis of tribal society while simultaneously assigning to its members differential access to strategic resources, it may be considered to be a transitional form between tribal and state organization. This is, of course, a general evolutionary statement. The first chiefdom appeared before the first state. In general, there has been a chiefdom phase—that is, one in which kinship and differential access were both important—in the specific evolutionary sequences which led to most archaic states. Let us consider more fully the chiefdom before turning to varieties of states.

The chiefdom

The chiefdom is like the band and the tribe in that kinship is still important in interpersonal relations. We owe a great deal of our knowledge of how chiefdoms work to ethnographic studies carried out in Polynesia, where chiefdoms were especially numerous at the time of European explorations. Depending on the island, the chiefs who ruled generally kept long genealogies, sometimes tracing their ancestry back as far as fifty generations. Everyone in a given chiefdom was related to everyone else, and all were believed to be descended from the common founding ancestor. To become chief it was necessary to demonstrate seniority in descent. Usually, seniority was based on being the eldest son of the eldest son of the eldest son and so on, to the common ancestor.

So intricate was the calculation of relative seniority in some areas of Polynesia that there were virtually as many gradations in rank as there were people. For example, the third son would rank below the second, who, in turn, would rank below the first. If their father was an eldest son, however, all three would rank above the children of their father's next younger brother, whose children would, in turn, outrank those of the other brothers in order of birth. Because everyone was related, when a Polynesian chief addressed even the lowest ranking man in his chiefdom, he was still dealing with a kinsman. The principle, therefore, determining access to rank, power, prestige, and strategic resources, was one of kinship and descent.

Since he lived in a kin-based society, the chief was expected to be generous. However, his generosity was different from that of the tribal big man. In a tribal society, the status of big man was created. Big men arose on the basis of personality. When someone wanted to establish himself as a big man, he set about doing it. Sometimes, there were no big men. The chief occupied an office, a permanent position in the social structure. There would be someone to replace him when he died. With his close kinsmen and advisers, the chief managed the entire system, and there was always a chief to do this. Included in his organization of the chiefdom were means of regulating production, distribution, and consumption of produce and products. The chief was normally a full-time political specialist; unlike the tribal big man, he was divorced from labor for subsistence. Other people supported him.

The chief could influence production by declaring taboos on growing certain crops or on cultivating certain areas of land. On the other hand, he could direct that certain crops be grown. He was important in regulating distribution and consumption because his office had means of collecting products and services from the population at large. There were times during the year when members of the population turned over some of what they had produced to the chief. They might, for example, offer him or one of his representatives (called a *steward*) the first fruits or some more substantial portion of their harvests. These products were transferred from lower-level to higher-level stewards until eventually they reached the chief. Then, once or more during the year, the chief might sponsor a feast or giveaway, in which he *redistributed* to the people some of what he had received. The flow of goods into and out of such a central office or storehouse is known as *redistribution*. In it, we see that a chief was still expected to demonstrate some of the generosity associated with big men, headmen, descent group leaders, and other figures of prestige in tribal societies. There are certain obvious economic advantages associated with redistribution. Since, as was stated previously, chiefdoms commonly administer an ecologically diverse population, different areas grow different crops and provide different goods and services to the center. The chief, through redistribution, made the specialized products of diversified zones available to the whole population of the chiefdom. Redistribution has another economic function. Sometimes famines occur in some areas but not others. The central storehouse can be viewed as a means of social security, directing resources from zones which have enjoyed a productive year to others in which production has fallen below normal expectations.

Differences between chiefdoms and states

There are some major contrasts between chiefdoms and states. States, first, are not usually kin-based societies. Their populations are divided into socioeconomic classes. In archaic states there are usually only two: upper and lower, elites and masses. Kinship ties do not extend from elites to masses. Generally, there is a tendency toward class endogamy. Most peasants marry other peasants; members of the elites marry other members of their own *stratum*, or class. Second, while there are some archaic states which have redistributive systems, generosity is underplayed in the state compared with the chiefdom. Why should this be so? In the chiefdom, everyone, depending on his particular line of descent, has a different status. The oldest son of the second son of an oldest son has a status different from the second son of the oldest son of the oldest son. Individual gradations in rank are gradual and continuous. It is difficult to draw a line dividing elites and masses. Yet states have done so, and, since chiefdoms

often develop into states, at many times and in many areas of the world where chiefdoms have become states, chiefs have been converted into kings by demoting former noble relatives to commoner status.

In archaic states, therefore, there is a division between elites and masses, and this division is maintained by a tendency toward *stratum endogamy*. Furthermore, in states, the elite class is more clearly demarcated in terms of its privileges and activities from the masses than are the chief and his close relatives. Most members of the elite take no part in subsistence activity. They have become state personnel with specialized functions to perform. They are administrators, tax collectors, judges, advisers to the king, and, with him, law makers; they may be military officials or members of a scholarly or priestly subsystem of the society. As the state grows, the elite group, the part of the population freed from direct concern with subsistence, also grows. In the archaic state, it is up to the population at large to support the elites. As in the chiefdom, this is accomplished through administrative intervention in production, distribution, and consumption of goods and services. The state decrees that a certain area is to produce certain goods. It forbids certain economic activities in other areas. It expropriates the produce and labor of members of the lower stratum.

In contrast to redistribution in the chiefdom, much of what the state gets in does not flow back to the population at large. Its wealth is used to feed, clothe, and generally support the life style of members of the elite. The king enlists peasants to build him a tomb which will mark his position in the afterlife. Peasants are sometimes called on to fight for territory which will provide the elites with items of no interest at all to the masses. The elite groups in states always enjoy *sumptuary goods*—jewelry, certain kinds of foods and drink, clothing which is reserved for those of their rank. As we shall see in Chapter 9,

when we discuss peasants, often the dietary needs of the masses suffer because state officials force them to cater first to the needs of the state and its elite. Life in a civilization is not necessarily a more fulfilling and happier experience for the majority of the population than life in a band or tribe. Obviously, the use here of the term *civilized* does not imply "better," "easier," "happier," "more valuable," or any other meaning which suggests superiority.

The contrast between chiefdom and state, then, pits a kin-based society in which generosity is still associated with prestige against a class-structured society in which the needs and prerogatives of the elite take precedence over those of the masses. With this in mind, let us consider some differences between archaic states.

Cities, Civilizations, and States

The first states appeared in the Old World: in southern Mesopotamia more than 5,000

years ago and slightly later in the lower (northern) Nile region of Egypt. Subsequently, states and civilizations were to develop independently of Egypt and Mesopotamia in the Indus River valley of India and Pakistan, in northern China, and in two areas of the New World—Middle America (Mexico-Guatemala) and the central Andes (Peru-Bolivia). One encounters a certain amount of terminological confusion among archeologists and other anthropologists in their use of the terms *civilization* and *state*, and in the relationship between these terms and *urbanism*— the presence of towns and cities. This reflects the fact that the first state, that which arose in southern Mesopotamia, was, according to criteria discussed here, also the first civilization. Furthermore, the world's earliest urban centers also grew up in Mesopotamia. Thus for Mesopotamia the origin of the state was the origin of civilization, and the origin of civilization was the rise of the city. But this was not so elsewhere.

Although "civilization" is derived from the Latin *civis*, which means "city," cities, or urban centers, are not characteristic of all civilizations. One can distinguish between two varieties of civilization: urban and nonurban. Most societies that exhibit the attributes of civilization are urban. Within their boundaries are cities—populations of 10,000 or more people concentrated in a small, continuous, compact (that is, *nucleated*) area. Cities are characterized by intense social differentiation based on variations in wealth, economic specialization, and power (Sanders and Price, 1968). The earliest civilization, Mesopotamia, was, throughout its evolution, an urban civilization, concentrated in a fertile area. Most of the classic civilizations which developed in both the New and the Old Worlds prior to the Iron Age were also urban centers. In the central highlands of Mexico, two urban centers, Teotihuacan, which thrived during the first six centuries A.D., and Tenochtitlan, capital of the Aztec

Empire at the time of the Spanish conquest in the early sixteenth century, had socio-economically differentiated populations in excess of 50,000. Towns and cities were equally characteristic of ancient Peruvian civilization. Chanchan on the northern coast and Tiahuanaco in the southern highlands were cities fully comparable in size and functions to those of central Mexico. On the other hand, cities, as we have defined them, were missing among the lowland Maya, who developed a civilization founded on shifting horticulture and regional trade. Nor were urban centers significant in the early evolution of ancient Egyptian civilization, during the Old Kingdom. Between the early urban civilizations of India and China, in Southeast Asia arose the Khmer nation, a civilization without cities.

In those areas where, more typically, cities and civilization arose together, an

The Pyramid of the Sun at Teotihuacan, in the central highlands of Mexico. *(Dr. Georg Gerster/Rapho Guillumette)*

important social distinction emerged between the city dweller and the rural inhabitant of the same society. Certain attributes and activities set the urban population off from inhabitants of the countryside. In the preindustrial world, it is in towns and cities that individuals who do not engage in agriculture, horticulture, fishing, pastoralism, or other subsistence activities typically have their homes. This does not mean that food producers never live in preindustrial cities. In fact, they often comprise a large percentage of its population. However, economic differentiation is the key attribute of cities. Marketplaces, scenes of an active commerce, are often characteristic of the preindustrial city. In the Sumerian civilization of ancient Mesopotamia, the city was the residence of rulers, administrators, government officials, priests, merchants, artisans, and others not directly connected with subsistence. In the rural zones lived the farmers, herdsmen, small-time merchants and traders, fishermen, and rural artisans. Contrasts in the life styles of these two diverse groups gave rise to the distinction between urbanites and country folk.

With civilization there arose what the anthropologist Robert Redfield (1955, 1956) called the distinction between the "Great Tradition" and the "Little Tradition." The Great Tradition oriented life in the cities. Its components were the art, music, manners, and codes of etiquette—in short, the customary behavior—of urbanites. Different was the culture of rural people in the same society—their so-called folk art and folk music, their rustic manners.

The contrast in life style between urbanite and country dweller provides one basis for social differentiation with urban civilizations. Other social distinctions—for example, those arising from occupation or from inherited wealth or power—are characteristic of civilizations and states in general, not just of those with urban centers. Some members of the population of a civilized society are born to spend their lives working in the fields. Others are born to rule, to enjoy wealth and power. No longer does an individual's achievement rest merely on his abilities. The determinants of prestige and success now have a hereditary basis.

Ascribed and achieved status

To clarify the tremendous difference between civilized society and social forms that preceded it, some definitions are in order. Anthropologists traditionally distinguish between ascribed and achieved status in any society. A *status* is simply a position in the social structure. The distinction drawn earlier between evolution and history will help explain what is meant by *social structure*. History, you will remember, has to do with individuals. Evolution has to do with forms. Every society may be said to have a form—its social structure. As individuals mature, they occupy different positions in the social structure. When they die, these positions are vacated, and others fill them. Status endures, even though the individual occupants change. Thus the social form endures, while at the same time there is historical change. There is history without evolution.

Some status is *ascribed*; this means position is determined for an individual, who has no say in the status he occupies. Sex is an obvious ascribed status (even though there are societies, including our own, in which an individual may change his sex). Age is also an ascribed status; an individual has little to say about growing old. *Achieved* status, on the other hand, is not gained automatically. In every hunting band there is a status called "best hunter." Individuals achieve this status through hunting skill. There is usually a ritual specialist in bands of foragers. Typically, certain individuals achieve this status.

Individual members of horticultural and pastoral populations in tribal societies may differ in wealth and power, but usually these differences are achieved rather than ascribed. As in the band society, where a man makes his reputation as a good hunter, in the tribal society, a man may make his reputation as a big man. As we have seen, generosity and the ability to attract supporters are important personality attributes of the big man.

In populations whose social organization is more complex, there are marked differences in wealth, prestige, and power. In many instances these are ascribed. Wealth is retained in families, so that one person may be born into a rich family, another into poverty. In many ancient civilizations, there was a paramount ruling status known as king or sovereign. This status conferred on its occupant great prestige and inspired great respect, not because the sovereign was a good ruler, but merely because he was sovereign. Often, too, people were taught that the sovereign was divine, or that his rule was divinely approved.

Differences between states and civilizations

The contrast between ancient civilizations and all previous forms of human social organization may be stated more generally as a contrast between state and nonstate organization. Hereditary differences in wealth, power, and prestige represent a common form of differential access to strategic resources, which is a universal attribute of state organization. As one may distinguish between urban and nonurban civilizations, one may also distinguish between states which are and are not civilizations. *State*, obviously, is the more inclusive term. Perhaps the most useful definition of state has been given by the anthropologist Morton Fried. Fried presents what he calls a "bare but essential list of state functions and institutions" (1960, p. 728). The primary functions of any state are to maintain general order and support the order of socioeconomic stratification. All states are stratified societies. That is, their populations are divided into two or more duosexual, multiage groups—strata which contrast in social status and economic prerogatives. One group, the *superordinate* stratum, enjoys privileged access to wealth, power, and other valued

resources. The other is *subordinate*, and its members' access to strategic resources is limited by members of the privileged group.

States develop means of accomplishing their primary functions which involve the creation of special-purpose parts and subsystems with a variety of secondary functions. Among them are the following: (1) population control, including the fixing of boundaries, establishment of categories of membership, and census taking; (2) the disposal of trouble cases, encompassing a system of civil and criminal laws, regular legal procedure, the appointment of judges and other regular officers of adjudication; (3) the protection of sovereignty, including maintenance of military and police forces; (4) taxation and conscription to support the foregoing functions.

The archeologist V. Gordon Childe (1950) has discussed the following attributes of early or archaic civilization: (1) increasing size and density of populations included within the same sociopolitical unit; (2) occupational specialization, including the appearance of a class of nonfood producers and full-time specialists in craft production as well as transport workers, merchants, officials, and priests; (3) regular expropriation from the subordinate stratum of tithes for a deity or taxes for a divine king, and management of this capital by priests or government officials; (4) construction of monumental public buildings; (5) existence of a ruling class consisting of priests and civil and military officials. Members of this ruling class are exempt from manual labor. They are, rather, planners and organizers and are fed and otherwise maintained by the tribute expropriated from the lower stratum; (6) a system of recording invented and used by the ruling class to manage vast revenues; (7) writing and science. Leisured clerks employ scripts and elaborate, exact, and predictive sciences—arithmetic, geometry, and astronomy; (8) art. Sculptors, painters, seal engravers, and other artists are employed full time to capture the like-nesses of persons and things and thus con-tribute to conceptualized and sophisticated art styles; (9) long-distance trade networks, involving the importation of luxuries des-tined for the ruling class as well as raw materials needed for industry or for agri-culture; (10) political identification. Mem-bership in socially and politically signifi-cant groups becomes a function of resi-dence rather than kinship.

There is little obvious correspondence between Fried's state and Childe's civiliza-tion. However, because the two men have emphasized different aspects of state or-ganization, our understanding of state organization has been enlarged. But now we must resolve the differences between states and civilizations.

Distinctive attributes of civilizations

Three of Childe's ten attributes of civiliza-tions (6, 7, and 8) can serve to distinguish civilizations from states in general. It is possible to have states without highly elaborated art styles. Similarly, there have been states without writing. For example, the kind of information preserved on writ-ten records was preserved orally in many precolonial states of the African interior. Traditions, myths, genealogies, and his-torical accounts were passed from genera-tion to generation by word of mouth. In the case of the territorially extended em-pires in the central Andes of Peru and Bolivia, dense populations and complex ac-tivities were managed by preliterate gov-ernment officials. Among the Incas, the census and other tasks which involved counting were facilitated by use of the *quipu*, a device of beads and string. Finally, there have been states which lack scientific or even protoscientific knowl-edge of arithmetic, geometry, astronomy, and astrology.

It is not surprising that states have existed without these attributes, for they are attributes not of state organization but

of a particular group—the elites—in a par-ticular variant of state-organized society—civilization. In archaic civilizations, for ex-ample, writing was typically a skill of the privileged class. Some states have been able to maintain central organization and distinctions between the elites and the masses in ways which do not involve such pronounced contrasts in life styles. In many of the states of sub-Saharan Africa, for example, although the king and his court enjoyed greater access to wealth, power, and prestige, because of kinship ties they were better able to relate to their peasant population than elite mem-bers in other ancient civilizations where contrasts between elites and masses were more marked.

Attributes of state organization

The other seven attributes of civilization which Childe lists apply, to some degree at least, to states in general and not just to the subtype known as civilization. In com-parison with kin-based societies, states tend to extend over larger territories with denser populations. They can organize and manage larger and denser populations be-cause their means of organization—parts and subsystems which fulfill Fried's sec-ondary functions of state organization—are more advanced. Special-purpose sub-systems commonly found in states include the following: military, religious, adminis-trative, legal, judicial, fiscal (tax collecting and others), and informational (spies may roam the land to gather information for the ruler). The functionally specialized subsystems, in turn, are integrated and regulated by a ruling subsystem, which, as Childe points out, may be composed of civil, military, and/or religious function-aries.

In states, membership in politically sig-nificant groups is based on residence rather than kinship. This is one of the most important differences, in human terms, between kin-based societies and states. In the kin-based society, a person resides with his relatives. In the band and tribe and even in the chiefdom, a person's social world consists of only two kinds of people: allies and enemies. A person's allies are his kinsmen. Nonkinsmen who are potential or actual enemies may be converted into friends by the creation of alliances. Common ways of establishing alliances are through marriage, through rites which convert nonkinsmen into (fictive) kinsmen, and through trading partnerships. In a state-organized society, on the other hand, a person may be born in a village, province, district, town, ward, or city. He grows up and lives out his life among *neighbors*, people with whom he claims common residence. People who live in the same territorial or political subdivision share common obligations to the state; ultimate decisions about their behavior and their lives are made and enforced not by their older kinsmen but by state officials.

In short, the individual's social world expands in the state-organized society. In markets, for example, he comes into contact with strangers—peasants and other food producers from different areas as well as a host of specialists. Occasionally, even the most insignificant peasant must deal with government officials. The closed

and often comfortable world in which kinship, marriage, and other personal relationships formed the idiom of interaction is gone.

States expropriate goods and services in taxes and labor from their subjects. States manage the funds which they collect, reallocating part for the public good and another part (often larger) to meet the subsistence and luxury needs and satisfy the aspirations of members of the elite. Corvée labor is often used to construct the monumental public works mentioned by Childe. Some of these public works may form part of a managed economy—irrigation systems, for example. Others, like temples, palaces, and tombs, can best be understood as structures where elites may reside and which stand as constant reminders of their prestige. State fiscal officials also supervise marketing and other trading activity, standardizing weights and measures and extracting taxes on goods that pass through the state.

Within their borders, state officials grant

Corvée labor in modern China. *(Marc Riboud/Magnum)*

safety to traveling caravans, to itinerant vendors, and to craftsmen—thus permitting exchange of goods and services over long distances. Often, in addition to regulation of occupational specialization by, for example, setting standards for artisanry and manufacturing, state officials must supervise ecologically diverse and productively specialized niches located in different parts of the state's circumscription.

In a host of ways, then, states contrast with kin-based societies. As a relatively new form of social organization (only 5,000 years old), states have competed successfully with populations organized on the basis of kinship, descent, and marriage in many parts of the world. They continue to supplant them. Their military organization undoubtedly enables states to compete successfully with neighboring tribes and chiefdoms. Yet this is not the only explanation for the spread of the state. In view of the hardships which it imposes on its populace, there must also be certain advantages which accompany state organization. The most obvious advantage is that its special-purpose subsystems permit order and peace to prevail within the state's boundaries. States curb feuding, often characteristic of tribal societies, and in so doing allow, and indeed encourage, higher levels of production.

The Origin of the State

Prime movers

Many scholars have turned their attention to the problem of the origin of the state. Several have offered what are basically *unicausal* explanations for the origin of the state, suggestions that a single variable, a *prime mover*, has contributed more to state formation than anything else. Even when they recognize that the prime mover whose importance they stress cannot explain every instance of state formation, these scholars still argue that their causal variable generally has been deter-

minative. Most of the prime movers which have been suggested are ecological, economic, or demographic. Let us examine some of them.

HYDRAULIC SYSTEMS   Karl Wittfogel (1957) has been foremost among those who argue that state organization emerges to organize the interrelationship between humans and water in an agricultural economy. In simplified form, Wittfogel's position is that state organization arises in arid areas to control large-scale hydraulic networks— systems of irrigation, drainage, and flood control, for example. According to the argument, state organization arises to regulate several problems and activities associated with large-scale hydraulic agriculture: the construction, enlargement, repair, and maintenance of hydraulic works; the allocation of water; the regulation of possible conflict between upstream cultivators, who are in a position to withhold water, and those downstream.

Casting doubt on hydraulic agriculture as a prime mover, anthropologists have investigated and described specific evolutionary sequences in which state organization has appeared before large-scale hydraulic systems and in which states have emerged without irrigation. However, while hydraulic agriculture is not the single cause of the evolution of the state, irrigation does have certain implications for state formation. First, irrigation is associated with permanent cultivation, sedentary communities, and dense human population. Second, irrigation is essential to productive plant cultivation in arid areas. In arid areas where irrigated land is limited, irrigation is correlated in complex ways with differential access to land and other strategic resources and with the emergence of territorial political organization. Even simple techniques of water control, small-scale canal systems and pot irrigation (drawing water from shallow wells to pour directly on plants) permit productive agriculture in arid lands. Irrigated agriculture leads to population growth. Population growth may lead to the enlargement of the hydraulic system. Growing

Hydraulic agriculture in Xochimilco. *(Dr. Georg Gerster/Rapho Guillumette)*

emphasis on hydraulic agriculture and its expansion supports increasingly larger and denser concentrations of people. Given such a process, problems involved in regulating interpersonal relations will increase. Conflicts over access to water, for example, will be more frequent. In this context, territory-wide means of controlling interpersonal relations and access to water and other strategic resources may arise. Thus a gradual growth in hydraulic systems may be associated with the evolution of political organization on a nonkin, supracommunity basis.

POPULATION INCREASE IN A CIRCUMSCRIBED ENVIRONMENT In order to explain why state organization has developed in some populations and not in others, the anthropologist Robert Carneiro (1968, 1970) has suggested that we consider whether the population occupies an open or a circumscribed environment. If the environment is open and population expands, excess population can be accommodated by fissioning

of social groups and colonization of new areas. On the other hand, certain environments are circumscribed. After a time, there is no place to go. There is no possibility of fissioning as an escape valve for excess population. Carneiro argues that if means of keeping population size constant are not employed, state organization will emerge to regulate the growing population and its access to strategic resources. Circumscription may be physical or social. Islands and alluvial plains in arid areas exemplify the former. Social circumscription exists when the possibility of fissioning is blocked by neighboring populations.

Carneiro's formulation is more general than Wittfogel's and therefore, I think, more valid, but there is a major question associated with it: Why should population increase? V. C. Wynne-Edwards (1962, 1964) and other experts on the ecology of nonhuman populations have demonstrated that it is rare for any population to be limited by starvation. Populations tend to stabilize, to develop means of limiting further increase at some level below the capacity of their environment and means of adaptation to support them. Human populations, like those of other animals, typically have *population policies*. Some common examples are infanticide and taboos on sexual intercourse for a certain length of time after the birth of a child.

Although Carneiro's formulation is useful, the association between population density and state organization is imperfect. Childe's first attribute of civilization declares that growth in population size and density is associated with state organization; and the anthropologist Robert Stevenson (1968) has demonstrated a correlation between high population density and state organization in sub-Saharan Africa. Yet increase in population and its density within a circumscribed environment is not the only factor in the origin and growth of states. Consider highland New Guinea, where, in certain valleys which represent socially or physically circumscribed environments, there are population densities comparable to those of states in many parts of the world. Nevertheless, no states have developed in highland New Guinea.

REGULATION OF ECOLOGICAL DIVERSITY It has also been suggested that states and the ruling systems and special-purpose subsystems associated with them arise in areas of ecological diversity. It is argued that states emerge in order to regulate the production and distribution of diverse products from a variety of environmental niches within the area which the state administrates. Central coordination, once established, is assumed to represent a more efficient adaptation to conditions of ecological diversity than other sociopolitical means; thus there is a tendency for it to grow, for states to evolve toward greater coordination and control.

Like other prime movers suggested, ecological diversity is often associated with state formation. Interzonal regulation does strengthen state organization. Ecological

diversity is not, however, sufficient in itself to explain state formation. States have originated in geographical areas where environmental diversity is not marked—ancient Egypt, for example. Furthermore, in other areas of environmental diversity, states have never emerged. Finally, one could argue that ecological diversity is as much a product of, as a prime mover in, the evolution of the state. As states grow, they typically create ecological and economic diversity, promoting areal specialization in the production of certain goods.

CONTROL OF LONG-DISTANCE TRADE ROUTES This prime mover is similar to ecological diversity. It has been suggested that states originate to regulate exchange of raw materials, manufactured products, and subsistence or luxury items produced in different areas. It has also been argued that states develop at supply or distributive nodes of long-distance trade networks, for example, at crossroads of caravan routes or in areas intermediate between two supply centers which are in a position to halt trade. Although long-distance trade has been important in the evolution of specific states, long-distance trade has come after, rather than prior to, the origin of the state in many cases. There are instances of long-distance trade without state organization. New Guinea provides several examples. Nevertheless, developed trade seems to be universally associated with state organization.

WARFARE It has been argued that situations of conflict or competition between neighboring human populations provide the selecting conditions for the origin of the state—that states develop as means of organizing military operations. Because central coordination represents a superior means of dealing with such situations, centrally organized groups enjoy an adaptive advantage over neighboring groups with no such organization. These neighboring groups are conquered and incorporated into the expanding state. Eventually, given continuation of conflict, the organization developed for military purposes becomes permanently established as a regulatory mechanism in ordinary life.

There is no doubt that states, by virtue of their military subsystems, enjoy an advantage in conflicts with nonstates. However, one still faces the problem of explaining why competition and conflict arose to begin with. If it is because of population build-up, this increase in population pressure must be explained.

A multivariate approach to the origin of the state

States have originated in different areas of the world for several reasons, and no single causal variable is sufficient to explain all these occurrences. In each case, the origin and evolution of the state involved the interaction of several ecological variables, the effects of one magnifying the effects of the others. Therefore, in each instance, the origin and evolution of the state was a unique example of specific evolution. This does not mean, however, that comparison of state origins and evolution in different parts of the world is impossible. In many cases, the ecological variables which have interacted to produce states have been comparable. Archeologists have documented some striking parallels in state formation in different areas of the world. To explain a particular instance of state formation, we must look into possible reasons for an increase in population size and density. In each situation, we must look for changes in the scale of regulatory problems and regulatory systems which have accompanied increases in population and density.

The origin of food production involved complex ecological factors and emerged gradually. The evolution of the state has also been gradual. In each case, it involved a long-time interaction between a human population, its adaptive means, and its environment. Changes in one of these components produced changes in the others, and the whole system was gradually altered. Because of the gradual nature of the transition from tribe or chiefdom to state, the decision on where to draw the line is arbitrary.

Economic foundations of state organization

The preceding discussion of prime movers suggests several ecological correlates of state organization, conditions that are more frequently associated with states than with kin-based societies. It is also possible to generalize about the economies of states. Populations of most archaic states relied heavily on agriculture for their food. Not all archaic states, however, had agriculture. In the tropical lowlands of Middle America, the Maya Indians created a state and civilization supported by horticulture. Horticultural systems also produced the crops of the indigenous states in many areas of precolonial Africa. It should be noted, however, that in all cases in which horticulture rather than agriculture was the predominant form of plant cultivation, state officials played an important role in the regulation of exchange systems. The Maya, for example, participated in long-distance trade networks which linked their own lowland country to the highlands of Middle America, and states in precolonial Africa were located along trade networks that linked West and North Africa.

Conquest states and colonialism

Some anthropologists—Morton Fried (1960), for example—distinguish between pristine and secondary states. *Pristine states*, according to Fried, are those which grew up purely out of internal conditions and independently of one another. Fried considers the world's only pristine states to be those which developed in Mesopotamia, Egypt, western India and Pakistan, northern China, Mexico, and Peru. He classifies as *secondary states* all those which subsequently evolved in other parts of the world, as a result of direct or indirect pressures emanating from already developed states.

It is certainly true that states may conquer non–state-organized populations and impose state organization there. There are many nineteenth- and twentieth-century examples to prove it. When this occurs, we are dealing with *conquest states*—the actual creation, through conquest, of state organization where previously there was none. Different are situations in which foreigners have conquered and replaced native elites in already existing states. An example is the Spanish conquest of the Inca Empire. Conquest has been offered as an explanation for the origin or the presence of states in some areas of the world. However, when a historian or an anthropologist accepts conquest as an explanation for the origin of a state, he must be careful to specify the means used by conquerors to create state organization. During the nineteenth and twentieth centuries, European nations created states through conquest in many areas of the world, and they incorporated already existing states into their colonial empires. The means whereby they accomplished this are clear: they involve superior military technology

SUMMARY

Tribal societies based on horticultural and pastoral economies accompanied the advent of food production in many areas. As food-producing techniques grew more productive, and as new environments, including arid areas, were occupied, new types of human organization—chiefdoms, archaic states, cities, and civilizations—appeared and spread. All are based on differential access to strategic and other socially valued resources. Chiefdoms differ from states in several respects. Retaining the kinship emphasis of tribal and foraging societies, chiefdoms often recognize genealogical ties between the chief and all other members of his circumscription. Some of the generosity associated with descent group elders and big men in tribal societies remains associated with the chief; he is expected to redistribute produce and products gathered from the population he administers. In a general evolutionary sense chiefdoms are intermediate and transitional between tribal and state organization.

States sever the kinship relationships between those who enjoy favored or unimpeded access to strategic resources, the elites, and members of subordinate strata. The primary functions of states involve maintenance of general order and of socioeconomic stratification. States accomplish these functions in a variety of ways, through population control (census); disposal of trouble cases (legislative and judicial subsystems); the protection of sovereignty (military and enforcement subsystems); and fiscal support (taxation).

Sources and Suggested Readings

CARNEIRO, R.
  1968   (orig. 1961) Slash-and-Burn Cultivation among the Kuikuru and Its Implications for Cultural Development in the Amazon Basin. In *Man in Adaptation: The Cultural Present*, ed. Y. Cohen, pp. 131–145. Chicago: Aldine. Links the origin of the state to population increase in a physically or socially circumscribed environment.

  1970   A Theory of the Origin of the State. *Science* 169: 733–738. Expansion of author's explanation for the origin of the state.

CHILDE, V. G.
  1950   The Urban Revolution. *Town Planning Review* 21: 3–17. A difficult-to-

and superior means of transporting men and supplies.

There is good reason to stress this point. In their approach to state formation, there is a bias among certain anthropologists and historians which is similar to the antievolutionary approach described in Chapter 2. It is a creationist bias. Scholars have attempted to explain the existence of states in many areas of the world not with reference to gradual modifications in adaptive relationships between human populations and their environments, but by making them the creations of alien invaders. If the means employed by conquerors are not specified, a fundamental question is immediately raised: If outsiders could create state organization, why couldn't insiders have done the same thing? In other words, might not an evolutionary rather than a catastrophist-creationist explanation be a better solution?

Not all states are civilizations, but all civilizations are states. Present in civilizations but not necessarily in states are the development of systems of recording; exact, practically useful sciences; writing; and sophisticated art styles. States and civilizations manage large and dense populations; promote occupational, economic, and ecological diversity and specialization; participate in long-distance trade routes; and, of course, have a ruling or administrative class which oversees the entire system.

Civilizations can be either urban or non-urban. Not all states or civilizations include urban centers. Functions and power relationships concentrated in cities and towns in some states may be spread out in others.

Scholars have speculated about reasons for the origin of the state. Problems of economic regulation, large-scale hydraulic systems within an agricultural economy, ecological and economic diversity, and long-distance trade routes have all been advocated as prime movers in state formation. Also linked to the origin of the state have been population increase in a physically or socially circumscribed environment; conflict and warfare; and conquest. However, a multivariate approach to the question of how the state originated explains more. Such an approach recognizes that several variables, ecological factors prominent among them, have interacted over protracted time periods to produce and elaborate socioeconomic stratification and the state.

locate article which discusses ten attributes of civilization.

FRIED, M. H.
1960   On the Evolution of Social Stratification and the State. In *Culture in History*, ed. S. Diamond, pp. 713–731. New York: Columbia University Press. Brilliant and influential article;

offers a sociocultural typology and examines different theories of the origin of the state, including some of Fried's own.

1967   *The Evolution of Political Society: An Essay in Political Anthropology.* New York: Random House. Useful introduction to major issues on the anthropology of political organization; includes a discussion of the origin of the state.

HARDING, T. G.
1967   *Voyagers of the Vitiaz Strait: A Study of a New Guinea Trade System.* Seattle: University of Washington Press. Field study of an intricate trade network in the absence of state organization.

LINTON, R.
1936   *The Study of Man: An Introduction.* New York: Appleton-Century. Early introduction to social anthropology, which distinguishes between ascribed and achieved status.

REDFIELD, R.
1955   *The Little Community: Viewpoints for the Study of a Human Whole.* Chicago: University of Chicago Press. How anthropologists study small rural communities where social relations are on a face-to-face personal basis.

1956   *Peasant Society and Culture.* Chicago: University of Chicago Press. Useful introduction to the anthropological study of peasants.

SAHLINS, M. D.
1958   *Social Stratification in Polynesia.* Seattle: University of Washington Press. Brilliant study of adaptive radiation through sociocultural means among related Polynesian populations, many of them chiefdoms.

1963   Poor Man, Rich Man, Big-Man, Chief: Political Types in Melanesia and Polynesia. *Comparative Studies in Society and History* 5: 285–303. Contrasts social and political organization, particularly authority structure, in Polynesia and Melanesia.

SANDERS, W. T., and PRICE, B. J.
1968   *Mesoamerica: The Evolution of a Civilization.* New York: Random House. State origins, evolution, and variations in Middle America.

SERVICE, E. R.
1971   *Primitive Social Organization: An Evolutionary Perspective.* 2nd ed.

New York: Random House. Provocative introduction to social and political organization of bands, tribes, and chiefdoms from a general evolutionary point of view.

SJORBERG, G.
1955   The Preindustrial City. *American Journal of Sociology* 60: 438–445. Contrasts social relations and economic organization of daily life in preindustrial and industrial cities, with emphasis on the formet type.

STEVENSON, R. F.
1968   *Population and Political Systems in Tropical Africa.* New York: Columbia University Press. Population density and state organization in sub-Saharan Africa.

STRUEVER, S., ed.
1971   *Prehistoric Agriculture.* Garden City, N.Y.: The Natural History Press. While emphasis is on early food-producing systems, some of the articles in this excellent reader deal with the origin of the state.

WITTFOGEL, K. A.
1957   *Oriental Despotism: A Comparative Study of Total Power.* New Haven: Yale University Press. Classic presentation of argument linking despotic states to tightly regulated hydraulic systems.

WYNNE-EDWARDS, V. C.
1962   *Animal Dispersion in Relation to Social Behavior.* Edinburgh: Oliver and Boyd. Influential work in animal ecology; observations of animal behavior suggest that animal populations are never limited by starvation, since means of dispersal intervene before pressure on strategic resources becomes critical.

1964   Population Control in Animals. *Scientific American* 211: 68–74. Other animal dispersal mechanisms; the work of Wynne-Edwards and other animal ecologists has prompted several anthropologists to interpret many social and cultural forms as means of dispersal of human populations.

5. Kinship and Descent

Students in introductory anthropology courses are often bewildered by what they perceive to be an overemphasis on kinship. Kinship symbols, charts, and genealogies of the sort which appear in this and subsequent chapters pervade the study of anthropology from beginning to doctorate end. The charge that anthropologists have devoted too much attention to the study of kinship is perhaps not totally unfair. Anthropology, like the people it studies, has a cultural tradition, one which emphasizes facility in kinship analysis. Such analysis has become an essential part of the esoterica of anthropology, and it continues to flourish as a means of distinguishing anthropology, a discipline whose interests and basic concepts touch on so many other disciplines, from these allied studies.

However, concern with systems of kinship and marriage arises naturally from the kinds of society anthropologists have traditionally studied. Kinship is vitally important as an orienting principle of everyday life in bands, tribes, and chiefdoms. In some archaic states, too, kinship is important, although, as will be shown in Chapter 13, its functions may be very different. Kinship is essential to ethnographers and ethnologists because of its meaning to the people whom they study. Therefore, to regard the analysis of kinship systems as merely an intellectual exercise would be unwarranted. Furthermore, it would be ethnocentric. Anthropologists use the term *ethnocentrism* to describe the universal human tendency to interpret and evaluate foreign beliefs and practices in terms of the values of one's own cultural tradition. Because kinship is not particularly important in contemporary American society, American students often ethnocentrically refuse to believe that it is important in other societies. Hopefully, by the time you finish this book you will understand better the importance of kinship, marriage, and descent in many human societies.

Kinship Groups and Kinship Calculation

The ethnographer soon recognizes that there are social divisions within any human population he chooses to study. In the course of his fieldwork, he refines his un-

Women of Colombe, Ecuador, work on the main road leading to their community. *(Guido Falconi/Rapho Guillumette)*

derstanding of socially significant groups by observing their activities and composition in much the same way that students of primate behavior observe the composition of troops of baboons or other nonhuman primates. The ethnographer, however, enjoys an advantage in the field which is not available to the behavioral primatologist. He can ask his primates questions. He can, for example, ask Sam why he is helping Harry, or why they live in the same village. In such a way, he can discover whether there are genealogical, or kinship, links between Sam and Harry and, if so, the nature of these links. Perhaps he may discover that socially significant groups are composed of all the descendants of a common grandfather. Members of such a group may live in adjacent houses, farm contiguous fields, and offer mutual assistance in a variety of everyday tasks. Other groups, the ethnographer discovers, come together less frequently. Socially significant groups based on actual or fictive kinship, including families and descent groups, will be discussed shortly.

In addition to the identification of kinship groups which are significant in a given society, anthropologists are also interested in *kinship calculation*, the system according to which individuals in the society reckon kin relationships. The study of kinship calculation requires the ethnographer to concentrate on individuals rather than groups. The ethnographer asks informants questions like "Would you tell me the names of all your relatives?" The ethnographer then poses additional questions to determine whether there are, in fact, genealogical relationships between these "relatives" and the individual who has named them. By asking the same question of several informants, the ethnographer develops a model of the extent and direction of kinship calculation in that society. Furthermore, he begins to understand the relationship between kinship groups and kinship calculation, seeing, for example, how individuals use kinship calculation to gain admission into groups and to create networks of personal ties with others outside their groups. The ethnographer also sees that there are some biological kin types who are considered to be relatives and others who are not.

Biological kin types and kinship calculation

At this point it is necessary to distinguish between relatives and biological kin types. Anthropologists designate biological kin types with letters and symbols of the sort shown in Figure 2.

The terms for biological kin types are usually not equivalent to those used for relatives in a given language. For example, in English we use the term "father" to refer to only one biological kin type, the genealogical father (although the word may also be used for an adoptive father). However, when you consider the term "cousin," you will see that it lumps together several different kin types. We distinguish between first, second, and third cousins, and so on; first cousin once re-

moved, second cousin once removed, and so on. But even the term "first cousin" includes several biological kin types. It includes one's mother's brother's son (MBS), mother's brother's daughter (MBD), mother's sister's son (MZS), mother's sister's daughter (MZD), father's brother's son (FBS), father's brother's daughter (FBD), father's sister's son (FZS), and father's sister's daughter (FZD). Thus "first cousin" lumps together eight biological kin types. There are other Indo-European languages—Portuguese, for example—which distinguish among first cousins on the basis of sex. In Portuguese, there are two terms, each lumping together four biological kin types: *primo* for all male first cousins and *prima* for all female first cousins.

Avoiding ethnocentrism means understanding that people with different cultures do not define their kinsmen in the same way that you do. The cultures of certain populations, for example, do not regard the biological father as a relative. Some cultures treat the father as a kind of in-law. For many cultures, only half of an individual's first cousins are deemed relatives. Some of the implications of these differences will be examined later.

The Nuclear Family

The *nuclear family*, which is only one of several kinds of kinship groups found in different human populations, is usually established by marriage and consists of parents and children. Some anthropologists also call it the elementary family or the biological family. Some other kinds of kinship groups are extended families and descent groups—lineages and clans. A *descent* group consists of people who believe, assert, or demonstrate that they all descend from a common ancestor. Descent groups are found in intermediate societies, tribal societies, and chiefdoms, and in some archaic states, among populations whose strategies of adaptation are based on horticulture, pastoralism, and agriculture.

FIGURE 2 Kinship symbols and notation.

△	Male
○	Female
▢	Individual regardless of sex
=	Is married to
≠	Is divorced from
│	Is descended from
⌐	Is the sibling of
●	Female ego whose kinsmen are being shown
▲	Male ego whose kinsmen are being shown
⊘ ◭	Individual is deceased
F	Father
M	Mother
S	Son
D	Daughter
B	Brother
Z	Sister
C	Child (of either sex)
H	Husband
W	Wife

A nuclear family. (Les Mahon/Monkmeyer Press)

There are major differences between the nuclear family and descent groups. Descent groups are permanent units which continue to exist even though their membership changes over time. The nuclear family, on the other hand, is impermanent. It lasts only as long as parents and their children reside together. When the parents die or all the children move away, the nuclear family dissolves.

There is another contrast between the nuclear family and descent group organization. Status as a member of a descent group is often ascribed at birth. An individual is born a member of a given descent group and remains a member throughout his life. On the other hand, he is normally a member of at least two different nuclear families at different times in his life. He is born into one consisting of his parents and siblings. Anthropologists call this the *family of orientation*. When he reaches adulthood, he normally marries and establishes a nuclear family which includes his spouse and eventually their children. Anthropologists call this the *family of procreation*. Since divorce exists in most human societies, some people may establish more than one family of procreation.

patrilineal descent

The definition of marriage

For a nuclear family to come into existence, a marriage must usually take place. Marriage is difficult to define. Reams have been written by anthropologists attempting to provide a definition of marriage which will apply to all human societies, but there is at present no universally accepted one—and perhaps there never will be. One of the most frequently quoted definitions comes from a basic book in anthropology, *Notes and Queries in Anthropology* (1951): "Marriage is a union between a man and a woman such that the children born to the woman are recognized as legitimate offspring of both partners." Although it certainly seems to accommodate marriage in the contemporary United States, the universal applicability of this definition seems doubtful for several reasons. As you will see in Chapter 6, it is not uncommon for marriages to involve the union of more than two spouses. When this is the case, we speak of plural marriages. In certain parts of the world, for example, a group of brothers may marry the same woman. This arrangement is called fraternal polyandry. Furthermore, in a few cultures that place a heavy premium on having heirs who will continue lines of descent, it is possible for one woman to marry another. In such a society which emphasizes patrilineal descent, the father of one of the women, having no male heirs, may declare his daughter a sociological male and arrange for her to take a bride. There is no sexual relationship between the two women. The bride is allowed to have sexual relations with men until she becomes pregnant. Her children are recognized as the legitimate offspring of her husband, who is biologically a woman but sociologically a man, and the descent line does not die out.

It would be possible to frame a revision of the *Notes and Queries* definition of marriage to take these deviations into account; however, the revision would be extremely cumbersome. The British social anthropologist Edmund Leach despaired of ever arriving at a universally applicable definition of marriage. Instead, he suggested that, depending on the social context, several different classes of rights may be transmitted by institutions which have been loosely termed "marriage." The rights transmitted vary from one society to another, and there is no single right which is so widespread as to provide a basis for defining marriage. Leach (1955, p. 183) lists ten classes of rights:

1. *To establish the legal father of a woman's children.*
2. *To establish the legal mother of a man's children.*
3. *To give the husband a monopoly in the wife's sexuality.*
4. *To give the wife a monopoly in the husband's sexuality.*
5. *To give the husband partial or monopolistic rights to the wife's domestic and other labour services.*
6. *To give the wife partial or monopolistic rights to the husband's labour services.*
7. *To give the husband partial or total rights over property belonging or potentially accruing to the wife.*
8. *To give the wife partial or total rights over property belonging or potentially accruing to the husband.*
9. *To establish a joint fund of property—a partnership—for the benefit of the children of the marriage.*
10. *To establish a socially significant "relationship of affinity" between the husband and his wife's brothers.*

Anthropologists should concentrate, Leach argued, on these and possibly other rights transferred through marriage rather than on what he regarded as the sterile problem of defining marriage.

Although Leach's list is useful in focusing attention on specific aspects of marital relationships in different societies, a loose definition at least is necessary to identify an institution which is found in some form in every human society. I suggest the following: marriage is a socially recognized relationship between a socially recognized male (the husband) and a socially recognized female (the wife) such that the children born to the wife are socially accepted as the offspring of both husband and wife.

Furthermore, the husband may be the actual genitor of the children, or he (or she) may be only the socially recognized father (*pater*, in anthropological parlance).

The Nuclear Family: Not a Cultural Universal

Since marriage exists in all human societies, and since it is necessary before a nuclear family can come into existence, some anthropologists have argued that the nuclear family is also a cultural universal. The intent of this section is to demonstrate that nuclear family organization is not a universal but a variable form of human social organization.

In most societies, adult men and women marry, live together, and have children. However, in some contemporary societies, particularly in the socioeconomically heterogeneous nations of the New World, many households are headed by a woman, with no permanent husband-father in residence. These are called *matrifocal* families or households, because the mother (*mater*) is the stable and constant parent and the household head. In many other societies, including most tribal societies and chiefdoms, larger kinship groups may overshadow the nuclear family.

In fact, there are only two kinds of society in which the nuclear family tends to be the most important kinship group: industrial nations and hunting and gathering societies. Why should these economies—so dissimilar—be associated with nuclear family organization?

Industrialism, stratification, and family organization

For most Americans, who live in a stratified nation-state, the nuclear family is not only the most important kinship group, it is the only kinship group. The isolation of the nuclear family is a product of geographical mobility associated with an industrial economy and, as such, is equally characteristic of many other industrial nations. A typical middle-class American is born into his family of orientation; he grows up and leaves home temporarily to go to college, but the break with his parents is underway. Eventually he marries, establishing a relationship which in most cases culminates in a family of procreation. Today, only 7 percent of the American population works in agriculture. Americans are not tied to the land, to specific localities. Like people in other industrialized nations, most Americans sell their labor on the market, and they move where jobs are available. Often, a married couple lives several hundred miles from the parents of either spouse. The place where one or both of the spouses work determines where they will take up residence. In Chapter 3, this practice was described as a cultural preference for neolocal postmarital residence. A middle-class couple is expected to establish a *new place* of residence—a home of their own—after they marry.

ACTUAL VERSUS IDEAL BEHAVIOR   It is necessary to introduce here a distinction which will be employed throughout the rest of this book. Anthropologists distinguish between cultural preferences, cultural rules, and ideal behavior, on the one hand, and statistical preferences, statistical rules, and actual behavior, on the other.

When you talk to members of a particular society, you will be told that certain things are considered appropriate in that culture, while others are not. People state *rules* of their culture. They tell you what people should do and how things should be. On the other hand, an anthropologist engaged in ethnographic fieldwork soon discovers that people do not obey prescribed rules all the time. For various reasons and to varying degrees, people deviate from the rules. An important part of the ethnographer's task traditionally has been to abstract from informants' statements a picture or a model of ideal behav-

ior, that is, cultural rules, preferences, and prescriptions in a society. Customarily, too, ethnographers describe the real situation, noting cases of, and reasons for, deviations from the ideal and the consequences of such deviations. The ethnographer's task, however, is hardly simple. Informants not only tell him what should be, they also describe to him what is. It often turns out that their perceptions differ significantly from those of the ethnographer. When this occurs, the ethnographer must determine why and to what extent discrepancies exist. Differences in perceptions that typically occur between actor and observer are summarized in Figure 3. Naturally, an ethnographer should be concerned about what actors—participants in the culture—think, perceive, and believe. But he must also be able to view the actors' world objectively.

This distinction may be applied to the cultural preference for neolocal postmarital residence in middle-class America. Studies of postmarital residence patterns and kinship organization carried out by social scientists have confirmed that, for middle-class Americans, the cultural rule is also the statistical norm. Most middle-class Americans strive to establish households and nuclear families of their own. We cannot always be sure, however, that the ideal and the actual will correspond so neatly.

It has been stressed that nuclear family organization and neolocal postmarital residence are cultural rules of the American middle class. Because most Americans are members of this group, its values are often accepted as typical, especially in the media. This should be obvious to anyone who has watched a great deal of American television. Yet in socioeconomically heterogeneous nations, that is, stratified societies,

FIGURE 3 The actor-oriented versus the observer-oriented approach to human behavior.

Actor-oriented	Observer-oriented
Cultural preference	Statistical preference
Ideal behavior	Actual behavior
Cultural rules	Statistical rules

Neolocality: Most middle-class American couples start postmarital households of their own. (*Mimi Forsyth/Monkmeyer Press*)

value systems do vary to some extent from class to class, and so does kinship organization. It is possible, for example, to point to significant differences in kinship values and relationships between lower-class and middle-class Americans. For example, many segments of the American lower class deem it perfectly appropriate for a newly married couple to reside with relatives. Furthermore, among members of the lower class in the United States and other stratified nations, the incidence of extended family households is significantly greater than it is among the middle class.

Extended family households come in several varieties. Most typically, they involve coresidence and mutual dependence of kinsmen representing at least three generations. However, they may also be collateral households, involving siblings and their spouses and children. Joseph Jorgensen (1972) and many other anthropologists who have done fieldwork in the contemporary United States have interpreted the high incidence of extended families in the lower class as an adaptation to economic marginality—that is, to poverty.

Unable to survive as independent family units, kinsmen band together in a single household and pool strategic resources.

A long history of poverty and powerlessness has caused the kinship values and attitudes of lower-class American Indians, blacks, Chicanos, Puerto Ricans, and other ethnic minorities to diverge from those of the middle class. Thus, when an American from a minority group achieves financial success, he or she often feels obligated to assist less fortunate kinsmen. This can involve inviting poorer kinsmen to join his own household. Kinship obligations may also be met through financial contributions to the households of less successful kinsmen.

Neolocal postmarital residence is therefore linked not only to the geographical mobility characteristic of industrial societies, but also to the distribution of income and other sources of wealth, to opportunities for achieving and maintaining financial independence. Neolocal residence isolates the nuclear family and makes it the only important kinship group in America today. The relationship between these factors is summarized in Figure 4, in which the arrows indicate the direction of causality.

Although the nuclear family is the only important group based on kinship for most middle-class Americans, Americans still recognize in their kinship calculations kinsmen other than members of their immediate family. Relatives living in other households or nuclear families are called mother, father, sister, brother, son, daughter, grandson, granddaughter, uncle, aunt, nephew, niece, and cousin.

The American kinship system recognizes relatives outside the nuclear family, but American kinship calculation is underdeveloped compared with those of most nonindustrial societies. This will become especially clear in Chapter 7, when systems of kinship terminology are discussed. At this point, it need only be stated that kinship calculation reflects the degree of importance kinship has in everyday life.

FIGURE 4 The relationship between industrial economy and kinship group organization.

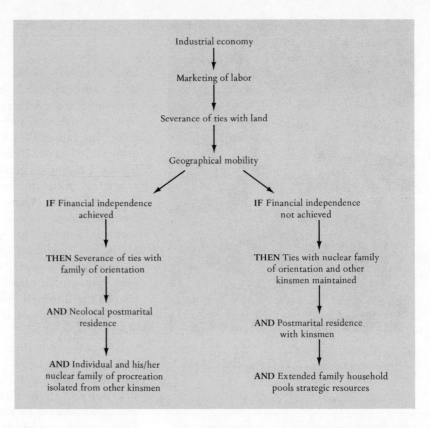

Industrial economy

↓

Marketing of labor

↓

Severance of ties with land

↓

Geographical mobility

IF Financial independence achieved

↓

THEN Severance of ties with family of orientation

↓

AND Neolocal postmarital residence

↓

AND Individual and his/her nuclear family of procreation isolated from other kinsmen

IF Financial independence not achieved

↓

THEN Ties with nuclear family of orientation and other kinsmen maintained

↓

AND Postmarital residence with kinsmen

↓

AND Extended family household pools strategic resources

In the contemporary United States, most of the people we see and interact with daily are either nonkinsmen or members of our nuclear family. Since other relatives are much less important to people in industrial societies than they are to people in bands, tribes, chiefdoms, and archaic states, it is easy to understand why American kinship calculation is comparatively rudimentary.

The nuclear family among foragers

Far removed from industrial societies on the evolutionary continuum are populations who pursue foraging strategies of adaptation. Yet here, again, the nuclear family is often the most significant group based on kinship. However, in no foraging society is the nuclear family the only group based on kinship. In Chapter 3 the two basic social units of foraging societies were identified as the nuclear family and the band. People who belong to the same band may be related by kinship, marriage, or fictive kinship.

In contrast to middle-class couples in industrial states, couples in foraging societies do not typically reside neolocally. In societies with band organization, they join a band where either husband or wife has relatives. A couple may shift from one band to another several times during their married years. Their nonadult children, and sometimes their adult children, follow them. Though nuclear families are ultimately as impermanent among foragers as they are in any other society, they are often more stable social groups than bands.

Many ethnographically documented foraging societies lacked year-round band organization. The Shoshone Indians of the Great Basin are an example. Among these people, strategic resources were so meager that during most of the year nuclear family units traveled alone through the countryside hunting and gathering. At certain times of the year, these families came together to take part in cooperative rabbit or antelope hunts. After a few months together as a seasonal band, they dispersed once again.

Different though they are, industrial and foraging strategies of adaptation have something in common. In neither case are people tied permanently to a specific area of land. Like people in industrial nations who sell their labor for wages, foragers are extremely mobile. This mobility and the emphasis on small, economically self-sufficient family units selects for the nuclear family as a basic kinship group in both foraging and industrial societies.

Functional alternatives to the nuclear family

The nuclear family does exist in intermediate societies with other strategies of adaptation. In these societies, however, it is often overshadowed in importance by larger kinship groups—extended families and descent groups. The anthropologist George Murdock (1949) believes that the nuclear family is a cultural universal. He has argued that it is so widespread in human society because its component relationships—wife-husband and parent-child—fulfill four essential social functions: sex-

ual, economic, educational, and reproductive. In discussing each of these functions, I will show that in intermediate societies other social units can assume many of the functions generally associated with the nuclear family. In other words, there are alternatives to the nuclear family.

SEX AND THE NUCLEAR FAMILY Murdock argues that because the nuclear family includes the husband-wife relationship, it fulfills a sexual function. It would be more accurate to attribute this function to marriage. Marriage institutionalizes and grants social approval to mating on a regular basis between a couple. However, there are very few human societies in which sexual intercourse is limited to the married pair. It could be argued that the institution of marriage has been selected for over many millenniums of human evolution because humans, unlike other primates, are sexually receptive all year round. Marriage is one way of establishing stable mating pat-

The nuclear family is widespread in human society. Here a Guatemalan farmer is shown having lunch with his wife and child. (*Paul Conklin/Monkmeyer Press*)

terns and thus preventing conflicts that might result if it were necessary for a new partner to be found every time there was a sexual urge. While I agree, therefore, with Murdock that marriage is a cultural universal, I would dispute his contention that it everywhere gives rise to nuclear family organization.

THE ECONOMIC FUNCTION AND THE NUCLEAR FAMILY The universality of the nuclear family has also been attributed to its economic function. In all human societies there has been a division of labor on the basis of sex. This is especially clear in hunting and gathering societies, where women gather and men hunt. From what we have learned through the work of the women's liberation movement, it should also be apparent to you that most industrial societies also have a sex-based division of labor. Although their role is changing now and certainly will change more in the near future, middle-class women in industrial societies have traditionally been housewives, and males have been expected to be the breadwinners. Please don't think that I am condoning this arrangement. But it does represent the cultural model which, as Kate Millett and others have pointed out, a male chauvinist society has used to raise its sons and daughters.

Obviously, then, the economic function of the nuclear family is especially important in those societies where the nuclear family is a rather self-contained unit of production and consumption. In intermediate societies, the division of labor is often more complex. Among the agricultural Betsileo in Madagascar, there are certain duties which are traditionally performed by adult women and others by adult men. But there are also jobs assigned on the basis of age and generation: grandfathers are expected to do certain jobs, adolescent boys and girls others. There is thus a more complex division of labor on the basis of age, sex, generation, and general social status. In such societies, the nuclear family does not encompass in microcosm all significant economic roles, as it typically does in a foraging economy. Other people are necessary to keep the economy functioning. In such societies, larger kinship groups linking at least three generations are characteristic.

THE EDUCATIONAL FUNCTION AND THE NUCLEAR FAMILY Before discussing this, it is necessary to distinguish between education and enculturation. *Enculturation* refers to the process whereby a child learns about his culture, learns how he is supposed to act and cultivates the abilities and habits appropriate in his society. *Education,* on the other hand, refers to the process whereby more formal knowledge is acquired. Education normally goes on in a place called a school. Education requires the individual to become familiar with relatively esoteric matters, a body of formal knowledge or

Enculturation in Japan. *(Grete Mannheim/D.P.I.)*

Education in Japan. *(Fujihira/ Monkmeyer Press)*

the lore of his society. In studying education cross-culturally, we note that it tends to be a correlate of state organization. Many nation-states maintain educational systems, but not everyone in the society is exposed to them. Knowledge imparted through the educational system is not of the sort that everyone must have to survive in the society.

There are exceptions to the general association between educational systems and state-organized societies. Certain populations in West Africa, and also the Tiwi, a hunting and gathering group of northern Australia (cf. Hart and Pilling, 1960), traditionally maintained bush schools in the hinterland where youths were taken for several years to receive instruction in tribal lore. Having completed bush school, these youths would be accepted as full adult members of their society. This was a kind of passage rite, a period during which individuals passed from one socially significant stage of their life to another.

It is apparent from this that education is not normally a function of the nuclear family but of some state or church organ. Nor is enculturation in any society an exclusive function of the nuclear family. In American society, it is not simply parents and siblings who teach a child how to be an "American," but friends, schoolmates, age peers, teachers, and neighbors. It should be obvious, too, that the enculturative function of the nuclear family is

most developed in those societies which isolate it. Among the Betsileo of Madagascar and other intermediate societies, grandparents, uncles, and other kinsmen play important roles in enculturating children. In Madagascar, grandparents sometimes spend more time with a child and have more to say about his or her upbringing than do the child's parents.

THE REPRODUCTIVE FUNCTION AND THE NUCLEAR FAMILY Murdock and others have argued that it is through the nuclear family that the population of a society is perpetuated. It seems to me that reproduction is more a function of marriage, which I do regard as a cultural universal, than of the nuclear family. It is true that marriage legitimizes the status of children and thus provides offspring who will enjoy full legal rights in the society into which they are born. There are some exceptions, however, which should be noted.

In the Trans-Fly region of New Guinea ethnographers have studied several tribes which are anthropologically unusual because homosexuality, rather than heterosexuality, is the cultural preference. The anthropologist Raymond Kelly has studied one of these groups, the Etoro, who taboo heterosexual intercourse for 295 days during the year (personal communication). The Dutch anthropologist van Baal (1966) has studied their neighbors, the Marind-anim. For various reasons, most notably because homo-

Tribesmen in the Trans-Fly region of New Guinea. *(Harold M. Lambert/Frederic Lewis)*

sexual relations are considered ideal, the birth rate is very low in both tribes. So low is it among the Marind-anim that in order to perpetuate their population, they must raid their neighbors. A large percentage of the children who grow up to be Marind-anim have been captured rather than born into Marind-anim society.

Another exception is provided by the Nayars, a group who live on the Malabar Coast in southern India. The Nayar kinship system is matrilineal; and there is no marriage, as we know it, among the Nayar. A woman, in adolescence, goes through a marriage ceremony with a man. Afterward, she returns home, in many cases without ever having had sexual intercourse with him. He goes back to his own household. Adult women then receive a succession of lovers. The children of these women are automatically admitted as full members of their mother's household and descent group. They are not considered to be relatives of their biological fathers, and some cannot even be sure who their biological fathers are. However, for children to be considered legitimate, a man, not necessarily their actual genitor, must go through a ritual acknowledging paternity. Thus Nayar society reproduces itself biologically, but not through nuclear family.

In summary, in certain populations the nuclear family is the only important kinship group. When this is the case, its sexual, economic, enculturative, and reproductive functions stand out. Yet enculturation never proceeds exclusively within the nuclear family, and in most societies there are economically important tasks which devolve on groups larger than the nuclear family. In a host of intermediate societies, kinship groups larger than the nuclear family share, and in some cases, take over, functions associated with it in others.

Lineages and clans

The nuclear family is a characteristic kinship group among some hunting and gathering populations and in most industrial states; the analogous group in intermediate societies is the descent group. "Intermediate" refers to societies whose strategies of adaptation are based on horticulture, pastoralism, or agriculture, or some combination of these. Thus tribal societies and some archaic states are included. Anthropologists recognize the existence of two principal varieties of descent groups—*lineages* and *clans*. Common to both is the belief that members all descend from the same *apical ancestor*, the individual who stands at the apex, or top, of their common genealogy.

There are some significant differences between lineages and clans. Lineage is based on *demonstrated descent*. Members of the descent group will cite the actual or believed descendants in each generation from the apical ancestor through the present. Clans, on the other hand, are based on *stipulated descent*. Clan members believe or assert that they are descended from the same apical ancestor, but they do not trace the genealogical links between themselves and that ancestor. In populations whose social organization includes both lineages and clans, clans generally have a larger membership and are distributed over a larger geographical area than lineages.

Sometimes the apical ancestor that distinguishes members of one clan from those of another is not a human at all, but an animal or plant. It is obvious that people cannot demonstrate their descent from a nonhuman. In both kinds of descent group, the common ancestor symbolizes the social unity and discrete identity of members, marking them off from others. Often, descent groups are exogamous. Thus the common ancestor also serves as a reference point, forcing people to seek their mates among members of other descent groups.

Among many populations, lineages are *corporate groups*. Like financial corporations in industrial nations, corporate descent groups manage an estate, a resource pool. In an agricultural society, this estate might include fields, rights to irrigation water, and house sites. Among pastoralists, herds might constitute the most significant estate item. Often, descent group members trace creation of their joint estate to their common apical ancestor.

In a modern industrial society, people become managers in a corporate enterprise by virtue of their own achievements or because of kinship ties. Corporation stock can also be bought on the open market. In contrast, descent rules regulate membership in corporate lineages, determining at birth who is to be a member and who is to be excluded. By virtue of descent rules, one enjoys or is excluded from access to the descent group estate.

Another attribute shared by industrial corporations and corporate descent groups is *perpetuity*. Descent groups, unlike nuclear families, are permanent and enduring units. New people become descent group members in every generation and eventually enjoy access to the corporate estate. Unlike the nuclear family, the descent group lives on even though specific members die.

Unilineal descent groups

Several principles may serve as cultural rules for admitting certain individuals as descent group members while excluding others. The descent rule may be patrilineal or matrilineal. Matrilineal and patrilineal descent are varieties of *unilineal descent*, because descent is based on one line only, either the female or the male.

Double unilineal descent

In some human populations, both matrilineal and patrilineal descent rules are used to assign people to discrete social groups

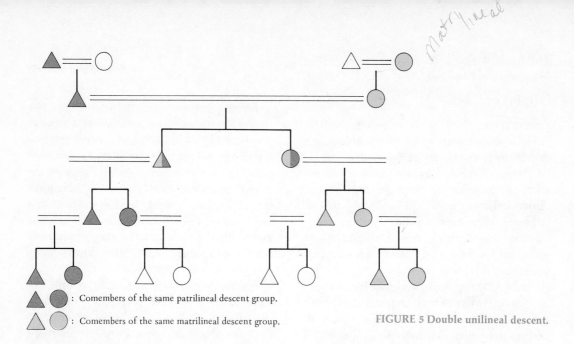

△ ○ : Comembers of the same patrilineal descent group.

△ ○ : Comembers of the same matrilineal descent group.

FIGURE 5 Double unilineal descent.

and to allocate rights to various kinds of resources. We call this *double unilineal descent*. An individual is a member of two descent groups, a matrilineal group through his mother and a patrilineal group through his father. In such a society, patrilineal and matrilineal descent serve different social and economic functions. For example, among the Yakö of West Africa individuals are entitled to farmland, house sites, and cooperative labor by virtue of their membership in patrilineal descent groups. Simultaneously, they inherit movable wealth, including currency, livestock, and harvested crops, as members of a matrilineal descent group (Forde, 1940). Note the difference between double unilineal descent and the kinship system prevalent in the contemporary United States. Americans calculate descent *bilaterally*, on both sides. In a bilateral system such as that of contemporary America, all grandchildren are considered to be equally close to the grandparents. The daughter's children and the son's children are equally the grandparents' relatives. In a society with double unilineal descent, on the other hand, there is a difference in the relationship with grandchildren. For a man, only his sons' children are members of his patrilineal descent group. His daughters' children are members of their father's patrilineal descent group. For a woman, her

daughters' children enjoy rights in her own matrilineal descent group, while her sons' children are excluded. Looking at ancestors rather than descendants, in a double unilineal society, your father's father is a member of your patrilineal descent group, and your mother's mother is a member of your matrilineal descent group. Your mother's father and father's mother belong to neither of these two descent groups. (See Figure 5.) In the United States, all four grandparents are equally relatives.

Flexibility in descent group organization

There are still other principles of descent which assign individuals to corporate or other socially significant groups. Anthropologists have described many societies with nonunilineal, or *ambilineal*, rules of descent. There are descent groups in such societies. Members are recruited on the basis of descent from a common apical ancestor. However, ambilineal groups differ from unilineal groups in that they do not automatically exclude either the children of sons or the children of daughters. It is easier to understand ambilineal descent groups if we regard them as merely being especially flexible instances of unilineal descent organization. In fact, most ambilineal descent groups tend to be either patrilineal or matrilineal. The difference is that

the descent rule does not apply automatically to individuals. With unilineal descent
rules, descent group membership is an
ascribed status. An individual is born a
member of his father's group in a patrilineal society or of his mother's group in a
matrilineal society (or of both in a double
unilineal society). He has no choice; he is
a member of that descent group for the
rest of his life.

In the following example, a patrilineal
descent group gradually converts into an
ambilineal descent group because of
demographic factors—lack of male heirs
to carry on the descent line. The example
is drawn from my work with the agricultural Betsileo in central Madagascar. The
changeover is illustrated in Figure 6.
Diagrammed is a localized corporate descent branch of a larger, geographically
dispersed, clanlike descent group called
the Wickered House people. The estate of
this branch consists of rice fields, irrigation sources, land used for secondary
crops, cattle pasture, areas for collecting

firewood, house sites, and a village area.

All the members of the localized descent
group trace their descent from an apical
ancestor called Harry, who lived on the
eighth ascending generation (P8) above the
lowest generation shown on the genealogy.
The descent line continued patrilineally
through three generations (P8–P6), from
Harry to Horace. Then, in the fifth ascending generation, the oldest son, Horace, had
two daughters, Cynthia and Zelda, but no
sons. Horace persuaded Cynthia's husband
Sam to come and live in her village rather
than take her to his own, a deviation from
the cultural rule of virilocal postmarital
residence among the Betsileo. Thus Cynthia and her husband Sam resided uxorilocally. Their children became full members
of the Wickered House descent group.

Zelda married and went to live with
her husband in his own village. However,
Zelda's father was still eager for male

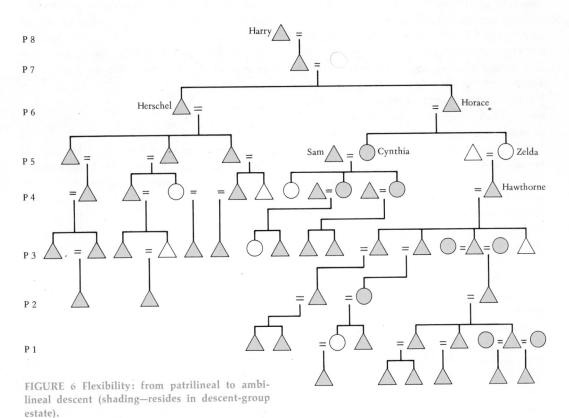

FIGURE 6 Flexibility: from patrilineal to ambilineal descent (shading—resides in descent-group
estate).

heirs. Thus he made an arrangement with Zelda's husband that their first son should return to Zelda's village and become a member of her group. In accordance with this arrangement, Zelda's son Hawthorne violated the cultural preference for affiliating with his father's group and joined the group of his maternal grandfather as a full member and as his heir.

How does the Wickered House descent group become even more ambilineal? It turns out that Cynthia bears three daughters but no sons. Cynthia's father, by this time very old and thoroughly distraught because he has no sons and only one grandson to farm his large estate, persuades two of his granddaughters' husbands to move to his village, stipulating that their offspring will be admitted as full members of his descent group. In the meantime, his brother Herschel has had three sons and four grandsons. The composition of the descent group on the P3 generation is certainly not exclusively patrilineal. Of the eleven descendants who are members of Harry's descent group, who live in his village, and who enjoy access to his estate, only four are full *agnates*, Harry's descendants through male links only. These are four of Herschel's P3 generation descendants. Four other members of this descent group include one female link in their descent from Harry. These are a P3 descendant of Herschel and the three sons of Hawthorne who affiliated with his mother's descent group. Finally, three P3 generation descent group members trace their descent from the apical ancestor through two female links. They are Cynthia's grandsons, who participate in their maternal grandmother's descent group estate.

There is reason to believe that, over the past 200 years, Betsileo descent rules really have gradually deemphasized patrilineality and have shifted toward ambilineality. While most Betsileo continue to join their father's descent group, and thus Betsileo descent groups remain statistically patri-

lineal in composition, ideology accommodates such demographic variations as the one just described, and ambilineality is considered culturally appropriate. Note finally that the Wickered House genealogy diagrammed in Figure 6 represents a descent *group* rather than a system of kinship calculation, that is, there is no ego/I as a single point of reference.

There is a dispute among anthropologists over how much difference there is between ambilineal and unilineal descent groups. Before 1950, descent groups were generally described simply as patrilineal or matrilineal. If a society tended toward patrilineality, the anthropologist classified it as patrilineal and left it at that. The recognition of ambilineal descent represented a formal admission that there is often a great deal of flexibility involved in descent systems. In even the most strictly patrilineal societies, there will always be cases where there are only daughters in a given generation. Something has to be done or the descent line will die out. From this I suspect that all descent systems are flexible, although some are more flexible than others. In other words, there is a quantitative rather than a qualitative difference between ambilineal and unilineal descent.

Adaptation, descent rules, and descent group composition

In order to explain variations of descent rules more clearly, we must distinguish between the ideology of descent—descent rules—and the composition of descent groups in a society. Here we are talking about a difference between cultural rules or preferences, on the one hand, and actual statistical norms, on the other. For reasons that are poorly understood, descent rules and descent group composition are not always concordant. In certain populations whose cultures place strong ideological emphasis on patrilineal descent, deviations away from patrilineal descent group composition may nevertheless be common. On the other hand, in populations whose ideology of descent is ambilineal, composition may be strongly patrilineal. The descent ideology of the Betsileo is, for example, very flexible. Betsileo assert that people should join their father's descent group, that the father's side is stronger. Yet they also say that all a man's descendants, through his daughters as well as through his sons, have rights in his group. Descent ideology is flexible among the Betsileo, tends toward ambilineality, but the composition of groups tends toward patrilineality. In contrast, among the Nuer who live in the Sudan in East Africa, there exists a fairly rigid ideological emphasis on patrilineal descent. Nuer descent groups, however, are actually considerably less patrilineal and more ambilineal in composition than those of the Betsileo and other populations with flexible ideologies.

The major lesson to be learned from this extended discussion of descent rules and descent group composition is that most systems of social organization are not totally inflexible. It should be stressed that flexibility is one of the major keys to the adaptive success of *Homo*; culture provides human populations with rules to live by. However, if conditions make it impossible to obey these rules all the time, people will violate those rules. If conditions continue to select for violation of a rule over time, then the ideology will probably change. In this case, cultural evolution has occurred. The selecting influences have changed, and the ideology has changed accordingly.

ECOLOGY AND DESCENT IN MADAGASCAR The population of Madagascar, the world's fourth largest island, is now about 7 million people. They belong to twenty different populations or ethnic units. Similarities in their languages and dialects, as well as other evidence, suggest that the twenty ethnic groups of Madagascar may be regarded as divergent descendants of an original population which began to settle the island around 2,000 years ago. Over time, the original population grew and dispersed; its offshoots settled contrasting environments. In the process, the original population of Madagascar underwent an *adaptive*

radiation. However, as you might expect, adaptive radiation has been accomplished through changes in social and cultural means of adaptation rather than through major biological alterations. As the people of Madagascar occupied new niches, they modified some of their customary behavior and beliefs. Whereas their ancestors had been a relatively homogeneous people with the same sociocultural heritage, the contemporary populations of Madagascar now differ from one another in noteworthy social and cultural features.

Variations in descent ideology and in composition of descent groups reflect this divergence. Some Malagasy populations have strict patrilineal ideologies and a very high incidence of patrilineal affiliation. Other ethnic units have more flexible descent rules, and their descent groups include significant numbers who are descended through females. Such variations in ideology and descent group composition are related to differences in population density and pressure on strategic resources in Madagascar. Patrilineal ideology is strongest, and descent groups are most patrilineal in composition, in some of the most densely populated agricultural areas. With land resources limited, strict ideological emphasis on patrilineal descent serves the adaptive function of limiting access to the land only to agnates, full members of the patrilineal descent group. If the children of female members do not inherit sufficient agricultural land from their fathers, they have to emigrate and seek their fortunes elsewhere. Patrilineal descent rules therefore function in such areas of Madagascar as a means of dispersing excess population which the land is incapable of supporting.

The Betsileo, too, are agriculturalists. However, pressure on agricultural land and other strategic resources does not appear to be as great for them. Population densities are typically lower. The Betsileo countryside is rugged and hilly. The most valuable agricultural land is located in valleys. Since the Betsileo irrigate their rice crop, sources of water are also valuable parts of descent group estates. Betsileo descent ideology is flexible. If a father's descent group cannot grant sufficient farmland to sustain a family because land is scarce, a child has the option of joining his mother's group, where land may be more abundant. So flexible, in fact, is Betsileo ideology that individuals can join the descent groups of any one of their four grandparents if need arises and have access to their estates. In the case of the Betsileo, flexible descent group ideology acts to distribute the population over the land by permitting people a larger number of options in terms of descent group affiliation and inheritance rights.

A third example of descent rule adaptation comes from the Bara, a population who dwell in a more arid area to the south of the Betsileo and whose strategy of adaptation is based on herding zebu, humped cattle. Population densities among the Bara are less than one-fifth that of the Betsileo. Bara orient their lives around their herds

rather than permanent plots of agricultural land. There is no problem of limited access to land, as there is when agriculture is the economic base and population is dense. The Bara are even more flexible than the Betsileo in their descent ideology and descent group composition. They can accurately be described as ambilineal. Individuals have full rights to affiliate with their father's or their mother's descent group or, in fact, with any group to which they can demonstrate a genealogical relationship.

Descent, ecology, and evolution

Some generalizations about relationships between descent groups, ecology, and the evolution of human populations are in order. There is a very definite relationship between ecological factors and principles of social organization, including kinship and descent. Because foraging societies live off nature rather than control it, there is no permanent tie between them and specific areas of land. In foraging populations with band organization, nuclear families may move from band to band during the year and throughout their lives. In populations whose strategy of adaptation has

SUMMARY

In the societies that anthropologists have traditionally studied, kinship is extremely important. A distinction is made between kinship groups, whose composition and activities can be observed and charted in the field, and kinship calculation, the manner in which individuals identify and designate their kinsmen. To study kinship calculation, we must distinguish between biological kin types and kinship designations in a given society.

A kinship-based group encountered in many societies is the nuclear family, which consists of a married couple and their children. Anthropologist George Peter Murdock has argued that the nuclear family is a cultural universal because its component

relationships (parent-child, husband-wife, sibling-sibling) fulfill what he regards as four functions essential to all human societies—sex, economics, education, and reproduction. However, two of these functions, sex and reproduction, are more appropriately attributed to marriage, which *is* a cultural universal, than to the nuclear family. Examples of functional alternatives to the nuclear family—social forms which replace or overshadow the nuclear family by assuming functions that would devolve on it in other societies—have been discussed.

This chapter has argued that the nuclear family is not a cultural universal but a variable form of social organization important in foraging and industrial societies.

changed from agriculture to industrialism, the relationship between humans and specific plots of land is also severed. Nuclear family organization becomes a cultural ideal when ties with the land are cut and the economy favors geographical mobility of individuals and their dependents.

Descent group organization is characteristic of intermediate societies, especially those whose strategies of adaptation involve a relatively permanent relationship between humans and estates. Descent, by admitting some and excluding others, is a means of regulating access to these estates. Descent must be understood as a flexible sociocultural means of adaptation. If there are too many people for a given estate to support, descent rules become stricter; if, on the other hand, the population exploiting the estate begins to fall, descent rules become less rigid. Principles such as descent that serve to maintain stable relationships between human populations and their resource base are known as *homeostats* because they maintain equilibrium, or homeostasis. Sociocultural homeostats are not limited to descent rules. Others are examined in subsequent chapters.

With these generalizations in mind, we might expect to find the most rigid descent rules operating in societies where there is great pressure of human population on estates. Densely populated agricultural societies would provide examples. Where the human population does not approach the carrying capacity of the land, however, or where other means of regulation are employed, descent rules should be weaker. We would therefore expect descent ideology to be more flexible and descent group composition more varied in sparsely populated, pastoral and horticultural societies where the relationship between the human population and specific plots of land is less permanent than it is among agriculturalists.

However, the matter of descent is not simply one of population pressure and ties with the land. Descent rules and descent group organization can serve other functions. The utility of descent as a means of political organization, for example, will be examined in Chapter 8, where we will see that factors other than population pressure on scarce resources can select for descent organization.

In neither type of society are permanent ties between people and specific areas of land characteristic. In horticultural, pastoral, and agricultural societies, on the other hand, there exist definite ties with the land, and other kinds of social groupings based on kinship and descent may overshadow the nuclear family in importance. In many contemporary nations, including the United States, the nuclear family is the characteristic kinship group for members of the middle class, while other kinship groups assume greater importance in different strata. Extended family households are more typically encountered among disadvantaged minorities in contemporary America. This form of household organization can be interpreted as an adaptation to poverty that involves pooling of strategic resources by people whose access to such resources is limited.

The descent group appears as the most important kinship group in many intermediate societies. Descent groups consist of people who maintain that they descend from the same ancestor. In contrast to nuclear families, descent groups are perpetual units; they endure over several generations. Often, members of the same descent group share access to and manage a common estate. Because of this, anthropologists compare descent groups to modern industrial corporations and call them corporate descent groups. Ethnographic studies have revealed several types of descent groups. Anthropologists distinguish between lineages and clans, the former based on demonstrated descent, the latter on stipulated descent. Different varieties of descent rules also exist: unilineal, including patrilineal and matrilineal, and nonunilineal, or ambilineal. With a patrilineal descent rule, only the children of male descent group members are admitted to the group, while the children of females are excluded. With a matrilineal descent rule, the children of male descent group members are excluded and the children of daughters automatically included. Sometimes both unilineal rules may operate in the same society, creating a system of double unilineal descent. In contrast are populations organized into descent groups, but

Sources and Suggested Readings

BAAL, J. VAN
  1966   *Dema: Description and Analysis of Marind-anim Culture (South New Guinea).* The Hague: M. Nijhoff. Field study of homosexual tribes in New Guinea.

BARNES, J. A.
  1962   African Models in the New Guinea Highlands. *Man* 62: 5–9. Differences between descent group organizations of Africa and highland New Guinea.

BOHANNAN, P., and MIDDLETON, J., eds.
  1968a   *Kinship and Social Organization.* Garden City, N.Y.: The Natural History Press. Classic articles on kinship and kinship terminology.

  1968b   *Marriage, Family and Residence.* Garden City, N.Y.: The Natural History Press. Articles on marriage and postmarital residence rules in several cultural settings.

BUCHLER, I. R., and SELBY, H. A.
  1968   *Kinship and Social Organization: An Introduction to Theory and Method.* New York: Macmillan. Comparative social organization; particular emphasis on theoretical approaches to kinship, descent, and marriage.

CLARKE, E.
  1957   *My Mother Who Fathered Me.* London: George Allen and Unwin. More personal than the average account of matrifocal family organization.

COULT, A. D.
  1964   Role Allocation, Position Structuring and Ambilineal Descent. *American Anthropologist* 66: 29–40. Argues for qualitative differences between unilineal and ambilineal descent.

DAVENPORT, W.
  1959   Nonunilineal Descent and Descent Groups. *American Anthropologist* 61: 557–572. Suggests similarities and differences between unilineal and ambilineal descent groups.

  1961   The Family System of Jamaica. *Social and Economic Studies* 10: 420–454. Field study of Jamaican family structure.

EVANS-PRITCHARD, E. E.
  1940   *The Nuer: A Description of the Modes of Livelihood and Political Institutions of a Nilotic People.* Oxford: Clarendon Press. Classic study of social structure (including segmentary lineage organization) and environment of a Nilotic population.

FORDE, D.
  1940   *Yakö Studies.* London: Oxford University Press. Field study of an African population with double unilineal descent.

FORTES, M.
  1953   The Structure of Unilineal Descent Groups. *American Anthropologist* 55: 17–41. Classic synthesizing article on corporate attributes of certain kinds of descent groups.

FRIED, M. H.
  1957   The Classification of Corporate Unilineal Descent Groups. *Journal of the Royal Anthropological Institute* 87: 1–29. Comparative analysis of descent group organization in several societies approximating different general evolutionary types.

GOUGH, K.
  1959   The Nayars and the Definition of

with no rule which automatically assigns descent group status at birth. Depending on the circumstances, a person may join his mother's, his father's, or perhaps another relative's group. The descent groups that result are called ambilineal.

Like other aspects of culture and social organization, descent rules may be seen as operating in the adaptation of human populations to their environments. Descent rules usually do not rigidly govern the lives of people in a society; rather, their observance often reflects considerable flexibility. The amount of flexibility, the extent of departure from the rules, and the variable functions of descent and descent groups can often be attributed to ecological differences associated with specific environments.

Marriage. *Journal of the Royal Anthropological Institute* 89: 23–34. Unusual marriage customs among the matrilineal Nayars of India. Definition of marriage offered which, author argues, includes the Nayar and all other known societies.

HARRIS, M.
1964   *The Nature of Cultural Things.* New York: Random House. Chapter 7 advocates an original and provocative approach to the study of social organization.

HART, C. W. M., and PILLING, A. R.
1960   *The Tiwi of North Australia.* New York: Holt, Rinehart and Winston. Case study of unusual population of polygynous and gerontocratic foragers.

HOBHOUSE, L. T.
1915   *Morals in Evolution.* Rev. ed. New York: Holt. Comparative view of social organization by an early anthropologist.

JORGENSEN, J. G., ed.
1972   *Reservation Indian Society Today: Studies of Economics, Politics, Kinship and Households.* Berkeley: University of California Press. Anthology with articles on the expanded household as an adaptation to poverty among contemporary inhabitants of reservations in North America.

KOTTAK, C. P.
1971a   Cultural Adaptation, Kinship and Descent in Madagascar. *Southwestern Journal of Anthropology* 27: 129–147. Relates variations in kinship calculation and descent group organization

to population pressure on strategic resources and other ecological variables.

1971b   Social Groups and Kinship Calculation among the Southern Betsileo. *American Anthropologist* 73: 178–193. Variations in descent group organization and kinship calculation according to socioeconomic stratum within an agricultural society of highland Madagascar.

LEACH, E. R.
1955   Polyandry, Inheritance and the Definition of Marriage. *Man* 55: 182–186. Polyandry in South Asia; argues against the cultural universality of marriage.

LOWIE, R. H.
1961   (orig. 1920). *Primitive Society.* New York: Harper and Brothers. Classic, chapter by chapter attempt to negate Morgan, 1963 (orig. 1877). Origins of clan organization and of age and sex-based groups, descent, marriage, and kinship terminology.

MORGAN, L. H.
1963   (orig. 1877). *Ancient Society.* Cleveland: World Publishing. One of the anomalies of this classic in anthropological theory is Morgan's argument linking the spread of exogamy to genetic improvement created by prohibition of inbreeding.

MURDOCK, G. P.
1949   *Social Structure.* New York: Macmillan. Classic use of statistics to resolve many problems and to raise many others in the anthropological study of social organization.

ROYAL ANTHROPOLOGICAL INSTITUTE.

1951   *Notes and Queries on Anthropology.*
6th ed. London: Routledge and Kegan
Paul. For years ethnographers have
carried this manual into the field;
includes a comprehensive list of questions about matters of interest to
social anthropologists.

SAHLINS, M. D.

1961   The Segmentary Lineage: An Organization of Predatory Expansion. *American Anthropologist* 63: 322–345.
Segmentary lineage organization as a
sociopolitical adaptive means of mo-
bilization among tribal populations.

1965   On the Ideology and Composition of
Descent Groups. *Man* 65: 104–107.
Some similarities and differences
between ambilineal and unilineal
descent groups.

1968   *Tribesmen.* Englewood Cliffs, N.J.:
Prentice-Hall. Kinship, descent, and
marriage in tribal societies.

SCHNEIDER, D. M.

1968   *American Kinship: A Cultural Account.* Englewood Cliffs, N.J.: Prentice-Hall. Impressionistic but often insightful account of American kinship as a cultural system.

SKINNER, E. P.

1964   The Effect of Co-residence of Sisters' Sons on African Corporate Patrilineal Descent Groups. *Cahiers d'Études Africaines* 16: 467–478. Widespread ambilineal elements in many supposedly patrilineal descent systems in Africa.

SMITH, R. T.

1956   *The Negro Family in British Guiana.* London: Routledge and Kegan Paul. Field study of family organization among Afro-Americans in the Caribbean area.

WESTERMARCK, E.

1894   *The History of Human Marriage.* London: Macmillan. Interesting early work; relates the incest taboo to fear of biological degeneration.

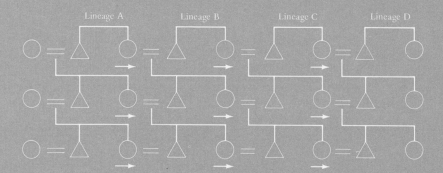

6. Marriage as Alliance

$$\triangle = O$$
$$\triangle = O \qquad O = \triangle$$

In previous chapters it has been suggested that the world of the primitive consists of two main social categories—friends and enemies. Marriage is one of the principal social institutions which converts potential or actual enemies into friends, which creates and maintains alliances. Fictive kinship and other institutions encountered less generally than marriage are others. The incest taboo forces people to be exogamous, to seek their mates outside of their own social groups. Exogamy has adaptive value. A child has peaceful relations with the social groups and kinsmen of both parents, and of different grandparents. Exogamy introduces the individual to a wider network of people who will nurture, assist, and protect him in times of need.

The Taboo against Incest

Incest involves having sexual relations with, or marrying, a close relative. In all societies there are taboos against it. However, although the incest taboo is a cultural universal, specific cultures define it differently. As an illustration, consider some implications of the distinction between two kinds of first cousins, cross cousins and parallel cousins. Children of siblings of the same sex are *parallel cousins*. Children of siblings of the opposite sex are *cross cousins*. Thus your mother's sister's children are your parallel cousins—the children of two sisters. Your father's brother's children are also your parallel cousins—the children of two brothers. Your father's sister's children are your cross cousins—the children of two siblings of the opposite sex. For the same reason, your mother's brother's children are also your cross cousins. (See Figure 7.)

The American kinship term *cousin* does not distinguish between cross and parallel cousins, but in many cultures, especially those in which there are unilineal descent groups, this distinction is essential. A society in which there are only two descent groups has what is known as *moiety* organization—from the French *moitié*, meaning half—because the society is bifurcated by descent rules, and everyone is a member of either one half or the other. Moieties may be patrilineal or matrilineal. Figure 7

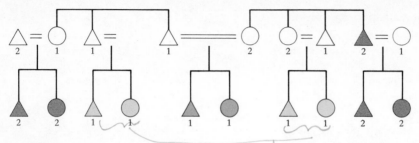

▲,● : Cross cousins.　▲● : Egos.

▲,○ : Parallel cousins.　1, 2 : Patrimoiety affiliation.

Parallel cousins belong to the same moiety as ego.
Cross cousins belong to the opposite moiety from ego.

cannot marry considered as brothers and sisters

depicts a society with patrilineal moieties. In Figure 8 the moieties are matrilineal. Notice that in both patrilineal and the matrilineal societies, all cross cousins are members of the opposite moiety and all parallel cousins are members of the individual's own moiety. In a patrilineal system, all individuals take their descent group affiliation from their fathers. In the matrilineal society, all people take their mother's descent group affiliation. You can see from these diagrams that ego's mother's sister's children (MZC) and his father's brother's children (FBC), that is, all his parallel cousins, belong to his group, while his father's sister's children (FZC) and his mother's brother's children (MBC) belong to the other moiety. In such societies, people consider their parallel cousins to be like siblings, and they cannot have sexual intercourse with, or marry, them. Parallel cousins lie within the incest taboo of these societies. In fact, people in such societies normally call their male and female parallel cousins by the same kinship terms that they use for their own brothers and sisters —indicating the closeness of the relation-

ship. Though this is completely foreign to the American kinship system, try to see that parallel cousins are, after all, members of the same generation and the same kinship group as ego's own siblings. Like siblings, they are considered too closely related to marry. Thus they are classified with brothers and sisters.

In such societies, cross cousins are members of the opposite group and not relatives. In fact, in many societies, one is expected to marry either his actual cross cousin or someone from the same social category as his cross cousins. In the case of moiety organization, spouses must belong to different moieties. Among the Yanomamo Indians of Venezuela and Brazil (see Chagnon, 1968 a & b), men anticipate the fact that they may one day marry their female cross cousins by calling them "wife" and their male cross cousins "brother-in-law." From early childhood, women, too, call their male cross cousins "husband" and their female cross cousins "sister-in-law." For the Yanomamo, as for many other societies with unilineal descent groups, sex with cross cousins is considered

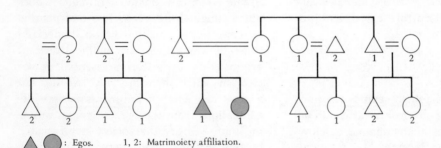

▲● : Egos.　1, 2: Matrimoiety affiliation.

Parallel cousins belong to the same moiety as ego.
Cross cousins belong to the opposite moiety from ego.

FIGURE 8 Matrilineal moiety organization.

perfectly proper, but with parallel cousins it is deemed incestuous.

A rarer phenomenon will further illustrate that people treat their biological kin types differently in different societies. In societies where the principle of unilineal descent is very strongly developed, people do not regard the parent who does not belong to their own descent group as a relative. In a strict patrilineal society, ego's mother is not a relative but a kind of in-law who has married a member of his group, his father. And in a strictly matrilineal society, ego may not consider his father to be a relative, since he is a member of a different matrilineal descent group.

The social organization of the Lakher of Southeast Asia is strictly patrilineal (Leach, 1961). Let us suppose that ego's father and mother have been divorced. Both ego's father and mother have remarried, and each has had a daughter by this second marriage. A Lakher always belongs to the father's group, and all members of this group are considered to be relatives. The Lakher consider agnates to be too close to marry. Therefore, ego cannot marry his father's daughter by his second marriage. On the other hand, ego's mother's daughter by her second marriage is fair game for him, since she is a member of her own father's descent group and not ego's. The Lakher illustrate particularly well that definitions of relatives differ from culture to culture. In the United States both half-sisters would be too close for mating and marriage. Among the Lakher, only one is considered a close relative and included within the Lakher version of the incest taboo. (See Figure 9.)

We may extend the observations based on the Lakher to strict matrilineal societies. If ego's parents divorce and his father remarries, ego may marry his paternal half-sister. On the other hand, if his mother remarries and has a daughter, she is ego's close relative and relations with her are taboo. People therefore regard relationships which are equivalent in a biological and genetic sense differently, according to the structure of their social organization and their culturally defined rules.

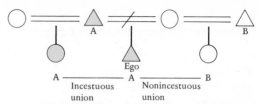

$\neq$: Separation or divorce.
FD by second marriage is a comember of ego's descent group and is included within the incest taboo.
MD by second marriage is not a comember of ego's descent group and is not tabooed.

FIGURE 9 Patrilineal descent-group identity and incest among the Lakher.

Explanations of the Incest Taboo

Instinctive revulsion

There is no simple explanation for the fact that prohibitions against incest exist in all human populations. Certain explanations can be rejected immediately, among them the one offered by the anthropologists L. T. Hobhouse (1915) and Robert Lowie (1961). They argued that since the incest taboo is found in all human societies, and since it is concerned with a biological act, sexual intercourse, it is a codification of instinctive revulsion. Following this line of reasoning, people everywhere have an instinctive aversion to mating with their close relatives. Thus, in all human societies, incest is intrinsically repulsive and is considered a crime.

There are several grounds on which to reject Hobhouse and Lowie's explanation, as Lowie himself did later. First, the mere fact that an institution is culturally universal does not mean that it is instinctively based. Fire making, for example, is also a cultural universal, and it is certainly not an ability transmitted by the genes. Furthermore, if there were indeed an instinctive horror of mating with close relatives, a formal taboo against incest would be unnecessary. No one would ever do it. Talk to social workers, judges, psychiatrists, and psychologists in our own society, however, and you will find that cases of incest are by no means rare. They occur in American families more often than you might suspect. Sometimes, they are hushed up;

patrilineal

sometimes, they are brought to the attention of the courts and punished.

The final objection to the instinctive revulsion theory is that it cannot explain why in some societies people can marry their cross cousins but not their parallel cousins, or why a Lakher can marry his mother's daughter but not his father's daughter. There is no known instinct capable of distinguishing between parallel and cross cousins. The specific kin types included within the incest taboo as well as the taboo itself have a cultural rather than a biological basis. Not only do cultural traditions define the specific relatives with whom sex is incestuous, they also punish individuals who violate these prohibited relationships in various ways, sometimes by banishment or imprisonment, sometimes by death, sometimes with the threat of supernatural retaliation.

Biological degeneration

The anthropologists Edward Westermarck (1894) and Lewis Henry Morgan (1963) each argued that the incest taboo originated because people everywhere came to recognize that biological deterioration—the appearance of abnormal or otherwise undesirable offspring—resulted from incestuous unions. To discourage such unions, early humans proscribed incest. So successful was the stock produced by human populations once the taboo came into existence that it spread everywhere. It is this argument against incest which most contemporary Americans accept. They believe that marrying close relatives leads to biological degeneration. However, from genetics we know that if harmful recessive genes exist in a population, inbreeding will increase the rate at which they are phenotypically expressed. Of course, it is only when harmful traits are phenotypical that natural selection can operate against them. Because of this, inbreeding may not be bad for a population. In fact, biologists cite it as one of the forces of evolution.

While the phenotypical expression of harmful recessives may not be bad for a population, it is never a happy situation for the individual who has a hereditary disease or for his parents. Like contemporary Americans, the Betsileo of Madagascar believe that marriage of close relatives leads to unwanted biological results. The Betsileo think that such marriages will produce nonviable offspring. My informants there cited one case of close relatives who had married and produced normal children, none of whom lived to adulthood. They claimed to remember other cases of related spouses whose offspring had died in childhood.

It is doubtful that fear of impaired offspring can explain the universality of the incest taboo, although in specific societies the phenotypical results of close inbreeding may have reinforced it. Certainly, neither instinctive revulsion nor fear of biological degeneration can account for the widespread custom of marrying a cross cousin.

Marry out or die out

Among anthropologists, perhaps the most widely accepted explanation for the incest taboo is that it forces people to marry outside their immediate kinship group. I believe it to be an adaptive means selected early in the evolution of *Homo*. Since to marry a member of a group with whom one is already on peaceful terms would be, in a sense, counterproductive, for an alliance already exists, there is more profit in extending peaceful relations to a wider group.

The first anthropologist to expound this argument was Sir Edward Burnett Tylor, foremost British anthropologist of the late nineteenth century. More recently, the American ethnologist Leslie White and the French social anthropologist Claude Lévi-Strauss have also emphasized the role of marriage in forming and maintaining alliances between social groups. White (1949, 1959) has stated the matter very simply: a group faces the choice of marrying out or of dying out. By forcing its members to marry out, a group increases its allies. Marriage within the group, on the other hand, would isolate that group and ultimately lead to extinction. Exogamy and the concomitant taboo against incest are among the best explanations for the adaptive success of the genus *Homo*.

Familiarity breeds attempt

The anthropologist Bronislaw Malinowski (1927), whose numerous books and articles based on his extended fieldwork among the Trobriand Islanders were published in the 1920s and 1930s, explained the universality of the incest taboo in terms of its relationship to enculturation and the family. Malinowski believed that the nuclear family was a cultural universal. Although he recognized that larger kinship groups existed and were important in several societies (including the Trobrianders), he stressed his belief that their functions were secondary. He emphasized instead the primacy of nuclear family relationships. Accordingly, Malinowski argued not only that the nuclear family was universal, but also that it was the essential agency through which the knowledge and sentiments upon which culture was based were transmitted across the generations. Smooth transmission of knowledge and values—that is, enculturation—required family emotions of reverence, dependence, and respect, strong affective bonds to the mother and submission to the leadership of the father. The formation of the family of procreation accommodated what Malinowski believed to be instinctive parental feelings of both the mother and the father.

Malinowski's view of the family as a complex of emotions, sentiments, and individual attachments reflects his interest in psychology, and particularly his familiarity with the works of Freud and other early twentieth-century psychologists. Freud offered a speculative and anthropologically absurd interpretation of the origin of the incest taboo, the Oedipal complex and infantile sexuality. His theories receive further consideration in Chapter 10. Malinowski, however, rejected what Freud had

regarded as universal attributes of the human mind, arguing instead that parent-child attitudes varied with different cultural traditions. Malinowski rejected the significance of sexual emotions prior to puberty. Instead, he stressed that sentiments like reverence, respect, and nonsexual affection were important within the family context. It was only at puberty, according to Malinowski, that sexual urges developed. Believing as he did in the closeness of family bonds, Malinowski argued that it would be natural for children to seek to gratify their emerging sexual urges with people who were already emotionally close to them. In other words, they would naturally seek out members of their nuclear family as sexual partners. To phrase it with a bad pun, familiarity breeds attempt. Malinowski argued that the incest taboo arose to repress and direct outward what he regarded as a universally encountered temptation toward incestuous unions. Were sexual urges of pubescent and postpubescent individuals to be satisfied within the family of orientation, conflict would be engendered which would impede its normal functioning. As Malinowski asserted, the fundamental pattern of all social bonds—the normal relationship of child to mother and father—would be destroyed, and it would be impossible for cultural transmission to continue.

There is much that seems reasonable in Malinowski's argument. As a child grows up, he or she learns that the roles of father, mother, brother, and sister within the family are different. A boy's attempt to emulate his father by having sexual relations with his mother would, in fact, destroy the role structure and the cohesion on which the family is based. You will note, however, that Malinowski's interpretation is not so satisfactory when it comes to the taboo against sexual intercourse between siblings. A more complete and satisfactory explanation of the incest taboo combines elements of several scholarly contributions. Exogamy and the alliances it engenders and maintains do have adaptive value. Close kinsmen do provide enculturative models for role differentiation on the basis of age and sex. Incestuous gratification of sexual urges would threaten the role structure encapsulated in groups of closely related kinsmen and would lead to conflict. Exogamy establishes alliances and guards against conflict. The incest taboo and exogamy therefore possess two selective advantages—prevention of conflict within the group and extension of peaceful relations beyond the group.

Endogamy

The function of the incest taboo and of rules of exogamy in creating and maintaining alliances between groups has been stressed. Exogamic rules push social organization outward, establishing and preserving bonds between groups. Endogamic rules prescribe that individuals choose mates from their own social groups. Such rules are less frequently encountered, but are still familiar to anthropologists. Most human societies are, in fact, endogamous units, although there may be no formal, cultural rule that an individual should choose as a mate someone from his own society. Note here the distinction between these cultural rules and the actual occurrence of exogamic and endogamic marriages in society.

It is perhaps obvious that in populations whose cultures include both exogamic and endogamic rules, these rules cannot apply to the same social unit. In stratified societies many people are to some degree enjoined to marry members of their own stratum. Yet each stratum may be divided into several descent groups or other social subdivisions, and each of these may be an exogamous unit. Exogamy links groups together; endogamy isolates groups and maintains them as distinct and exclusive units. Rules of endogamy are often found in stratified societies. Along with other devices, they act to maintain social, economic, and political distinctions, to preserve differential access to strategic and other culturally valued resources.

Caste

An extreme case of endogamic prescriptions is the caste system of India. Castes are stratified groups in which membership is ascribed and life long. Castes are usually endogamous groups. However, endogamy is not the critical feature in the definition of caste. More significant is the fact that a caste system has rules which automatically and unambiguously classify a person at birth. A person has no choice about his caste affiliation. The major difference between castes and unilineal descent groups, which also automatically and unambiguously recruit members at birth, is that castes are stratified.

The major Indian castes are *horizontal* groups; that is, their membership is spread across India and not confined to certain villages, towns, or regions. Some castes, however, are *vertical* groups, and their membership is limited to certain parts of the Indian subcontinent. Indian villages, towns, and cities are typically multicaste communities, and Indian society as a whole is intricately subdivided into thousands of castes with distinct names and myths of origin.

Occupational specialization serves to demarcate one caste from another. Some of the major horizontal castes are those of priests and warriors. A rural community may include castes of agricultural workers, merchants, artisans, priests, sweepers, and others. Indian untouchables are castes whose ancestry, ritual status, and occupations are considered so abject that members of higher castes consider even casual contact between themselves and untouchables to be defiling.

Important in maintaining caste endogamy is the ideology that intercaste marriages result in a state of ritual impurity for both partners. The Indian caste system therefore places great emphasis on intracaste marriage. As an illustration of the relationship between endogamy and exogamy, however, note that although Indian castes are endogamous groups, many of them are internally subdivided into exogamous groups. An Indian is expected to select as his mate a member of another descent group within his own caste.

A long history, an elaborate ideology which includes notions of ritual purity and contamination, and intricate occupational and economic distinctions buttress the Indian caste system. Yet the principle of caste, with these cultural and historical embellishments absent, is widely encountered in stratified societies. For example, the two groups that Americans call "black" and "white" are castelike groups. A dual hierarchy exists in the United States. There is a class structure, consisting of the lower, middle, and upper classes and their subdivisions. To a certain extent class status in the United States is achieved. The American ideal of the self-made man, the rags-to-riches stories we have all heard, stress and value individual achievement as a means of moving up in the class structure. Yet there is a second dimension of the American stratification system—the black-white dimension—in which membership is ascribed rather than achieved. Many American states once prohibited marriages between blacks and whites—the way Indian culture still prohibits marriages between castes. However, the really critical cultural and legal rule which has created and perpetuated the American caste system is the rule of hypodescent. Such a rule is essential to a caste system. Hypodescent automatically, unambiguously, and nonbiologically assigns the children of intercaste unions to membership in the subordinate group—in this case the black caste.

Royal incest

Similar to caste system endogamy, particularly to that of India, is privileged royal incest. Well-known examples are provided by the Incas of Peru, the ancient Egyptians, and the royalty of aboriginal Hawaii. In these archaic states, royal brother-sister marriages were allowed. Privileged endogamy, a violation of the incest taboo which applied to the masses in these societies as elsewhere, was a means of differentiating between rulers and subjects.

MANIFEST AND LATENT FUNCTIONS   To understand why rulers and their near relatives did not observe the same prohibitions as others against marrying their close relatives, it is necessary to distinguish between manifest functions of behavior patterns and latent functions. The *manifest function* of an institution or custom refers to the reasons that people in the society give for that behavior. The *latent function* refers to an effect which that behavior has for the society, which people do not mention or may not recognize.

The institution of privileged royal incest illustrates the distinction between manifest and latent functions. Aboriginal Polynesians believed in an impersonal force or substance distributed throughout the world, which they called *mana*. Mana could reside in things or people, in the latter case marking them off from other people and making them divine. In ancient Hawaiian ideology, no other human concentrated as much mana in his person as the sovereign. The amount of mana depended on closeness of genealogical connections. The individual whose concentrated mana was surpassed only by the king's was his sibling. Thus the most appropriate spouse for the ruler was his own full sister. Note that brother-sister marriage also meant that the children born of the marriage were as mana-ful, or divine, as it was possible to be. The manifest function of royal incest in ancient Hawaii was related to notions of mana and divinity.

It is also possible to point out certain latent functions of royal incest. Royal sibling marriages had repercussions in the political domains of these ancient states. The ruler and his spouse had the same parents. Since mana was transmitted from parents to child, they were almost equally divine. When the king and his sister married, their children were indisputably divinest in the land. No one could contest their right to rule the kingdom. If, on the other hand, the king had taken a wife who was not his sister, and the sister a husband who was not the king, the children of the two couples would present problems. Both sets of children could argue that they were equally divine and that they had equally valid claims to rule. Royal sibling marriage thus served to limit conflicts over succession by restricting the number of people with valid claims to rule. This political function has, of course, been accomplished differently in other states. It is possible, for example, to specify that only the eldest son of the reigning monarch will succeed him. As commonly, rulers can kill or banish claimants to succession who rival their favorite heirs.

Recognize, too, the latent function of royal incest in economic spheres. If both ruler and his sibling had equal rights to the ancestral estate, their marriage to each other, again by limiting the number of heirs, tended to keep it intact. Power often rests on wealth, and royal incest tended to ensure that royal wealth remained concentrated in the same line.

Brazilian plantation society

Cases of royal incest are extreme examples of the functions of endogamy as a means of limiting and preserving access to wealth and power. Cases of marriages between close kinsmen, although not as a rule sister and brother, mother and son, or daughter and father, are not infrequent. In Brazilian plantation society as recently as the nineteenth century, it was common for first cousins to marry. In fact, among families owning sugar and coffee plantations, cousin marriages were often considered ideal unions. Plantation society was composed of ambilineal descent groups centered around estates consisting of land, slaves, equipment, and other resources. Brazilian inheritance law granted estate rights both to sons and daughters and to

their descendants. Marriages of heirs to the same estate, including cousins and, on occasion, uncles and nieces, represented conscious attempts to keep estates intact. In the case of Brazilian society, the function of endogamous unions in limiting access to wealth is therefore manifest. Note, however, that it was only partially successful. Endogamous unions only inhibited, they did not stop, fragmentation of estates. With laws granting equal inheritance rights to all descendants of large plantation families, severe fragmentation has taken place.

Patrilateral parallel cousin marriage

Functionally analogous to marriage of close kinsmen in Brazilian society is parallel cousin marriage among Islamic, or Moslem, populations of the Near East and North Africa, particularly the Arabs. Arabic society is structured by patrilineal descent. All Arabs ultimately trace their descent patrilineally from Abraham in the Bible. This common genealogy provides a basis for the Arabs' distinctive ethnic identity in the form of a patrilineal segmentary lineage structure. Although the origin of their cultural preference for marriage between patrilateral parallel cousins—the children of two brothers—has not been explained, Arabs say that men marry their father's brother's daughters in order to keep property in the family. Such a manifest function follows from the imposition of Islamic inheritance laws on a social organization in which inheritance was formerly patrilineal. The Koran, the Islamic bible, stipulates that daughters and sons must share in their parents' estates. However, daughters' shares are only half those of sons. In some Islamic areas, patrilateral parallel cousin marriage does function to prevent fragmentation of estates.

As Fredrik Barth (1954) has pointed out, patrilateral parallel cousin marriage may also serve a political function, cementing solidarity among brothers in factional disputes. Furthermore, the anthropologists Robert Murphy and Leonard Kasdan (1959) have suggested still another function for such a marriage preference. They argue

[margin handwritten note: Marrying in family — mean of keeping property — wealth in doors]

that because it closes small social groups—brothers and their children—in on themselves, it functions to maintain political factionalism and disunity among the Arabs. In inverse form, it illustrates the function of exogamy which has been repeatedly stressed in this book: to extend social ties outward, to establish and maintain peaceful intergroup relations. Endogamy, on the other hand, isolates social groups and contributes to an atmosphere of factionalism.

Stratum and descent group endogamy

Endogamic tendencies also function in the stratified society of the Betsileo. During the eighteenth and nineteenth centuries, Betsileo society became stratified into nobles, senior commoners, junior commoners, and slaves. Members of these stratified groups differed in access to wealth, power, and prestige. Although slavery among the Betsileo was abolished early in the twentieth century, slave ancestry still conveys a social stigma. Traditional Betsileo strata were castelike groups, with nobles expected to marry other nobles, senior commoners other senior commoners, junior commoners other junior commoners, and slaves other slaves. The rule that no freeman marry a slave was most rigorously enforced. However, nobles were occasionally allowed to marry senior commoners, and senior commoners sometimes chose their spouses from the junior commoner stratum.

In theory, patrilateral parallel cousin marriage was permitted among nobles and senior commoners. In fact, and for reasons related to preservation of wealth and power, nobles tended to marry closer relatives. Among senior commoners there appears to have been both a cultural and an actual preference for descent group endogamy. However, descent group endogamy usually involved marriages between different local branches of the same named, and territorially dispersed, descent group. While endogamy was allowed in the clanlike group as a whole, it occurred far less frequently within localized branches. The manifest function of descent group endog-

amy, the explanation that Betsileo themselves offer for their ancestors' behavior, concerns the purity and appropriateness of marriage among people with the same status. Members of the Wickered House descent group chose other members as their spouses because the parents and kinsmen of each spouse were familiar with the marital history and ancestry of the other. In this way, the Betsileo say, their ancestors could be sure that their spouses had no ancestors who were slaves or members of another socially stigmatized group. A latent function served by descent group endogamy, when the descent groups were territorially dispersed and based on stipulated rather than demonstrated descent, was to reinforce political alliances among relatives.

The Betsileo permit marriage of patrilateral parallel cousins, though I have never been able to discover a case of it among them. Betsileo ideology also allows a man to marry his matrilateral cross cousin, his MBD. Note that in a strictly patrilineal society this is not a case of descent group endogamy, since the MBD belongs to the mother's rather than the father's patrilineal descent group. However, as was noted earlier, Betsileo society is incompletely patrilineal. Individuals have rights to join their mother's descent group. In cases where these rights have been activated, MBD marriage represents descent group endogamy. However, such marriages seem to have been just as rare as those involving the children of two brothers. According to the Betsileo, the preference that a senior commoner choose his spouse from a branch of his own descent group is a corollary of a more general rule that individuals marry members of their own stratum. Therefore, if a marriage could be arranged with another senior commoner descent group whose genealogy was known to be pure according to Betsileo standards, this was fine, too. As a result, Betsileo males sometimes sought as spouses women from their mother's descent group, perhaps from the mother's actual descent branch, perhaps from another branch. The Betsileo say of this custom, "if cattle find the grazing good in a pasture one day, they will return to graze there on another."

This discussion of marriage among the Betsileo is meant to illustrate that in many ethnographic cases it is difficult to distinguish between endogamy and exogamy. If, in a nonunilineal society, an individual is a member of his father's descent group and marries another member of that descent group, the ethnographer can speak of descent group endogamy. The same is true if a person who is a member of his mother's descent group marries another member of that group. However, although the stipulated descent groups of Betsileo senior commoners could be, and often were, endogamous, as long as intracaste marriages were arranged, stipulated descent groups also could be exogamous. Furthermore, in the great majority of cases, local descent groups were exogamous. Among the Betsileo, endogamy functioned to maintain the castelike structure of stratification, while local descent group exogamy functioned to establish and maintain intracaste alliances. Local groups whose members had intermarried were usually political allies, and these alliances also carried obligations of economic support.

Exogamy

Here we leave the discussion of endogamy, which serves to isolate social groups, and return to the discussion of exogamy, which serves to incorporate them into larger networks. Among many populations of the world, there is a great deal of flexibility in rules of exogamy, but in tribal populations, the rules regulating exogamy are often rigid and specific. For example, certain populations with strongly developed unilineal descent organization not only strictly prohibit descent group endogamy, but also dictate exactly where a person is to seek his spouse.

Generalized exchange

The French anthropologist Claude Lévi-Strauss (1969) has been most instrumental in directing anthropological attention toward such societies. He has described and analyzed exogamic rules which give rise to what he calls *generalized exchange* systems. Among populations who practice generalized exchange, there is a definite marital relationship between exogamous descent groups. For any descent group B, there is a group C of wife receivers and a group A of wife givers. A, B, and C are each different descent groups. The men of B always take as their wives women of group A, and women of group B always marry men of group C. Note, too, that generalized exchange is associated with patrilineal descent organization and virilocal postmarital residence. The assumption is that the men stay put and the women marry out. A system of generalized exchange may arrange several descent groups in a closed circle, so that women of A always marry men of B, women of B always marry men of C, women of C always marry men of D, and so on through n, the number of descent groups in the circle. The women of n−1 will marry the men of n, and the women of n, the men of A; and so the circle continues. This variety of gen-

FIGURE 10 Circulating connubium.

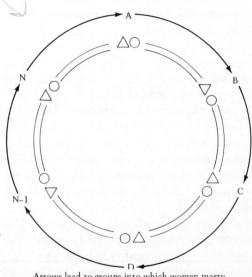

Arrows lead to groups into which women marry.

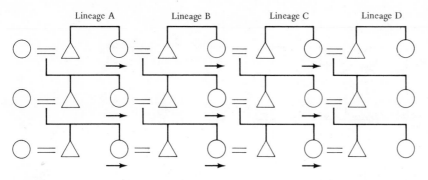

Lineage A   Lineage B   Lineage C   Lineage D

FIGURE 11 Generalized exchange system (male marries his MBD and female her FZS).

Exogamy marriage in differ descent grps.

eralized exchange system is often called *circulating connubium*. (See Figure 10.)

Note that if men of B always marry women of A and if descent is patrilineal, a man who shares his father's descent group affiliation B will also take his wife from group A. This is, in fact, his mother's descent group. Aside from his mother, another female member of his mother's descent group is his MBD (mother's brother's daughter). In some societies with generalized exchange systems, cultural preferences actually favor a man's marriage to his own MBD. Far more commonly, however, a man is expected to marry either his true MBD or any other female of his mother's group who is of appropriate age. A hypothetical, generalized exchange system involving marriage of men to their MBD is shown in Figure 11. Note that from a woman's point of view, she is marrying her FZS (father's sister's son). Some anthropologists use the term *matrilateral cross cousin marriage* to describe such systems. The use of the term "generalized exchange" is preferable, since it avoids viewing marriage from only the man's point of view and implying that first cousins are supposed to marry.

Marriage in Intermediate Societies

Among people who do not live in industrial societies, marriage is often more of a relationship between groups than individuals. In American society, marriage is an individual matter. Certainly, the bride and groom often look to their parents for approval, but the final choice is with the marrying pair. It is they, after all, who plan to spend their lives together. The con-

cept of love in industrial societies symbolizes this relationship between an individual female and an individual male.

In intermediate societies, marriage is a group affair. A man does not simply take a bride, he takes a brother-in-law. In societies with descent groups, he marries a descent group. The same is true for a woman. In a society where typical postmarital residence is virilocal, a woman must leave the community where she was born; she must leave her kinsmen and members of her own descent group. She faces the prospect of living the rest of her life in her husband's village, with her husband's kinsmen and their wives. She may even transfer her major allegiance from her own group to her husband's. Thus if there are disputes between her group and her husband's, she may side with him.

Bridewealth

Typically in societies with descent groups, a man cannot enter marriage alone. He calls on other members of his descent group for help. In many societies there is an institution known as bride price, or *bridewealth*. Wealth of some sort is passed from the husband's group to the wife's. The term "bride price" is unfortunate, since it suggests that the wife is being sold. In most societies with bridewealth institutions, people do not regard the transfer of such wealth as a sale. Certainly, they do not think of marriage as a relationship between a man and an object that can be bought and sold. Alternatively, several explanations are offered for the custom. Sometimes it is said that payment compensates the bride's group for the loss of her

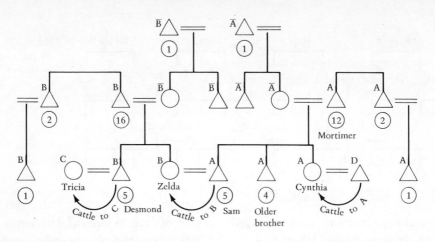

FIGURE 12 Bridewealth. The majority of cattle entering group A from daughter Cynthia's marriage are initially collected by Cynthia's father, Mortimer, and subsequently used as the major part of Sam's bridewealth payment for Zelda. Other close agnates also contribute to Sam's bridewealth payment. The cattle pass to Zelda's group, B, where the majority are conserved by Zelda's father to be used as bridewealth when Desmond marries. The cattle then pass to group C, where Tricia's father (not shown) stores most of the herd until it is needed for bridewealth payment for the marriage of his own son or another of Tricia's close agnates. $\overline{A}$ = not A, descent group other than A; $\overline{B}$ = not B, descent group other than B; ① = number of cattle received or donated.

companionship and economic labor. Far more often, however, people point to the role of bridewealth in making children born to the woman full members of her husband's group. It is for this reason that some anthropologists prefer to call the institution *progeny price*. It is the children whom the woman will bear, rather than the woman herself, who are being permanently transferred to the husband's group.

Whatever we choose to call it, such an exchange of wealth on the occasion of marriage is common in intermediate societies. It tends to be found in societies with patrilineal descent rules, or in societies with a tendency toward patrilineal descent group composition. In matrilineal societies, where children are automatically members of the mother's group, there is no reason to pay a progeny price. Although the institution of bridewealth exists in many different parts of the world, there are differences in the nature and quantity of goods transferred at marriage. In many African societies, cattle are the major item in bridewealth payments. There are, however, variations from society to society in the number of cattle given. The following discussion should illustrate some reasons for bridewealth. As the value of bridewealth increases, marriages become more stable;

bridewealth may be good insurance against divorce.

Imagine a patrilineal society, represented in Figure 12, in which a marriage normally involves the transfer of twenty-five cattle from the groom's group to the bride's group. Figure 12 demonstrates where the cattle come from and where they go to. Sam, a member of descent group A, and Zelda, a member of descent group B, are going to get married. Sam must seek the assistance of his kinsmen in assembling bridewealth. He expects help from his close agnates, that is, his older brother, his father, his father's brother, and his patrilateral parallel cousin. Representatives of Sam's mother's group, his mother's father or his mother's brother, may also contribute as a token of a continuing alliance established one generation earlier. Sam's marriage is the concern of his entire corporate lineage, and especially of his father. His father or, if his father is dead, his older brother or his father's brother, may actually assemble the cattle. Some of the cattle have come from natural increase in the herds of Sam's descent group. Others have come in as bridewealth for female members of Sam's descent group, for example, Sam's sister Cynthia and other sisters and his father's married sisters.

The distribution of the cattle once they have been turned over to Zelda's group mirrors the manner in which they were assembled. Zelda's father, or oldest brother if her father is dead, receives Zelda's bridewealth. Most of the cattle remain with him; he will use them as bridewealth to acquire wives for his sons and other close agnates. However, a share in Zelda's bridewealth also goes to those whom her father will expect to help him when one of his sons gets married. Cattle may also be passed to Zelda's mother's father or mother's brother.

When Zelda's brother Desmond gets married, therefore, many of the same cattle may pass to a third group, C, his wife's group. Similarly, they are transmitted through the institution of bridewealth to still other groups, as men use bridewealth derived from their sister's marriages to obtain wives of their own. In a decade, the cattle which Sam's group gave to Zelda's group may have been dispersed among so many different groups and over so large a territory that Sam's group have lost track of their whereabouts.

With marriage, there is a covenant between two descent groups. Various cultural traditions define the roles of husband and wife differently. The marriage covenant is an understanding between the two groups that neither Zelda nor Sam will deviate too far from behavior expected of a married couple. The covenant also specifies what Zelda owes to Sam's group and what she can expect from Sam and from his agnates. In populations whose members think of bridewealth principally as a device which entitles a woman's children to full membership in her husband's descent group, the woman's major obligation is to bear children, to ensure the continuity of her husband's group.

Several problems may threaten the fulfillment of the marriage covenant between the two groups. Zelda, for example, may find that Sam is not at all what she expected in a husband; she may not be able to get along with him or with his agnates. She may consider leaving him and returning home. If she convinces her kinsmen

that she has been treated badly, if the amount of bridewealth was small and it is within their means, her kinsmen may return it. Thus a divorce takes place. However, marriages in intermediate societies are not usually so soluble. It is common for a woman's kinsmen to try very hard to convince her to return to her husband. This is especially true if the amount of bridewealth was large and it has been distributed among a number of Zelda's agnates and other kinsmen, or if most of it has been used to obtain a wife for Zelda's brother or another close male agnate. In such a case, Zelda may try again to make her marriage work. To generalize, the more difficult it is to reassemble bridewealth, the more stable is marriage, and the rarer divorce.

If Zelda and Sam try again and again to make their marriage a success but fail, both sets of agnates may conclude that the marriage cannot survive. In such circumstances it becomes especially obvious that marriage in bridewealth societies is a relationship between groups as well as individuals. If Zelda has a younger sister, or her brother a daughter, either is a member of Zelda's descent group. To avoid the return of the bridewealth, Zelda's and Sam's descent groups may agree that Zelda is to be replaced by one of these women. There is another possibility. When a woman divorces a man, he may claim her brother's wife. And why not? After all, the cattle which Sam gave to Zelda's father may have been used subsequently to obtain a wife for Zelda's brother Desmond. Since Sam's cattle served as her brideweath, Sam has a claim on Desmond's wife (Figure 12). Such a custom exists among the Ba-Thonga of Mozambique in Southeast Africa.

Marital problems other than incompatibility occur in populations with the institution of bridewealth. It may turn out that Zelda bears no children. Clearly, in this case, neither she nor her group has fulfilled their part of the marriage contract. If the relationship between groups is to be maintained, Zelda's group must furnish a woman, perhaps her younger sister, perhaps another female agnate, who can have children. So important is this consideration among the Betsileo that it is often only after a young woman has become pregnant that the marriage takes place and bridewealth is transferred. There is a period of trial marriage in which the young woman lives in her husband's village. During this time she demonstrates her fertility and also learns whether she and her husband and others in his village are compatible. If after she becomes pregnant, the couple does not wish to get married, the child has the right to become a full member of its mother's descent group.

Among populations whose social organization includes descent groups and bridewealth, any marriage is a contract between descent groups. If a woman cannot have children, her group will be obliged to return the progeny price or to provide a substitute wife. The original wife may sometimes be allowed to remain in her husband's village. Perhaps she will someday have a child. Perhaps, in recognition of her companionship and labor and because it has received two women rather than only one, her husband's group will add a bit to the bridewealth. If the first wife stays on, her husband will now be involved in a plural marriage. Most intermediate societies allow plural marriages, or *polygamy*. There are two varieties, one common, the other very rare. Common, especially in intermediate societies, is *polygyny*, in which a man has more than one wife. Rare is *polyandry*, in which a woman has more than one husband. Therefore, if an infertile wife remains married to her husband after he has taken a substitute child bearer provided by her descent group, this is polygyny. Reasons for polygyny other than infertility are discussed shortly.

Durable alliances: sororate

It is possible to exemplify the group nature

of marriage in intermediate societies by examining still another common practice—continuation of group marital alliances in the event one of the spouses dies. What would happen if Zelda died young? Again, Sam's group might call on Zelda's to provide a substitute, perhaps the sister of his deceased wife. This custom is known as the *sororate*. What, you may wonder, happens if Zelda has no sister, or if all her sisters are already married? Quite simply, another marriageable female member of Zelda's group may be available—Zelda's older brother's daughter or some other patrilineal relative. Sam marries her; there is no need to return the bridewealth; and the alliance between the two groups continues. The sororate is found both in matrilineal and patrilineal societies. In a matrilineal society with uxorilocal postmarital residence, a widower may remain with his wife's group by marrying her sister or some other female member of her matrilineage. (See Figure 13.)

Levirate, widow inheritance, and other arrangements

So far, marriage as a relationship between groups rather than individuals has been illustrated only by cases in which the wife reneges on the marriage contract. Obviously, however, a breach can also originate with the husband. What happens, for example, if the husband dies? In many societies, a woman will marry a brother of her deceased husband, or a man, the widow of his deceased brother. This custom is known as the *levirate*, and like the sororate, it rep-

Sororate

Levirate and Widow Inheritance

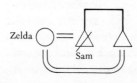

FIGURE 13 Sororate and levirate.

resents a kind of continuation marriage. It continues the alliance between descent groups by replacing the deceased husband with another member of his group. Any children sired by the woman's new husband are socially and legally recognized as those of the deceased rather than of his brother, the actual genitor. In this way, a man who dies childless can still be identified as an ancestor in future generations. (See Figure 13.)

Similar to the levirate, and serving an equivalent function in preserving alliances, is *widow inheritance*, whereby a widow's subsequent children are socially and legally deemed offspring of the brother who inherits her rather than of the deceased (cf. Middleton, 1965).

The implications of the levirate and widow inheritance vary with the age of the widow. Returning to Sam, Zelda, and company, what happens if Sam dies after Zelda's child-bearing years are over? When Sam and Zelda married, it was understood that Sam's group would be obliged to care for Zelda if Sam died. She has fulfilled her part of the marriage contract: she has borne children for Sam's descent group. Now that Sam is dead and gone, who is to care for her? The levirate assigns her to one of Sam's brothers. If he already has a wife, he will now become polygynous. He is obligated to care for Zelda and to treat her as his wife. Depending upon the difference in their ages, their marriage may or may not involve sexual relations.

If a husband has no brother, another member of his descent group may want to marry his widow. In some patrilineal and polygynous societies, when a man who has no brothers dies, his sons, his closest living agnates, may inherit his widows. Under no circumstance, however, does a son inherit his own mother. If Sam had two wives, Zelda and Millie, Zelda's son may get Millie, and Millie's son, Zelda.

There are ways of taking care of widows other than the levirate. Among the Betsileo, for example, a widow is not expected to marry her husband's brother. If she has sons, she may remain in her husband's village where they will support her.

Alliances end, conflict begins

The relationship between groups is not always maintained. Particularly in populations that exchange bridewealth, divorce may not only end an alliance, it may actually trigger conflict. Consider what could happen if Sam argues that Zelda is not behaving like a good wife and Zelda argues that Sam is mistreating her. Sam's group believes and supports him and Zelda's group believes and supports her. Zelda's group may refuse to provide another woman for a louse like Sam; or Sam's group may declare that it does not want another wife from a group which has done such a bad job in training its women. With both groups convinced that not only the individual marriage but the group relationship should end, the matter of the bridewealth comes up. Zelda's group may be reluctant to return it, since they feel that the fault lies with Sam. To his group, Zelda is clearly to blame. In societies which lack judicial systems to settle such disputes, open conflict between the two groups may break out.

Plural Marriages

In the contemporary United States, as in most industrial nations, polygamy is against the law. Perhaps this is partly because divorces are fairly easy to obtain. Relationships between individuals may be more soluble than those which ally social groups. As divorce becomes more common, both men and women may become involved in what anthropologists call *serial monogamy*: an individual has more than one spouse in his lifetime, but never, legally, more than one at the same time.

As was stated earlier, there are two forms of polygamy: polygyny and polyandry. Polygyny is far more common than polyandry, which is accepted in very few societies. Populations of the Marquesas Islands in Polynesia, and certain groups in Tibet, India, and other parts of southern Asia provide some of the rare examples of polyandry in practice.

Polygyny

Before examining some of the reasons for polygyny, it is necessary to distinguish between the social approval of plural marriage in a given society and its frequency in that society. People in many societies—and in most intermediate societies—attach no stigma to polygynous unions; in fact, it may be considered good to have more than one wife. However, even in societies where polygyny is encouraged, most men and women are involved in monogamous unions. Polygyny is characteristic of only a fraction of the marriages in that society. Why?

EQUAL SEX RATIOS In the contemporary United States, there are approximately 105 males born for every 100 females. However, by adulthood the ratio of men to women is equalized, and later it is reversed. In the United States, the average female lives longer than the average male. In some nonindustrial societies, the sex ratio, if it favors males at birth, may be reversed by adulthood. This is because in many societies the activities traditionally allocated to males are more dangerous than those deemed appropriate for females. Men have to climb coconut trees; repair roofs; hunt tigers or sea mammals; take part in raiding parties and warfare; fish, sail, and travel, possibly into alien territory. Where male tasks are dangerous and often fatal, the practice of female infanticide may be considered appropriate.

Infanticide is a means of population control common among populations who do not employ birth control. For example, the horticultural Tapirapé Indians of Brazil customarily controlled their population by killing every fourth baby (see Wagley, 1971). Each couple was allowed to have two girls and a boy or two boys and a girl. If the third child was of the same sex as the previous two, it was killed. If it was of a different sex, the fourth child was always killed. This custom permitted the Tapirapé population to maintain itself, for

infant mortality and death from natural causes further reduced the population.

Populations such as the Eskimos, which assign especially dangerous jobs to males, practice female infanticide. The practice of killing female infants ensures that there will be approximately equal numbers of adult female and male Eskimos.

There are some demographic reasons why polygyny is more common than polyandry. If there is no female infanticide and there is a disparity in the dangers associated with male and female tasks, the adult sex ratio favors females, and polygyny is the cultural adaptive result. Polygyny is also found in populations where men typically marry later than women. Among the Kanuri of Bornu in Nigeria (Cohen, 1967), men customarily marry for the first time between the ages of eighteen and thirty. Many women, on the other hand, marry between twelve and fourteen. Because of the age disparity between spouses, there are more widows than widowers. Most of the widows remarry or are inherited by their deceased husband's agnates. Some become wives in polygynous unions. Among the Kanuri, and in other polygynous societies, widows constitute a large number of the women involved in polygynous unions (cf. Hart and Pilling, 1960).

SOME EXPLANATIONS FOR POLYGYNY Shifting our orientation from observers' to actors' explanations, we find that the reasons people give for practicing polygyny vary from society to society. Perhaps the most common response is a variant of the following: "We are polygynous because our ancestors were polygynous, and that is the way things should be." Related to this is the answer: "It is the custom of our people for men to marry as many women as they can support." Among many populations, including the Kanuri, the number of a man's wives is a measure of his prestige and social position. The Kanuri live in composite households headed by men. Also residing in the household are the man's wives and unmarried children, and, because residence after marriage is virilocal, his married sons and their wives and

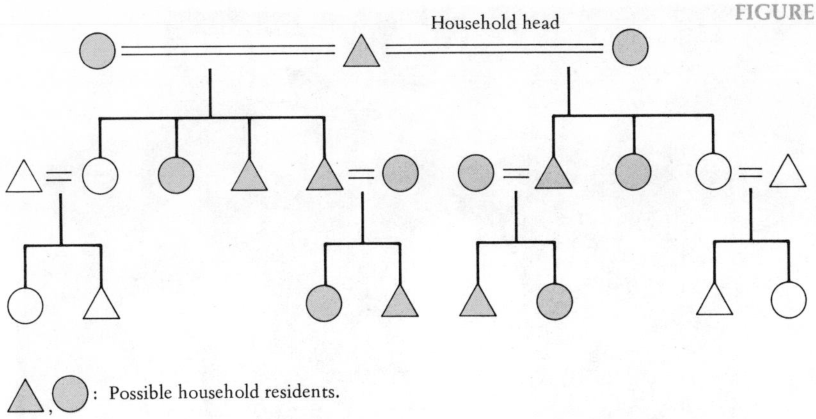

FIGURE 14 A Kanuri household.

Household head

△,○ : Possible household residents.

children. The household is the major productive unit among the Kanuri. The more wives, the more productive workers in a household. Increased productivity means more wealth for the household head; more wealth attracts additional wives. Wealth and wives mean greater prestige for the household and its head, and were it not for the fact that Kanuri marriages are highly unstable, with a high incidence of divorce, there would be a progressive differentiation of Kanuri households. (See Figure 14.)

Informants in several societies have told ethnographers that the additional wife or wives have been obtained at the request of the first wife to help her with household work and other burdens. In such cases, the status of the second wife is commonly below that of the first: there are a senior wife and junior wives. Often, it is actually the senior wife who chooses the second wife. She may be a close kinswoman who has not yet married—a younger sister, for example, whom the senior wife is reasonably sure that she can control.

The anthropologist Robert Murphy reports that an informant among the Tuareg, a pastoral population whom he studied in Niger in West Africa, gave him the following explanation for having taken a third wife: "I married my third wife because my first wife and my second wife found it hard to get along most of the time. When they agreed, it was usually to team up against me with some complaint. I wanted a third wife to mediate. I also wanted to have someone to spend a few hours with to get away from the constant bickering."

When I asked some of my Betsileo informants in Madagascar about their ancestors' reasons for practicing polygyny, they pointed out that the different wives always lived in different villages. A man's first and senior wife, called "Big Wife" in Malagasy, lived with him in the ancestral village where he cultivated his principal rice field and spent most of his time. However, the Betsileo inherit from several different ancestors and cultivate rice fields in several different areas. Prestigious men with several rice fields customarily established wives and households in hamlets near each rice field. They spent most of their time with their senior wife, but visited the others as they tended additional fields throughout the year.

Plural wives often play political roles in archaic states. The king of the Merina, a population of more than 1,500,000 located in the highlands of Madagascar north of the Betsileo, established official residences for each of his twelve wives in different provinces of his kingdom. He stayed with them as he traveled throughout his kingdom, and they were his local agents, overseeing and reporting on events in the provinces. The king of Buganda, a highly developed state during the eighteenth and nineteenth centuries in what is now Uganda, East Africa, took his wives from among all the commoner clans in his nation. The child of one of his wives would eventually become king. Thus all clans in the state were in-laws of the king, and all had a chance to provide the next king. This seems to have been an effective way of

The wedding of a Kabaka of Buganda, Uganda. *(Dr. Georg Gerster/Rapho Guillumette)*

giving the common people a stake in the administration of the state.

From these examples, it should be apparent that it is foolhardy to seek a single explanation for polygyny. Its function varies from society to society and even within the same society. Some men are polygynous because they have inherited a widow from a brother or another close kinsman. Others take plural wives because they seek prestige or greater productivity for their households. Still others establish wives in different areas to supervise their estates in those regions. Recall, too, that marriage is a political tool, and it may also be a means of economic advancement. Men with political and economic ambitions cultivate alliances which serve their aims. Polygyny by a monarch to increase his power is a very different matter from polygyny by a commoner who is obliged to care for his older brothers' widows.

Polyandry

Because polyandry is so rare, it is necessary to point to the very specific conditions under which it is practiced. The great majority of ethnographically documented polyandrous marriage systems come from South Asia—from Tibet, India, Nepal, and Ceylon. In contemporary India, the most consistent practitioners of polyandry are certain groups that live in the lower ranges of the Himalayas in northern India. Collectively, these people are known as Paharis, which means "people of the mountains," and they have been studied extensively by the anthropologist Gerald Berreman. In particular, Berreman (1962) has completed a comparative study of two Pahari groups, one located in Jaunsar Bawar in the western foothills of the Himalayas, the other in Garhwal in the central foothills. Berreman noted a high incidence of polyandrous marriages in Jaunsar Bawar, but no cases at all in Garhwal.

The western and the central Paharis are historically, genetically, and linguistically related. They speak dialects of the same Indo-European language. Western and central Paharis may be viewed as divergent descendants of a common ancestral population which has undergone an adaptive radiation. The polyandrous inhabitants of Jaunsar

Bawar represent adaptation to an area of the lower ranges of the western Himalayas, those of Garhwal to the lower ranges of the central Himalayas. Noting extensive similarities in other aspects of their cultural traditions and social organization, Berreman addressed himself to the question of why one group practiced polyandry while the other did not.

The major reason for the difference appeared to be demographic. The sex ratios of the two areas were very different. In Jaunsar Bawar, the polyandrous area, there was an unusually great shortage of females (789 females per 1,000 males), while in nonpolyandrous Garhwal, the ratio favored females (1,100 females per 1,000 males). Berreman was unable to explain the shortage of females in Jaunsar Bawar. Female infanticide has not been documented in the area. He thought that neglect of female children might be a more likely explanation.

Berreman's work documents that there is variation among polyandrous marriage systems as there is among polygynous systems, and such systems occur for different reasons. Polyandry in Jaunsar Bawar is exclusively fraternal; when there are multiple husbands they are always a group of brothers. Typically, the oldest brother arranges the marriage. The marriage ceremony establishes all the brothers as socially recognized husbands of the wife. Subsequently, the brothers may marry additional women. All such wives, however, are considered wives of all the brothers. Brothers have equal sexual access to their common wife or to all other wives, and all wives have sexual access to each brother. Children born to the wives call all the brothers "father," disregarding biological paternity.

Among the related people of Garhwal, where the sex ratio favors females over males, 85 percent of the unions in Berreman's sample were monogamous, and 15 percent were polygynous. Despite prohibitions against polyandry in Garhwal, Berreman found striking similarities in the actual operation of polyandry in Jaunsar Bawar, and monogamy in Garhwal. In Garhwal as in Jaunsar Bawar, a group of brothers jointly contribute to the bride-wealth given for the wife of any brother. Furthermore, in Garhwal brothers also have sexual access to each other's wives. The major difference seemed to be that children in nonpolyandrous Garhwal recognize only one father. Needless to say, with the common sexual rights of brothers, a child's socially recognized father is not necessarily his true genitor.

In other areas of South Asia, informants and ethnographers have pointed to other reasons why polyandry may be selected for. Among some polyandrous groups, marriage of plural men to a single wife has been interpreted as adaptation to geographical mobility associated with male economic tasks. It has been argued that when men travel a great deal to engage in trade, commerce, or military operations, polyandry ensures that there is always a male at home to care for the wife and children and to maintain a viable household. Polyandry also represents an adaptation to scarcity of strategic resources. Like Americans plagued with poverty, a group of brothers who have inherited access to a limited patrimony also often pool their resources in expanded households. In these cases, polyandry, by restricting the number of wives, also limits the number of heirs who must compete for the same meager estate. In still other cases, the practice of polyandry appears to be related to a distribution of wealth in which women as well as men are property owners and dowry, a parcel of property rights, is brought into a marriage by the wife. Given such conditions, the anthropologist E. R. Leach (1955) has argued that polyandry serves to keep property of the husbands and wife intact, to be passed on to children with minimal fragmentation. Note, therefore, that fraternal polyandry can serve as a functional alternative to endogamy.

The selecting conditions for polyandry also were specific among the Marquesan Islanders of Polynesia. In contrast to polyandry in South Asia, however,

Marquesan polyandry was typically non-fraternal. During the nineteenth century, following contact with Europeans, the Marquesan population fell drastically. Over eighty years, the population of one of the Marquesan Islands was decimated. Intertribal skirmishes and warfare with the European explorers appear to have played a part in population decline. However, smallpox and famine were even more devastating (Otterbein, 1968). Population decline affected males and females differently. By the end of the nineteenth century the sex ratio was about six females to five males. Polyandry, in a variety of guises, was the cultural adaptive response.

Otterbein has identified four types of Marquesan marital arrangements: (1) monogamous; (2) simple polyandrous unions involving a woman and multiple husbands; (3) polygynous-polyandrous households in which a married man married a married woman (the new wife and her husband joined the household of the new husband, who was always a richer man, and all spouses had sexual rights to the spouses of the opposite sex); (4) composite households including a core representing one of the other three marital arrangements, to which unmarried males had attached themselves. They did not marry, but had sexual access to the wife or wives of the household. (See Figure 15.)

The Marquesan case represents an example so rare as to be considered only

SUMMARY

Taboos against incest are encountered in all human societies. However, incest taboos in different societies proscribe marriage with different biological kin types. Various reasons have been suggested for the taboo's universality: (1) it codifies instinctive human revulsion against such unions; (2) it results from recognition of biological degeneration that follows from such unions; (3) it possesses a selective advantage because of the exogamic alliances it promotes; and (4) it is necessary to maintain the role structure of the nuclear family and thus the cohesion of society. While no single explanation can totally account for the taboo's universality, anthropologists Edward Tylor, Leslie White, Claude Lévi-Strauss, and Bronislaw Malinowski have offered valuable clues to understanding it. The incest taboo does promote exogamy, therefore increasing networks of friends and allies. Furthermore, mating between close kinsmen, especially parents and children, would create conflict which could impair sociocultural cohesion and continuity.

The major adaptive advantage associated with exogamy is to extend social ties outward. This is confirmed by a consideration of endogamy, marriage within the group. Endogamic rules are often encountered in stratified societies. Perhaps the most familiar example is India, where castes, though endogamous units, are often subdivided internally into descent groups which are themselves exogamous. People therefore may follow both endogamic and exogamic prescriptions in the same society, but with reference to different groups to which they belong. The stratified system of the United States is structurally similar to the Indian caste system, although it lacks many of the cultural embellishments.

In certain archaic states, royal incest was allowed and even encouraged, even though the incest taboo applied to commoners. The manifest functions of royal incest in ancient Hawaii, for example, were related to their ideology of mana. However, royal incest also served certain latent functions in the political and economic spheres—limiting succession struggles and reducing fragmentation of wealth which accompanied royal status. Marriage of close relatives in Brazilian plantation society demonstrates some of the same functions. Preferential

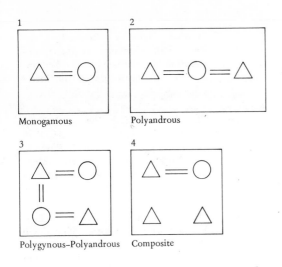

1 Monogamous
2 Polyandrous
3 Polygynous–Polyandrous
4 Composite

FIGURE 15 Four types of households among the Marquesans.

as a curiosity. Like marriage in South Asia, however, it does serve to illustrate that there is no simple trichotomy of monogamy-polyandry-polygyny. All three marriage types can coexist in the same society as part of a flexible set of traditional rules. The practice of polygyny or polyandry among different populations represents a kind of convergence—the appearance of similar forms though the selecting conditions may have been different. Cultural forms like polyandry may be adaptive solutions which serve functions analogous to those which other forms, such as endogamy, serve in different cultures.

marriage of brothers' children in the Near East and North Africa, particularly among Arabs, illustrates some additional functions and effects of endogamy.

Cultural rules of many tribal societies not only forbid people from marrying within their own group, but also rigidly dictate their choice of spouses. What Lévi-Strauss has called generalized exchange is a common variant of such prescriptive exogamic marriage systems. Generalized exchange links exogamous descent groups in a set series of marital relationships, such that women from group B always marry men from group C, while men from group B always take their wives from group A.

There is a major contrast between marriage in intermediate and industrial societies. Especially among populations with descent group organization, marriage must be understood as a relationship between groups as well as between spouses. Populations with descent group organization often follow a custom known as bridewealth, whereby wealth of some sort is assembled by the groom and his relatives and transmitted to the bride and her relatives before marriage. A relationship between bridewealth and divorce has been suggested: as the value of the bridewealth increases, the frequency of divorce declines. The amassing and distribution of bridewealth demonstrates that marriages in intermediate societies ally groups, as do other customs such as sororate, whereby a man marries the sister of his deceased wife, and levirate, whereby a woman marries the brother of her deceased husband. Certain replacement marriages in the event of incompatibility of specific spouses also confirm the importance attached to maintenance of group alliances.

Among many human populations, including those of most intermediate societies, plural marriages are considered culturally appropriate. Two varieties of polygamy are recognized: polygyny, marriages involving multiple wives; and polyandry, marriages involving multiple husbands. No single reason can account for the practice of polygyny or polyandry in the variety of social and cultural contexts in which they occur. Polygyny occurs far more commonly than polyandry. Demographic and ecological reasons for plural marriage systems have been discussed.

Sources and Suggested Readings

BARTH, F.

1954   Father's Brother's Daughter Marriage in Kurdistan. *Southwestern Journal of Anthropology* 10: 164–171. Argues for a political function of marriage of children of brothers among the Kurds.

BERREMAN, G. D.

1962   Pahari Polyandry: A Comparison. *American Anthropologist* 64: 60–75. Similarities and differences in the marriage systems of two related Himalayan populations.

BOHANNAN, P., and MIDDLETON, J., eds.

1968   *Marriage, Family and Residence.* Garden City, N.Y.: The Natural History Press. Articles on variant forms of marriage, incest, and exogamy, and family and household organization.

BUCHLER, I. R., and SELBY, H. A.

1968   *Kinship and Social Organizaion: An Introduction to Theory and Method.* New York: Macmillan. One of the best general works on social organization; includes a good discussion of descent and alliance.

CHAGNON, N.

1968a   Yanomamo Social Organization and Warfare. In *War: The Anthropology of Armed Conflict and Aggression,* ed. M. H. Fried, M. Harris, and R. F. Murphy, pp. 109–159. Garden City, N.Y.: The Natural History Press. Relationship of Yanomamo marriage and trade patterns to their warfare.

1968b   *Yanomamo: The Fierce People.* New York: Holt, Rinehart and Winston. Marriage practices and descent group organization with concrete examples of Yanomamo behavior and ideology.

CHANCE, N. A.

1966   *The Eskimo of North Alaska.* New York: Holt, Rinehart and Winston. Case study of contemporary Eskimos.

COHEN, R.

1967   *The Kanuri of Bornu.* New York: Holt, Rinehart and Winston. Case study includes interesting discussion of patrilocal, polygynous households and marital instability.

FIRTH, R.

1940   The Analysis of Mana: An Empirical Approach. *The Journal of the Polynesian Society* 49: 483–510. Variations in the *mana* doctrine in Oceania.

FREUD, S.

1950   *Totem and Taboo,* translated by J. Strachey. London: Routledge and Kegan Paul. Contains fanciful reconstruction of early human social organization and the origin of the incest taboo.

FREYRE, G.

1956   *The Masters and the Slaves: A Study in the Development of Brazilian Civilization,* translated by S. Putnam. New York: Knopf. Idealistic examination of social relations in plantation society of northeastern Brazil.

HARRIS, M., and KOTTAK, C. P.

1963   The Structural Significance of Brazilian Racial Categories. *Sociologia* 25: 203–209. Contrasts Brazilian and North American racial classification systems with reference to the rule of hypodescent.

HART, C. W. M., and PILLING, A. R.

1960   *The Tiwi of North Australia.* New York: Holt, Rinehart and Winston. Case study of unusual degree of polygyny among North Australian foragers.

HOBHOUSE, L. T.

1915   *Morals in Evolution.* Rev. ed. New York: Holt. Comparative view of social organization by an early anthropologist.

HOEBEL, E. A.

1954   *The Law of Primitive Man.* Cambridge: Harvard University Press. "Law" in different cultures; social organization of the Eskimos and several other groups.

HOMANS, G., and SCHNEIDER, D. M.

1955   *Marriage, Authority and Final Causes.* Glencoe, Ill.: The Free Press. Interprets marriage of a man to his mother's brother's daughter as following from the affection he feels first toward his mother, and then extends to his mother's brother, and finally to his daughter.

HUTTON, J. M.

1951   *Caste in India: Its Nature, Functions and Origins.* 2nd ed. London: Oxford University Press. Classic study of caste, based on personal knowledge of India.

JOSSELIN DE JONG, J. P. B.

1952   *Lévi-Strauss's Theory on Kinship and Marriage.* London: E. J. Brill. Long and comprehensive review of Lévi-Strauss, 1969 (orig. 1949).

KOTTAK, C. P.

1971   Social Groups and Kinship Calculation among the Southern Betsileo. *American Anthropologist* 73: 178–193. Includes analysis of marriage patterns among the Betsileo.

LEACH, E. R.

1955   Polyandry, Inheritance and the Definition of Marriage. *Man* 55: 182–186. Argues that marriage is not a cultural universal.

1961   *Rethinking Anthropology.* London: Athlone Press. Stimulating collection of articles; most deal with marriage systems.

LÉVI-STRAUSS, C.

1969   (orig. 1949). *The Elementary Structures of Kinship.* Boston: Beacon Press. Classic account of marriage, particularly generalized exchange, in non-Western societies.

LOWIE, R. H.

1961   (orig. 1920). *Primitive Society.* New York: Harper and Brothers. Classic, chapter by chapter attempt to negate Morgan, 1963 (orig. 1877). Origins of clan organization and of age and sex-based groups; descent, marriage, and kinship terminology.

MALINOWSKI, B.

1927   *Sex and Repression in Savage Society.* London: International Library of Psychology. Role of the father among the matrilineal Trobrianders of the South Pacific.

MERTON, R. K.

1957   *Social Theory and Social Structure.* Rev. ed. Glencoe, Ill.: The Free Press. Sociological discussion of manifest and latent functions included.

MIDDLETON, J.

1965   *The Lugbara of Uganda.* New York: Holt, Rinehart and Winston. Case study of an East African tribe, particularly strong in analysis of social organization.

MORGAN, L. H.

1963   (orig. 1877). *Ancient Society.* Cleveland: World Publishing. Classic contribution to social and political theory by an early American anthropologist.

MURPHY, R. F., and KASDAN, L.

1959   The Structure of Parallel Cousin Marriage. *American Anthropologist* 61: 17–29. Links marriage of children of brothers in the Near East and North Africa to factionalism; exemplifies in inverse form the alliance functions of exogamy.

OTTERBEIN, K. F.

1968   (orig. 1963). Marquesan Polyandry. In *Marriage, Family and Residence,* ed. P. Bohannan and J. Middleton, pp. 287–296. Garden City, N.Y.: The Natural History Press. Using secondary sources, author reconstructs four household types, some including polyandrous marriages, among this Polynesian population.

TYLOR, E. B.

1889   On a Method of Investigating the Development of Institutions: Applied to Laws of Marriage and Descent. *Journal of the Royal Anthropological Institute* 18: 245–269. Classic article advocating quantitative approach to anthropological comparison, particularly in the study of marriage and other aspects of social organization.

WAGLEY, C.

1969   (orig. 1951). Cultural Influences on Population: A Comparison of Two Tupi Tribes. In *Environment and Cultural Behavior,* ed. A. P. Vayda, pp. 268–279. Garden City, N.Y.: The Natural History Press. Cultural means of limiting population growth among two related South American Indian populations.

1971   *An Introduction to Brazil.* Rev. ed. New York: Columbia University Press. Social organization of a complex society, particularly kinship and marriage of upper- and middle-class Brazilians.

WESTERMARCK, E.

1894   *The History of Human Marriage.* London: Macmillan. Interesting early work; relates the incest taboo to fear of biological degeneration.

WHITE, L. A.

1949   *The Science of Culture.* New York: Farrar, Strauss and Company. Includes famous essay on the adaptive functions of the incest taboo and exogamy.

1959   *The Evolution of Culture.* New York: McGraw-Hill. Alliance functions of exogamy and variation in social organization among several non-Western populations examined from a general evolutionary viewpoint.

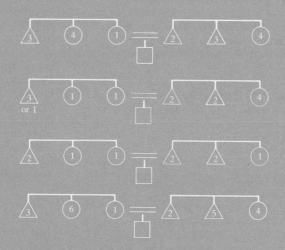

7. Kinship Terminology

In the discussion of the incest taboo in Chapter 6, it was asserted that people in different societies define their relatives in various ways. Contemporary Americans believe that a person is equally related to all his first cousins, to his father and mother, to his uncles and aunts, to all four grandparents, and to all his grandchildren. This belief is related to the cultural and actual preference for nuclear family organization in the contemporary United States.

Just as people with different cultural orientations define their relatives differently, they also use different patterns of kinship terminology to refer to them. Consider kinship terminology in the United States. Our term *first cousin* applies to any one of eight biological kin types. The term *cousin* includes an even larger number of biological kin types, because it lumps together first through fifth cousins, first through third cousins once removed, distant cousins, and, in certain regions of the United States, "kissing cousins." Similarly, our term *uncle* lumps together at least two kin types: mother's brother and father's brother. Our term *aunt* applies equally to

a mother's sister and a father's sister. *Grandfather* includes mother's father and father's father.

In any society, the terminology used to designate relatives is a classification system, a taxonomy or typology. However, it is not a classification system which has been developed by an anthropologist. Rather, it is a native taxonomy, a native classification system developed over generations by the people who live in that society. You have already seen that the native taxonomy of racial differences encountered in contemporary America is peculiar to us. It is therefore not surprising that the way we classify our kinsmen is also an American convention, although convergent systems do exist among other populations with prominent nuclear family organization.

A native classification system is based on how people perceive similarities and differences in the things being classified. When Americans use the term *uncle* to refer both to mother's brother and father's brother, it must be because we perceive both as being basically the same kind of relative. By lumping together these two biological kin types under the term *uncle*, we are distinguishing between these two kin types and another, F, whom we call "Father," "Dad," or "Pop." We never, however, use the same term for our father and our uncle. You may be surprised to learn that it is also common to call a father and a father's brother by the same term. This chapter examines several systems of kinship terminology encountered in different populations and attempts to suggest explanations for some of the differences and similarities between them.

To clarify the matter, let us return to the distinction between our terms *uncle* and *father*. The nuclear family has been described as the only important group based on kinship in many contemporary industrial nations. Its organization was explained in terms of an industrial economy, geographical mobility associated with lack of permanent ties to the land, sale of labor for cash, financial success, and neolocal postmarital residence. In this social context, it is perfectly reasonable for middle-class Americans to distinguish between those who belong to their nuclear families of orientation and procreation, and those who do not. We normally grow up living with our mother and father, but not with our aunts or uncles. We normally see our parents everyday; we see our uncles and aunts less frequently. Often, uncles and aunts live in different towns and cities, perhaps hundreds or thousands of miles from us. We expect to inherit our parents' property. The children of our uncles and aunts, our cousins, have first claim to inherit property from their parents.

Similar observations apply to the family of procreation. We raise and live with our children, see them virtually every day until they leave our households; they are our heirs. We are closer to them than we are to our nieces and nephews. We mean more to them than their aunts and uncles; they mean more to us than our nieces and nephews.

Native classification systems are based on differences and similarities as native members of the society perceive them. The term *uncle* distinguishes between the kin types MB and FB, on the one hand, and the kin type F, on the other. Yet it also lumps together; it uses the same term for MB and FB, two different kin types. Why? American kinship is bilateral; it extends equally on the mother's and the father's side. Both kinds of uncle are siblings of our parents. We think of both as roughly the same kind of relative. "No," some of you will object, "I feel closer to my mother's brother than to my father's brother." That may be. But for everyone who feels closer to his mother's relatives, there is another who feels closer to his father's relatives. In a large sample of American college students, we would probably find that approximately equal numbers favor each side. This is what the term *bilateral kinship* means: in the population as a whole, kinship is calculated equally on both sides.

Similar observations apply to such things as interaction with, residence near, and rights to inherit property from more distant relatives. Americans usually do not inherit from uncles on either side. However, on the whole, if they do inherit, there is an equal chance that they will inherit from one as from the other. Americans usually do not live near or in the same household with either of their uncles, but, if they do, the chances are approximately the same that it will be their father's brother as their mother's brother. The same rule applies to other aspects of social life based on kinship in this society.

FIGURE 16 Kinship classification on the first ascending generation.

	FZ	FB	F	M	MB	MZ
Lineal	4	3	1	2	3	4
Bifurcate merging	4	1	1	2	3	2
Variant	3	1	1	2	2'	2
Generational	2	1	1	2	1	2
Bifurcate collateral	4	5	1	2	3	6

Several considerations will determine differences in the way people treat, interact with, and classify their biological relatives in different societies. For example, do two biological kin types customarily reside together or apart? If they live apart, how far apart? How often do they see one another? What kind of behavior is appropriate between them? What kinds of rights do they have in each other? What benefits do they derive from one another and what are their obligations? With these questions in mind, let us examine other systems of kinship terminology.

Kinship Terminology on the Parental Generation

Lineal kinship terminology ✦

Figure 16 applies to biological kin types on the generation above ego, the first ascending generation. Letters at the top identify six biological kin types. Numbers indicate the manner of classification. Where the same number appears in a line under two biological kin types, they are called by the same term. The American system of kinship classification is called the *lineal system*. The number 3, which appears below the biological kin types FB and MB, stands for the term *uncle*, which is applied both to FB and to MB. (See Figure 17.)

Lineal terminology is found in societies where the nuclear family is the only or the most important social group based on kinship. The strategies of adaptation of such populations are generally industrialism and hunting and gathering.

Bifurcate merging kinship terminology ✦

Bifurcate merging kinship terminology is the most common way of classifying biological kin types on the first ascending generation. (See Figure 18.) It is found among

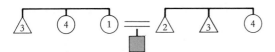

FIGURE 17 Lineal kinship terminology.

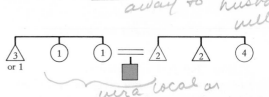

FIGURE 18 Bifurcate merging kinship terminology.

populations who follow unilocal rules of postmarital residence. It is also found in populations with unilineal descent. Recall that in a particular society the unilocal residence rule may be either virilocal, residence with the husband's group, or uxorilocal, residence with the wife's group. Similarly, patrilineal and matrilineal are the two varieties of unilineal descent rules. Thus bifurcate merging is generally found in societies with patrilineal or matrilineal descent rules, virilocal or uxorilocal residence patterns, or a combination of these rules.

What are the conditions that determine bifurcate merging kinship? If there is a virilocal rule of postmarital residence, men will bring wives into their own village, and women born in that village will marry out. You will grow up in the village where your father was born. Your father's brother will also live there with his wife. Your mother's brother, on the other hand, will live in another village, the one in which your mother was born. Your father and his brother are your two closest male kinsmen in the first ascending generation. You perceive them as similar enough to designate by the same term.

In a society where postmarital residence is uxorilocal, your mother and her sister will have brought their husbands to the same village, the place they were born. Your father's sister will be living somewhere else, in the place where she was born. Her husband will live there with her. Your mother and her sister are your closest female relatives in the generation above you who share your place of residence. You perceive them as similar, and you call them by the same term. In your kinship terminology, you differentiate between them and your father's sister, who resides in another locality.

Note that this explanation for bifurcate merging kinship terminology is incomplete. With uxorilocal residence, your father is living in his wife's—that is, your mother's—place of birth, and your father's brother is residing in his own wife's village. They will reside in the same place only if they marry women from the same place. Similarly, in a society with virilocal postmarital residence, there is no guarantee that your mother and her sister will reside in the same village after they marry. They do so, obviously, only when they marry men from the same village. Why, then, in a society with virilocal postmarital residence, do you call your mother and your mother's sister by the same term? And why, in a society with uxorilocal residence after marriage, do you call your father and your father's brother by the same term?

A partial explanation is offered here. If, in a unilocal society, it is customary for siblings of the same sex to take spouses from the same village or local group, then father and father's brother will, in fact, reside together in an uxorilocal society, and mother and mother's sister will marry into the same local group in a virilocal society. When the population has not only a unilocal rule of postmarital residence, but also a unilineal rule of descent, it is easier to see the logic of bifurcate merging kinship terminology. With unilineal descent groups, every individual in that society is a member of one descent group. In a patrilineal society, ego's father and father's brother are members of the same descent group, of the same sex and of the same generation. Since most patrilineal societies also have rules of virilocal postmarital residence, father and his brother also will be permanent residents of the same local group. Since they share so many attributes which are socially relevant in the society in question, it is fairly simple to see why ego regards them as sociological equals.

What about the mother and the mother's sister in a society with patrilineal descent? As full siblings, they are members of the same descent group, their father's. They are also of the same sex and the same generation. In many cases, though not always, they marry into the same village. These factors in conjunction may be sufficient to explain the use of the same term for both.

Similar observations apply to societies with matrilineal descent groups. Consider a society with two matrilineal clans, called the Wombats and the Aardvarks. Ego is a member of his mother's clan, the Wombat clan. Ego's father is a member of the Aardvark clan. His mother and her sister are both members of the Wombats, of the same sex and generation. If there is uxorilocal residence, as there often is in matrilineal societies, they will also reside in the same local group after they marry. Ego's father and father's brother are both members of the other descent group, the Aardvarks. They are of the same sex and generation. The fact that they share these attributes may be sufficient to explain why ego uses a single term to describe them. Marrying women of the same clan and residing after marriage in the same local group will serve to reinforce this usage.

Generational kinship terminology

Like bifurcate merging, generational kinship terminology merges parents and their siblings, but the lumping is more complete. (See Figure 19.) There are really only two terms for relatives on the parental generation. We may translate them as "father" and "mother," but more accurate translations would be "male member of the parental generation" and "female member of the parental generation." Of interest in generational kinship terminology is the fact that it does not distinguish between mother's side and father's side. It lumps together father, father's brother, and mother's brother. Note that in neither a matrilineal nor a patrilineal society are all three kin types members of the same descent group. Similarly, generational kinship terminology uses a single term for mother, mother's sister, and father's sister, relatives who, in a unilineal society, would never be members of the same descent group. Yet the terms

FIGURE 19 Generational kinship terminology.

suggest closeness between ego and relatives in the first ascending generation, much more closeness, in fact, than exists between aunts and uncles and nephews and nieces in America. From this we might expect generational terminology to be found in societies where kinship is much more important than in our own, but where there is no rigid distinction between father's side and mother's side.

It is no surprise, then, that generational kin classification is the typical kinship terminology of populations with ambilineal descent. Recall that in such societies there are descent groups centered around estates. Members of the descent group have access to its estate. However, in contrast to unilineal descent, ambilineal descent is not fixed at birth. An individual has a choice about which descent group he will join. Still other kinds of flexibility are characteristic of societies with ambilineal descent. In some, an individual may change his descent group membership during his lifetime. Furthermore, he may be a member of two or more descent groups simultaneously.

How does generational terminology fit in with these conditions? The individual's use of kin terms allows him to maintain close personal relationships with all relatives on the first ascending generation. In a rough way, he exhibits the same kind of behavior to them that he exhibits to his biological parents. Someday he will have to make a choice about the descent group he joins. Relevant, too, is the fact that in societies with ambilineal descent, postmarital residence is not usually unilocal but *ambilocal*—the married couple may reside either with the husband's or the wife's group. Consider the implications of cultural rules which allow individuals considerable leeway in where they can live after they marry. Ego's father and mother may be residing in ego's father's natal community. If ego decides to join his father's descent group and live in his father's local

group, he may become a permanent resident of the village where his father and his mother are residing. However, his father's sister, like his father, may have brought her spouse to her own village. His father's brother may or may not be residing in the village where he was born. Possibly he has moved to his wife's community. Similarly, if ego decides to join his mother's descent group, his father and mother may be there if they decided to reside uxorilocally after marriage. His mother's brother may be residing there with his wife, or he may have joined her in her village. His mother's sister may be there with her husband, or she may have followed her husband to his own community. In short, because of ambilocal residence and ambilineal descent, it is impossible for ego to know during his childhood which of his relatives on the first ascending generation will be closest to him throughout most of his later life. By calling everyone on that generation either father or mother, he can avoid the problem.

It is also significant to note that generational principles appear in the kin classification systems of some hunting and gathering populations with band organization, for example, certain groups of Bushmen and several of the Indian populations of aboriginal North America. Why? There are similarities between hunting and gathering bands and ambilineal descent groups in both their composition and rules of affiliation. In either type of social organization, ego has a choice about which group he will join. Furthermore, individuals shift their band affiliations quite commonly. When an adult establishes his own family of procreation, he may decide to join a band other than the one of his own parents. During his lifetime, he may be a member of several different bands. As in ambilineal, ambilocal societies, generational kinship terminology in populations with band organization establishes close personal relationships with several relatives whom ego may in time use to gain entry into different bands.

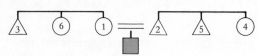

FIGURE 20 Bifurcate collateral kinship terminology.

 Bifurcate collateral kinship terminology

Of all the systems designating kinsmen on the parental generation, bifurcate collateral is the most specific: it has separate kin terms for each of the six kin types on the first ascending generation. (See Figure 20.) Bifurcate collateral kinship terminology is not as common as the others that have been discussed. In fact, a large number of the populations employing this variety of kin terminology are concentrated in a specific part of the world—northern Africa and the Near and Middle East. Many are related genetically, that is, they are offshoots of the same ancestral group. They are geographically close, and in many cases, they have been affected by the same events.

How, then, is bifurcate collateral kinship classification to be explained? Could it be that the kinship terminology simply arose as a quirk in one society in this region and was subsequently transmitted to all the others? Such an explanation assumes that a cultural practice has been *diffused* from one society (or by way of neighboring societies) to others. Or could it be that bifurcate collateral kinship terminology arose accidentally in an ancestral group and now exists in several offshoots that share a common cultural heritage? In other words, was bifurcate collateral terminology invented by the remote ancestors of these populations and culturally transmitted over generations to their descendants? If this is the case, it exemplifies what anthropologists call a *genetic* explanation. Genetic and diffusional explanations are grouped under a common category: *historical explanations*. Social institutions or cultural practices exist among two or more different societies because they shared a period of common history or have been exposed to common sources of information.

Anthropologists have thus far come up with no satisfactory explanation for bifurcate collateral kinship terminology. It is possible, however, to suggest a *functional explanation*, which is similar to those that have been offered for the other kinds of kinship terminology. Functional explanations attempt to relate specific practices to other aspects of behavior in the society being examined. Are certain aspects of human behavior so closely related that when one of them changes, the other will change too? What are the social correlates of bifurcate collateral kinship terminology?

Descent group organization is found among many of the North African and Near Eastern populations who employ bifurcate collateral kinship terminology. Descent rules are generally patrilineal, but this is only a tendency. In composition, many of the descent groups could be classified as ambilineal. I suggest therefore that bifurcate collateral kinship terminology can serve some of the same functions that generational terminology serves. With generational terminology, ego maintains the same formal relationship with all members of the parental generation. In bifurcate collateral, he maintains distinctive but close relationships with all his kinsmen on the parental generation. In either case, he has established and maintained, through kin terms, close relationships based on kinship. He may change his descent group or local group affiliation at different times during his life. Establishing close and distinct kinship relations with kinsmen on the generation above him will facilitate such changes in group affiliation.

Classification of Same-Generation Kinsmen

Some of the same principles which determine the system of kinship terminology for parental generation kin types also affect the classification of ego's kinsmen on his own generation.

Eskimo kinship terminology ~~similar to lineal terminology~~

Eskimo terminology on ego's generation is similar to lineal terminology on the first

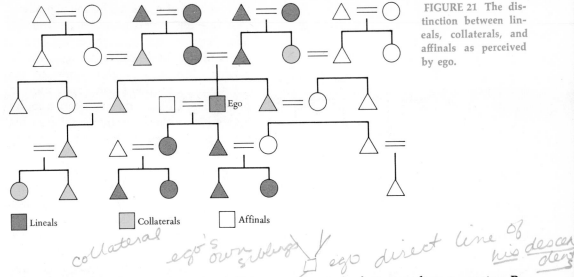

FIGURE 21 The distinction between lineals, collaterals, and affinals as perceived by ego.

| ■ Lineals | ▨ Collaterals | □ Affinals |

collateral   *ego's own siblings*   *ego direct line of his descendents*

ascending generation. (See Figure 21.) Eskimo kinship terminology separates members of the nuclear family from other kin types. The most important thing about Eskimo terminology, however, is that it clearly distinguishes lineal relatives from collateral relatives. A *lineal relative* is an ancestor or descendant, anyone on the direct line of descent which leads to and from ego. Thus ego's lineal relatives are his direct ancestors: his parents, grandparents, great-grandparents, great-great-grandparents, and so forth. Equally lineal relatives are his children, grandchildren, great-grandchildren, and so forth. Collaterals are any other biological kin types. They are ego's own siblings and their descendants, and the siblings of his lineals and the descendants of those siblings. His brothers and sisters, nieces and nephews, aunts and uncles, are collateral relatives. Eskimo terminology has two terms comparable to brother and sister in English for kin types on ego's own generation who are members of his nuclear family of orientation. It lumps together under a single term analogous to cousin the children of parents' collaterals, who are members of different nuclear families.

Iroquois kinship terminology — *bifurcate terminology*

Iroquois kinship terminology is found among many of the populations who employ bifurcate merging kin terms for kin types on the first ascending generation. Recall that bifurcate merging kinship terminology uses the same term for mother and mother's sister. People also refer to their father and their father's brother by a common term. It is easy to understand Iroquois terminology if you think of it in the following way. You call your mother and your mother's sister by the same term, "mother," a loose translation. You also call your father and father's brother by the same term, "father." The child of anyone whom you call "father" is "brother" or "sister." The child of anyone you call "mother" is also "brother" or "sister." Thus your mother's sister's children and your father's brother's children are called "brother" and "sister," that is, by the same terms you use to refer to your own siblings. You use a different term for the children of your father's sister and your mother's brother, your cross cousins. In Iroquois terminology, the same term (or terms if a sex distinction is made in referring to male and female children) is used for father's sister's children and mother's brother's children. In many populations, however, kin terms distinguish between the father's sister's children and the mother's brother's children.

Omaha kinship terminology

The Omaha system of kinship terminology differentiates between two kinds of cross

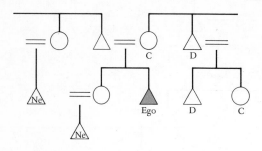

FIGURE 22 An Omaha man speaking. Ne: FZS, ZS, or any other son of a female member of my patrilineage. (See also Figure 23 for meaning of C and D.)

cousins. However, this is not its most significant characteristic. Omaha kinship classification tends to be found in populations with strongly corporate patrilineal descent groups. In such societies, people think of marriages as alliances between descent groups, and only secondarily as relationships between individuals. Imagine that such a marriage has taken place and there is a son, ego, shown in Figure 22. Ego is a member of his father's descent group. When his father married his mother, their descent groups entered into an alliance. Ego is not a member of his mother's group. In fact, she, her brother, and the other members of her group are related as in-laws or *affinals* to ego and to all members of his own patrilineage.

Ego uses the same term to refer to his mother and his mother's sister. They are, after all, members of the same descent group, of the same sex, and of the same generation. Often, the term which ego uses to refer to his mother's brother is some variant of the term he uses for his mother. We may translate it as "male mother." Thus, for the parental generation, ego uses one of three terms—"mother," "male mother," or "uncle"—to refer to his mother and her siblings. He calls his true brothers and sisters, "brother" and "sister." However, he also calls his mother's sister's children "brother" and "sister," as he would in Iroquois terminology, because they are

the children of a woman he calls "mother." The difference between Omaha and Iroquois terminology lies in the terms used for mother's brother's children. Ego calls his mother's brother's daughter "mother" and his mother's brother's son "male mother" or "uncle." He uses the same terms to designate his mother's brother's children that he uses to designate his mother and his mother's brother.

This system seems less peculiar when you think of the kind of society in which ego lives. He is a member of one corporate descent group, and his mother and her brother are members of another. In his terminology, ego shows that he tends to view his mother's group as a group. The fact that certain biological kin types in her group are members of that group is more significant to him than their generation, than the biology or genealogy of the relationship. For members of his mother's group, he employs either "mother," "male mother," or "uncle." Again, the terms "mother," "male mother," and "uncle" are misleading. A better translation would be "a female member of my mother's descent group" and "a male member of my mother's descent group." Ego calls all kin types who fulfill this requirement by those terms. Who are these kin types? On the parental generation, they are his M, MZ, and MB, on his own generation, his MBS and MBD. His mother's children are his sisters and brothers and are members of his own group. His mother's sister's children are members of their father's group. On the next generation down, the children of his MBS are also called "mother" and "uncle." They are male and female members of his mother's patrilineal descent group. The same terms may also be used for relatives on the grandparental generation: the term for MF and MB may be the same; they are, after all, both male members of his mother's descent group.

Now consider the other side of the genealogy, the father's side. Ego calls his father and his father's brother by the same term. There is a different term, which I shall translate as "aunt," for his father's sister.

His father's brother's children will be his brothers and sisters, children of someone he calls "father." His father's sister's children, his patrilateral cross cousins, on the other hand, belong to a different descent group, that into which his father's sister married. They are children of a female member of ego's descent group, and not themselves members of that descent group. Other people related to ego biologically also share this attribute. Ego's sister's children fall into this category. It is not surprising, then, that ego refers to father's sister's children and sister's children by the same term, distinguishing only on the basis of sex. We can translate these terms as "niece" and "nephew," but this is deceptive. A better translation for the term used to refer to the FZS and ZS is "son of a female member of my own descent group." For FZD and ZD, the term may be translated as "daughter of a female member of my group."

Omaha kinship terminology is logical. To appreciate this, note that some of the terms are reciprocal. Make Sam the first ego in Figure 22, but now let us shift our attention to Harry. Harry is Sam's mother's brother's son, and Sam calls him "uncle," "male mother," or "male member of my mother's descent group." Now make Harry the ego. What does Harry call Sam? Sam is Harry's father's sister's son. He calls him by the same term he uses to designate his own sister's son, that is, "son of a female member of my descent group." Thus Harry, whom Sam calls "uncle," calls Sam "nephew" or "sister's son."

To summarize, Omaha terminology exists in societies where there are strongly corporate patrilineal descent groups. Perceptions of group relationships are more important than perceptions of individual relationships. Marriages, for example, are conceived of as relationships between groups. These social facts are revealed in kinship terminology. On his mother's side, ego uses two basic terms to refer, respectively, to all the male and all the female members of that group. On his father's side, ego applies the same terms to the

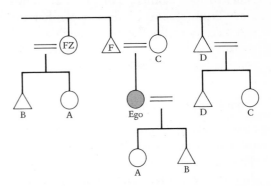

FIGURE 23 An Omaha woman speaking (mirror image of a Crow man speaking).

A: my own daughter or daughter of another female member of my patrilineage
B: son
C: my own mother or other female members of my mother's patrilineage.
D: my own mother's brother or other male members of my mother's patrilineage

children of all closely related female members of his group, sister, father's sister, and sometimes his own daughter.

In contrast to other systems of kinship terminology which have been examined in this chapter, Omaha exhibits a difference in kinship terms depending on whether ego is a man or a woman. Figure 23 illustrates Omaha kinship terminology with a female ego. Note that while on the mother's side, the kinship terminology is the same as for male egos, on the father's side, it is different. In patrilineal societies, women bear children who will be members of their husband's rather than their own descent group. For females, Omaha terminology lumps together their own children with those of other female members of their lineage. Thus a female ego uses the same term for her own S, her FZS, and her ZS. Like her own son, all are offspring of women who are members of her patrilineage. Note, too, that kinship terminology is also reciprocal for a female ego. Sophie is the ego in Figure 23. She calls Trudy, who is her MBD, "mother." Now look at things from Trudy's point of view—make her the ego. Trudy calls Sophie "daughter." If someone calls you "mother," isn't it reasonable for you to call her "daughter"?

Crow kinship terminology

Crow kinship terminology does some of the same things that Omaha classification does. Like Omaha, it lumps members of different generations under the same terms. Like Omaha, too, it is found in societies with strongly developed unilineal principles and strongly corporate unilineal descent groups. As in Omaha, membership in a descent group is more important than genealogical or biological position in terms of ego. Crow kinship is found in matrilineal rather than patrilineal societies. In Figure 24, ego is a member of his mother's descent group. The ego in Figure 24 is shown to be a male member of that group. Who else is a male member of that group? His mother's brother, for one. In Crow terminology, ego calls his mother's broth-

FIGURE 24 A Crow man speaking.

S, D: my son or daughter or the son or daughter of other male members of my matrilineage

F, FZ: my own father or father's sister or other members of my father's matrilineage

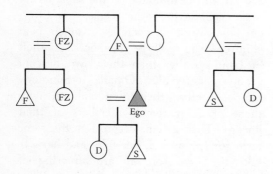

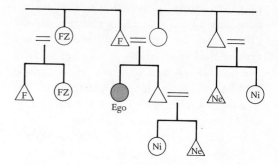

FIGURE 25 A Crow woman speaking.

F, FZ: male or female member of my father's matrilineage

Ne, Ni: son or daughter of male member of my matrilineage

er's children "son" and "daughter," the same terms he uses for his own children. A better translation might be "child of a male member of my own descent group." Ego's own children fill the bill; so do his mother's brother's children, his mother's mother's brother's, and his sister's son's children. They are children of male members of ego's group, but none are themselves members of that group. All belong to their own mother's groups.

Compare Figure 24 with Figure 23. Figure 24 illustrates Crow terminology with a male ego. In a matrilineal society, a man's children are not members of his own descent group but of his wife's. Figure 23 shows Omaha terminology from the point of view of a female ego. In a patrilineal society, a woman's children are not members of her own descent group. It should not be surprising, therefore, that Crow for male egos is the counterpart of Omaha for female egos.

Examining Figure 24, if ego calls his mother's brother's son "son," then his mother's brother's son should call ego "father." A better translation would be "male member of my father's matrilineage." In fact, as you can see in Figure 24, ego uses only two terms to refer to the members of his father's matrilineal descent group. This is a descent group to which ego's own descent group is joined by marriage, specifically, by the marriage of ego's mother and father. He calls all the male members of that descent group—his F, FZS, and FZDS—by the term he uses for his father. All the female members of that group are called by the term he uses for father's sister.

Figure 25 shows Crow terminology with a female ego. As is the case when ego is male, two terms, translated as "father" and "father's sister," are used to designate all members of ego's father's matrilineage. If you call someone "father's sister" or "aunt," it is reasonable for her to call you "brother's daughter" or "niece." Female ego, therefore, applies the terms "niece" and "nephew" to the children of all male members of her matrilineage. The kin types to which the term "niece" applies include brother's daughter, BD, and matrilateral cross cousin, MBD, among others.

Thus there are three common ways of designating biological kin types on ego's own generation—Iroquois, Crow, and Omaha—among populations with bifurcate merging kinship terminology on the parental generation. We might designate two of these, Crow and Omaha, as *unilineal kinship terminology* because they occur in societies with strong matrilineal or patrilineal descent groups, and they clearly identify the members of those descent groups to which ego's own is joined by marriage.

Hawaiian kinship terminology

If ego calls all his uncles and aunts by the same terms he uses for father and mother, there are only fathers and mothers on the first ascending generation. The children of any father or mother are brother and sister. Ego therefore uses one term for his brothers and male first cousins and another for his sisters and female first cousins. This system of classifying relatives on ego's own generation is known as Hawaiian kinship terminology, and it resembles generational kinship terminology on the parental level. The logic of such kinship terminology is

clearly to bring ego in close relationship with all his kin and enable him to create especially close ties with any one of them he chooses.

Descriptive kinship terminology

Ego may employ separate terms for each kin type on his own generation: B, Z, MBS, MBD, MZS, MZD, FBS, FBD, FZS, FZD. The first filial generation can also illustrate this descriptive principle (bifurcate collateral), with distinct terms for S, D, BS, BD, ZS, ZD, and perhaps the sons and daughters of each first cousin. When kinship terminology is this descriptive, ego usually refers to many of his kinsmen by their names rather than by any kinship term. Kinship terms are used by ego to identify kinsmen when someone asks about a specific relationship.

Relevance of Kinship Terminology

Anthropologists spend a great deal of time analyzing the kinship terminology of the people they study. There are many good reasons for this. Kinship is extremely important in the societies traditionally of interest to anthropologists. Most anthropologists assume that a population's kinship terminology will reveal information of value in understanding its social relationships and interactions. If two biological kin types are designated by the same term, it is probable that they share some attribute of significance in that population's social structure. The anthropologist attempts to determine how categories employed in language are significant in social life.

Several scholars who have studied principles of social organization cross-culturally have found that kinship terminology is one of the slowest-changing aspects of social organization. Ownership and inheritance patterns, postmarital residence rules, and descent principles all appear to change more easily and more rapidly. Because patterns of nonverbal and verbal behavior change at different rates, the anthropologist expects to find some cases in which the association between kinship terminology and other aspects of social structure does not hold. If he finds generational kinship terminology in a society with virilocal postmarital residence and patrilineal descent groups, for example, he may have to conclude that changes in kinship terminology are lagging behind changes in residence and descent. In such a case the expectation is that the kinship terminology of the society will change ultimately to bifurcate merging.

A final observation about the relationship between kinship terminology and so-

SUMMARY

[handwritten annotation: Lineal terminology = nuclear fam. industrial - foraging socie]

Kinship terminologies, as distinct from biological kinship designations, represent native taxonomies, cultural ways of dividing up the world based on perceived characteristics. Although kinship terminologies belong to specific cultures, comparative research has demonstrated that different cultures always employ one of a limited number of classification systems. Anthropologists' interest in kinship classification reflects the importance of kinship-related institutions in societies that they have traditionally studied. Furthermore, comparativists have discovered general relationships between kinship terminology and other aspects of social organization. To a certain extent, we may predict kinship terminology from knowledge of other aspects of culture and social organization.

Four basic classification systems, each widely distributed throughout the world, exist to categorize kin types on the parental generation. Lineal terminology, associated with importance of the nuclear family, is the characteristic kinship terminology of many foraging and industrial populations. Bifurcate merging kinship terminology, perhaps the most commonly encountered of the four, is found among populations with unilocal rules of postmarital residence and unilineal descent groups. Generational terminology is associated with ambilineal descent group organization and ambilocal postmarital residence, while bifurcate collateral kinship terminology, a system concentrated in the Near East and northern Africa, may also be associated with ambilineal descent.

Sources and Suggested Readings

BUCHLER, I. R., and SELBY, H. A.

 1968 *Kinship and Social Organization: An Introduction to Theory and Method.* New York: Macmillan. Introduction to comparative social organization; several chapters on interpretations of kinship classification systems.

GRABURN, N., ed.

 1971 *Readings in Kinship and Social Structure.* New York: Harper and Row.

Several important articles on kinship terminology.

KROEBER, A.

 1909 Classificatory Systems of Relationship. *Journal of the Royal Anthropological Institute* 39: 77–84. Classic attack on Morgan's analysis of kinship terminologies. Kroeber was wrong in one of his major criticisms, but article provided inspiration for

cial structure is in order. Certain correspondences between kinship terminology on the first ascending generation and on ego's own generation have been discussed. Often, however, anthropologists encounter societies in which the classification systems for these generations do not correspond. Bifurcate merging, for example, may be used for the parental generation and Hawaiian principles may be used for ego's own, rather than the Iroquois, Omaha, or Crow systems we would normally expect. Such anomalies may indicate that both kinship terminology and the social and economic factors which influence it are undergoing a change of form—that is, an evolution.

Bifurcate - post marital residence unilocal

Generational : Ambilineal descent group ambilocal post marital residence

There are six traditionally recognized types of kinship classification for ego's own generation. Eskimo terminology, employed by contemporary Americans, makes a classificatory distinction between lineal and collateral relatives. Iroquois terminology is characteristically associated with bifurcate merging on the parental generation and is generally found in populations with unilocal rules of postmarital residence and unilineal descent groups. Omaha and Crow terminologies are typically found among populations with strongly corporate unilineal descent groups—patrilineal and matrilineal. Hawaiian terminology is normally associated with generational terminology on the parental generation and is found among populations with ambilineal descent groups and ambilocal patterns of postmarital residence. Descriptive kinship terms, often associated with bifurcate collateral, are concentrated in the Near East and northern Africa.

Anthropologists have demonstrated that kinship terminology usually changes more slowly than certain other aspects of social organization, such as inheritance patterns, patterns of postmarital residence, and descent group organization. Thus there is often an incomplete correlation between kinship terms and social structure and between the classification principles which operate for different generations. The study of kinship terminology reveals differences and similarities in the social categories deemed important in human populations, suggesting research problems and increasing knowledge about such variations.

the componential analysis approach to kinship terminology.

LOUNSBURY, F.

1964   A Formal Account of Crow- and Omaha-Type Kinship Terminologies. In *Explorations in Cultural Anthropology: Essays in Honor of George Peter Murdock*, ed. W. H. Goodenough, pp. 351–387. New York: McGraw-Hill. Intriguing attempt to

state rules which generate all variants of Crow and Omaha systems.

LOWIE, R. H.

1948   *Social Organization.* New York: Rinehart. Useful attempt to update his 1920 book; good introduction to kinship terminology included.

1961   (orig. 1920). *Primitive Society.* New York: Harper and Brothers. Classic which examines use of kinship terms and offers a classification of kinship terminologies.

MURDOCK, G. P.

1949   *Social Structure.* New York: Macmillan. Influential statistical examination of kinship, marriage, and descent; includes Murdock's well-known typology of systems of classification of kinspeople on ego's own generation.

1957   World Ethnographic Sample. *American Anthropologist* 59: 664–687. Data on social organizational variables, including kinship terminology, for 565 cultures.

MURDOCK, G. P., ed.

1962–present. Ethnographic Atlas. In *Ethnology.* Coded quantitative data on a large sample of world cultures, including their kinship terminologies.

RADCLIFFE-BROWN, A. R.

1950   Introduction to *African Systems of Kinship and Marriage,* ed. A. R. Radcliffe-Brown and D. Forde, pp. 1–85. London: Oxford University Press. Excellent introduction to kinship and classification systems.

1965   (orig. 1952). *Structure and Function in Primitive Society.* New York: The Free Press. Includes essay on the study of kinship systems.

SCHUSKY, E. L.

1965   *Manual for Kinship Analysis.* New York: Holt, Rinehart and Winston. Good elementary introduction to systems of kinship terminology.

SERVICE, E. R.

1971a   (orig. 1960). *Cultural Evolutionism: Theory in Practice.* New York: Holt, Rinehart and Winston. Collection of essays; see especially "Kinship Terminology and Evolution" for an innovative approach to kinship terminology in general evolutionary perspective.

1971b   *Primitive Social Organization: An Evolutionary Perspective.* 2nd ed. New York: Random House. Includes theoretical discussion, from general evolutionary point of view, of kinship terms in bands, tribes, and chiefdoms.

WHITE, L. A.

1939   A Problem in Kinship Terminology. *American Anthropologist* 41: 566–573. Association of Crow and matrilineal descent; Omaha and patrilineal descent.

1958   What Is a Classificatory Kinship Term? *Southwestern Journal of Anthropology* 14: 378–385. Demonstration that Kroeber was wrong and Morgan right about a basic difference between primitive and nonprimitive kinship terminologies.

1959   *The Evolution of Culture.* New York: McGraw-Hill. Kinship terminologies in general evolutionary perspective.

8. How Anthropologists Study Political Organization

Anthropologists and political scientists share an interest in political organization. Data gathered from populations outside the industrial West have provided a framework for the comparative study of such organization, and for as long as there have been anthropologists, they have speculated about such matters as the differences between law and cultural rules, between crime and deviation from social norms; the nature of relationships between groups in societies; reasons for disputes and means of resolving them in different social and cultural contexts; variations in power and authority systems of different peoples.

In the mid-nineteenth century, before anthropology emerged as a separate discipline, anthropologist-sociologists such as Lewis Henry Morgan, Herbert Spencer, and Sir Henry Maine wrote extensively about the evolution of political society. Their works, particularly Maine's *Ancient Law*, published in 1861, and Morgan's *Ancient Society*, published in 1877, related not only to the evolution of political systems, but also to the evolution of society in general. It is, in fact, particularly diffi-cult to distinguish early contributions to political anthropology from contributions to social and cultural anthropology.

Why? The major reason is that in many nonindustrial populations, particularly those that lack state organization, the *polity*, the political order, does not exist as a separate institution as it does in our own. Rather, it is submerged in the social order. When polity is part of society, it may be very difficult to characterize an act or event as political rather than merely social. Recognizing that political organization is but an aspect of social organization, Morton Fried has offered the following definition (1967, pp. 20–21): "Political organization comprises those portions of social organization that specifically relate to the individuals or groups that manage the affairs of *public policy* or seek to control the appointment or activities of those individuals or groups [italics added]."

This definition certainly applies to political organization in the contemporary United States. Under "individuals or groups that manage the affairs of public policy," you can fit in the whole apparatus of federal, state, and local governments; and under "or seek to control the appointment or activities of those individuals or groups," a mass of interest groups and individuals ranging from the John Birch Society and Radical Lesbians to John Wayne, Barbra Streisand, and Henry Ford. However, Fried's definition is weak in terms of societies which lack state organization. There is a question in my mind about whether there is any "public policy" in certain kinds of society, particularly those whose strategy of adaptation is hunting and gathering. It is also difficult to apply the word "manage" to most of what goes on in everyday life among foraging bands.

At the risk of overgeneralizing, I prefer to delineate the area of study of the political anthropologist more broadly: political anthropology is the study of the interrelationships between groups or their representatives. As elsewhere in ethnology, in the political sphere the anthropologist may study the polity—interrelationships between groups—in a single society, in a single kind of society, within a typology of societies, or in society in general. However, it is difficult to see how he could make too many nontrivial statements about the political organization of society in general. Perhaps he could generalize that no society is totally egalitarian, because there are always differences in station, prestige, and respect which result from differences in sex, age, and personality. Another trivial generalization might be: no society can survive if its social order is in complete disarray.

Imagine yourself an ethnographer who plans to study the political organization of a society, or suppose you are undertaking a cross-cultural study of political organization. You will be using my definition of political organization to start you on your research. What do you do? First, you identify the groups that are significant in the society or societies included in your sample. Second, you determine what kind of people represent those groups on particu-

lar occasions. Now you are well on your way to the central question: What kinds of relationships prevail among these groups and their representatives?

In the remainder of this chapter we will follow these steps. We will examine in detail several populations, representing different general evolutionary types and different strategies of adaptation. For each we will indicate the significant social groups, their local or dispersed nature, means of tying them together, how they represent themselves to one another—in short, the system of interrelationships between groups in each society. The discussion of each population will also be concerned with the nature of leadership roles; reasons for disputes; means of resolving these disputes; presence or absence of a public policy embodied in a law code; means of enforcing this code; and legal sanctions, rewards, and punishments.

Two distinctions are paramount here: (1) disputes over property are confined to certain kinds of society and (2) there is a tremendous contrast between bands and tribes on the one hand, and states, on the other, in aspects of political organization, law, and order. Here we recall Fried's definition: in states the individuals and groups who manage the affairs of public policy stand out from other members of the population. Furthermore, many of them are full-time political functionaries occupying permanent offices. Other implications of state organization will become apparent as the following cases are considered.

The first step in studying the political organization of a particular society is to identify the social groups which are significant in that society. This is a matter which has been discussed in several previous chapters. The kinds of groups that exist in a society will depend on its general evolutionary type and on its strategy of adaptation. For example, previous chapters have examined the groups that exist in band-organized societies (general evolutionary type) and in societies with foraging strategies of adaptation. In most foraging societies, there are only two kinds of significant social groups: the nuclear family and the band or local group. Among many hunters and gatherers, the band does not exist as a permanent group throughout the year but forms seasonally, as its component nuclear families, which vary from year to year, assemble.

Political Organization among Foragers

The Eskimos and the Bushmen exemplify the political organization of foraging societies. The bands or local groups found among foraging populations typically are linked together not through group ties but through the webs of personal relationships established by individuals. Individuals generally marry outside their band. Band exogamy creates personal ties between individuals living in different bands. Bands are also tied together through bilateral kinship networks. Since an individual's mother and father, and perhaps all four grandparents, come from different bands, he may be related to several different bands. Trade between individuals from different bands also links the local groups together. Finally, there may be fictive kinship connections between individuals residing in separate bands. The Bushman namesake system has been mentioned—individuals with the same name are regarded as relatives. Sam I and Sam II are like brothers. The relatives of Sam I call Sam II by the same kinship term that they apply to Sam I. Sam II also uses the same kinship terms as his namesake to refer to the latter's relatives.

Among the Eskimos of the Arctic, members of different bands have trade partners whom they treat as quasi-brothers. A man extends the hospitality of his home, including sexual access to his wife, to his trading partner. The aborigines of Australia had a similar institution known as the section system.

Larger kin groups such as clans and lineages are not usually found among foraging populations. Because of this paucity of social groups, the political organization of band-organized society is very rudimentary. Bands are usually unstable in their membership. When we encounter a band

headman in a foraging society, he is usually simply the most permanent member of that band, a social core around whom other individuals and their families may group for various lengths of time.

The Eskimos

Among foragers, there is nothing that could accurately be called law in the sense of a legal code, including machinery of adjudication and enforcement, that applies to all members of the population. In some foraging societies, there may be a great deal of disorder. The Eskimos can serve as a good example. There are approximately 20,000 Eskimos, and the population extends over approximately 6,000 miles in the extreme north, the Arctic region from eastern Siberia to eastern Greenland. The only significant social groups among Eskimos are the nuclear family and the local band. Bands are tied together through personal relationships established by each member individually. Some of the bands have headmen. There are also shamans, diviners, in Eskimo bands. These positions confer little power on those who occupy them.

Why do disputes arise among the Eskimos? Most involve males, and most originate over women. Wife stealing and adultery are common causes for disputes. Although it is acceptable for one man to have intercourse with another man's wife, access is by invitation only. If a man discovers that his wife has been having sexual relations without his sanction, he considers himself wronged, and he is expected to retaliate against the male offender. The manner of retaliation will be examined after discussion of a related reason for disputes —wife stealing.

The Eskimos, you will remember, practice female infanticide. There are several reasons for this. The male's role in Eskimo subsistence activity is primary; people prefer to have sons who can care for them when they become old. Furthermore, men have to travel on land and sea, hunting and fishing in a bitter environment. Their tasks are much more dangerous than those of women. Female infanticide regulates the size of the Eskimo population: since the male role in the division of labor takes more lives, there would be an excess of females over males in the adult population if a proportion of female infants were not killed. Even with female infanticide, however, slightly more females survive than males. This demographic imbalance accommodates polygyny. Some men take two or three wives. Usually, it is a successful hunter-fisherman who marries plural wives. The ability to support more than one wife confers a certain amount of prestige. Yet, it also encourages envy. If it becomes obvious that a man is marrying plural wives merely to increase his status, he is likely to have one of his wives stolen by a rival. This, like adultery, can lead to conflict.

A wronged man has several alternatives. Community opinion will not let him ignore the offense; one way of avenging his tarnished honor is to kill the man who has stolen his wife. However, if he does this, he can be reasonably sure that one of the close kinsmen of the dead man will try to kill him in retaliation. Consider an example. Sam has two wives, Cynthia and Tricia. Irving, a younger man from another local group, manages to steal Tricia and take her home. Sam's social status and honor have now been tarnished. He must avenge himself in some way. One way of doing it is to kill Irving. However, Sam knows that Irving has a brother, and if he kills Irving, Irving's brother will be bound by kinship to kill Sam. Sam also has a brother who will then be obliged to kill Irving's brother. One dispute could escalate into several deaths.

Once such a *blood feud* develops, there is no state authority to intervene and stop it. However, an aggrieved individual always has the alternative of challenging the offending party to a song contest. This is a means of regaining lost honor. The two

parties in the dispute make up insulting songs about one another. The audience listens and judges the insults. At the end of the song match, one of the two is declared the winner. If the man whose wife has been stolen wins the song contest, there is no guarantee that his wife will return to him. The woman appears to have a good bit to say about where she will remain. Sometimes, she will decide to stay with her abductor.

There are several acts of killing which are deemed crimes in the contemporary United States and in other state-organized societies but which are not considered criminal among the Eskimos. Individuals who feel that, because of age or infirmity, they are no longer economically useful may kill themselves or ask others to kill them. An old person or invalid who wishes to die will ask a close relative, a son perhaps, to end his life. It is necessary to ask a close relative to be sure that the kinsmen of the deceased will not take revenge on his killer.

Occasionally among the Eskimos we encounter something suggestive of law, the enforcement of a decision for the public good. An individual who has committed a single homicide is apt to be attacked and perhaps killed by a close kinsman of his victim. Suppose, however, that before the avenger can kill him, he kills the avenger instead. He has now committed two murders. The Eskimos fear individuals who murder more than once. In such cases, there may be a meeting of adult male members of the offender's local group. It is apparently the headman of the group who initiates this meeting. If there is unanimous agreement that the individual must die, then one of his close relatives is usually chosen to carry out the execution. Again, this is to avoid the possibility of revenge by kinsmen. There is some possibility, too, that the headman may do the killing.

To summarize, most disputes which arise among the Eskimos are related to the disposition of women. Murders must be avenged in some way, often leading to the blood feud. However, peace may be restored through a song contest. The group may decide to execute a repeated murderer, per-

"Personalty" describes the relationship between material items, such as those depicted in this surreal painting by Magritte, and the individual who owns them. René Magritte, Personelles, 1952 / Collection Harry Torczyner, New York. *(Photo courtesy Marlborough Gallery, New York)*

ceived as a public threat. Disputes also arise if individuals believe that others are practicing sorcery on them, and Hoebel (1954) reports that certain individuals have been killed because they are chronic liars.

Perhaps you have noted a major and significant difference between Eskimo conflicts and our own. Theft is not a problem for the Eskimos. Access to resources needed to sustain life is open to everyone. By virtue of his membership in a band, every individual has the right to hunt and fish and to manufacture all the tools he needs for subsistence activities. Individuals may even hunt and fish within the territories of other local groups. Conspicuously absent is the notion of private ownership of strategic resources. To describe the property notions of people who live in non-stratified societies, the anthropologist Elman Service (1966) coined the term *personalty*. Personalty describes items other than strategic resources which are indelibly associated with a specific individual, things like the arrows he makes, the pouch he uses to carry his tobacco, his clothes. Service chose this term to point to the personal relationship between material items and the individual who owns them. So tied to specific

individuals in public opinion are personalty items that for another to steal them would be inconceivable. It may be that the grave goods found so often in pre-Neolithic archeological sites represent items of personalty, things which could not be passed on to heirs, so definite and inseparable was their association with the deceased.

Thus, in band-organized society, there is no differential or impeded access to strategic resources; private property is personalty, and if one individual wants something which is owned by another, he simply asks for it and it is given. According to Hoebel, one of the basic postulates of Eskimo life is that "all natural resources are free or common goods." One of the corollaries of this is that "private property is subject to use claims by others than its owners [Hoebel, in Middleton, 1968, p. 96]."

Political Organization in Intermediate Societies

The Yanomamo

In his book *Yanomamo: The Fierce People*, the anthropologist Napoleon Chagnon (1968b) has described the political system of the Yanomamo Indians of southern

Yanomamo tribesmen of southern Venezuela, arguing over a trade item. *(Napoleon Chagnon)*

Venezuela and adjacent Brazil. The Yanomamo live in approximately 125 dispersed villages, each with a population of between 40 and 250 people. Chagnon estimates the total Yanomamo population at about 10,000.

The Yanomamo are tribal horticulturalists whose staple is the plantain, a fruit much like the banana. More social groups are significant for Yanomamo than for the Eskimos or the Bushmen. There are nuclear families; local patrilineal descent groups; groups of two intermarrying local descent groups known as moieties; villages; and geographically dispersed patrilineages. Yet there is no state; there is no central authority capable of maintaining order in Yanomamo society. In fact, the Yanomamo appear to be exceedingly bloodthirsty. Warfare involving raids in which as many males as possible are killed and as many females as possible are captured, is endemic.

The intensity of warfare among the Yanomamo appears to be related to the shortage of females in that society. The Yanomamo practice a form of female infanticide, but, according to Chagnon, they do not realize that their infanticide selects against females. The Yanomamo prefer sons to daughters, especially as first-born children. Thus, if the first-born is a girl, it is killed, and if a boy, allowed to live.

This influences the sex ratio among children in favor of males. Females are also killed in warfare, as Chagnon shows, so that in the adult population, too, there are more males than females (449 to 391 in seven villages he studied). The shortage of females is made even more obvious by the practice of polygyny. Despite the fact that the number of Yanomamo women is insufficient to provide just one mate for each Yanomamo man, 25 percent of the men are involved in polygynous unions. Thus the reason for frequent raiding to capture women becomes obvious. Once established, the pattern of Yanomamo warfare perpetuates itself, as is shown in Figure 26.

The Yanomamo illustrate in extreme form earlier statements that in primitive society the world is divided into two categories: allies and enemies. The Yanomamo use several social mechanisms—trading, feasting, and marriage are principal among them—to convert potential or actual enemies into allies. Marriage is the strongest (and trading the weakest) alliance that may link two villages. Only after a relationship based on trade and feasting has been established, however, will two villages begin to exchange women. On the other hand, feast and trade do not always lead to marriage.

Notable in Yanomamo social organization is the absence of solidarity based on descent. Demonstrated descent does not extend very far into the past, and lineages are not named. Lineage membership is

FIGURE 26 Continued selection for warfare among the Yanomamo.

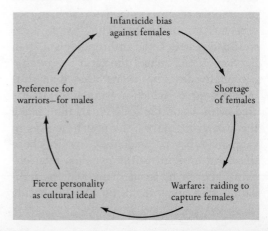

usually spread out among multiple villages, and it may cover a large territory. Membership in the same lineage is no basis for friendly relations or solidarity. In fact, disputes break out frequently even among close kinsmen. Chagnon documents several disputes involving full brothers and a case of a violent fight between son and father. In most other societies, kinship establishes peaceful relationships. Why then is this not the case among the Yanomamo?

The answer, again, is related to the shortage of women. Among the Yanomamo brothers determine whom their sisters will marry. To the Yanomamo, the ideal form of marriage is brother-sister exchange. (See Figure 27.) Sam, a member of patrilineage A, gives his sister to Joe, a member of patrilineage B, and Joe gives his own sister to be Sam's wife. What happens, however, if Sam and Joe have brothers? Each of the brothers is competing with the other to give away their sisters in marriage, so as to gain wives for themselves. Sam's father, too, may undertake to pledge some of his daughters, Sam's sisters, in marriage. The father's motives may be different; presumably, he already has a wife. He may simply use his daughters to establish a personal alliance with another village. Or his motives may be the same; he may be seeking a second wife. In either case, he is competing with Sam. It is no wonder then, that, as Chagnon observed, groups allied by marriage enjoy friendlier relationships than those allied by descent. Members of a descent group compete to dispose of the same women in order to obtain wives. On the other hand, two lineages who regularly exchange women have everything to gain from one another.

The fact that alliances are based on marriage rather than on descent is also important in determining the way a single village divides. Imagine a village in which there are two exogamous descent groups, A and B. Each descent group is divided into two branches, A_1 and A_2, B_1 and B_2. A_1 exchanges women with B_1, and A_2 with B_2. When the village fissions, A_1 and B_1 move to a new site together, while A_2 and B_2 remain in the original village or settle a new site on their own. In some cases, according to Chagnon, it only takes a few years for the two villages to begin raiding one another. Solidarity results from exchange of women; hostility results from competition over them.

Each Yanomamo village has a headman. As is characteristic of many tribal societies, the role of the headman in influencing others is very limited. Because he is expected to be more generous than any other villager, the headman cultivates more land. His plot will supply a great deal of the food consumed when his village hosts a feast for another village. He gets nothing from his position other than the right to give away more. His ability to issue commands is strictly limited. He may issue orders to his wives, children, and younger brothers. On the other hand, he may not command his brothers who are his age peers, full adults who are "already fierce," as the Yanomamo say. Nor may he issue orders to other adults in the community.

The Yanomamo headman represents his village in its dealings with other villages. Sometimes he may travel to another village to arrange a feast. He hosts feasts held in his village. Chagnon stresses that the headmanship is an office devoid of authority. The way a given individual conducts himself in the headmanship is a function of his personality and the number of supporters he can muster among the villagers.

FIGURE 27 Brother-sister exchange.

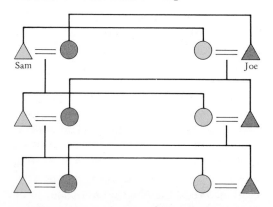

Chagnon relates a few cases in which one village headman, Kaobawa, intervened in a dispute between a man and his wife and prevented the husband from killing the wife. The same headman also guaranteed safety to a delegation from a village with which one of his covillagers was eager to initiate war. Kaobawa is probably a particularly effective headman. He has a large number of brothers and other supporters in his village. He has demonstrated his fierceness in battle. Chagnon points out that he diplomatically exercises his influence in such a way as not to offend other villagers. There is no one in the village with a better personality claim to the headmanship and with more supporters. If certain segments of the village population are dissatisfied, they have open to them the option of leaving the village and founding one of their own.

The Yanomamo believe, and they would appear to be right, that a shortage of women is the principal reason for the frequency of their raids. It is also the case that most disputes which arise between and within villages are related to women. As villages grow larger, according to Chagnon, the incidence of adultery also increases. There is nothing to stop an enraged husband from killing both his wife and the adulterer. If he is not killed, the adulterer may leave the village. As village size increases, intravillage feuding over women and other matters will eventually increase to such a point that the village will break up.

Warfare between villages arises in several ways. Raiding may begin when people from one village attack individuals or small groups outside the territory of another village. Individual women may be abducted, their husbands killed. If an epidemic kills many people in one village but few in another, people in the former may believe that people in the latter are practicing sorcery against them. This may precipitate raids. People from village A may raid the unprotected gardens or the fruit trees of

village B, again leading to revenge raiding. In any event, there is no outside authority which can stop intervillage warfare once it has begun. There is no law, no threat of legal sanctions, no fear of feud—in short, no state among the Yanomamo.

The segmentary lineage system

The Nuer are a population numbering some 200,000 people who inhabit the region of the upper Nile River in the Republic of the Sudan. They are one of many Nilotic populations. The Nuer were studied ethnographically by the British social anthropologist E. E. Evans-Pritchard in the 1930s and are described in his book *The Nuer* (1940) and in other books and articles by him. Their economy revolves around cattle pastoralism, but they also cultivate some crops horticulturally. Their social organization includes many of the institutions you have been led to expect among tribal populations, including descent groups, marriage relationships that emphasize group alliance, and progeny price. The Nuer have attracted considerable attention among anthropologists because of their type of patrilineal descent structure, known as *segmentary lineage organization*.

The Nuer's segmentary lineage structure is not unique. The Tiv, a Nigerian population numbering approximately 1 million, share this form of descent organization, as did certain populations of North Africa and the Near East including the Arabs and the ancient Jews. In societies with segmentary lineage systems, political organization is based on descent rules and genealogical reckoning. Descent rules of populations with segmentary lineage systems tend toward patrilineality. In the ideology of these populations, an individual should be a member of his father's group.

The Tiv believe that all Tiv are ultimately descended from the same apical ancestor, a man called Tiv who settled their present homeland, Tivland, several generations ago. The Tiv trace the line of descent leading from Tiv to the present, listing lineal ancestors in each intervening generation. While the Nuer do not claim to be able to demonstrate patrilineal ancestry that far back, they do believe that they have a common ancestry that distinguishes them from the neighboring Dinka and other Nilotic populations.

Evans-Pritchard reports that four levels of descent group segmentation are significant in Nuer social organization. Nuer clans are composed of segments called lineages. The segments of *maximal* lineages are known as *major lineages*. Major lineages are composed of several *minor lineages*, and the latter are subdivided into *minimal lineages*, whose members are descended over three to five generations from the same man. In contrast to the larger descent groups, which are territorially dispersed, minimal lineages are usually coresident groups, that is, members of the same minimal lineage usually reside in the same local group.

Over time, minimal lineages grow into minor, minor into major, and major into maximal. The genealogy in Figure 28 illustrates the segmentary principle. The core of Figure 28 is a major lineage founded by an individual called Anthony Smithley-Nurnspratt. Anthony is dead and has become the common apical ancestor for two minor lineages known, respectively, as the Smithleys and the Nurnspratts. Kaobonga Smithley, dead too, has become the apical ancestor for two minimal lineages, the Smiths and the Lees, who reside in separate but neighboring villages. Mo'valuta Smith is now the leader of the Smiths, and Rooster Lee heads the Lee homestead. Once Mo'valuta Smith and Rooster Lee die, and as their descendants increase, their sons and grandsons will become apical ancestors for new minimal lineages, and the former

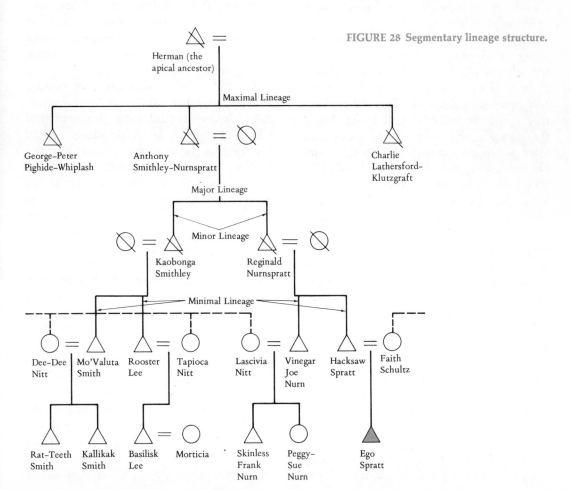

FIGURE 28 Segmentary lineage structure.

minimal lineages will become minor, the minor major, the major maximal.

Note that while the Smithleys have been segmenting into Smith and Lee minimal segments, the Nurnspratts have been doing the same thing. Vinegar Joe Nurn is the apical ancestor of the newly formed Nurn segment, and Hacksaw Spratt heads the Spratt minimal lineage.

The lineage illustrated in Figure 28 is somewhat idealized. In fact, new minimal lineages form only when individuals move away from their natal local groups and establish new settlements. In Figure 28, all the male agnates in each generation have founded new settlements. In reality, most or perhaps all sons in some generations would stay in the parental settlement, and new and discrete minimal lineage segments would bud off only after a few generations of common residence.

Unlike the Yanomamo, the Nuer seem to suffer no shortage of women. Moreover, the relationship between brothers appears to be very close in societies with segmentary descent organization. This is especially true when the father is still living. He is the manager of his sons' joint estate and attempts to curb quarreling among them. He also uses bridewealth which his daughters bring in to obtain wives for his sons. When the father dies, the brothers may continue to live together, or one may choose to take his share of the herds and found a settlement of his own. His brothers remain, however, his closest allies. Thus he will establish his local group as close as possible to his brothers'. Even if the brothers stay together following their father's death, segmentation may take place in the next generation, as some of the grandchildren establish new homesteads. Each of the grandsons, however, will try to remain as close to home as possible, settling nearest to his full brothers but nearer to his agnatic first cousins than to any more distant relative.

From this discussion you can perhaps comprehend the basic principle of solidarity among the Nuer: the closer the agnatic relationship, the greater the solidarity. The more distant the shared patrilineal apical ancestor, the greater the potentiality for hostility. This is extended right up the genealogy; there is a greater chance that maximal lineages will engage in disputes than there is in the case of major lineages.

The anthropologist Marshall Sahlins (1961) has argued that segmentary lineage organization and belief in a common apical ancestor represent cultural adaptive means that have enabled Nuer and Tiv to expand at the expense of their neighbors. The common genealogy, Sahlins argues, provides a basis for tribal solidarity, enabling Nuer and Tiv to present, when need arises, a common front against outsiders—people who claim different ethnic identity. In the absence of state organization and centralized authority, segmentary lineage structure is the most effective political device encountered in tribal societies. It possesses a selective advantage in terms of increase in numbers and expansion of range where several tribal populations are competing for the same living space.

The Arabs, who also have segmentary lineage structure, claim to demonstrate their descent patrilineally from biblical Ishmael. There is an Arab adage, "I and my brother against my cousin [father's brother's son]; I, my brother, and my cousin against all other Arabs; I, my brother, my cousin, and all Arabs against all the world [cf. Murphy and Kasdan, 1959]." Interestingly, the Jews believe themselves to be descended from Isaac, half brother of Ishmael. So one generation up, the Jews and the Arabs share a common ancestor, Abraham, father of both Ishmael and Isaac.

Among Nuer, Tiv, and other populations with segmentary lineage organization, then, there are correlations between closeness of common agnatic ancestry, geographical proximity, and degree of social solidarity. We have seen how belief in common descent may serve as the basis for a political structure and provide a means of unifying one tribal population against others that lack such belief. Principles of segmentary descent are also important in understanding the nature of disputes and their resolution.

If a dispute breaks out between two Nuer men who share a common living ancestor, he intervenes to settle the dispute. As head of the minimal descent group which includes the disputants, he backs his authority with the threat of banishment. But what happens when no common agnatic ancestor of the two disputants is alive? There is the possibility of a blood feud.

Disputes among the Nuer do not appear to arise over access to strategic resources. An individual acquires land and cattle as a member of a lineage. Belonging to a minimal descent group, he has a right to its estate. No adult appears to be limited in his access to strategic resources. Adultery, however, does lead to disputes among the Nuer. Furthermore, if an individual murders or brings bodily harm to another, a feud may develop. Conflicts also arise over the disposition of progeny price in the event of divorce. If a woman leaves her husband before providing his group with what they regard as an adequate number of children, her husband's group may press for return of part of the bridewealth. If her own group is unwilling to meet these demands, a dispute may ensue.

Figure 28 can be used again to illustrate different ways in which disputes are resolved depending on whether or not the disputants share a common, living patrilineal ancestor. The common ancestor of Rat Teeth Smith and Kallikak Smith is alive. He is Mo'valuta Smith, their father. Should Kallikak kill his brother, Rat Teeth, all members of their group will be shocked. It is, after all, unthinkable for a Nuer to kill his brother or another close kinsman. However, should such an event take place, Kallikak will not be killed in retribution. The group's rationale for letting him live is that one member has already been lost; it cannot afford to lose another.

Now consider a dispute involving the Smiths and the Lees. Their common ancestor, Kaobonga Smithley, is dead. The dispute developed after Basilisk Lee found his wife, Morticia, committing adultery with

Rat Teeth Smith. There is no common ancestor to settle the dispute, but the fathers of the disputants are brothers, and they will probably be able to work out a settlement. The adulterer will probably pay damages in cattle to Basilisk.

Now assume that Basilisk commits adultery with the wife of Skinless Frank Nurn, and Skinless Frank surprises them in the act. He is furious and kills Basilisk. What happens? The nearest common ancestor of Basilisk and Skinless Frank is Anthony Smithley-Nurnspratt, their common great-grandfather. The Lees, who have lost Basilisk, may be willing to forgo a revenge killing and accept damages in cattle from the Nurns. They can use the cattle to acquire a wife for a man of their lineage who will provide children to replace the dead Basilisk. The Nurns and the Lees may be able to work out an arrangement satisfactory to both, and the dispute may thereby be settled. On the other hand, should they find themselves unable to come to terms, there is then the possibility of a blood feud between the Lees and the Nurns.

The importance of close common agnatic ancestry as a basis for sociopolitical solidarity emerges here. The Smiths are expected to help the Lees since they share a more recent common ancestor, Kaobonga Smithley, than any Smith or Lee does with any Nurn or Spratt. The Spratts, for the same reason, will help the Nurns.

There is an alternative to a blood feud. The parties may consult the leopard-skin chief, so-called because he wears a leopard skin over his shoulders. "Chief" is actually a misleading translation for this position in Nuer society. The Nuer have no true chiefs. Leopard-skin chiefs are individuals who perform certain ritual duties, but whose most important functions involve mediation of disputes. Skinless Frank Nurn and the elders of his lineage may ask a leopard-skin chief to mediate the dispute, to try to convince the close agnates of Basilisk Lee to accept a certain number of cattle as recompense for their murdered kinsman.

The leopard-skin chief, who performs various duties for the Nuer. (*Kay Lawson/Rapho Guillumette*)

While the mediator attempts to get the parties to agree to a peaceful settlement, the murderer, Skinless Frank, may take refuge in the leopard-skin chief's homestead, which offers him sanctuary until the leopard-skin chief resolves the dispute or withdraws.

The leopard-skin chief, like the Yanomamo village headman, must rely primarily on his talents for persuasion. He cannot make a decision imputing right or wrong to either side, nor can he hold up the threat of physical enforcement. He merely uses the threat of supernatural retribution. If, after seeking the mediation of a leopard-skin chief, the parties to the dispute remain recalcitrant, the chief may withdraw his services as mediator. If one of the segments is especially adamant, he may, in disgust, threaten to curse that segment. The ethnographer of the Nuer, however, was unable to discover a single case in which a leopard-skin chief's curse had been invoked. Presumably, this is because once both parties submit their quarrel to his mediation, they are genuinely interested in reconciliation. Negotiations involve the individual parties to the dispute, the elders of their segments, and other close agnates. Disputes involve full and free discussion, and normally there is considerable agreement among the discussants before settlement is made. Such negotiations provide a way out for the individual parties to the dispute, who may be readier to modify their positions in accordance with the collective opinion of the mediator and the elders than they had been previously.

Should the mediator withdraw, however, Skinless Frank would lose his sanctuary and wander out into a world of bloodthirsty Smiths and Lees. In the ensuing feud to avenge the murder of Basilisk, a Smith or Lee might kill a Nurn or Spratt. A Nurn or Spratt might then kill a Smith or Lee, and so on, until the feuding groups grew tired of conflict and settled the dispute themselves or called on the leopard-skin chief again. By that time each party would be more willing to resolve their differences.

In the event of a dispute, then, each Nuer is expected to help his closest patrilineal kinsmen against more remote agnates. All the descendants of Anthony Smithley-Nurnspratt would, for example, band together as allies against all the descendants of Charlie Lathersford-Klutzgraft if the dispute involved Skinless Frank Nurn and Winston Klutz, great-grandson of Charlie Lathersford-Klutzgraft. And so it goes, each one allied against another, up to the maximal lineages of Nuer society. Finally, the Nuer as a group would also unite against neighboring populations on the basis of their belief in common descent.

Here you see that among populations with segmentary lineage organization, alliance is relative. No man has a set group of allies. Rather, his allies vary from one dispute to another, depending on the genealogical distance of the parties to the dispute. Although the peace-making abilities of the leopard-skin chief are greater than anything found among either Yanomamo or Eskimos, the blood feud still exists among the stateless Nuer.

The Ifugao are a population of wet rice cultivators living in the northern part of Luzon, one of the islands in the Philippines. Their political organization, particularly their "law," was the subject of a book by R. F. Barton in 1919. The Ifugao may be classified as agriculturalists because they cultivate their rice on permanent, irrigated plots within monumental terracing systems. The Ifugao countryside is extremely rugged. Generations of Ifugao have carved their terraces into the steep mountainsides of their homeland.

In contrast to the populations considered previously, the Ifugao, some 120,000 people around 1920, do conceive of private property in strategic resources. Access to agricultural land and water used in irrigation is held by individuals. The Ifugao have no descent groups. The most basic kinship group is the nuclear family, and inheritance is equal among sons and daughters, with preference, however, given to the eldest child. The only other significant social group is the hamlet or village, and these are located on the hillsides near the rice terraces. Ifugao are linked to other Ifugao as individuals, through networks based on bilateral kinship.

Rice cultivation by the Ifugao of the Philippines. *(John Launois/ Black Star)*

It is among the Ifugao that disputes related to strategic resources are encountered for the first time. Since individual plots are limited in size and all children may inherit, disputes may arise over fragmented shares that each heir receives. Furthermore, the rice fields of different owners often share access to the same source of water, perhaps a spring high on the hillside. Cultivators above may threaten to cut off one's water supply or, eager to transplant their own rice, may divert the water first into their own fields. Other disputes arise over murder, bodily injuries, and debts.

The Ifugao also contrast with the other societies just examined by virtue of their well-formulated ideas about crime and its consequences. Over the centuries, the Ifugao have developed an unwritten code of justice, stipulating a range of damage compensations due victims of criminal acts. Thus if a murder has taken place, the Ifugao know precisely what is due the

An Ifugao village, built on a hillside near the rice terraces cultivated by the villagers. *(John Launois/ Black Star)*

closest bilateral kinsmen of the murder victim. The problem, however, is deciding on the nature of the crime. In the United States, a given act may be judged self-defense, manslaughter, second- or first-degree murder. For example, in the trial of Lieutenant Calley, accused of war crimes and found guilty of premeditated murder, the punishment was legally specified as either death by hanging or life imprisonment. Had the jury sentenced Calley to death, the judge might well have lowered the crime to second-degree murder or manslaughter, in which case a different penalty would apply.

What happens when there is a dispute between two Ifugao? First, the plaintiff, the defendant, and their close kinsmen may try to negotiate a settlement. If they are unable, however, to assign fault or agree on the nature of the crime, they may call in a mediator. Usually, mediators have reputations as successful warriors. The Ifugao were head hunters; successful warriors were those with many heads to their credit. The usefulness of prowess in warfare for the role of mediator will be seen in a moment.

The mediator's job is to travel back and forth between the defendant and the plaintiff and try to get them to agree to a solution. If the dispute is settled peacefully, he will receive a part of the damages paid the plaintiff. The tools of the mediator's trade are few. He, like the Yanomamo headman and the Nuer leopard-skin chief, relies on his abilities to persuade the parties to agree. As he travels from one to the other reporting concessions, he also transmits another kind of information. By the time the plaintiff brings in the mediator, he has also notified his bilateral kinsmen that he is involved in a dispute. They know that they must ready themselves in case mediation fails and a blood feud breaks out. The defendant also informs his kinsmen of the dispute. During his visits back and forth, the mediator conveys to each how many are pledged to defend the other. This may have some influence on both parties' decision to settle. Sometimes, there is a negotiated peace. However, it is also possible that one day the mediator will get fed up, decide he has done all he can do, and withdraw from the affair.

If he does this, the blood feud can begin. Although the Ifugao lack descent groups, they regard close kinsmen as substitutes for themselves in cases of dispute. Thus if Daryl is the plaintiff and Joe the defendant, Daryl or one of his kinsmen may kill Joe or one of his kinsmen. The matter is, of course, not settled here. One death breeds desire for revenge. The blood feud is in full swing. According to Barton, such feuds were terminated only by a marriage linking the disputants or their relatives, or by a ritual involving animal sacrifice. The blood feud continually reinforced the pattern of warfare and head taking among the Ifugao. It is possible to speculate that warfare has been an essential part of the Ifugao's adaptation to their environment. It would appear to have checked population increase in a region where population is dense and there is great pressure on strategic resources. A state organization can regulate internal feuding, but there are obstacles to state control in the rugged terrain where the Ifugao live. Other means of population control—or expansion of the Ifugao territory—would have to emerge in the context of state organization, for, as you are about to see, the blood feud is anathema to state organization.

Law and Order: the State

It could reasonably be argued that the state ranks alongside exogamy, symbolic communication, and tool making as a major achievement of human evolution. This is not to say that the state is a good thing. It is merely a very significant thing. There are tremendous differences between state-organized societies and tribal and band societies. In fact, the gap between state-organized and stateless societies is so great, it may be compared to the one between human and nonhuman primate society. As an inhabitant of an industrial state, you would find that life in even an archaic state is far more familiar to you than life in a band or tribal society.

The National Guard, agents of the military subsystem, on parade in Peru in 1964. *(Paul L. Doughty)*

Attributes which define the state will be recalled briefly here. All societies with state organization also have socioeconomic stratification, although, as the Ifugao document, the converse is not always true. Certain individuals and groups in states enjoy unimpeded access to strategic resources; others are deprived of such access. Morton Fried (1960) regards the state as a form of political organization which has two principal functions. First, the state apparatus acts to maintain the socioeconomic contrasts within the population it governs, to preserve the stratified order. The major concerns of its rulers are defense of the idea of hierarchy, property relations, and the power of the law. These are familiar in our own society as private property and law and order.

The second principal function of state organization is broader. It maintains the entire social order for the population it rules. There are two expressions of this function: (1) internal disorder is suppressed; the state's population is controlled; and (2) the state is defended against external threats. There are subsystems which guard against internal threats—police, secret services, and the FBI are examples—and there are subsystems which guard against external threats—the Army, the Navy, and the Department of Defense are examples. Sometimes, however, the duties of the agents of internal and external order overlap, as, for example, when the National Guard, theoretically a military organization, is used to suppress student rebellions and ghetto uprisings.

To accomplish its two major functions, the state has additional, secondary functions. There are four broad categories of these according to Fried: population control subsystem; judicial subsystem; enforcement subsystem; and fiscal subsystem.

The state controls its population by knowing whom it governs; it takes censuses, and the population is enumerated. It also establishes and maintains boundaries to demarcate its territory from that of other populations. Customs officials and coast guard are stationed at these boundaries to regulate passage from one state to another. Even in archaic states, there may be boundary maintenance forces. In the African state of Buganda, located in what is now Uganda in East Africa, the king rewarded faithful military commanders with estates in the outlying provinces. The military leaders and their followers who settled in such areas acted as guardians against intrusions by alien populations.

The state also controls population through administrative circumscriptions: provinces, districts, states, counties, subcounties, parishes, and so forth. Specific state officials oversee the population and territory of each of its subdivisions.

Finally, the state controls its population by establishing categories of citizenship. The principal contrast is between the citizen and the noncitizen, whose rights and obligations with respect to the state are different. In the United States, specific governmental agencies oversee the activities of aliens. Distinctions among the native-born population of the state are also common. In most archaic states, state nationals include at least three socially distinct categories of people. There are nobles, commoners, and slaves. The rights and obli-

gations of each group are different. Those familiar with the history of the United States before the Emancipation Proclamation are aware that the same laws did not apply to slaves and freemen. Furthermore, in areas where European colonial rule was established, there were usually separate courts to judge disputes involving only natives and those which involved Europeans.

Among the Merina of central Madagascar, founders of one of the major states in the tropics, the state's laws were very clearly aimed at maintaining the social categories of the state. Merina legal codes made it a crime against the state for a nobleman or woman to marry a commoner, or for any freeman or woman to marry a slave.

In the United States, there is no division into nobles, commoners, and slaves, but there are differences in, for example, the rights and obligations of civilians and members of the armed forces. A military code of justice and a military court system exist alongside the civil judicial hierarchy.

Fried distinguishes a second broad category of secondary functions, one which includes aspects of the judicial system. In all states there is a body of rules and precedents which tends toward codification. In other words, there are legal rules based on precedent and on proclamations of the state's legislative bodies. In states which lacked writing, laws were preserved in oral tradition. The king's chief justices or council of elders might be the officials charged with remembering the laws. An oral tradition is also true of some societies which have had writing for a long time. England is the most familiar example.

We have been told in the United States that laws are made to be observed, to regulate conduct in society. Violation of the legal code constitutes a crime. Specified punishments or ranges of punishments are attached to conviction for any crime. However, as among the Ifugao, it is possible here for a given act, for example, the killing of one or more human beings, to be treated legally in different ways.

To deal with crimes and disputes, all states have courts and judges. Courts exist at different levels. In the United States there are city courts, county courts, state courts, federal courts, and the Supreme Court. In certain African states there are subcounty courts, county or district courts, and finally, a court consisting of the king and his advisers. In most states, appeals are possible to higher court officials, though often people are encouraged to resolve their disputes on the local level.

Important in the contrast between states and band or tribal societies is intervention in family matters. The state intervenes to stop blood feuds. It must, after all, maintain internal order, and it has the ability to do this. Private matters enter the domain of public law, as they are subjected to the adjudication of state-appointed officials.

Decisions of judicial systems, once appeals have been exhausted, are binding. There are governmental agencies which are charged with carrying out court decisions. These belong to the third of Fried's categories of secondary functions of the state: the enforcement subsystem. For crimes punished by death, executioners are needed; for confinement, jailers are needed. State officials supervise confiscation of property and collect fines.

Fourth of Fried's categories is the fiscal subsystem. Kings, nobles, officials, and specialists of various sorts constitute a large body of non–food producers that must be supported. Taxation supports these state officials by pumping food into their bellies; but it also supports the political structure, the offices of the state itself. Kings use taxes to make state control more secure by expanding its civil and military apparatus. States also call on their subject population for labor. Forced labor has been used in different archaic states to build public works, to maintain irrigation and drainage canal systems, to build great walls, and to erect pyramids.

The attributes just discussed, which Fried regards as a "bare but essential list," collectively define the state as a different form of society. How does life in the state differ from life in band and tribal societies? One advantage is apparent—the blood feud is ended. Should a Yanomamo state come into existence, no longer would Yanomamo fierceness be allowed to find expression in internal raids. However, although states curb internal conflict, they are certainly not warless societies. War, probably a side effect of the food-producing revolution, continues, with states fighting other societies. Industrial states, in fact, carry on the most virulent forms of warfare known to man. Lacking world government, individual states today are like Yanomamo villages. They are locked in conflict which no one seems able to stop. They fight over economic interests, political empires, and sometimes ideological issues—to maintain certain philosophies of government, to subdue the infidel, to stop the threat of creeping communism, to halt capitalist imperialism. People who live in nation-states enjoy little respite from war.

Other disadvantages are associated with life in states. Stratification is constant, and there may be very little chance for an individual born in a lower stratum to move up socially or economically. Taxation and state labor demands often deprive members of the subject population of basic resources. In band and tribal society, a person typically shares his labor and his wealth with kinsmen, in-laws, and fictive kinsmen, all people who mean something to him personally. In states, a person often shares labor and its fruits with unknown bureaucrats and rulers, to accomplish ends that are theirs. Obviously, the state does not mean greater freedom or greater leisure for most of its population.

In a work first published in 1877, anthropologist Lewis Henry Morgan characterized band and tribal society as *societas*, distinguishing it from state organization, which he called *civitas*. Morgan pointed to an important distinction in social relations between the two. In *societas* a man interacts daily and throughout his life within a limited social world. He sees, works, and spends his leisure hours with his kinsmen, his relatives by marriage, people with whom he has personal relationships. He has enemies too. They are people not included within these close categories.

With the advent of *civitas*, there is a change. States promote geographical mobility. Many times they actively sever ties between people and the land. In Buganda, for example, kings could transfer heads of descent groups from their ancestral estates to distant villages. Some of their followers went with them. Over the years, however, descent group members became widely dispersed throughout the state's territory. Administrative units subject to state rule—

hamlets, villages, wards, towns, and cities—became significant social groups, and the importance of descent as a means of sociopolitical organization diminished. The people living in such settlements were not necessarily, or even usually, kinsmen or in-laws. They were neighbors, people living and working together not on the basis of kinship, marriage, or other personal associations, but because state organization had somehow placed them together. With impersonal and external, rather than personal and internal, bases for association, solidarity often waned. In contemporary industrial nations, where geographical mobility is accentuated, people identify themselves by nationality, dwelling place, occu-

SUMMARY

Since the nineteenth century, anthropologists have contrasted political organizations in primitive, non-Western, and Western populations, concerning themselves with the kinds of groups significant in the different societies, the determinants of leadership, the nature of interrelationships between groups or individuals, the reasons for disputes between individuals or groups, and the means available for resolving these disputes. Human populations representing different general evolutionary types and strategies of adaptation are contrasted to illustrate some characteristic differences in political organization.

Bands and nuclear families are characteristic social groups among foragers. Individuals, families, and bands are linked together through personal networks. There is little differential power among foragers; band headmen are merely first among equals and can employ no means of enforcing decisions. Among the Eskimos, as among foragers in general, disputes do not arise over access to strategic resources, since the means of production are open to all. Rather, most Eskimo disputes originate in cases of adultery or wife stealing.

Aggrieved individuals may kill offenders, but their actions will trigger blood feuds, in which a kinsman of the victim may kill a murderer, only to face the prospect of being killed by one of the murderer's kinsmen. No governmental authority exists to intervene and halt such blood feuds. There are, however, certain customary means of resolving disputes among the Eskimos.

The Yanomamo Indians of Venezuela and Brazil are tribal horticulturalists. Ethnographically unusual because of the intensity of their raiding and warlike behavior, the Yanomamo value aggressive male personalities. Their principal ethnographer, Napoleon Chagnon, links Yanomamo disputes to a shortage of females and demonstrates that the pattern of raiding and killing perpetuates itself through cultural mechanisms. Yanomamo sociopolitical organization includes a larger variety of significant groups: villages, localized and dispersed patrilineal descent groups, and groups of intermarrying descent groups. Descent ties provide no basis for solidarity. Differential authority is more developed among the Yanomamo than among forag-

pation, political party affiliation, religion, team or club affiliation, but rarely with reference to kinship.

Despite similarities which enable states to be classified within the same sociopolitical category, all states are not equally successful in terms of effective control over their territory and their subject population. There are states in which the government supervises the economic order; there are also states like ours in which private economic interests jockey for political power and can exercise considerable influence on governmental decisions.

There is a certain amount of truth to the popular belief that government is strong and is continually growing stronger. Means

of control employed by various branches of the American government, for example, including computers and other aspects of industrial and atomic technology, are more sophisticated than anything previous states have employed. But consider the recent past: the nineteenth century and the Wild West. Many western towns were virtually ruled by local marshals, who were more like Yanomamo headmen than lawmen in some ways. And in the Appalachians in the early decades of this century, Hatfields and McCoys engaged in a blood feud that would put the Nuer to shame.

ers, yet village headmen, their major political figures, have no absolute power; they must lead by example and have no way of ensuring that their wishes will be followed.

The Nuer, tribal pastoralists of the Upper Nile, along with the horticultural Tiv of Nigeria, have a different kind of sociopolitical organization based on the segmentary lineage. Like the Yanomamo, Nuer and Tiv are organized into patrilineal descent groups; however, unlike the Yanomamo, a Tiv's or Nuer's closest allies are his agnates. The term segmentary describes the organization of descent groups into segments at different genealogical levels. Nuer belong to minimal lineages which are residential units: groups of these units constitute minor lineages; groups of minor lineages make up major lineages; groups of major lineages make up maximal lineages; and groups of maximal lineages make up clans. Although Nuer clans do not trace descent from the same ancestor, they do believe that they share a common ethnic origin separate from their neighbors. Among populations with segmentary descent organization, alliance is relative, de-

pending on genealogical distance. Social solidarity is directly proportional to the closeness of common agnatic ancestry and to geographical proximity. The Nuer have disputes over murder and bodily injuries, adultery, and disposition of bridewealth in cases of divorce. If a dispute involves two agnates, other agnates will support the individual with whom they share a more recent common ancestor. Disputes may be mediated by figures who can invoke only supernatural sanctions. Again, in the absence of state organization, there is no sure way of halting blood feuds.

Like the Nuer, the Ifugao, stateless agriculturalists of the Philippines, have mediators. But unlike the Nuer and the other populations that have been discussed, the Ifugao have differential access to strategic resources, and many of their disputes are related to the disposition of land and water. The Ifugao do not belong to descent groups; their significant social groups are villages, hamlets, and nuclear families. However, individuals reckon kinship bilaterally, and an Ifugao may rely on kinsmen in the event of a dispute. If mediation does not succeed, a blood feud may erupt.

State organization makes private disputes a matter of public concern, subject to state authority. States, societies characterized by socioeconomic stratification, include administrative and territorial subdivisions in addition to the villages and kinship groups characteristic of the other societies examined. States maintain special purpose subsystems: a population control

Sources and Suggested Readings

BARTON, R. F.

1969 (orig 1919). *Ifugao Law.* Berkeley: University of California Press. Classic ethnographic study of legal custom among stateless agriculturalists in the Philippines.

BEATTIE, J.

1960 *Bunyoro: An African Kingdom.* New York: Holt, Rinehart and Winston. Case study of an African state; social as well as political organization.

1964 *Other Cultures: Aims, Methods, and Achievements in Social Anthropology.* New York: The Free Press. Good introduction to British social anthropology; chapters on political organization especially recommended.

BOHANNAN, L., and BOHANNAN, P.

1953 *The Tiv of Central Nigeria.* London: Oxford University Press. Field study of Nigerian horticulturalists with a segmentary lineage system.

BOHANNAN, P., ed.

1967 *Law and Warfare: Studies in the Anthropology of Conflict.* Garden City, N.Y.: The Natural History Press. Good collection of articles on law, custom, conflict, and war.

CHAGNON, N.

1968a Yanomamo Social Organization and Warfare. In *War: The Anthropology of Armed Conflict and Aggression,* ed. M. H. Fried, M. Harris, and R. F. Murphy, pp. 109–159. Garden City, N.Y.: The Natural History Press. Relationship between warfare, economy, and social and political organization among horticultural Indians of Venezuela and Brazil.

1968b *Yanomamo: The Fierce People.* New York: Holt, Rinehart and Winston. Account of the Yanomamo, who are more aggressive than most tribal peoples; fascinating to most beginning anthropology students.

COHEN, R., and MIDDLETON, J., eds.

1967 *Comparative Political Systems: Studies in the Politics of Pre-industrial Societies.* Garden City, N.Y.: The Natural History Press. Political organization in different parts of the world.

EVANS-PRITCHARD, E. E.

1940 *The Nuer: A Description of the Modes of Livelihood and Political Institutions of a Nilotic People.* Oxford: Clarendon Press. Classic field study of people with segmentary lineage organization.

FRIED, M. H.

1960 On the Evolution of Social Stratification and the State. In *Culture in History,* ed. S. Diamond, pp. 713–731. New York: Columbia University Press. Major contribution to the theory of state origins and development; argues against the existence of law in stateless societies.

1967 *The Evolution of Political Society: An Essay in Political Anthropology.* New York: Random House. Valuable introduction to political anthropology.

subsystem which enumerates population and defines and maintains boundaries and internal subdivisions; a legal subsystem with laws and law officers to adjudicate disputes; an enforcement subsystem to ensure that laws are obeyed and penalties are carried out; and a fiscal subsystem to support the officials and special machinery of state organization.

FRIED, M. H., HARRIS, M., and MURPHY, R. F., eds.
1968   *War: The Anthropology of Armed Conflict and Aggression.* Garden City, N.Y.: The Natural History Press. Anthology on warfare in cross-cultural perspective written during the Vietnam War.

HOEBEL, E. A.
1954   *The Law of Primitive Man.* Cambridge: Harvard University Press. Counters Fried's view that law exists only in state-organized societies; "legal" customs of several societies discussed, case by case; unique in its field.

1968   (orig. 1954). The Eskimo: Rudimentary Law in a Primitive Anarchy. In *Studies in Social and Cultural Anthropology*, ed. J. Middleton, pp. 93–127. New York: Crowell.

KOTTAK, C. P.
1972   Ecological Variables in the Origin and Evolution of African States: The Buganda Example. *Comparative Studies in Society and History* 14: 351–380. Attempt to demonstrate and explain independent evolution of a state in East Africa.

MAINE, H. S.
1861   *Ancient Law.* London: J. Murray. Classic comparison of ancient and modern legal systems; a major evolutionary work of the nineteenth century.

MORGAN, L. H.
1963   (orig. 1877). *Ancient Society.* Cleveland: World Publishing. Classic treatment of social and political evolution, including private property and the state.

MURPHY, R. F., and KASDAN, L.
1959   The Structure of Parallel Cousin Marriage. *American Anthropologist* 61: 17–29. Social and political repercussions of the custom of marriage of children of brothers.

SAHLINS, M. D.
1961   The Segmentary Lineage: An Organization of Predatory Expansion. *American Anthropologist* 63: 322–345. The role of the segmentary lineage as an effective means of political organization in stateless societies.

1968   *Tribesmen.* Englewood Cliffs, N.J.: Prentice-Hall. More general treatment of political organization among tribal peoples.

SERVICE, E. R.
1966   *The Hunters.* Englewood Cliffs, N.J.: Prentice-Hall. Survey of social and political organization of several contemporary or recent foraging populations.

SPENCER, H.
1873   *The Study of Sociology.* New York: D. Appleton. Early sociological contribution to the theory of comparative political organization.

1873–1933 *Descriptive Sociology.* New York: D. Appleton. Monumental attempt to gather data on societies of the world.

9. Anthropologists Study Economies

Like political anthropology, economic anthropology is a subdivision of ethnology, and its relationship to economics is similar to the one between political anthropology and political science. However, economic anthropology is an even more ethnographic study than political anthropology. Anthropologists traditionally study primitives and peasants. Economists, on the other hand, concentrate on the industrial nations, and principally on the capitalist, or "free enterprise," systems found in the United States and Western Europe, and on the managed economies found in the Soviet Union and other socialist states. It has remained for the anthropologist to broaden economics by gathering data on primitive and peasant economies.

To understand and evaluate the contributions of economic anthropologists, definitions of "economy," "economics," and "comparative economics" are needed. Anthropologists have argued for several different meanings. The ones I find most useful are the following: The *economy* of a population is its system of production, distribution, and consumption of material resources. *Economics* is the study of such systems. *Comparative economics* is the study of such systems in different societies. It is in this last area that anthropologists have made the greatest contribution.

To economic anthropologists of different "schools," one or the other of these two questions is viewed as paramount. What are the differences and similarities in the organization of production, distribution, and consumption between different societies? Here the focus is on systems of human behavior and the organization of these systems. What motivates people in different societies to produce, to distribute or exchange, and/or to consume? Here the focus is not on systems of behavior but on the individuals who participate in these systems. Motivation is a concern of psychologists, but it has also been, implicitly or explicitly, a concern of anthropologists and economists. Anthropologists, of course, are interested in culturally conditioned motivations: traditional systems of beliefs and values that orient personality formation and cause individuals to behave in different ways.

Economizing and Maximization

Although the relevance of motivation to economics may not be immediately clear, assumptions about motivations are basic to economic theory. In fact, the subject matter of economists is often defined as "economizing"—that is, the allocation of scarce means or resources to alternative ends or uses. What does this mean? Classical economic theory assumes that human wants are infinite and that human resources are always limited. Since means to ends are always scarce, individuals have to make choices. They must decide to what uses they will put their scarce resources—their time, their labor, their money, their capital. Because Western economists have concentrated on capitalist systems, they have tended to assume that, when confronted with alternative ends, individuals usually choose the one which maximizes profit. In other words, the profit motive is supposed to be the principal motivation of Western man.

That individuals usually act to maximize profits was a basic assumption of the classical economists of the nineteenth century, and many contemporary economists in the United States still believe it. However, during the twentieth century, certain economists have also recognized that individuals may be motivated by other ends. They may, for example, seek to enhance their prestige. Anthropologists have shown that in many non-Western societies still other considerations and motivations may guide individual choices on how to use scarce resources.

Depending on the society, people may strive to maximize several things: profits, wealth, reputation, overall prestige, pleasure, social harmony. Their efforts in producing and exchanging material resources, in short, may be directed at many different ends. Again depending on the social context, individuals may strive to realize their personal ambitions or those of some social group to which they belong.

Alternative ends

To illustrate some of the factors which may determine how individuals allocate their scarce resources, differences between primitive and peasant societies will be discussed. The term *primitive* is used to refer to societies with band or tribal organiza-

Maintaining technology.
(Cornell Capa/Magnum)

tion. By *peasant* is meant rural inhabitants of archaic states. Peasants are generally agriculturalists. Occasionally, however, they may be involved in other strategies of adaptation, horticulture, for example. In northeastern Brazil there are ocean fishermen whose economic activities revolve around fishing; nevertheless, these rural Brazilians share many aspects of their culture and social organization with rural agriculturalists and horticulturalists living in nearby communities. These marine fishermen can therefore be considered peasants. Later on, they will be discussed in this context.

To what ends do people in primitive and peasant societies allocate their scarce resources? In his book *Peasants* (1966), Eric Wolf points out that throughout the world people devote some of their time and energy toward building up what he calls a *subsistence fund*. In other words, they have to work to eat, to replace the calories they expend in daily activity. People must also invest their limited resources in a *replacement fund*. A hoe or plow breaks; a person must invest his own time and energy or part of his capital in repairing or replacing it. People must maintain their technology. They must also replace items essential not to production but to everyday life: clothing and shelter, for example.

Both primitives and peasants also have to invest in a *social fund*. They have to help their kinsmen, their fictive kinsmen, their affinals, and, especially among peasants, their unrelated neighbors. In many societies it is useful to distinguish between a social fund and a *ceremonial fund*. The latter refers to expenditures of scarce resources on ceremonies or rituals. To prepare a festival honoring the ancestors, for example, requires time and work and often the outlay of wealth.

In state-organized societies, individuals must also allocate their time, energy, and wealth to what Wolf calls a *rent fund*. Americans think of rent as a payment, usually in money, for the use of someone else's property. Following Eric Wolf, however, rent fund has a wider meaning. It

Sharecroppers in the United States. (*Kenneth Murray/Nancy Palmer*)

refers to scarce resources which a subordinate is required to render to a superordinate. In all states, industrial as well as archaic, subjects must allocate a part of their time, energy, and wealth to the controllers of resources, the agents of administration, and the wielders of power. The subordinate may be a tenant farmer or a sharecropper. He must then either pay rent or allocate a portion of his produce to the owner of the land he farms. The peasant generally has to worry not only about providing rent to landlords, but also about his obligations to the state. He pays taxes in money or in kind, and often the state appropriates his time and labor for state ends. The major distinction between the primitive and the peasant, between band or tribal society and the state, is the existence of the rent fund, the requirement that individuals must allocate part of their scarce resources to superordinates.

The rent fund is not simply an additional obligation for the peasant; often, it becomes his primary obligation. There is no evidence that peasants in archaic states enjoy better nutritional standards than primitives in tribal societies. The peasant's foremost and unavoidable obligation is to pay rent, and sometimes, to meet this obligation, his own subsistence needs, his intake of basic nutrients, may suffer. Demands of superordinates may divert scarce resources from the subsistence, replacement, social, and ceremonial funds.

The social and ceremonial funds may also assume new and different functions in the state. States often convert ceremonial events into occasions for gathering rent. Consider an example. Today the government of Madagascar levies a tax on every steer sacrificed in a ceremonial context. In the Merina state, circumcision, formerly a ritual and social event, became a device for collecting taxes and carrying out a census. In prestate times, circumcision had been an affair involving the boy, other members of his household, and his close kinsmen on his mother's and father's sides. Among the Betsileo, southern neighbors of the Merina, the ritual of circumcision affirmed kinship between the boy, usually a member of his father's group, and his maternal kinsmen. Traditionally, the maternal uncle was expected to swallow the foreskin. There are indications that the ritual of circumcision was similar among the early Merina. As the Merina state developed, however, the king institutionalized circumcision and made it a concern of the state. All boys every seventh year were circumcised. Their circumcision sponsors, similar to Western godparents, had to pay a sponsoring fee to the agents of the state. Other examples of ways in which states have modified the functions of social and ceremonial events will be examined in Chapter 13.

Thus among different societies, several factors may determine how an individual disposes of his scarce resources. Because of obligations to pay rent, peasants may be investing in ends which are not their own at all but those of the managers of the state. Anthropologists and economists —and introductory students, too—should be aware not only that motivations differ from society to society, but that often individuals lack freedom of choice in allocating scarce resources.

Production

Organization in nonindustrial populations

Comparative economics has been defined as the study of systems of production, distribution, and consumption of material resources in different societies. In previous chapters, certain aspects of production and some aspects of exchange systems, particularly those related to marriage, have already been discussed. For example, the strategies of adaptation defined in Chapter 3 and discussed throughout the book are actually based on the system of production which predominates in a particular population. It is difficult to generalize about the production systems of societies employing the same broadly defined strategy of adaptation. For example, in certain hunting and gathering populations, cooperative hunting, a production activity, takes place seasonally or on an irregular basis; in others, cooperation in production goes on throughout the year. In this case, production may depend on the habits of the game exploited. Gathering, usually the work of women, is often a more individualistic activity than hunting. Fishermen may be solitary, or they may fish in crews.

It is also difficult to generalize about organization of production among horticulturalists or pastoralists. In Chapter 3 you learned that while a division of economic labor on the basis of age and sex is characteristic of all human societies, the specific tasks assigned to each sex and to individuals of different ages vary. The cultures of some horticulturalists assign a major productive role to women, while others make male labor primary. Similarly, among pastoralists men generally tend large animals, but in some cultural traditions milking is considered a woman's task. Tasks which are accomplished in certain horticultural populations by cooperative work parties consisting of kinsmen, age peers, and neighbors are carried out in others by smaller groups or people working individually over a longer period of time. Understanding differences and similarities in the organization of production among human populations with similar adaptive strategies requires detailed study of the specific environments to which these groups have adapted.

Within a given population, the organization of production may change over time. Among the Betsileo, there are two stages of cooperative labor in the cycle of wet rice cultivation: transplanting and harvesting. Both activities involve work parties, which vary in number according to the size of the field. Within these work parties, there is a marked division of labor on the basis of age and sex. The first group activity in the transplanting stage is the trampling by cattle of a flooded rice field. Young men and boys drive humped zebu cattle around and around in the plot. The effect is to mix the earth and the water into a soil of even consistency for transplanting. As the tramplers leave the plot, older men move in. With their spades they break up the clumps of soil which the cattle have missed. Meanwhile, the owner of the land or other adult members of his household have pulled the seedlings from the nursery bed and transported them to

the field. Young married women now plant the seedlings in plots which have been trampled and spaded. At harvest time, four to five months later, young men cut the rice on the stalk; young women transport it to a cleared area above the field; older women arrange and stack it; and old men and women stand on the stack, stomping and thus compacting it. Three days later, young men thresh the rice, beating the stalks against a rock to remove the grain. Older men beat the threshed stalks with sticks to make sure that all the grains have fallen off.

Most of the other tasks involved in Betsileo rice cultivation are accomplished by the owner and members of his household. Adult males maintain and repair the irrigation and drainage systems and the earth walls which separate one plot from the next. Men also till, with spade or plow, and harrow. All noninfant members of the household help weed the rice field.

Nowadays, the Betsileo do not use cooperative labor in maintaining the irrigation and drainage systems—hydraulic systems— essential to rice cultivation. Each man cleans the sections of the canals which irrigate and drain his own rice field. However, my Betsileo informants report that in the past, hydraulic work was cooperative. Irri-

The transplanting cycle of wet rice cultivation by the Betsileo. *(Conrad P. Kottak)*

gation systems, consisting of stone dams built across shallow parts of rivers and canals sometimes seven miles long and irrigating the rice fields of as many as thirty individuals in the area, were originally constructed by work parties organized by political officials. Local officials also convoked male labor to repair these hydraulic systems during the year.

Small-scale hydraulic systems can grow over time into massive networks of canals and drainage ditches. As the economist Karl Wittfogel pointed out in his provocative book *Oriental Despotism* (1957), large-scale hydraulic systems are often associated with strongly developed political structures—with states. Where this is true, water control becomes one of the principal concerns of the state administration. State officials organize cooperative work groups to clean and repair the irrigation and drainage systems and to reinforce walls for flood control, and they also oversee the allocation of water to the fields that depend on it. But hydraulic systems formerly regulated by political officials can be maintained without cooperative labor, as is true of the present-day Betsileo system.

Factors of production: territory

Some significant contrasts between industrial and nonindustrial economies involve the factors of production. In primitive and peasant societies there is a more intimate relationship between the worker and the factors of production—land, labor, technology, capital—than in industrial nations. Among foragers ties between individuals and specific areas are usually less permanent than in food-producing societies. Though hunting bands are associated with territories, boundaries are not typically marked, and there is no way that they can be enforced. The hunter's stake in the game animal he is stalking or which he has hit with a poisoned arrow or spear is more important than territorial considerations—that is, where the animal finally dies.

A man acquires the right to exploit the band's territory, to hunt—and a woman, to gather—by being born a member of the band or by joining it through some tie of kinship, marriage, or fictive kinship. Among the Bushmen, women, whose labor provides over half the diet, may have access to a tract of berry-bearing trees or some other specific area of wild vegetation. But when a woman moves from one band to another, she will be assigned a new gathering area.

Consider for a moment the relationship between marine fishermen and specific fishing areas. Marine fishermen often simulate property by marking fishing spots. The deep sea fishermen I studied in Brazil say that they use physical features on the land—landmarks—to pinpoint rocky areas of the ocean floor where fishing has been especially good. But like the territory of bands, fishing spots are very different from property as Americans define it. There is no way, other than by fighting, in which one fisherman may keep another from using his spot. Furthermore, any individual with good eyesight can mark as many spots as he likes, and two individuals may, on different days, fish at a spot they have both marked. Fishermen discover good fishing areas all the time. The major value of the fishing spot seems to be that it may save the fisherman a few minutes in deciding where to fish on a given day.

In tribal societies, as among foragers, individuals acquire rights to land and other factors of production as members of social groups. An individual born into a descent group has, like all other descent group members, a right to use the estate of his group. If the adaptive strategy is horticultural, the estate includes garden and fallow land essential to shifting cultivation. By virtue of his birth and membership in a local group, an individual also acquires access to an estate where he may engage in hunting, gathering, and other, secondary economic activities. As a member of a descent group, a pastoralist has access to animals to start his own herd, to grazing land, to garden land, and to other factors of production.

An individualistic economic activity: Camel herding in Kenya. *(Dr. Georg Gerster / Rapho Guillumette)*

Among the Nyoro of Uganda and in several other East African states, the king claimed to own all land within the borders of his state. Nevertheless, in many communities descent group status remained important, and individuals continued to acquire rights to land for cultivation and grazing through their membership in a localized, corporate descent group.

In states, however, the factors of production are usually unequally distributed; there is differential access to strategic resources, thus the existence of a rent fund. Notions of private property arise in states. In some cases, nobles, close relatives of the king, receive grants of land along with peasants to work the land. These peasants are exploited by nobles, who use peasant labor to work their own land and then keep part of the peasants' taxes. Nobles may or may not have the right to dispose of their own estates; usually, the sovereign must confirm inheritance or transfer of estates he has granted to nobles or officials.

Depending on the state, several factors may be involved in the allocation and distribution of lands owned or used by peasants. In many African states, as has been suggested, land and other factors of production continue to be allocated on the basis of membership in a descent group or other local group. Often, the estate cannot be alienated, that is, pass from descent group hands. Among the Betsileo, for example, after two centuries of life in nation-states, the role of descent in allocating land has weakened considerably. In the past, rice fields were part of a descent group estate to which individuals normally gained access through patrilineal ties. Today, estates in rice land are held in common by, and distributed among, members of minimal descent groups, individuals who share the same grandfather. However, a Betsileo has the legal right to terminate the condominium (joint holding) at any time and register his share of the rice field as private property. If he does so, he also may sell his rice field. However, Betsileo continue to discourage sale of rice fields to individuals who are not members of the owner's descent group. If a Betsileo wishes to sell his rice field and still maintain good relations with his kinsmen, he will sell it to a member of his own descent group.

Labor

The preceding discussion of factors of production has concentrated on the natural environment which humans exploit, most specifically, on land. However, in primitive and peasant societies access not only to land but also to labor is acquired through social position. Coworkers are kinsmen, affinals, fictive kinsmen, and, in peasant societies, often neighbors. Mutual aid in production is merely one aspect of a social relationship that is continuous and expresses itself on several different occasions in ongoing social life.

The individual is born and grows up in a world where some economic activities are traditionally cooperative, others traditionally individualistic. When he succeeds his father or another relative as cultivator

A cooperative economic activity: Women grinding maize. *(Victor Englebert/Photo Researchers)*

of a field, many of the same people who have assisted the father in cooperative tasks in previous years will continue to help him. The individual also gains access to labor through a social network consisting of his relatives on both sides, his affinals, his fictive kinsmen, his age peers, and perhaps his neighbors.

Specialization

Primitive and peasant societies also contrast with industrial nations in terms of another factor of production—technology. In fact, it is to some extent because their technologies are rudimentary that anthropologists have applied the term "primitive" to certain human populations. Manufacturing specializations are not characteristic of band and tribal societies. Manufacture of tools and other material items is generally regulated on the basis of age and sex. Depending on the society, women may weave and men manufacture pottery, or vice versa. Most people of a given age and sex

share the technical knowledge associated with that status. If married women customarily make baskets, most married women know how to make baskets. Neither technology nor technical knowledge is specialized as it is in industrial nations or among human populations involved in far-flung trade networks. However, there are certain exceptions to this generalization.

In some tribal societies, there is specialization in local units. Among the horticultural Yanomamo Indians of Venezuela, for example, certain villages specialize in the manufacture of clay pots, others in the preparation of different items. You might suppose that villages specialize because the raw materials from which their products are made are located near their villages. Chagnon (1968) asserts that this is not the case. Clay suitable for making Yanomamo pottery is available in all villages. People in most villages know how to make pots. But they do not do so. Chagnon relates craft specialization to the social and political environment rather than the natural environment. Trade is the first step in creating an alliance which may eventually convert enemy villages into allies. Village specialization promotes trade. Trade, like marriage, promotes alliance.

Among the Trobriand Islanders studied by Malinowski (1961), only two of many villages manufactured certain ceremonial items important in a regional exchange network. As with the Yanomamo, this manufacturing specialization did not appear to be related to the natural occurrence of raw materials. Rather, the existence of traditionally specialized villages was part and parcel of an exchange system known as the Kula-ring, which ultimately linked the inhabitants of several different communities and islands.

Alienation and impersonality in industrial economies

To conclude this discussion of production, some of the major contrasts between industrial and nonindustrial economies will be summarized. It is often—and accurately—said that the factory worker in the contemporary United States or Western Europe is alienated from the item he produces; that is, he feels no strong personal identification with it. This is not so among nonindustrial populations, where the manufacturer, that is, the individual worker, usually sees his work through from start to completion and feels pride, or at least accomplishment, in the finished item.

Another contrast involves relationships between coworkers. In nonindustrial societies, the economic relationship is merely one aspect of the social relationship. In the industrial nation, people usually do not work with their kinsmen and neighbors. However, if their colleagues are also their friends, the relationship is usually founded on their common occupation rather than on a broader tie of kinship or fictive kinship.

The relationship between the factory worker and what he produces is impersonal, as are his relationships with his coworkers and his employer. In fact, it is in industrial nations that we can most appropriately speak of "employer-employee relationships." People sell their labor for cash. They do not give it to their kinsmen or other members of their personal networks as readily or as frequently as they do in tribal societies. They do not, without remuneration, give their time and energy to fulfill an obligation to a landlord or a political official, as they would in peasant societies. Even privates in the

American army receive monetary compensation. In primitive societies, people work for their kinsmen; they share community goals. This is also true in some peasant societies where people work for the state. The goals of the factory owner, however, often seem to have little bearing on the goals of the factory worker or the consumer.

In short, in industrial societies there are economies. In primitive societies, there are relations of production, distribution, and consumption—social relationships with economic aspects. The economy is not a separate entity, to be studied by economists and manipulated by advisers and government officials. Rather, the economy is, in the words of many anthropologists, *embedded* in the society.

The Comparative Study of Distribution or Exchange

Economic anthropologists have recently concentrated more on exchange or distribution than on production or consumption. The impetus for stressing exchange comes from an economist, Karl Polanyi. Chief among the exponents of Polanyi's theories have been the anthropologist-economist George Dalton and the anthropologist Paul Bohannan. The cross-cultural study of ex-

In industrial societies the relationship between workers and what they produce is usually impersonal, as in this poultry processing plant in Georgia. *(Ron Sherman/Nancy Palmer)*

change has been further stimulated by the French anthropologist Claude Lévi-Strauss, who has written extensively on marriage as an exchange system which promotes alliance between social groups—a point of view which is in agreement with the stress on exogamy and its adaptive functions presented in Chapter 6. As Lévi-Strauss has suggested, alliances may be formed on the basis of exchange in marriage. Communication may also be regarded as a kind of exchange. Finally, we may study the exchange of material items, goods and services.

The market principle

To study exchange cross-culturally, Polanyi defined three principles orienting exchanges: reciprocity, redistribution, and the market principle. These principles may all be present in the same economy, but they will govern different kinds of transactions. However, in a specific society, one of them usually predominates. The principle of exchange usually considered to be predominant is the one which allocates the factors of production. In the industrial West the market principle is dominant. Thus in the United States, the factors of production—land, labor, natural resources, technology, and capital—are distributed by the operation of the market principle. In the words of George Dalton:

Market exchange refers . . . to the organizational process of purchase and sale at money price which is the mechanism of transacting material products, labor and natural resources.

. . .

The distinguishing feature of a market-organized economy, then, is the special nature of interdependence: all material livelihood is derived from selling something through the market mechanism; resource and labor ingredients of production are organized for purchase and sale as are produced material items; market prices rearrange labor and resource uses [1968, pp. 144, 145].

The law of supply and demand operates in this Sudanese market.
(George Rodger/Magnum)

When exchanges are governed by the market principle, the value of an exchangeable item is determined by the "law of supply and demand." Items enter the market to be bought and sold, their value determined by supply and demand, a variable related to such factors as inflation and summed up in such economic concepts as the "gross national product (GNP)." Characteristic of exchanges oriented by the market principle is bargaining—involving a kind of behavior which Polanyi called "higgling-haggling." Both buyer and seller try to get their "money's worth." However, bargaining does not necessitate a verbal exchange between buyer and seller. It may merely involve "shopping around."

Redistribution

Redistribution is the major exchange mode in chiefdoms and many archaic states. This principle operates when goods, services, or their equivalent move from the local level to a center. In states, the center is often a capital. In chiefdoms, it may be a storehouse near the chief's residence. Goods move up through a hierarchy of officials to be stored at the center. Some are consumed along the way and at the center by state or chiefly personnel and dependents. But the principle of exchange here is *redistribution*. Goods also flow out from the center, down through the hierarchy, and back to the peasants. An exchange principle similar to redistribution predominates in contemporary managed economies.

Reciprocity

Reciprocity, as Polanyi defined it, is "movements between correlative points of symmetrical groupings [Polanyi, 1968, p. 128]." Reciprocity is exchange between social equals not governed by the market principle. Since reciprocal exchange is between social equals, you would expect it to be the characteristic form of exchange in relatively egalitarian societies—foragers, horticulturalists, and pastoralists living in tribal societies which lack the office of chief.

The anthropologists Marshall Sahlins, in his book *Tribesmen* (1968) and elsewhere, and Elman Service, in his book *The Hunters* (1966), have drawn on their knowledge of ethnography to show that reciprocal exchange is not as simple as Polanyi made it seem. Sahlins and Service have identified three degrees of reciprocity, generalized reciprocity, balanced reciprocity, and negative reciprocity. These may be considered as areas on a continuum. *Generalized reciprocity* is characteristic of exchanges between closely related individuals; by *balanced reciprocity*, social distance increases; and at *negative reciprocity*, social distance is greatest. Generalized reciprocity occurs in exchanges between close relatives and fictive kin. One party gives to the other and may expect nothing concrete or immediate in return. Examples are the gifts parents bestow on their children. People view such exchanges not as economic transactions but as normal parts of a personal relationship. They often expect no immediate repayment; affection, respect, or loyalty will suffice. Good parents ultimately breed good children who will, as adults, honor their culture's conventions regarding obligations to aging parents.

In exchanges between more distantly related individuals, there is a balanced reciprocity. A person presents a gift to someone in another village—perhaps a lineage mate, a trading partner, a brother's wife's brother, or a brother's fictive kinsman. The bestower expects something in exchange for his gift—perhaps not immediately, but the social relationship will be strained and may terminate if, ultimately, there is no return.

Finally, at the outer limits of the social worlds of foragers and tribesmen is the domain of negative reciprocity. Exchange is still usually between social equals—free trade, freely entered—but it is impersonal. At this end of the continuum belongs intertribal trade, as well as exchanges between distant or hostile groups in the same tribal society. To a tribesman or forager, whose life is mostly lived in a world of close personal relations, exchanges on the fringes are permeated with ambiguity and distrust. Trade is a form of alliance, but such alliances are tentative and as close to being purely economic as any exchanges which ever take place in tribal society. Not only do people expect to receive something in return for what they have to offer, but, as in the market-oriented economy, they are concerned with getting their money's worth. Polanyi's term "higgling-haggling" could certainly describe the behavior which often attends such exchanges.

By recognizing three degrees of reciprocity, it is possible to see how negative reciprocity grades into behavior characteristic of economies oriented by the market principle. We are still dealing with reciprocity—the partners to the exchange are social equals. This is the major contrast with market economies, in which exchanges are not only impersonal and characterized by a concern with getting one's money's worth, but also often involve individuals who are unequal in social status and economic position.

Ethnographers have observed exchanges characterized by negative reciprocity among many tribal populations. One of the most frequently cited examples of inter-tribal trade is the silent trade or barter between groups of Pygmy foragers of the African equatorial forest and the horticultural villagers who live on the fringe of the forest. Silent trade represents a recognition of the potential for hostility in face-to-face economic transactions involving members of two culturally different populations. In silent trade, there is no personal contact involved in the exchange. A Pygmy hunter leaves game, honey, and other forest products at a site. Villagers then come to collect his offering and leave horticultural produce in exchange. A bit of silent bargaining may take place in these exchanges. If one party feels that the return is not equivalent to his own contributions,

he may reject it by simply leaving it at the trading site. If the other party wishes to continue the relationship, he will augment the offering in time for its collection the following day.

Sahlins and Service regard their three varieties of reciprocity as quantitatively rather than qualitatively different. As a person exchanges with more and more distantly related people, he moves along the continuum away from generalized reciprocity in the direction of negative reciprocity. But because the differences are in degree rather than kind, exchange relationships may shift as personal relationships change. A good example, which also illustrates the role of exchange in establishing alliances, comes from the Yanomamo Indians. Chagnon reports that two hostile villages may initiate an alliance by beginning to engage in reciprocal exchange. The first step is exchange of products in which each of the villages specializes. The next step involves the exchange of food and hospitality with each village inviting people of the other to a feast. By this time, intervillage exchanges have moved from the domain of negative reciprocity, in which immediate return and equivalence were characteristic, toward balanced reciprocity, in which gifts may be returned later. Certainly, it takes time to reciprocate a feast. However, there may still be bargaining in the relationship. Anyone who doubts this should see Chagnon's excellent ethnographic film *The Feast*. In it, an old man must be persuaded to bestow his dog on a man from another village as a village feast comes to an end.

Mutual feasting does not guarantee that an alliance between Yanomamo villages will last, but it represents a closer relationship than one based on intervillage trade of arrows, pots, and hammocks. The final stage in establishing an alliance between two villages comes when they begin to intermarry. As noted previously, many Yanomamo marriages result from an arrangement called sister exchange. If two men have unmarried sisters, they may exchange them, each losing a sister but gaining a wife. The notion of equivalence is involved in sister exchange; a man exchanges a sister for a wife. Once the marriages have taken place, however, subsequent exchanges between brothers-in-law fall in the domain of generalized reciprocity, for a close personal relationship has been established. From Chagnon's data, it seems possible that people could fall out of alliance the way individuals in our own society fall out of love. Villages may split and stop exchanging women with groups they once married into. They continue to feast for awhile and to engage in trade. Finally, one village may invite the other to what Chagnon calls a "treacherous feast," in which the hosts attack and try to kill their guests. The alliance terminated, no longer is there even negative reciprocity. There is open hostility and a state of feud.

Coexistence of modes of exchange

In the United States, the market principle predominates, governing the distribution of factors of production and most other exchanges, for example, those involving consumer goods. On the other hand, there is also redistribution in our society, though it is underdeveloped. We pay taxes. Our taxes flow from the local level to the Internal Revenue Service, a branch of the federal government. Many states also levy an income tax; they maintain their coffers at the state capital. A great deal of our tax money goes to support governmental apparatus, but some of it does come back to us in the form of social services, educational funds, highway funds, and other goods and services to the taxpayers.

There are even reciprocal exchanges in our society. Generalized reciprocity is characteristic of most exchanges between parents and children, although even here the American market mentality is strong. Recently, for example, a mother wrote "Dear Abby" to ask how much she should charge her son, a serviceman returning from Vietnam, for his room and board. Exchanges of gifts, cards, and dinner invitations are examples of American reciprocity, though generally of balanced reciprocity. Who has not heard remarks like, "Since they invited us to their daughter's wedding, when our daughter gets married, we'll have to invite them to hers"? Or, "Herman, we gave Gail Smith twenty-five dollars for a wedding present, and the Smiths only gave our Susan a fruit bowl. I don't think we should invite them to our dinner party next week."

I can even think of examples of negative reciprocity. One of my teachers in grade school thought it would be a good idea for her students to exchange Christmas presents. We drew lots. People were pleased when they drew a friend's name. On the last day of classes before the Christmas vacation began, gifts were exchanged. I was one of many, some even shouting, who felt that their gifts had not been properly reciprocated. I halted trade with the classmate who had given me one of her old comic books, and never said a word to her again.

Money and Spheres of Exchange

Money is of such overwhelming importance in the contemporary United States that it is difficult for us to conceive of societies without it. Some of the same scholars who have spread Polanyi's theories among anthropologists have also tried to ascertain what money is. They have argued, plausibly, that money is not a cultural universal: there are moneyless societies and economies.

The anthropologist Paul Bohannan (1963) has pointed out that money has several different functions. First, money may be a means of exchange. In the United States, it is the most common means of exchange. We don't give food to a bank teller and expect cash in return; we don't give the cashier a dozen roses in exchange for a sirloin steak; we do give money to the supermarket in exchange for food. Second, money may function as a standard of value. It is the principal standard that Americans use to evaluate relative worth. A washing machine is worth $200, not

225 chickens or 40 hours of work. A third function of money is as a means of payment. We pay money to the government, often not in exchange for anything but simply to satisfy some obligation, for example, a parking ticket.

In discussing things which seem to serve as money in different populations, we have to examine the functions they are serving. American money, like currency of other contemporary nation-states, serves all the functions just mentioned. Paul Bohannan calls such currency *general purpose money*. Any currency which does not serve all three functions is *special purpose money*. Among certain populations, for example, a cow can be used as a means of exchange but not as a standard of value. In societies with the institution of progeny price, it would be ridiculous to question people about how many cattle a wife and two children are worth.

Still another complication arises in the cross-cultural study of money. Anthropologists have encountered many populations whose exchange systems are organized into different categories or spheres. One of the most thoroughly analyzed examples of spheres of exchange comes from Bohannan's (1955) work among the Tiv of Nigeria. Items which Tiv exchanged were divided into three spheres. Tiv evaluated each sphere and the items within it differently. There was, first of all, what may be called the *subsistence sphere*. Items within it were normally exchanged for one another. Included within the subsistence sphere were foods, small livestock, household utensils, some tools, and raw materials used to produce any item in this category.

The second sphere was the *prestige sphere*. Within it were slaves, cattle, a type of large white cloth, and metal bars. The third sphere of exchangeable items was what Bohannan called the "supreme and unique category of exchange values [1955, p. 62]." It included only one "item"— women.

How did such a *multicentric* exchange system work? Normally, items in a given category were exchanged only for other items in that category. Examples would be exchange of yams for pots, an exchange within the subsistence sphere, or exchange of cattle or brass rods for slaves, an exchange within the prestige sphere. In the final and supreme sphere, Tiv believed that the only appropriate exchange item for a woman was another woman. The exchange of women was not based on sister exchange, as it is among the Yanomamo, but on what appears to have been a rather elaborate system of wardship whereby men tried to obtain as many wards, females, as possible, and to arrange marriages for them. In return, they themselves received wives.

With multiple spheres of exchangeable items, exchange becomes a moral problem. It is considered right, proper, and normal to exchange items in a given category for other items within that category. Bohannan calls such exchanges *conveyances*. On the other hand, Tiv told Bohannan that it was wrong to exchange items in one sphere for those in another. Bohannan calls exchanges between spheres—for example, brass rods for food—*conversions*. While Tiv apparently considered conveyances to be normal and conversions abnormal, individuals who had been able to convert their subsistence goods into prestige items were very pleased with their luck in the exchange. Of course, those who had to trade prestige items for subsistence items, or women for prestige items, were sorry that circumstances had forced them to make these downward exchanges.

Although the Tiv exchange system was organized into spheres with different moral values, the Tiv also had a general-purpose money. It was, according to Bohannan, metal bars, which were used simultaneously as a means of exchange, a standard of value, and a means of payment. However—and here is the difference between multicentric economies and our own—use of the general-purpose money was restricted to the prestige sphere. In conversions, metal rods sometimes functioned either as a means of exchange or as a standard of value, but not as both.

The Adaptive Relevance of Multicentric Economies

Tiv considered conversions abnormal and improper, and individuals were sorry when they had to exchange items for lower category goods. While not always so clearly defined, spheres of exchangeable items, multicentric economies as Bohannan calls them, have existed among populations other than the Tiv. Now let us consider some of the ways in which maintenance of normally distinct spheres of exchange helps humans adapt to their immediate environments in populations other than the Tiv.

Multicentric exchange systems usually are bifurcated into at least prestige and subsistence spheres. While most exchanges are conveyances, conversions do take place. The intent of the following discussion is to demonstrate that in societies which lack banks, prestige spheres assume some of the functions that banks serve in industrial nations. On the one hand, individuals may convert momentary surpluses in subsistence resources into higher level, prestige goods. On the other hand, in times of need they may reconvert prestige into subsistence. Thus in multicentric economies, as in our own, people save for a rainy day. However, the context of saving is personal, and the situations in which saving and spending take place are social and ceremonial. Consider the following ethnographic case.

One of the most famous of the institutions described by ethnographers is the *potlatch*, or blowout, of the Indians on the Northwest Coast of North America. Potlatching tribes included the Coast Salish of Washington and British Columbia and the Kwakiutl, who live further north. The potlatch was generally a festive event. Assisted by other members of his community, its sponsor gave away food and blankets, pieces of copper, and other

wealth items. In return for this, he received prestige. To give a potlatch was a socially recognized means of enhancing his reputation, and his prestige grew directly with the magnitude of the potlatch, the volume of goods given away in it.

The tribes on the northwest coast, and especially the Kwakiutl, began to trade extensively with Europeans during the nineteenth century. There is every indication that the volume of their wealth increased while trade was going on. At the same time, Kwakiutl population size appears to have declined drastically because of European diseases. The effect of increased wealth and reduced population was to extend the prerogative of sponsoring a potlatch to a larger segment of Kwakiutl society than had been the case in the past.

Both the Salish and the Kwakiutl had multicentric economies. It is possible to recognize a subsistence sphere. Above it was what may be called a sphere of wealth. Finally, the supreme sphere contained a nonmaterial item—prestige. Included in the subsistence sphere were several varieties of foods. Although the tribes on the northwest coast were hunters and gatherers, compared to contemporary foraging populations such as the Bushmen, Shoshone, and Eskimos, they were more like food producers. Anthropologists usually speak of tribal rather than band organization when referring to these populations. For one thing, their natural environments were not marginal. In fact, these populations tapped a wide variety of naturally occurring resources on the land and sea. The most important foods of the Kwakiutl appear to have been salmon, herring, candlefish, and berries, and, to a lesser extent, mountain goats, seals, and porpoises (Piddocke, 1969).

Because of microenvironmental variations, there appear to have been minor differences in the types of food consumed by the Salish and the Kwakiutl. Likewise, the items included in their spheres of wealth differed. Among the Salish, blankets, shell ornaments, hide shirts, and fine baskets were wealth items. The Kwakiutl wealth sphere included slaves, canoes, dressed elk skins, blankets, and pieces of copper. Finally, among both tribes, people could convert wealth into prestige by giving away, on the occasion of the potlatch, wealth items. With European trade, increased wealth, and decreased population among the Kwakiutl during the nineteenth century, people could also convert wealth into prestige by destroying wealth items such as slaves and pieces of copper (Vayda, 1968).

Until recently, most anthropologists who described the potlatch interpreted it as an example of uneconomic, irrational, and competitive behavior—the result of a culturally inspired drive for prestige and status. The destruction of property in the potlatch was stressed to support the contention that in some societies individuals are much more interested in maximizing their prestige and social status than in preserving economically valuable resources.

Ecologically oriented anthropologists, on the other hand, have developed a new interpretation which also applies to similar blowouts in populations elsewhere. Wayne Suttles, Stuart Piddocke, and Andrew Vayda, among others, have determined that there are significant fluctuations from year to year and from place to place in the natural resources available to the human foragers on the northwest coast. Salmon and herring runs up rivers, for example, are not equally abundant from year to year in a given locality. Furthermore, one village may be enjoying a good year while another village is experiencing a lean one. Later, however, the situations of the two villages may be reversed. Thus while the overall natural environment of the northwest coast is more favorable than elsewhere, there are microenvironmental and microecological variations in time and place.

In this context, the potlatch and the multicentric economies of the Kwakiutl and Salish had adaptive value. A village enjoying an especially good year had a surplus of items in the subsistence sphere, which it could then exchange for wealth items. It was possible among the Salish at least to convert food directly into prestige. A sponsor, drawing on his own wealth and contributions from other members of his community, gave away food and wealth to people from other communities who needed it. In return, the individual and his community were attributed prestige. The decision to potlatch was related to the economic situation of the community in the year the blowout was given. If there had been a surplus of subsistence items and, thereby, a build-up of wealth over several good years, it could afford a potlatch converting wealth into prestige.

The adaptive value of this behavior becomes clear when we consider what happened when a community which had enjoyed a good foraging period encountered a lean year. At this point, its members began to accept invitations to attend potlatches in other communities which were faring better. People in the unfortunate community would now accept wealth items and food from potlatching communities. In doing so, they lost some of the prestige they had formerly accumulated, because they became recipients rather than bestowers of gifts. Later, if the community's fortunes continued to decline, its people could exchange their wealth items for food, for example, slaves for herrings or canoes for cherries (Vayda, 1968). Hopefully, over time, the fortunes of the community would be reversed, and the process of converting up could resume.

Thus multicentric economies have adaptive value. They are like our banks because they enable people to convert a perishable surplus into a more durable one while providing for other communities in need. As fortunes fluctuate, food is converted into wealth and prestige, wealth into prestige, prestige back into wealth and food, and wealth back into food. Potlatching linked together the local groups along the northwest coast, establishing an alliance system and an interdependent relationship which in the long run had adaptive value. We can perceive the ecological function of potlatching and multicentric exchange regardless of the motivations of the individual participants. The anthropologists who stressed prestige and status rivalry among the Kwakiutl were not wrong in doing so; they merely emphasized the motivational rather than the systemic aspect of the behavior they were describing.

The use of feasts to enhance individual and community reputations and to redistribute wealth within a population is not peculiar to the Kwakiutl and the Salish. There are numerous other ethnographic examples, particularly from tribal populations. In fact, we might accurately classify the adaptive blowout as an institution of tribal society. Among foraging populations living in marginal environments, resources are too meager to support intercommunity feasting on this level. Further along the general evolutionary continuum, in chiefdoms or states, there are more effective and permanently established means of redistributing strategic resources among local groups. There are storehouses and administrative hierarchies. In Chapter 13, some of the very different functions which blowouts or community feasts assume in nation-states will be considered.

The Future of Economic Anthropology

As a result of work by Polanyi, Dalton, Bohannan, Sahlins, Service, and various ecological anthropologists, comparative understanding of exchange systems is now well established. Anthropologists know that in human populations with non-Western cultural traditions, individual behavior is influenced by motivations, incentives, and considerations which may not be the same as our own. They also know that many populations lack the unitary exchange system which money makes possible in the industrial world. And they understand ways in which the institutionalized exchange systems of different societies assist populations in adapting to their environments.

While anthropologists have learned a great deal about the sociocultural factors which motivate people in different cultures to produce and exchange, they need research designed to establish a firmer basis for the comparative study not of motivations but of economic systems. In concluding this chapter, some of the research problems in comparative economics which have begun to engage anthropologists will be mentioned.

There are signs that future ethnographers will be more concerned with gathering quantifiable data on production, distribution, and consumption, as well as on other matters of interest to anthropologists, for example, aspects of social organization. During my own field work among the Betsileo, I became interested in their economic system. In studying production, I measured rice fields and plots where the Betsileo grew their secondary crops. I weighed harvests and was able to determine yields of different crops and soil types. I computed the nutritional value of food produced by the Betsileo in terms of calories, protein, vitamins, and minerals. I observed work patterns and obtained information on the number of personnel, their ages and sex, and the hours they worked at different tasks involved in rice cultivation. On the basis of these and other inquiries, I can make much more than an impressionistic assessment of the Betsileo system of production.

As comparable data become available from other societies, it will be possible to determine differences and similarities between human populations in terms of several questions traditionally of interest to economic anthropologists. The output of an economy in terms of calories can be measured if the caloric value of each food is known and the total yield of all foods produced is approximated. Likewise, the calorie can be used as a unit to measure energy expended in production. As we all know, some tasks are harder than others; when we do harder work we expend more energy, more calories. There are devices with which fieldworkers can measure the calories expended in different kinds of tasks. If we know how many people work for how many hours on what kinds of productive activities, we can establish the total cost, in calories, of production in a given population. With estimates of energy expended and energy produced, we can answer such questions as, What is the ratio of input to output and of labor invested to yield in different populations? Computer analysis will help us in analyzing and manipulating comparative data as well as data gathered from a single society.

Such data will enable us to answer several other comparative questions. What is the relative contribution of males and females, of people of different ages and statuses, to production in the different societies of our sample? Is productive labor allocated on the basis of kinship, marriage, or other ties? How does the amount of labor contributed vary with genealogical or other social distance? When quantitative data are also available on other aspects of life in the populations being compared, it will be possible to pinpoint relationships between such areas as economic, societal, and political organization.

Similarly, a quantitative approach will increase our knowledge of exchange systems in different societies. Ethnographers must begin to monitor exchanges in the populations they study. Answers to questions such as the following will help to resolve some of the problems raised and confirm some of the generalizations made here. What is exchanged, between whom, how often, and in what way? What is the value of the goods or services exchanged (in terms of, say, energy in calories or time required to produce)?

Finally, quantitative ethnographic research will raise and help to resolve questions about the third aspect of economy, consumption. As in most anthropological discussions of comparative economics, consumption has been neglected in this chapter in favor of production and exchange. Ethnographers are beginning to gather quantitative data on consumption of subsistence items and other resources in the societies they study. In Chapter 14 a recent example of collaboration between an ethnographer and a nutritionist which demonstrates a relationship between diet

SUMMARY

Economics focuses on the economies of industrial nations; economic anthropology studies systems of production, distribution, and consumption of material resources in cross-cultural perspective. Economists commonly define economics as the science of allocating scarce means to alternative ends. Western economists often assume that in choosing alternatives, individuals strive to maximize profit—that they obey the "profit motive." However, in nonindustrial contexts, people may attempt to maximize values other than individual profits; furthermore, people often do not have free choice in allocating their scarce means.

Among populations with band and tribal organization, individuals must invest their time, energy, and liquid wealth into funds described as subsistence, replacement, social, and ceremonial. In states there is also a rent fund: individuals must render a portion of their labor or its fruits to religious or secular authorities or to other superordinates. The rent fund often becomes primary, and subsistence may suffer. In addition, social and ceremonial obligations may serve different functions in state and tribal societies.

The adaptive strategies discussed in Chapter 3 are actually productive strategies. Among nonindustrial populations, production proceeds in a personal context;

and social structure will be discussed. An ethnographic study of production will overlap but usually not totally coincide with a study of consumption. Even if we know the total yield of all food resources in a given household, for example, we cannot be sure that all the food which is produced is also consumed within that household. A portion may be sold; another part may be converted into a nonsubsistence sphere; some items may end up in state coffers. Goods produced by members of household A may be consumed in household B. Ecologically oriented ethnographers have gathered information about diet by monitoring, during their stays in the field, all food consumed by members of sample households. Ideally, studies of production and consumption should extend over several years so that seasonal, annual, and longer term fluctuations in yield and diet may be determined. Although there are obvious limitations to this type of study, only when such studies have been carried out will we be able to confirm many of our generalizations about consumption.

Since collecting quantitative data has not traditionally been the major aim of ethnographers, descriptions of particular societies, and the data which enter cross-cultural studies, have had a qualitative, often impressionistic, basis. Most of the generalizations made in this book are based on qualitative data, and many of them cannot be validated statistically at this time. Such generalizations are, however, common in ethnology. Moreover, it would be incorrect to suggest that anthropologists should wait until all the data have been collected before they dare to generalize. This would be a futile endeavor, since ethnographic and ethnological data are indefinitely expansible. Because new data raise new problems for research, anthropology will never see a time when all the data have been gathered. The present suggestion is merely that anthropologists pursue new research problems and employ quantitative techniques more extensively. It is probable that, as the fruits of this new strategy are circulated and compared, a surprisingly large number of generalizations based on impressions and qualitative data will turn out to be valid. After all, people could tell the difference between a gorilla and a chimpanzee before geneticists began to measure the contrasts.

relations of production are merely aspects of continuous social relationships. A person acquires rights to strategic resources through membership in bands, descent groups, villages, and other social units, and not impersonally through purchase and sale. Labor, too, is recruited through personal ties, and the sharing of labor is merely one aspect of social relationships that are expressed in a variety of social and ceremonial contexts. While not as developed as it is in states, manufacturing specialization may exist in tribal societies, serving to promote trade and alliance between groups. In nonindustrial societies there is typically a personal relationship between producer and commodity, in contrast to the alienation of labor, product, and management in industrial economies.

Economic anthropologists have been more concerned with description, analysis, and comparison of systems of distribution and exchange than with production and consumption. Economist Karl Polanyi introduced a distinction between three principles of exchange—the market principle, redistribution, and reciprocity. The market principle, governing exchanges dictated by supply and demand, is the dominant principle in the United States and other industrial societies, as well as in many archaic states. It involves impersonal purchase and sale, getting one's money's worth, and exchanges among social unequals; and it allocates the factors of production in industrial nations. Redistribution is the characteristic exchange mode in chiefdoms and some archaic states. It also exists in rudimentary form in the United States and in many modern nations. Goods are collected at a central place, and part of what is collected is eventually given back, or redistributed.

Reciprocity, a principle governing exchanges among social equals, is the characteristic mode of exchange in band and tribal societies. Anthropologists Marshall Sahlins and Elman Service have suggested that there are different degrees of reciprocity which ultimately grade into exchange behavior characteristic of the market principle. With generalized reciprocity, there is no immediate expectation of return. With balanced reciprocity, characteristic of exchanges involving more distantly related people, individuals expect their gifts to be returned but not immediately. Exchanges on the fringes of the social systems in band and tribal populations are governed by negative reciprocity, reminiscent of the market principle but involving social equals. There is concern about immediate return of exchanged items and getting one's money's worth. Reciprocity, redistribution, and the market principle may coexist in the same society, but the primary exchange mode in any society

Sources and Suggested Readings

BARNETT, H. G.
1938   The Nature of the Potlatch. *American Anthropologist* 40: 349–358. The famous blowout among the Indians of the Northwest Coast of North America.

BEATTIE, J.
1960   *Bunyoro: An African Kingdom.* New York: Holt, Rinehart and Winston. Case study written for undergraduates; includes some aspects of the economy of an African state.

BELSHAW, C. S.
1965   *Traditional Exchange and Modern Markets.* Englewood Cliffs, N.J.: Prentice-Hall. Exchange systems in cross-cultural perspective.

BOHANNAN, P.
1955   Some Principles of Exchange and Investment among the Tiv. *American Anthropologist* 57: 60–70. A multicentric economy in Nigeria.

1963   *Social Anthropology.* New York: Holt, Rinehart and Winston. Useful statements of many central problems in economic anthropology, including multicentrism, money, and modes of exchange contained in Chapters 13–15.

BURLING, R.
1962   Maximization Theories and the Study of Economic Anthropology. *American Anthropologist* 64: 802–821. Economic and noneconomic motivations.

CHAGNON, N.
1968   *Yanomamo: The Fierce People.* New York: Holt, Rinehart and Winston. Discussion of political functions of specialization in the manufacture of trade items is especially interesting.

CODERE, H. S.
1950   *Fighting with Property*, monograph 18. New York: American Ethnological Society. History of potlatch.

COOK, S.
1966   The Obsolete "Anti-Market" Mentality: A Critique of the Substantive Approach to Economic Anthropology. *American Anthropologist* 68: 323–345. Provocative criticism of view of economic anthropology espoused by P. Bohannan, G. Dalton, and K. Polanyi.

DALTON, G.
1968   (orig. 1961). Economic Theory and Primitive Society. In *Economic Anthropology: Readings in Theory and Analysis*, ed. E. E. LeClair and H. K. Schneider, pp. 143–167. New York: Holt, Rinehart and Winston. Defines the "substantive" approach in economic anthropology, and advocates concentrated study of exchange systems in different societies.

is that which allocates the factors of production.

Economic anthropologists distinguish between general purpose monies—currencies which serve simultaneously as standards of value, means of exchange, and means of payment—and special purpose monies—currencies which do not assume all these functions. Economic anthropologists have also described multicentric economies, organized into different spheres of exchange. Spheres including subsistence items, wealth items, and prestige are usually characteristic of multicentric economies, and such spheres are most often found in populations with tribal organization. Multicentric economies have adaptive relevance: conversions of subsistence goods to wealth or prestige and reconversions to subsistence represent ways of saving in tribal societies.

Concentrating on production and exchange, anthropologists have slighted systems of consumption. However, ecologically oriented anthropologists have recently monitored diets of sample households and other family units. With similar quantitative data on production and distribution, anthropologists are laying a basis for a statistical approach to economic anthropology, one which will make it possible to compare inputs and outputs in different societies and to confirm or invalidate some of the existing generalizations in economic anthropology.

DALTON, G., ed.
1967   *Tribal and Peasant Economies.* Garden City, N.Y.: The Natural History Press. Articles on production and distribution in different societies.

1968   *Primitive, Archaic and Modern Economies: Essays of Karl Polanyi.* Garden City, N.Y.: Doubleday. Essays with considerable influence on economic anthropology, especially Polanyi's typology of modes of exchange.

FIRTH, R., and YAMEY, B. S., eds.
1963   *Capital, Savings and Credit in Peasant Societies.* London: Allen. Articles discussing these institutions in a peasant context.

FORMAN, S.
1970   *The Raft Fisherman: Tradition and Change in the Brazilian Peasant Economy.* Bloomington: Indiana University Press. Field study of Brazilian raft fishermen, their system of production, and their exchanges with the outside world.

HERSKOVITS, M. J.
1952   *Economic Anthropology.* New York: Knopf. Thorough textbook statement of one position in economic anthropology, from one of its major proponents.

KNIGHT, R.
1965   A Re-examination of Hunting, Trapping and Territorialty among the Northeastern Algonkian Indians. In *Man, Culture and Animals: The Role of Animals in Human Ecological Adjustments*, ed. A. Leeds and A. P. Vayda, pp. 27–42. Washington, D.C.: American Association for the Advancement of Science. Important contribution to long-running anthropological dispute about the existence of private property among certain Indian foragers prior to European impact on interior North America. Links development of private property notions to trade with Europeans.

LEE, R. B.
1969   (orig. 1966). Kung Bushman Subsistence: An Input-Output Analysis. In *Environment and Cultural Behavior*, ed. A. P. Vayda, pp. 47–79. Garden City, N.Y.: The Natural History Press. Creative analysis of subsistence among these famous foragers.

LÉVI-STRAUSS, C.
1969   *The Elementary Structures of Kinship.* Boston: Beacon Press. Classic examination of marriage systems in primitive societies. Groups can be allied through the exchange of women as well as material items.

MALINOWSKI, B.
1920   Kula; the Circulating Exchange of Valuables in the Archipelagoes of Eastern New Guinea. *Man* 51: 97–105. First description of what has become the best-known exchange system in the world ethnographic stockpile.

1961   (orig. 1922). *Argonauts of the Western Pacific.* New York: Dutton. Classic ethnographic examination of the behavior of Trobrianders on a trading expedition; as rich in data about ritual and myth as about economic behavior.

MAUSS, M.
1954   (orig. 1925). *The Gift: Forms and Functions of Exchange in Archaic Societies.* New York: The Free Press. Uses comparative data to emphasize the positive value of giving. Influence on the theoretical work of Lévi-Strauss and generations of anthropologists, especially French.

NASH, M.
1966   *Primitive and Peasant Economic Systems.* San Francisco: Chandler. Short introduction to economic anthropology.

PIDDOCKE, S.
1969   The Potlatch System of the Southern Kwakiutl: A New Perspective. In *Environment and Cultural Behavior,* ed. A. P. Vayda, pp. 130–156. Garden City, N.Y.: The Natural History Press. Ecological interpretation of potlatching.

POLANYI, K.
1968   (orig. 1958). The Economy as Instituted Process. In *Economic Anthropology: Readings in Theory and Analysis,* ed. E. E. LeClair and H. K. Schneider, pp. 122–143. New York: Holt, Rinehart and Winston. Most comprehensive reader on economic anthropology; this article is a clear statement of Polanyi's position on the comparative study of exchange.

SAHLINS, M. D.
1968   *Tribesmen.* Englewood Cliffs, N.J.: Prentice-Hall. Exchange and other issues in economic anthropology.

1972   *Stone Age Economics.* Chicago: Aldine. A major authority in economic anthropology offers a collection of his ideas, new and old.

SERVICE, E. R.
1966   *The Hunters.* Englewood Cliffs, N.J.: Prentice-Hall. Economies based on hunting and gathering.

SUTTLES, W.
1960   Affinal Ties, Subsistence and Prestige among the Coast Salish. *American Anthropologist* 62: 296–305. Innovative view of the potlatch as an adaptive institution.

TURNBULL, C.
1961   *The Forest People.* New York: Simon and Schuster. Popular account of the Pygmies of the Ituri forest in equatorial Africa; relationships of these foragers to their horticultural neighbors.

1965   The Mbuti Pygmies of the Congo. In *Peoples of Africa*, ed. J. L. Gibbs, Jr., pp. 279–318. New York: Holt, Rinehart and Winston. More complete account of Pygmy subsistence techniques in a collection of articles about African populations.

VAYDA, A. P.
1968   (orig. 1961). Economic Systems in Ecological Perspective: The Case of the Northwest Coast. In *Readings in Anthropology.* 2nd ed., vol. 2, ed. M. H. Fried, pp. 172–178. New York: Crowell. Brief but persuasive attempt to interpret the potlatch in ecological terms.

VEBLEN, T.
1953   (orig. 1899). *The Theory of the Leisure Class.* New York: New American Library. The potlatch used as a comparative case to bolster argument of the importance of prestige in human motivation.

WITTFOGEL, K. A.
1957   *Oriental Despotism: A Comparative Study of Total Power.* New Haven: Yale University Press. Famous and controversial attempt to link the origin of despotic states with management of hydraulic systems.

WOLF, E. R.
1966   *Peasants.* Englewood Cliffs, N.J.: Prentice-Hall. Fascinating theoretical and comparative introduction to peasants.

10. Religious and Ritual Behavior

When, why, and how did religion begin? Before considering some of the speculations of social scientists and philosophers on the origin of religion, we need a definition of religion, and the anthropologist Anthony F. C. Wallace has provided a good one. Religion is "a kind of human behavior ... which can be classified as belief and ritual concerned with supernatural beings, powers, and forces [1966, p. 5]."

This definition has several implications. First, religion is a kind of human behavior. Religious behavior may be verbal or nonverbal. The nonverbal aspects of religious behavior might involve religious rites, religious personnel, and specific religious acts and activities. The verbal aspects of religious behavior might include beliefs, mythology, ethical standards, conceptions of the supernatural, and religious ideology. Second, religion is broad enough to apply to all populations of *Homo sapiens*; religious behavior, as described, is encountered in all human societies. Religion, then, is a cultural universal. Finally, religion is concerned with the supernatural. The supernatural is the non-natural, the more than natural, a realm outside of the everyday world, the strange, the mysterious, that which is inexplicable in ordinary terms. Supernatural beings—gods and goddesses, ghosts, and souls—are beings not of this world. Extraordinary powers and forces are those which people believe affect them, perhaps control them. Some are personal, wielded by supernatural beings. Others are impersonal; they simply exist. These powers are beyond the ordinary forces controlled by human beings. In some societies, people believe that humans can gain a measure of control over supernatural forces, that individuals can benefit from, or become imbued with, supernatural powers.

Speculations about the Origin of Religion

When did religion originate? The fact that Neanderthals buried their dead and often interred objects in their graves has convinced many anthropologists that *Homo sapiens Neanderthalensis* was a religious creature concerned about the afterlife. The earliest archeological suggestion of religion dates from the Neanderthal burials. There

is no way of knowing if religion pre-
dates the Neanderthal, however. Some
scholars have gone so far as to speculate
that religion is precultural, that chimpanzees engage in rituals and may even experience emotions akin to those evoked in
humans by certain stimuli. Jane van Lawick
Goodall, for example, has reported her observation of what she called a "rain dance"
by a group of male chimpanzees in Tanzania. This display of rapid and violent
behavior was triggered by a tropical cloud-
burst and thunder. During their rain dance,
the chimpanzees raced down a hillside, hit-
ting the ground as they went, tearing off,
brandishing, and flinging branches, while
the females and juveniles looked on.

Most anthropologists would have difficulty including the chimpanzee rain dances
with human rituals. Perhaps such chimp
behavior is conditioned by environmental
factors such as a fall in barometric pressure. The safest position, since neither
chimpanzees nor our remote ancestors can
tell us the reasons for their actions, is that
any statement about when, where, why,
and how the first religion arose, or about
its nature, is pure speculation. Nevertheless, though such speculations can tell us
nothing conclusive about the origin of religion, many reveal some of the more important functions that religious behavior
serves. Several of these undemonstrable
theories—some probable, others not—will
be examined now.

Tylor, animism, and explanation

One of the founders of the anthropology
of religion was Sir Edward Burnett Tylor,
an Englishman who lived during the late
nineteenth and early twentieth century.
Like many other scholars who speculated
on how religion began, Tylor thought that
in order to discover the origin of religion,
it was necessary to get into the mind of
primitive man. Spurred by his knowledge
of the ethnography of his time, Tylor let
his mind wander along that path back

through time. Primitive man, thought
Tylor, must have wondered about many
things not explained by daily experience.
He was particularly intrigued by death,
dreaming, and trance. In dreams and
trances, the individual experiences a form
of suspended animation; yet on waking,
he recalls events, people, animals, places,
and things from his dream or trance.

Tylor (1873) argued that speculation
about the events associated with dreams
and trances led primitive man to the notion of the double, the soul. In my body,
said primitive man, are two beings, me,
active during the day, and my double, active when I sleep and when I enter a trance.
They are in complementary distribution.
They never meet. But one is essential to the
other. When the double, the soul, permanently leaves the body, the whole personality, the human being, dies. Death is departure of the soul. From the Latin word
for soul, *anima*, Tylor named what was in
his opinion the most primitive form of
religion: *animism*. He offered a broad definition of religion as the belief in spiritual
beings.

In addition to being a speculative anthropologist, Tylor was a unilineal evolu-
tionist; he believed that mankind had
evolved through a set series of stages, one
by one, from a primitive condition to civilization. Thus he applied a unilineal evolutionary model to his speculations about religion. Out of simple animism, the original
religion according to Tylor, came higher
religious forms: polytheism and, ultimately, monotheism. Remember, however,
that Tylor thought that religion, the belief
in spiritual beings, had been invented by
man to explain things he could not understand in terms of his experiences in the
natural world. The major function of religion, then, was to explain. Tylor thought
that religion would diminish in importance
as science encroached on its explanatory
domain. To an extent, he was right. We
now accept without thinking scientific explanations for events that religious doctrines explained during the nineteenth century. Yet religion persists. Why? It must
be because religion does something more

than explain the mysterious. Religion must, and does, have other functions. Other early contributions clarified some of them.

Marett, mana, and animatism

Another early speculator about the origin of religion was Robert R. Marett. In his book *The Threshold of Religion* (1909), Marett took issue with Tylor's assumption that animism, rudimentary belief in spiritual beings, was the most primitive form of religion. Marett argued that a different conceptualization of the supernatural was even more fundamental. According to Marett, early man and primitive man conceived of the supernatural as a domain of raw, impersonal power, influencing man but, under certain conditions, able to be controlled. For Marett, this conceptualization of the supernatural, which he called *animatism*, was primary, the most rudimentary form of religious conception. It was only later in the evolution of man and of religion that people had added spiritual beings to their theologies.

Why did Marett regard animatism as more ancient than animism? At the beginning of the twentieth century, there was gradually accumulating a body of ethnographic reports by missionaries from several different areas of the world. Some of these reports were excellent descriptions of life in primitive areas. Among them was a work by British missionary Robert Codrington, who had from 1864 spent twenty-four years in Melanesia. You will recall from our discussion of incest (Chapter 15) that the aboriginal Polynesians believed in mana, an impersonal force which existed in the universe. The Melanesians shared this belief, but in slightly different form. Codrington (1891), in describing religious practices and beliefs among the aboriginal Melanesians, stressed the importance of their doctrine of mana. The Melanesians believed that mana could reside in people, animals, plants, and sometimes inanimate objects. In some ways Melanesian mana was like our own notion of luck. Thus Melanesians explained the success of individuals in their society by their possession

of quantities of mana. Individuals could acquire mana in different ways. When they performed magical rites, they enlisted mana on their behalf to accomplish what they had in mind. Objects containing mana could change the luck of an individual if they came into his possession. A charm or trophy that had belonged to a successful hunter was believed to convey his mana to the next individual who possessed it. A man might place a rock in his horticultural garden and find that his yields suddenly improved dramatically. The explanation was believed to be mana, the sacred force contained in the rock.

Mana was the impersonal force which Marett had in mind when he wrote of animatism. Mana-like notions exist in several different parts of the world, though the specifics of the religious doctrines vary. The difference between Polynesian and Melanesian mana is related to the greater socioeconomic stratification characteristic of many Polynesian societies. It is like the distinction between ascribed and achieved status. In Melanesia, individuals had approximately equal access to mana; it could come to them by chance or because some worked harder at getting it than others. On the other hand, in Polynesia mana was attached to offices in the political structure. The rulers and other members of the nobility were believed to have greater concentrations of mana than ordinary people. In fact, so charged with mana were members of the royal family that contact with them was dangerous to commoners. Mana is analogous to electricity; it is not inherent in people or things, but can move; it flows from one person or thing to another. Polynesians believed that the mana of the king flowed out of his person everywhere he walked; it could infect the ground, making it dangerous for ordinary mortals to walk in his footsteps. It could flow from his person to the containers and utensils he used in eating. Bodily contact between king and commoner was dangerous to the commoner because mana could have an

Approaching the supernatural: A female witch doctor conducts a baptismal ceremony. *(E. Cole/Rapho Guillumette)*

effect very like electrical shock. Ordinary people simply could not support as much sacred current as royalty. Rites to purify exposed individuals were necessary.

Mana is related to the notion of taboo. Because of the mana residing there, the king's person was considered taboo. There was an injunction against contact between royalty and commoners. The concept of mana has also been found in aboriginal North America, Africa, and Japan.

While it is, of course, impossible to say whether animism or animatism was the original form of religion, Marett, like Tylor, in speculating about the origin of religion, increased our understanding of the nature of contemporary religions. The contributions of both men are incorporated in Anthony F. C. Wallace's definition of religion quoted at the beginning of this chapter. Religion consists of behavior related to supernatural beings, forces, and powers. For Tylor the supernatural world of the primitive was peopled with spiritual beings. For Marett it consisted of an impersonal force or power. In fact, both spirits and impersonal forces are found in the

supernatural conceptions of most populations of the present and the recent past.

Frazer, magic, and religion

One of the most famous treatises on the origin of religion is *The Golden Bough* (1911–1915), by the British anthropologist Sir James Frazer. In abridged form, this monumental, twelve-volume work has long been one of the anthropological studies most familiar to laymen. Frazer denied that early man had religion. He argued that religion evolved out of magic, that early man first approached the supernatural through magical means. Frazer thought that magic among primitive populations was analogous to the science of civilized nations. Magic was a body of techniques designed to accomplish specific aims. Included among the techniques of the magician were such things as spells, formulas, and incantations. Frazer further argued that religion was born when humans finally discovered that magic was ineffective. Instead of continuing to try to control the supernatural through spells and formulas, humans now began to supplicate, to pray to, to cajole, and, in general, to make themselves subservient to, the supernatural.

Frazer went on to draw a distinction—which is still accepted as valid today—between two types of magic: imitative and contagious. *Imitative magic* is based on what Frazer called the "Law of Similarity." The magician believes that he can produce the desired effect merely by imitating it. If one wishes a person injured or dead, he may imitate the injury or death on an image representing the person. Sticking pins into effigies is an example of such behavior. On the other hand, *contagious magic* is based on what Frazer calls the "Law of Contact or Contagion." Whatever is done to a material object will affect the person who was once in contact with that object. In some cases the magician uses effluvia from the person of his victim—his nails or hair, for example. The spell performed on the effluvia is believed eventually to reach the person and to work the desired result.

While Frazer is important for introducing a classification of magical techniques which remains valid today, most anthropologists reject his speculations about the evolution of religion out of magic. There are several reasons for this. Aspects of magic and religion may, for example, be found in the same society, and even in the same rites. Contrary to Frazer's argument, too, there is nothing simpler or more primitive about magical beliefs and practices than about animism or animatism.

Note that the speculations of Tylor, Marett, and Frazer are similar in one respect: All are concerned with the role of supernatural conceptions within cognitive systems, that is, within the world views, the ideologies, of human populations. For Tylor and Marett religious doctrines and beliefs serve to explain. The belief in souls explains what happens in sleep and after death, and how the supernatural world becomes populated. Mana, especially in Melanesia, explains differential success which people are unable or unwilling to explain in ordinary, natural terms. It serves to place success on a superhuman level. Some individuals are less successful at hunting, warfare, gardening, or other activities not because they are lazy, stupid, or inept, but because success, like grace, comes from the supernatural world. Frazer's primitive supernaturalism, magic, is also part of the cognitive system, consisting of a body of techniques whose mastery enables individuals to accomplish specific ends.

Hopi Indian kachina dolls, carved from cottonwood root to represent ancestral spirits. *(Robert Davis / Photo Researchers)*

Malinowski, magic, science, and religion

Other anthropologists have discussed religious beliefs and actions in the context of human emotions. On the basis of his ethnographic fieldwork in the Trobriand Islands, Bronislaw Malinowski (1948, 1958) addressed himself to some of the same questions that occupied Frazer. Malinowski distinguished between magic, science, and religion. He disagreed with Frazer that magic was the science of primitive man, for Malinowski actually found science among the Trobriand Islanders. "As soon as man developed the mastery of environment by the use of implements, and as soon as language came into being, there must also have existed primitive knowledge of an essentially scientific character [Malinowski, 1958, p. 87]."

Thus primitive man has developed techniques which enable him to deal with everyday problems involved in making a living. But there are certain aspects of his life over which he has no control; it is when he is confronted with these, according to Malinowski, that he turns to magic.

But however much knowledge and science help man in allowing him to obtain what he .wants, they are unable completely to control chance, to eliminate accidents, to foresee the unexpected turn of natural events, or to make human handiwork reliable and adequate to all practical requirements [1958, p. 88].

Malinowski pointed out that among the Trobrianders magical activities were usually associated with sailing, which is a very hazardous activity. Humans have no control over winds, rough weather, or the availability of fish. In such situations they turn to magic. "Magic is to be expected and generally to be found whenever man comes to an unbridgeable gap, a hiatus in his knowledge or in his powers of practical control, and yet has to continue in his pursuit [1958, p. 93]."

Religion, on the other hand, "is not born out of speculation or reflection, still less out of illusion or misapprehension, but rather out of the real tragedies of human life, out of the conflict between human plans and realities [Malinowski, 1958, p. 97]." Malinowski stressed religion's role in giving comfort to the individual at certain times during his life, particularly when he faced crises. "Primitive religion is largely concerned with the sacralization of the crises of human life. Conception, birth, puberty, marriage, as well as the supreme crisis death, all give rise to sacramental acts [1958, p. 99]."

Malinowski emphasized the roles of magic and religion in reducing anxiety. Magical solutions resolve anxiety which develops when events are beyond human control; religion provides a familiar way of getting through the crises of life and facing death.

Radcliffe-Brown and the social functions of ritual acts

While Malinowski stressed the roles of magic and religion as means of reducing anxiety, of allaying fears, the British social anthropologist A. R. Radcliffe-Brown (1965) argued for what he considered an opposite interpretation. He asserted that rites may actually create fears. Malinowski's theory, according to Radcliffe-Brown,

is based on a hypothesis as to the psychological function of a class of rites. The theory is that in certain circumstances the individual human being is anxious about the outcome of some event or activity because it depends to some extent on conditions that he cannot control by any technical means. He therefore observes some rite which, since he believes that it will insure good luck, serves to reassure him. . . .

I think that for certain rites it would be easy to maintain with equal plausibility an exactly contrary theory, namely, that if it were not for the existence of the rite and the beliefs associated with it the individual would feel no anxiety, and that the psychological effect of the rite is to create in him a sense of insecurity or danger [1965, pp. 148–149].

Radcliffe-Brown was being argumentative. In fact, there is no necessary incompatibility between his and Malinowski's interpretations; they are complementary. Different kinds of explanations may be given for the same rites in a society. From the point of view of the individual born into that society, raised within its cultural tradition, performance of the rite does relieve anxiety; often, it is the socially approved means of doing so. But Radcliffe-Brown was also right. In many cases, a kind of displaced anxiety may arise *because* a rite exists. As examples, Radcliffe-Brown discussed certain ritual acts he observed in the Andaman Islands, where he did fieldwork. The Andamanese customarily prohibit expectant parents from eating certain foods. The Andamanese also taboo the use by others of the personal names of the expectant father and mother. The individual may be anxious about carrying out culturally required ritual actions in the culturally appropriate way.

Radcliffe-Brown did not concern himself with distinguishing between magic and religion. His major interest was in specifying the social functions of certain rites and attitudes encountered among non-Western populations. Both he and Malinowski, however, were more concerned with the functions of religion in society than with its origin. Malinowski was interested in the psychological functions which magic and religion serve for the individual—allaying fears and anxiety. Radcliffe-Brown, on the other hand, was interested in the social functions of religion. For him, the social function of institutionalized behavior consisted of the part that behavior played in maintaining a stable orderly society.

Müller and naturism

Because of their concern with the functions of institutionalized behavior in human societies, both Malinowski and Radcliffe-Brown have been called *functionalists*. The nineteenth-century German linguist Max Müller (1878) emphasized the emotional aspects of religious experiences. Müller thought that the inception of religion lay in certain emotional attitudes. He argued that the genesis of religion lay in spontaneous emotional reactions, awe, for example, evoked in early humans by natural events. This school of thought is known as *naturism*. Imagine primitive man awakening one morning, looking up at the sun, and being filled with awe at this wonder of nature. Other natural phenomena presumably awe inspiring were the moon, the stars, and catastrophic events such as earthquakes, hurricanes, and volcanic eruptions. The naturists argued that early humans had begun to worship the sun and moon because of such spontaneous emotional reactions. This nature worship eventually became more complex, with the appearance of deities of thunder and lightning and a host of beings responsible for a myriad of natural events. There are, of course, several objections to Müller's explanation for the origin of religion. Why, we might ask, should early man experience fear and awe in the presence of that most ordinary of everyday sights—the sun?

Spencer and the ancestors

Herbert Spencer, nineteenth-century sociologist, also speculated in 1896 that the origin of religion was related to human emotions. For Spencer the earliest form of religion was ancestor worship, based on the continuing emotional involvement of living individuals with their departed kin. The major objection to this thesis is that ancestor worship is not normally associated with very simple societies. Most hunters and gatherers do not worship their human ancestors. The Australian aborigines hold ceremonies honoring totems, stipulated ancestors who are plants or animals rather than humans. Most hunters and gatherers do not even remember their ancestors more than two generations back. Ancestor worship is typically found in populations where descent groups are important. The ancestors of living members of the descent group once enjoyed access to the group's estate. One of them may be remembered as founder of that estate. Worship of the ancestors serves to reinforce the continuing solidarity of the descent group by creating a link between the world of the living and the world of the dead.

Freud and the incestuous horde

In a discussion of emotionalistic approaches to the origin of religion, we cannot omit Sigmund Freud. As you might imagine, Freud related the origin of religion to the Oedipus complex. In *Totem and Taboo*, first published in 1918, Freud developed a completely fictional picture of the social life of early man. He saw our prereligious, precultural ancestors as living within a social organization which we now recognize as similar in some respects to that of the baboon troop. An old man, a primitive patriarch, headed a group composed of women and their children. There was no incest taboo at this time, and the old man had sexual access to all females, including his own sisters and daughters. According to Freud, the patriarch's sons were deprived of access to women. Resenting this, sexually jealous of their father, they decided to unite and slay him. They did this, and then they ate him. The deed done, they immediately began to feel guilt and remorse. To atone for their sin, they created the incest taboo, eschewing their father's wives, their mothers and sisters, for women of different groups. And they did something else. They began to worship their father. At first they worshiped him in the form of a totem (Freud regarded the Australian aborigines as contemporary representatives of this stage). Annually, they held totemic ceremonies, in which they reenacted the original deed by ceremonially killing and eating their totem. The rest of the year there was a taboo against hunting or consuming the totem. Over time, according to Freud, the totemic substitute for the

father was replaced by a more accurate identification: God.

From information provided in Chapter 1, you know that there is no reason to suppose the social organization of early humans conformed to Freud's speculation. There are numerous other problems. As Malinowski argued, the Oedipus complex does not appear to be a cultural universal. Malinowski documented, on the basis of his work in the Trobriand Islands, that the resentment and strain often encountered in the father-son relationship in Western Europe is not a function of sexual jealousy but of the authority structure. In a patriarchal society, such as that in which Freud grew up, the father is the authoritarian figure. On the other hand, among the matrilineal Trobrianders, it is the mother's brother, male representative of ego's descent group on the first ascending generation, who is the authority figure. There is resentment and strain in this relationship, but the relationship between son and father, who are members of different descent groups, is free and easy and involves considerable affection.

Society worships itself

Many of the theories on religion which have just been discussed are psychological. They make reference to attempts by humans to explain the world, to the cognitive systems of different human groups, to their techniques for accomplishing individual ends, to their emotions, and to their psychological adjustment to the external world. The French sociologist Emile Durkheim argued that religion should be studied as a social rather than a psychological phenomenon. Durkheim thought that much could be learned about the origin of religion by examining the religious beliefs and practices of the most primitive contemporary human populations. Studying the present for clues to the past is known as the *comparative method*, and it has been much criticized by anthropologists. While the method, if used judiciously, can undoubtedly tell us something about the past, most anthropologists agree that Durkheim made a serious error in concentrating on the religion of the Australian Aborigines. The native Australians are hunters and gatherers employing a very rudimentary technology, and in this sense they are among the most primitive living populations. Nevertheless, many features of their social organization and religion are not at all typical of other contemporary hunters and gatherers.

Durkheim focused on totemism, important in the religions of aboriginal Australia. He argued that since the aborigines are otherwise so primitive, totemism must be the simplest form of religion. Totems are animals and plants, and, rarely, geographical features like rivers and the sky. Totemites assert that they are descended from this totem and customarily observe a taboo on killing or eating it. This taboo may be suspended once a year, when totemites assemble to take part in ceremonies dedicated to the totemic animal or plant. It is believed that these annual ceremonies are necessary for the maintenance and continued reproduction of the totemic population.

Durkheim offered an explanation for the origins of totemism, and, therefore, for religion. He asserted that the principal role of religious rites and beliefs is to affirm and thereby maintain the social solidarity of the adherents of that religion. When people worship their totem, a sacred emblem which symbolizes their common social identity, they are actually worshiping society—the moral and social order without which, according to Durkheim, individual life would be impossible. In Durkheim's argument, such a moral and social order is too abstract to be worshiped in itself. It is necessary to substitute something less abstract. Thus the totem. In totemic rites, people come together to worship their totem, which stands for their own social unity, and in so doing, they maintain that unity which the totem symbolizes. There is, as virtually everyone who has read Durkheim points out, a certain amount of circularity in his argument.

Radcliffe-Brown attempted a modification of Durkheim's interpretation of totem-

ism. Like Durkheim, who influenced his own anthropological approach, Radcliffe-Brown also viewed the annual ceremonies as functioning to maintain social solidarity and the social order. But his analysis is easier to grasp. Groups—subdivisions or segments of society—have different totems. The totems are animals and plants, which are part of nature. Humans are members of social groups; as such they relate themselves to nature through their totemic association with natural species. Each group has a different totem. Groups are thereby divided as are species of plants and animals. The natural order becomes a model for the social order. Yet although totemic plants and animals occupy different niches in nature, on another level they are united because all are part of nature. In the same way, social groups are united and made solidary in the social world of man. Thus the unity of the social order is preserved by symbolic association with, and imitation of, the natural order. Note that Radcliffe-Brown was again not interested in the origin of religion. He specifically avoided conjecture about the past. He was concerned with ascertaining the social functions of totemism and other religious practices and beliefs.

Demons, devolution, and degeneration

There is yet another approach to the origin of religion to be examined. It is theological, and would not belong in an anthropology text were it not for the fact that certain clerics have also been anthropologists. In many cases their religious preconceptions have influenced the ways in which they have interpreted data from different cultures. One of these clergymen-anthropologists was Father Wilhelm Schmidt, a Jesuit priest. Schmidt's anthropological theories on religion were influenced by Andrew Lang, whose own speculations about the origin of religion are contained in *The Making of Religion*, published in 1898. Lang's intent was to dispute assertions and assumptions of Tylor and other unilineal evolutionists that monolatry and monotheism were lacking in primitive cultures. Examining ethnographic data from different parts of the world, Lang concluded that *monolatry*, primary worship of a single god, if not *monotheism*, exclusive worship of a single, eternal, omniscient, omnipotent, and omnipresent god, was indeed characteristic of some primitive cultures.

An early twentieth-century school of Jesuit ethnologists known as the Kulturkreislehre and headed by Father Schmidt, followed Lang's lead, and, in so doing, brought Christianity right into anthropology. They argued that God had originally revealed himself to early man. Subsequently, the devil had been working against God. Where they were allowed to, diabolical forces modified the beliefs of certain primitives away from the true religion. This explains religious diversity. Kulturkreislehren argued that there had been a steady degeneration of monotheism until the Second Revelation, which was the coming of Christ, whereupon certain civilizations had adopted Christianity and had returned to the monotheistic fold. On the other hand, prior to the coming of Christ, and among non-Christian populations, there was a direct correlation between general evolutionary advance and the extent of digression from the original monotheism. The non-Christian populations whose religions were purest and truest would be the most primitive—the most isolated from degenerative influences.

Despite their mixture of orthodox Christianity with anthropology, it could be argued that these priest-anthropologists aided the comparative study of religion. Their major contribution seems to have been recognition of *devolution*, which they termed degeneration. There is no reason to suppose that religions cannot move from class A to class B to class A again, or from simple to complex to simple. What the anthropologist must do, when possible, is to specify the exact changes that have taken place and try to explain why they occurred.

The origin of religion remains foggy, but the origin of the degeneration theory is obvious. If, as Tylor argued, there had been evolution from animism through polytheism to monotheism and Christianity, this meant that religion could change—and had. For Christianity, which is held to be the "true" religion, the implications are obvious: degeneration provided an explanation for the existence of other "less true" religions.

Social Correlates and Functions of Religion

State religions

The functions of religious beliefs and practices vary with the society. Karl Marx called religion the opiate of the masses. This, however, cannot be a universal function of religion. For religion to serve thus, there must be masses; and there are masses only where there are elites, that is, in state-organized, stratified societies. One of the attributes of many archaic states is the existence of a state religion. Associated with the state religion are religious functionaries, often priests. The priesthood generally has elite status. Traditionally, in archaic civilizations with writing some or most members of the priesthood were literate. Thus priests functioned to preserve sacred lore and texts as well as more obviously utilitarian information. In ancient Mesopotamia, members of the priesthood kept records of agricultural production, exchanges, and other economic transactions.

In archaic states with writing, the priesthood was distinguished from the masses by virtue of its privileged access to sacred lore and, along with other members of the elite, to the skills necessary to record the history and culture of that society. In Chapter 4 a distinction was drawn between great and little traditions, the music and art of the elite as opposed to the folk arts of the masses. A similar distinction applies to religion. Though members of the priesthood often actively engaged in promoting state religion, folk religious beliefs and rites persisted in the countryside. Ancestor worship and beliefs in sacred attributes of certain spots in the countryside might exist alongside a monotheistic or polytheistic state religion.

On many occasions and in diverse populations, state religion has served as a means of supporting the state structure. Like the other attributes of state organization, state religion often functioned to maintain the general social order, including socioeconomic stratification. In this sense, Marx's observation that religion has been an opiate of the masses does apply. Subjugation, subordination, and slavery could be borne more easily if the unfortunate believed that there was an afterlife which held better things in store.

Religious doctrines can, then, serve as ideological struts of state organization, maintaining the status quo. However, this is not true in all states, for some of them lack state religions. The Merina of Madagascar provide an instructive example. During the eighteenth and nineteenth centuries they developed a state which covered approximately 150,000 square miles and ruled over approximately 2 million people. All the attributes of state organization mentioned previously were present, but not state religion. In the early nineteenth century Protestant missionaries began to arrive in Madagascar from England. They brought to the Merina elite writing skills and, naturally, religion. Christianity was rapidly accepted by members of the Merina nobility and promulgated among its subject population. So ripe was Madagascar for a state religion that today 5 million out of a total population of 7 million are nominal Christians—representing one of the most successful missionary endeavors in sub-Saharan Africa. Of course, as is true in other archaic states, elements of the prestate religions of Madagascar, ancestor worship and indigenous ceremonials, remain. Prospective missionaries take heed: if you are interested in quick acceptance of Christianity, try spreading it in an archaic state with no established state religion. Some of the same factors were probably involved in the rapid spread of Islam among archaic states in West Africa.

Religion and general evolution

Related to this discussion of state religions are Leslie White's observations about the evolution of religion in *The Evolution of Culture* (1959). White argues that there is a characteristic difference between the ideologies and pantheons of non–food-producing and food-producing populations. Foragers, according to White, generally have *zoomorphic* gods—animals and plants; or they may worship natural phenomena—the sun, moon, stars. On the other hand, as man gains greater control over his environment through food production, his greater mastery is reflected in his deities. Anthropomorphic gods appear. They are supermen and women who control certain natural phenomena, such as thunder and lightning, soil fertility, or the earth itself. White also discusses some of the attributes of state religions. In imperial, expansive states, according to White, gods serve as sacred arms of imperialism. There are gods of war or, as was the case during a certain epoch in ancient Egypt, gods of all the universe. The use of religion to justify the policies of nation-states has occurred throughout history. Religious fervor inspired Christians on crusades against the infidel and led Moslems to undertake *jihads*, holy wars against non-Islamic peoples. I can remember being told as a boy that God would not let the United States lose a war.

Is it possible to generalize about the relationship between religion and culture? White, Tylor, and others before them tried, as has Guy Swanson, a sociologist whose book *The Birth of the Gods* (1960) is one of the most carefully documented works on comparative religion. Swanson confirmed the hypothesis that there is a relationship between general evolutionary status and conceptualization of deities. Analyzing data from several societies, he found that there was a correlation between level of social complexity and belief in high gods. Generally, high gods, whose at-

tributes included omnipresence, omniscience, and omnipotence, were found in complex societies and were absent in primitive groups.

Swanson's work is important because it represents a quantitative and statistical approach to comparative religion. It demonstrates—in terms of one aspect of religious belief—what many anthropologists suspect, namely, that there is a general evolutionary relationship between social forms and certain religious forms. As you will see shortly, it is also possible to demonstrate relationships between religious beliefs and practices, on the one hand, and adaptation of human populations to their environments, on the other. In fact, later in this chapter religious behavior and ideology will be discussed as sociocultural means of adaptation to specific environments.

Religion and stability

Having examined several scholarly contributions to this study of religions, we may now summarize some of the functions that religion serves. From Tylor we know that religion can explain the unexplainable. Religious beliefs and doctrines function within cognitive systems of human populations. The supernatural doctrines of a population often provide solutions to problems and queries which cannot be solved in terms of ordinary experiences. Religious

doctrines provide explanations for individual success or failure. As Malinowski contended, religion also functions to allay anxieties and fears of individuals. Yet the existence of rites and ritual prohibitions which must be performed or observed in prescribed ways itself creates fears and anxieties which can be allayed only through ritual observance.

As Durkheim, Radcliffe-Brown, and Marx pointed out, religion functions to maintain the social order. For Durkheim and Radcliffe-Brown, common religious sentiments and ritual activity promote and maintain social solidarity and thus preserve the cohesion of society. Marx wrote about nation-states in which religion functioned to maintain a stratified social order, to discourage rebellion against, and questioning of, the social and economic order.

It is obvious that religion creates and maintains social solidarity; yet perhaps less obvious is the fact that it also creates and maintains divisions. In a population subdivided into multiple social groups on the basis of religion, there may be conflict. You are familiar with social divisions between Christians and Jews, Catholics and Protestants, in your own society. You have heard about the conflict between Protestants and Catholics in Northern Ireland, between Jews and Moslems in Palestine, and, of course, between other religious groups in other places and at other times. Often, religious divisions are institutionalized, as they are, for example, in the different totems of the Australian aborigines. Other social ties also link members of different groups and discourage the outbreak of hostilities between religious affiliations.

Religion and change

The role of religion in maintaining the established social order has been stressed above. However, religion may also be an instrument of change, sometimes even of revolution. The anthropologists Ralph Linton (1943) and particularly Anthony F. C. Wallace (1956, 1966, 1970) have examined such religious phenomena, which Linton called *nativistic movements* and Wallace, *revitalization movements*. Especially in times of rapid social change, religious leaders may emerge and undertake to alter or revitalize a society in some way. Jesus Christ, for example, was one of several prophets who preached new religious doctrines while the Near East was under Roman rule. All such doctrines represented rearrangements of preexisting religious doctrines, but usually with some new overall orientation. This was a time when foreign powers ruled the land, a time of social unrest and upheaval. Christ, of course, succeeded in inspiring a new, enduring, and major religion; his contemporaries were not so successful.

Wallace (1966) has recounted the genesis in 1799 of the Handsome Lake religion among the Iroquois Indians of New York State. Handsome Lake, the prophet and founder of the revitalization movement, was a chief of the Seneca, one of the Iroquois tribes. By the end of the eighteenth century the Iroquois had been adversely affected by their support of the French against the British during the French and Indian war. Warfare and the British victory produced a major change in the Iroquois environment. To accommodate expanding European colonization, the Iroquois were dispersed among several small reservations. Unable to pursue their traditional way of life, horticulture and hunting, in their ancestral homeland, they became heavy drinkers and frequently quarreled among themselves.

Handsome Lake himself had been a drunkard until he began to receive a series of visions which he and his followers believed to be from heavenly messengers. He related his visions and the supernatural messages they contained to his fellow tribesmen. The spirits had told him that unless the Iroquois changed their ways, they would eventually suffer total destruction. Handsome Lake's visions contained specific moral injunctions to be followed if destruction was to be averted, a plan for adjusting to the new moral and social order. Witchcraft, quarreling, and drinking were to be forsaken. The Iroquois were told to copy the white man's farming techniques, which, unlike traditional Iroquois horticulture, stressed male rather than female work in the fields. Furthermore, Handsome Lake preached that his fellow tribesmen should abandon the communal houses and matrilineal descent groups of their ancestors in favor of more permanent marriages and residence in individual family households. The teachings of Handsome Lake formed the basis for a new church and a new religion, one which still has adherents in New York and Ontario. As a result of this revitalization movement, the Iroquois survived in a drastically modified environment and have gained a reputation among their non-Indian neighbors as sober family farmers.

Events in the life of Handsome Lake were recorded by missionaries who actually witnessed the formation of the new religion as well as by his own followers. Recalled only in myth is another Iroquois revitalization movement which, according to Wallace, took place around 1450. The name of its leader and prophet—Hiawatha —is probably familiar to you. According to myth, Hiawatha lived at a time of great social conflict, of blood feud and warfare among different Iroquois tribes. Hiawatha's wife and children were killed by raiders; thereafter he took refuge in the forest and became a cannibal, preying on travelers. Like other revitalization leaders, Hiawatha underwent moral regeneration as a result of contact with a deity, an Iroquois god born to a virgin mother. Hiawatha became the spokesman of the deity and traveled from village to village attempting to establish intertribal peace. According to myth, Hiawatha was responsible for the formation of a political confederation by the formerly warring tribes, the famous League of the Iroquois. The five major tribes, whose members spoke related languages and had similar cultural traditions, thereafter settled grievances through compensation rather than the blood feud. Later, during the seventeenth and eighteenth centuries, the league provided a basis of political unity for the Iroquois in their dealings with the European invaders.

Taboos and Adaptation

Some of the functions which religious beliefs and practices may serve for societies and for individuals have already been indicated. Religion will now be approached from a different point of view. The remainder of this chapter will be concerned with what religion does for humans as *biological* organisms. That is, what functions do beliefs and rituals serve in the adaptations of human populations to specific environments?

Totems and taboos

Consider first interpretations of food taboos, important religious prohibitions in many human populations. In interpreting the totemism of the Australian aborigines, Durkheim and Radcliffe-Brown attempted to show its role in maintaining social solidarity. Might totemism also aid Australian populations in adapting to their natural environment? Noting that different social groups have taboos on killing and consuming different plants and animals, an anthropologist might investigate the possibility

that such a system of taboos functions as a primitive conservation device. Might not taboos protect certain species otherwise in danger of dying out? Could not annual ceremonies during which totemic animals are killed be a means of reducing these same animal populations if their increase has been too rapid? Since, as far as I know, no one has attempted an investigation of the ecological functions of totemism to test these hypotheses, it is impossible to assess the ecological relevance of Australian totemism.

The adaptive significance of sacred cattle in India

The adaptive significance of a ritual prohibition against slaughter and consumption of a certain animal is more easily demonstrable, however, in the case of India's sacred zebu cattle. Indian cattle are protected by the Hindu doctrine known as *ahimsa*, which prohibits the consumption of beef. Several anthropologists, economic developers, and economists have cited this taboo as an example of the extent to which the non-Westerner is culture bound. After all, these individuals are ignoring a potentially valuable economic resource because of cultural or religious traditions, when, as any American knows, beef is not only good but nourishing. The economic developers also tell us that Indians do not know how to raise proper cattle. To illustrate their contention they point to the scraggly beasts, the Indian zebus, that wander about in town and country. Western techniques of animal husbandry, they assert, could certainly improve the size of Indian cattle, yielding more beef and more milk. But, they lament, the Indian is set in his ways. Bound by culture and tradition, he will not change.

An anthropologist could identify errors in these assumptions and thereby warn the economic developers against potentially disastrous interference in an Indian ecosystem which represents the present culmination of millenniums of specific evolution. In his article "The Cultural Ecology of India's Sacred Cattle," Marvin Harris

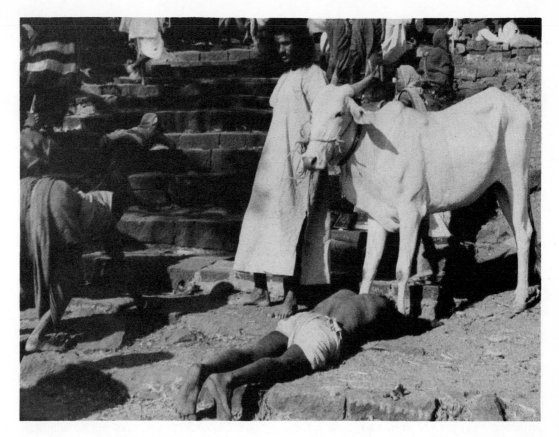

An Indian worshipper prostrates himself before a sacred zebu while women crawl up the steps to a shrine. *(P. R. Shinde/Black Star)*

(1966) demonstrated some of the adaptive functions of ahimsa. Most Indian peasants are poor agriculturalists. They use some of their cattle—bullocks—as draft animals to pull plows and carts. In short, the use of cattle as cultivating machines is an essential part of the technology of traditional Indian agriculture. Thin cattle pull plows and carts well enough, yet they do not eat the peasant out of house and home. The larger animals that many European developers want Indians to breed would require more food per animal. But how could an Indian peasant, whose diet is already marginal and whose land, and therefore productive potential, is limited, feed a supersteer unless he took food away from himself and his family?

Furthermore, Indians collect a portion of the dung from their cattle and use it to manure their fields. Not all dung is collected, however, since Indians do not carefully superintend their cattle, but allow them to wander around the countryside during certain seasons. As they wander, the zebus deposit dung. When the rains come, some of the dung from the hillsides is swept into fields below. Cattle, therefore, are employed directly and indirectly as fertilizing machines. India's supplies of fuel coal are very low. What do Indians use for warmth and to cook their food? Again the sacred cow is the answer. Slow-burning, dry cattle dung is one of India's most basic cooking fuels.

Far from being economically useless, the sacred cow is, in fact, vital to the Indian ecosystem. Biologically adapted to poor pasture land and a marginal environment, the zebu provides fertilizer and fuel, is indispensable in farming, but can still be supported by the peasant. There are good ecological reasons for maintaining the religious doctrine of ahimsa. It is a sociocultural means of adaptation to the Indian environment.

Yams for the ancestors

Another frequently cited example of economically irrational, culture-bound behavior is based on ethnographic data from Melanesia. The yam-growing horticulturalists of the Trobriand Islands customarily overproduce. They plant, weed, and harvest more yams than they can possibly eat. At harvest time, they consecrate surplus yams to the ancestors and store them in a yam house, where they are left to rot. Westerners have regarded this cultural practice as irrational behavior. We all know that gods and dead ancestors cannot eat yams. Clearly Trobrianders overproduce because they are slaves to their cultural rules, to their religious beliefs.

But wait, says the ecologically oriented anthropologist. Might seemingly irrational production of more yams than can possibly be eaten be a means of adaptation to the environment? To answer this question, long-term study would be necessary. However, on the basis of what we already know about the Trobrianders, the argument would seem to have some merit. It turns out that most years bring good harvests to the Trobrianders, and there are sufficient yams for the ancestors. But islands are particularly vulnerable to environmental fluctuations such as drought and natural disasters such as typhoons. At least once every ten years a drought destroys a good portion of the normal Trobriand yam crop. In these lean years, people have only a token sacrifice to give to the gods. Yet they cannot anticipate when they plant how large a crop they are going to get. If conditions are normal, they will have a surplus for the ancestors. If not, they will slight the ancestors that year but still have enough yams to eat themselves. This practice, then, may be viewed as a cultural means of adaptation to minimal conditions, conditions that are not present every year but only occasionally. Yet if the people gave it up, they would face starvation when the limiting event took place.

Another aspect of Trobriand culture illustrates adaptation to minimal conditions. In Trobriand sociopolitical organization, there is a rudimentary distinction between chiefs and commoners. Certain foods are tabooed to commoners. Yet in times of drought, the taboo is relaxed, and commoners have access along with the chiefs to such foods. The ecological interpretation of this taboo is that it is a means of keeping a food reserve for times of need, of preventing overexploitation under ordinary conditions, and of regulating, over time, the relationship between the Trobriand population and its environment.

Ritual regulation of population size

It is possible to suggest ecological functions for many other ritual injunctions besides food taboos. Taboos may act to maintain population size at a fairly constant level. Throughout the primitive world various forms of infanticide are ritually sanctioned. But there are other taboos which also appear to limit population size. In many cultures sexual intercourse is proscribed while a mother is still nursing an infant. Common, too, are taboos on sexual relations prior to hunting or raiding parties. Sometimes, cultural traditions seem to carry this kind of taboo to maladaptive extremes. Recall the homosexual tribes of the Trans-Fly region of New Guinea. The Etoro, one of the most inappropriately named tribes in the lore of anthropology, observe a taboo on heterosexual intercourse 295 days out of the year. Homosexuality is the culture's sexual preference. There is every indication that the Etoro population is falling rapidly. Perhaps the taboo started out as a means of maintaining population size, but the sexual preference which it eventually engendered has led to widening of the taboo and now threatens to bring the Etoro to a biological end.

Some cases in which ritual action serves a function in mediating relationships between human populations and their immediate environments will now be examined. In the previous section the emphasis was on ideology; here it is on behavior. Of course, people engage in specific rituals because they hold certain beliefs. But in the following discussion the ecologically relevant results of these rituals, rather than the beliefs that underlie them, will be emphasized.

Betsileo ceremonial

The first example comes from my fieldwork among the Betsileo. The Betsileo grow wet rice, using cattle as draft animals in its cultivation. The Betsileo settlement pattern is one of dispersed hamlets and villages. Formerly, hamlets were small settlements with an average of two or three households, but over time many have grown into villages. There are ancestral tombs in all Betsileo settlements.

The tomb is extremely important to the Betsileo; its construction usually represents a much larger investment of capital than a house. After all, the Betsileo say, it is right to spend more on the tomb for this is where one spends eternity. One's house, on the other hand, is a temporary residence. A Betsileo has the culturally recognized right to be buried in the same tomb as any one of his eight great-grandparents. If a Betsileo woman bears her husband children, she also has the right to be buried in his tomb, and most wives are. Most Betsileo men affiliate with their father's descent group, live in his village, and are buried in the tomb of their agnates. However, throughout their lives Betsileo participate in ceremonials involving all the tombs of their ancestors, because they have potential rights to be buried in all of them.

There are several kinds of Betsileo ceremonials which focus on the tomb. Most rice is harvested in April and May. The Malagasy winter, our summer, the time of year when agricultural work is least, is the ceremonial season. The major ceremonials honor the ancestors. The Betsileo open their tombs and do one of two things: simply rewrap the corpses and bones of their ancestors in new shrouds; or remove

The ceremonial opening of a Betsileo tomb. *(Conrad P. Kottak)*

all the corpses and bones from the tomb, dance awhile with them, and then wrap them in new shrouds and return them to their beds in the tomb. When a new tomb is constructed, ancestral remains are moved to it from one or more of the old tombs. Transfer of remains is also a winter activity.

During these ceremonials, cattle are slaughtered, and a part of the meat is offered to the ancestors. The participants in the ceremonial consume the rest. After the beef has been consecrated to the ancestors, the living remove it from the ancestral altar and eat it, too.

The ceremonial slaughter of cattle evolved among the Betsileo at a time when there were no markets in Betsileo country and population was dispersed among small hamlets. It is in this context that we must seek its ecological origin. Though cattle are used for sacrifice, they still provide animal protein important in Betsileo nutrition. In the past, such ceremonial events represented the only source of beef available to the Betsileo. It was not feasible to slaughter and consume a whole steer in a small hamlet. There were simply too few people to eat it up. Betsileo could not buy meat in markets. They obtained meat by attending ceremonials in villages where they had ancestral connections, relations by marriage, or fictive kinship.

Betsileo also slaughter cattle in a ceremonial context when there are funerals. Again, part is dedicated to the ancestors and eventually consumed by the living. Betsileo have the right to attend funerals of neighbors, kinsmen, relatives by marriage, and fictive kinsmen. Because the funerary slaughter of cattle takes place throughout the year, Betsileo have access to beef and thus to necessary animal protein on a fairly constant basis.

Although deaths occur throughout the year, they tend to cluster in certain seasons, and especially from November to February. This is the rainy season. It is also a lean period, because the rice stored in the granary following the harvest in March or April has dwindled and, for some peasants, may be virtually exhausted. Of interest to the study of Betsileo ecology is the fact that a large number of funerals, occasions on which beef and rice are distributed ceremonially, occur at precisely that time of the year when Betsileo are hungriest. Funerals tide people through the lean season.

Related to the ceremonial slaughter of beef at funerals is another Betsileo ceremonial. Traditionally, when a Betsileo gets sick, he, or a close kinsman, consults a curer. The curer normally prescribes some native medicine. If the health of the afflicted individual does not improve, and if ancestral displeasure is diagnosed as the cause of the illness, the curer may advise the household head to slaughter one of his cattle as an offering of appeasement. To this event he invites kinsmen, affinals, fictive kinsmen, and neighbors. Again, sicknesses cluster in the hungry period; some may be nutritional in origin, others involve greater susceptibility to disease because of nutritional inadequacies. The ceremonial distribution of beef and rice as a response to illness is also a means of getting the Betsileo through the lean season.

Today, though Betsileo settlements are larger and there are now markets in the Betsileo homeland, the ceremonials persist. However, I am told that there are fewer big winter ceremonials now than in previous years. Naturally, any discussion of the ecological functions of Betsileo ceremonials raises the question of whether Betsileo began the ceremonials because they recognized these functions. The question is instructive. The answer is that Betsileo take part in these ceremonials to honor, commemorate, or appease their ancestors, relatives, fictive kinsmen, affines, and neighbors. However, each Betsileo has the right to attend several ceremonials throughout the year. He chooses to attend some ceremonials but not others. If a distant kinsman or acquaintance dies at a time of the year when his granary is full and he is eating well, he might decide not to go. On the other hand, if an equally distant kinsman dies during the lean period, our

Betsileo may decide that he would enjoy nothing more than a day or two of communal feasting on rice and beef, with a little Malagasy rum thrown in. Some of my Betsileo informants, usually those with small parcels of land, were veritable funeral hoppers during the lean season, activating virtually all of their personal ties to attend funerals and other ritual events throughout the countryside.

Ritual regulation of environmental relations

Roy Rappaport has documented another example of the ecological functions of ritual action. Rappaport conducted fieldwork among the Tsembaga Maring of the highlands of New Guinea. In his book *Pigs for the Ancestors* (1968) and in several articles (1967, 1971), he has been concerned with the ecological significance of their ceremonial slaughter of pigs. He points out that the ritual slaughter of pigs functions within two levels of ecosystems in which Tsembaga Maring are involved: The first level is the *local ecosystem*, consisting of the Tsembaga, their territory, and its flora and fauna; the second, a wider or *regional ecosystem*, consisting of the Tsembaga and other Maring groups, along with the territory and flora and fauna of a wider geographical region. Rappaport focuses attention on the Maring as a human ecological population jointly participating with other, nonhuman populations in these ecosystems.

Some of the ways in which Maring ritual functioned in local and regional ecosystems may now be examined. Until the Australian government brought them under control in 1962, the Maring, like the Yanomamo but with less intensity, engaged in intratribal warfare. That is, Maring groups such as the Tsembaga warred on other Maring, generally their neighbors. Usually, a period of fighting between two Maring groups ended in a truce. Occasionally, however, one group prevailed, and the other vacated its ancestral territory.

When the fighting ended, either because a truce had been established or one group had withdrawn, the group or groups remaining in ancestral territory performed a

ceremonial act known as planting the rumbim plant. Associated with this was a ceremonial slaughter of most of the group's pig herd. In fact, all nonjuvenile pigs were slaughtered. Their meat was distributed among the allies of the group, to repay them for their aid in war. The slaughter also had a ritual dimension. The Tsembaga believed that they were killing pigs to repay their ancestors for military assistance.

But their obligations to their ancestors and allies were not fulfilled by this pig feast. When they planted the rumbim, the Tsembaga vowed to the ancestors that they would hold a *kaiko*, a larger pig festival, when the pig herd was once again sufficiently numerous. This could take as long as twenty years.

The kaiko was more a ritual period than a single feast; pigs were slaughtered ceremonially throughout the year of the kaiko. The period terminated when the people uprooted the rumbim. By doing this, they signalled that they had repaid their ancestors and their allies. They also were ready to fight again. A Maring group might not engage in hostilities with another group as long as the rumbim remained in the ground. Rappaport argues that this interdiction on battle until the ancestors were repaid served to limit the frequency of hostilities among the Maring. Thus it functioned to introduce periods of relative peace within a society which lacked state organization. Recalling the Yanomamo, we might speculate that they could benefit from such a ritual device.

This function of the pig festival was significant within the regional ecosystem because it regulated interrelationships between different Maring groups. However, the local ecosystem must be examined in order to ascertain what factors determined when the kaiko was held and also to discover how the local ecosystem articulated with the regional ecosystem. In addition to the ceremonial slaughter of large numbers of pigs, the Maring also killed individual pigs when members of their group fell ill or were injured. Rappaport argues that illness and injury bring physiological and psychological stress to the individual and increase his protein needs. The afflicted individual and members of his own and related households consumed the pork. Not only did it contribute to the recovery of the sick individual if his illness had nutritional origins, it also made available high quality animal protein to those closest to him. If his own diet had been inadequate, it is likely that the diets of individuals whose crops came from the same or nearby gardens were also deficient. Remember that there is an analogous custom involving cattle among the Betsileo.

The rate of increase in the pig herd was affected by ritual demands of this sort. The pig herds of healthier populations increased faster. Maring women fed the pigs substandard tubers from their gardens. Pigs were allowed to roam through the village and its territory during the day; they were collected at night. As the pig herd grew, Maring found that there were simply not enough substandard tubers for their pigs to eat. They were forced to take some of the tubers destined for human consumption and give them to pigs. They were also forced to plant additional plots to satisfy the dietary needs of the human population. At this point, the Maring, especially Maring women, were working for the pigs.

Another problem arose as the pig herd grew. Pigs began to invade gardens. Again they were competing with humans for food. The owner of the garden might shoot a pig that had ravaged his crops. The pig's owner might then shoot the garden owner, his wife, or his pig.

At this point disputes between inhabitants of the same village were frequent. Women were also complaining to their husbands that they had more pigs than they could handle. Horticultural labor demands had increased. It was time for the kaiko. Usually, it was the women's complaints and demands for a kaiko that led their husbands to meet to plan the festival. The men issued invitations to their allies. The kaiko lasted a year. During this time, groups of allies arrived in the territory of the local group; they danced; they traded; they arranged marriages. They ate pork and took it home to their own local groups. Once all but the juvenile pigs had been sacrificed to the ancestors, the men uprooted the rumbim. They could now engage in war again.

You now have enough information to understand the role of the ritual cycle in regulating the relationship between humans and their environment in the larger,

SUMMARY

Religion, a cultural universal, designates human belief in supernatural beings, powers, and forces, and ritual behavior associated with such belief. Speculation about the origin of religion was a dominant concern of early anthropologists. Although it is impossible to discover when, why, and how religion first appeared, the comparative studies of early anthropologists help us to understand some of the functions of religion in varied sociocultural contexts. Edward Tylor speculated that the most rudimentary form of religion was animism, belief in souls. For Tylor, religion functioned principally to explain, and it evolved from animism through polytheism to monotheism. He believed that as science provided better explanations for things and events, religion would decrease in importance and eventually disappear. R. R. Marett disputed Tylor's contention that belief in spiritual beings was the most elementary form of religious conception. Instead, he speculated that animatism,

regional ecosystem. Once it uprooted the rumbim, the local group could occupy any territory vacated by its adversaries in the last fighting period. Planting rumbim was a way of validating a claim to a territory. Since the adversary had vacated its territory, it was unable to plant rumbim. Its members had dispersed into other local groups, where they had joined kinsmen and affines. By this time, they might have participated with members of their new local groups in rumbim planting. According to Rappaport, "if one of a pair of antagonistic groups is able to uproot its rumbim before its opponents can plant their rumbim, it may occupy the latter's territory [1967, p. 26]." The Maring believed that the ancestors of the vanquished group, like the group itself, had left its former territory. Among the Maring, then, the ritual cycle gradually functioned to adjust the distribution of the human population over Maring territory.

The Ecological Approach

By adopting an ecological approach, anthropologists have been able to suggest new interpretations for religious beliefs and practices. More important, the ecological approach focuses attention on the human population as a biological unit. It demands that we consider basic biological variables. It places man in the animal kingdom and shows that many of the laws and generalizations which apply to other animals also apply to man. By taking a new look at many practices formerly regarded as irrational and wasteful, ecological anthropology has shown that principles of Darwinian evolution apply to the study of social as well as physiological development in man. Taking specific human populations as units of analysis and focusing on their local and regional ecosystems, ecological anthropologists have been able to identify sociocultural means—ritual, for example— whereby these populations adapt to their environments.

Of course, not all sociocultural traits are adaptive. However, it is possible to evaluate whether a trait is adaptive or maladaptive with reference to biological and demographic variables. If a population is dying out because of some aspect of its culturally determined behavior, that aspect of behavior can well be called maladaptive. On the other hand, there are many more cases of traits that anthropologists formerly called economically wasteful or irrational, but which turn out to have a specific, demonstrable, selectively determined, and maintained function in adaptation.

conceptualization of the supernatural as a domain of raw, impersonal power which under certain conditions could be controlled, was more fundamental. James Frazer argued that religion evolved out of magic, attempts by primitives to control the supernatural through rites and spells. Bronislaw Malinowski argued that magic originated as an attempt to deal with potentially hazardous situations over which humans had no control. Religion, he argued, surrounded major life crises—birth, puberty, marriage, and death—and functioned to relieve anxiety caused by transitions from one life condition to another. Another functionalist anthropologist, A. R. Radcliffe-Brown, disputed Malinowski's contention. According to Radcliffe-Brown, the existence of customary rites and observances actually created anxiety—anxiety that only the observance of these rites could dispel. Both Malinowski and Radcliffe-Brown were addressing themselves to the psychological functions of religion. Naturism, another school which attempted to explain the origin of religion, also invoked psychological variables, linking the origin of religion to spontaneous emotional reactions by early humans to the sun, moon, stars, and so forth.

Sociologist Herbert Spencer believed that religion originated as ancestor worship. Sigmund Freud related the origin of religion to the origin of the incest taboo and to what he believed was universal guilt. Eschewing individual psychology, French sociologist Emile Durkheim offered a sociological approach to the origin of religion, considering the totemism of native Australians the most elementary religious form.

Though the reasons for the origin or origins of religious behavior will never be known, anthropologists, through their comparative research, have demonstrated several of the correlates and functions of religion. Swanson and others have demonstrated relationships between religious forms and general evolutionary status. Religion's role in social change has been clarified.

Sources and Suggested Readings

CODRINGTON, R. H.
  1891   *The Melanesians: Studies in Their Anthropology and Folklore.* Oxford: Clarendon Press. Early, very rich account of tribal life and customs in the South Pacific.

COHEN, Y. A., ed.
  1971   *Man in Adaptation: The Institutional Framework.* Chicago: Aldine. Best reader in cultural anthropology available; many articles relate to the analysis of ritual.

DURKHEIM, E.
  1961   (orig. 1912). *The Elementary Forms of the Religious Life.* New York: Collier Books. Major figure in French sociology and social anthropology tried to find the most primitive form of religion among the Australian Aborigines, and in doing so developed a sociological analysis of religion which has influenced anthropologists Radcliffe-Brown, Lévi-Strauss, and many others.

EVANS-PRITCHARD, E. E.
  1965   *Theories of Primitive Religion.* Oxford: Clarendon Press. View of primitive religion by British social anthropologist.

FRAZER, J. G.
  1911–1915 *The Golden Bough: A Study of Magic and Religion.* 3rd ed. 2 vols. London: Macmillan. Monumental collection of data from around the world on religion, myth, magic, and other rituals. The abridged version is recommended.

FREUD, S.
  1950   (orig. 1918). *Totem and Taboo,* translated by J. Strachey. New York: W. W. Norton. Links the origin of religion to primeval patricide guilt, and the origin of the incest taboo.

GEERTZ, C.
  1960   *The Religion of Java.* New York: The Free Press. Sensitive portrayal of religion in Indonesia.

HARRIS, M.
  1966   The Cultural Ecology of India's Sacred Cattle. *Current Anthropology* 7: 51–66. Adaptive functions of the Hindu doctrine of *ahimsa.*

LANG, A.
  1898   *The Making of Religion.* London: Longmans Green. The place of high gods in primitive religion.

LESSA, W. A., and VOGT, E. Z., eds.
  1972   *Reader in Comparative Religion: An Anthropological Approach.* 3rd ed. New York: Harper and Row. Major articles in the anthropology of religion.

LINTON, R.
  1943   Nativistic Movements. *American Anthropologist* 45: 230–240. The use of religion to forge social solidarity in times of crisis, particularly of social change.

MAIR, L.
  1969   *Witchcraft.* New York: McGraw-Hill. Good analysis of social contexts and functions of witchcraft and witchcraft

While anthropologists have traditionally stressed functions of religion for individuals and for societies, religious beliefs and practices also function in the adaptation of human populations to their environments. For example, ecological explanations have been offered for several food taboos and for cultural rules that serve to control population size.

The effects of ritual action on ecology have also been described. Among the Betsileo of Madagascar several rituals centered around tombs maintain stable relationships between a human population and its environment. Ritual involving the cere-monial slaughter of pigs among the Tsembaga Maring of New Guinea also demonstrates the function of ritual prohibitions in regulating such ecological relationships. While ecological explanations are not the only or even necessarily the best explanations for religious behavior, they do serve to place in comparative, evolutionary terms many practices that hitherto have been called irrational. In this way they serve to increase our respect for the diversity of human customs.

accusations; relies heavily on African data.

MALEFIJT, A. DE WAAL
1968   *Religion and Culture: An Introduction to the Anthropology of Religion.* New York: Macmillan. Historical survey of anthropological studies of religion.

MALINOWSKI, B.
1920   Kula; the Circulating Exchange of Valuables in the Archipelagoes of Eastern New Guinea. *Man* 51: 97–105. Role of ritual in the kula ring, an exchange system.

1927   *Sex and Repression in Savage Society.* London: International Library of Psychology, Philosophy and Scientific Method. Role of the father and ignorance of physiological paternity among the matrilineal Trobrianders.

1948   *Magic, Science and Religion, and Other Essays.* Boston: Beacon Press. Includes distinctions between and discussions of science, magic, and religion.

1958   (orig. 1931). The Role of Magic and Religion. In *Reader in Comparative Religion: An Anthropological Approach,* ed. W. A. Lessa and E. Z. Vogt, pp. 86–99. Evanston, Ill.: Row, Peterson. Differences between functions of magic and religion.

1961   (orig. 1922). *Argonauts of the Western Pacific.* New York: Dutton. Myth and ritual in sailing and on the land.

MARETT, R. R.
1909   *The Threshold of Religion.* London: Methuen. Argues that animatism is the most primitive form of religion, and examines its expression in several societies.

MIDDLETON, J., ed.
1967a   *Gods and Rituals.* Garden City, N.Y.: The Natural History Press. Articles on religion by anthropologists.

1967b   *Magic, Witchcraft and Curing.* Garden City, N.Y.: The Natural History Press. Articles on sorcery, witchcraft, dreams, curing, and divination in several societies.

1967c   *Myth and Cosmos.* Garden City, N.Y.: The Natural History Press. Articles on symbolism, myth, and aspects of world view.

MÜLLER, F. M.
1878   *Lectures on the Origin and Growth of Religion.* London: Longmans Green. A naturist views religions in different societies.

NORBECK, E.
1961   *Religion in Primitive Society.* New York: Harper and Row. Introduction to the anthropology of religion; discussions of major theorists are balanced with case analysis.

RADCLIFFE-BROWN, A. R.
1964   (orig. 1922). *The Andaman Islanders.* New York: The Free Press. Field study of role of religious observances

and ceremonies in maintaining social solidarity.

1965   (orig. 1952). *Structure and Function in Primitive Society.* New York: The Free Press. Includes essays on totemism and taboo.

RAPPAPORT, R. A.

1967   Ritual Regulations of Environmental Relations among a New Guinea People. *Ethnology* 6: 17–30. Ecological interpretation of ceremonial slaughter of pigs in a highland New Guinea society.

1968   *Pigs for the Ancestors: Ritual in the Ecology of a New Guinea People.* New Haven: Yale University Press. Demonstrates the role of ritual in regulation of local and regional ecosystems; also includes impressive field data on diet and work.

1971   Ritual, Sanctity and Cybernetics. *American Anthropologist* 73: 59–76. General theoretical treatment of some of the ecological and other functions of ritual and various aspects of religion.

SCHMIDT, W.

1931   *The Origin and Growth of Religion,* translated by H. J. Rose. London: Methuen. Extreme diffusionist approach to comparative religion, written by a cleric.

SPENCER, H. L.

1896   (orig. 1876). *Principles of Sociology.* 3 vols. London: Williams and Norgate. This nineteenth-century sociologist includes speculations about the origin of religion.

SWANSON, G. E.

1960   *The Birth of the Gods: The Origin of Primitive Beliefs.* Ann Arbor: University of Michigan Press. Statistical approach to comparative religion; demonstrates relationship between general evolutionary type and conceptualization of high gods.

TYLOR, E. B.
1873 *Primitive Culture: Researches into the Development of Mythology, Philosophy, Religion, Language, Art, and Custom.* 2nd ed. 2 vols. London: John Murray. In the second volume of this classic, Tylor offers a minimal definition of religion as belief in spiritual beings, and examines animism in several societies.

WAGLEY, C.
1968 (orig. 1943). Tapirapé Shamanism. In *Readings in Anthropology.* 2nd ed., vol. 2, ed. M. H. Fried, pp. 617–635. New York: Crowell. Case analysis of behavior of practicing shamans among an Indian tribe in interior Brazil.

1969 (orig. 1951). Cultural Influences on Population: A Comparison of Two Tupi Tribes. In *Environment and Cultural Behavior,* ed. A. P. Vayda, pp. 268–279. Garden City, N.Y.: The Natural History Press. Supernatural sanctions are important in the popu-

lation policy of the Tapirapé, one of the two tribes discussed.

WALLACE, A. F. C.
1956 Revitalization Movements. *American Anthropologist* 58: 264–281. Religious movements as means of revitalization of societies at times of social crisis.

1966 *Religion: An Anthropological View.* New York: Random House. Excellent survey of anthropological approaches to religion.

1970 *Culture and Personality.* 2nd ed. New York: Random House. Revitalization movements and some of the psychological functions of religion.

WHITE, L. A.
1959 *The Evolution of Culture.* New York: McGraw-Hill. Relates religious conceptions to general evolutionary type of society.

11. Diversity in Language

The Origin of Language

Communication systems of subhuman primates

Language has been cited by many students of human behavior as one of the distinctive attributes of man. While it is true that only humans speak languages, evidence is accumulating that man's linguistic ability represents a quantitative rather than a qualitative difference between him and other primates, especially the great apes.

Among no other living hominoid population has anything approaching the complexity of human languages evolved. Yet observations of the natural communication systems of chimpanzees and other primates are revealing a far greater complexity in verbal signals than was once supposed. Furthermore, while no chimpanzee or other nonhuman primate has been taught to talk—that is, to speak a human language—recent research has shown that chimps at least have the ability to understand and to manipulate nonverbal symbols based on human language. Chimpanzees and perhaps other hominoids as well share with man, apparently through genetic inheritance from their common ancestor, a tendency toward linguistic ability, toward complex communication systems. Among contemporary great apes, the tendency is present only in rudimentary form. In the course of human evolution, the communication systems of our ancestors gradually became more and more complex and eventually turned into language.

Since the communication systems of our remote ancestors are not preserved in the fossil record, it is impossible to know when they first began to qualify as language. Although speculation about the origin of language can never be conclusive, there is every reason to assume that the hominids which gave rise to man gradually perfected the tendency toward complexity in communication into true language.

Nonhuman primates communicate through *call systems*. Anthropologist Jane van Lawick Goodall has identified at least twenty-five distinct calls used by chimpanzees living in the Gombe Stream Reserve in Tanzania. Though she was able to classify these calls into seven categories, depending on the broad situations that evoked them, each of the twenty-five carried a distinct message. Goodall noted the situations that evoked each call and the responses of other chimpanzees to a given message. She also noted that, like other nonhuman primates and man, chimpanzees communicate both verbally and nonverbally, through a rich array of facial expressions and bodily movements.

Observations of gibbons, macaques, and other primates demonstrate that they, too, communicate through a limited number of acoustically distinct calls evoked by environmental stimuli. The calls convey discrete messages to other members of the primate's species—his *conspecifics*. There is a question concerning the extent to which nonhuman primate calls are instinctive or learned. Many of them—for example, those uttered by macaques when threatening conspecifics and those emitted by gibbons in situations of danger—may be varied in intensity. Variation in intensity, duration, and repetition of a given call increases the amount of information conveyed to conspecifics about the environmental stimulus.

The argument that the calls of nonhuman primates are instinctive or genetically programmed is based on the observation that they are automatic and discrete, that is, they cannot be combined. If a nonhuman primate encounters simultaneously two environmental stimuli for which calls are available, he will choose only one call. He cannot combine the calls for food and danger into a single call signifying that both food and danger are present. If, by chance, he did, the message would probably not be understood. At some point in the evolutionary line leading to man, however, such call combinations began to take place and to be understood. It is likely that there was also an expansion in the number of calls; the number of meaningful verbal forms uttered and understood by man

has increased throughout his evolution. Eventually, the number of calls became too great to be transmitted genetically, and the ability to communicate became a function of learning. The matter of when in man's evolution the ability to communicate changed from instinct to a function of learning remains, however, a subject for speculation and dispute.

Recent evidence of the chimpanzee's ability to learn language comes from an experiment conducted by two scientists, Beatrice and Allen Gardner (1969), at the University of Nevada. They raised a female chimpanzee, Washoe, from infancy. Washoe never heard a spoken word. The Gardners and their associates always used sign language when communicating in front of the chimp. The Gardners taught Washoe to distinguish between more than 200 gestures representing English words. Even more impressive than Washoe's vocabulary, which is far more extensive than her cousins' in the wild, is the fact that when she was two years old she independently began to combine the different symbols she had learned into rudimentary sentences such as "Give me water." As she grew, Washoe learned to combine as many as four symbols into sentences or statements. On the other hand, though she can combine several basic terms to express complex meanings, Washoe demonstrates no notion of grammar. In a given sentence, she arranges the basic words at random, so that "Give me water quickly" may easily be expressed as "Water quickly give me."

A similar experiment performed several years ago by another wife and husband team was not nearly so successful. They tried to teach their chimp, Viki, to speak. She was able to learn only three words. Thus, while chimpanzees appear capable of acquiring the rudiments of human language, of remembering a large number of basic, meaningful units and combining them to form sentences, they contrast with humans in their inability or unwillingness to mimic human speech and to communicate grammatically. However, the Gardners' experiment with Washoe once again questions what was once assumed to be a unique ability of man. It suggests that the ability to remember and to combine a large number of meaningful expressions is latent in hominoids other than man. In the evolutionary line leading to man, this latent ability was elaborated and eventually became the basis for language. Although differences in the verbal communication systems of contemporary human and nonhuman primates are great, they are, nevertheless, differences of degree. Language did not develop either spontaneously or miraculously. Human linguistic ability emerged over millions of years of evolution, as call systems similar in many ways to those of contemporary apes were transformed, gradually, into language. Nevertheless, contrasts between fully evolved language and call systems are obvious and significant. Perhaps most important is man's ability to displace speech. Each of the calls or messages emitted by nonhuman primates is tied to a specific environmental stimulus—food, water, and so forth. Calls are uttered only when the stimulus is present. Humans, however, freely speak of danger or food when neither is present. We are not obliged to perceive the actual referents as we emit the verbal forms. Our conversations are not bound by place; we can talk of the past, of the future, of the experiences of others, even of things and events which have never existed. We can even talk about talking, which is what I am doing now.

An additional difference between the language of contemporary humans and the call systems of nonhuman primates is the *productivity* of language. We are able to use the rules of sound and meaning in our language to bestow meaning arbitrarily, to create entirely new expressions. It is possible for me to coin the word "baboonlet" to refer to a baboon infant. I do this by borrowing from other words in which the suffix "let" is used to designate the young of a species. Everyone who speaks my language can immediately understand the meaning of the new form. No ape could perform such a linguistic feat. In contrast to human language, call systems are closed. Tied to environmental stimuli, they lack the ability to bestow meaning on forms arbitrarily.

Finally, all language shares what linguists call *duality of patterning*. This means that all language has two structures—a phonological structure, the sound system, and a formal structure, a system of verbal forms with meaning. Man's ability to connect the two is learned, not instinctive. In the phonological system are a limited number of sounds which lack meaning by themselves but which distinguish between meaningful units. Consider the English words "pit" and "bit." They vary only in their initial sounds *p* and *b*. Neither *p* nor *b* has meaning in itself, but preceding the sound represented by *it*, they serve to differentiate meaning, to keep meanings distinct. Within the second structure, the formal system, are the verbal forms which carry meaning in isolation, that is, by themselves. "Pit" and "bit" are verbal forms which designate things and events. They are meaningful forms composed of certain conventional arrangements of sounds which are meaningless in isolation.

Although it required hundreds of thousands of years to evolve, language represented a tremendous adaptive advantage to the genus *Homo*. Along with technology, reliance on the manufacture and use of tools, language is a basic part of man's nonbodily, or extrasomatic, means of adaptation. Because of language, the amount of information stored by any human group far exceeds that of any nonhuman primate group. Language is a uniquely successful vehicle of learning. Because we can speak of things and events which we have never experienced, we can anticipate responses before stimuli are encountered. In short, reliance on language increases learning ability, man's unique capacity to adapt through learned behavior patterns rather than solely through genetic or bodily change. Adaptive change in man can therefore occur more rapidly because man's adaptive means are more flexible than those of the other primates.

Speculation about the origin of language

All statements about the ultimate origin of language are speculative. During the nineteenth century, linguists and other scholars occasionally offered explanations for the origin of language. Some of them proposed what has been called the "bow-wow" theory, according to which humans first began to speak by imitating the sounds encountered every day in their environment, the calls of various animals, the sounds made by moving objects. In other words, human speech originated as imitation of sounds heard in nature.

Speculation about the origin of language is not fashionable among contemporary linguists. In fact, one could argue that such speculation reflects an antievolutionary bias, because if one believes that it is possible to discover the ultimate origin of anything, he is assuming that there was a sudden change. Evolutionary studies, on the other hand, emphasize continuous change. In this context, it seems reasonable to argue that in the evolution of *Homo*, call-systems similar to those found among other primates gradually developed more and more in the direction of language. While it is not possible, therefore, to determine the ultimate origin of language, and, in fact, there may have been no single origin, it is possible to document gradual changes in form among languages of the recent past.

A distinction recognized in previous chapters between study of phenomena at a single point in time and study of phenomena over time is also characteristic of the study of language. In a subdivision of linguistics known as *descriptive linguistics,* scholars study, describe, and analyze a language as it exists at a given point in time. Most of the languages which have been studied by methods of descriptive linguistics are contemporary, spoken languages. If there are written records of languages which are no longer spoken, or which are used only in a limited context—

for example, Church Latin and Sanskrit—descriptive linguistic techniques may also be applied. Linguists have a term, *speech community,* for the collectivity of speakers of a given language. Linguistic habits of a speech community may also be studied over time. This domain of the study of language is known as *historical linguistics.* By examining written texts, and by using other linguistic techniques, it is possible to chart changes which have taken place in speech patterns over an extended period of time. Historical linguistics can compare, for example, the English of Chaucer's time with modern English.

One of the techniques most basic to historical linguistics is known as the comparative method. By using the comparative method, historical linguists are able to learn a great deal about the languages of a relatively distant past, to extend their analysis back beyond written texts. The comparative method is not simply the comparison of two or more languages chosen arbitrarily. It involves the study of two or more *related* languages—languages which belong to the same family or stock and which represent the divergent end results of centuries or millenniums of linguistic evolution.

The Subsystems of Language

Linguists have traditionally recognized the existence of three linked subsystems of any language: phonology, grammar, and lexicon, or vocabulary. *Phonology* is the study of sounds used in human speech. *Grammar* is the arrangement of sounds into longer sequences of speech, or, in linguistic parlance, into longer utterances. In addition, there is *lexicon,* the meaning system of the language. People who study foreign languages are aware of these three aspects of language study. You must master pronunciation and grammar, and you must attempt to increase your vocabulary in the language you are learning.

Techniques of descriptive linguistics have contributed to many programs which specialize in teaching foreign languages quickly. Knowledge of descriptive linguis-

A linguist using a tape recorder for field work in Peru. *(Cornell Capa/Magnum)*

tics has long been considered an essential part of training in anthropology, both at the graduate and undergraduate levels. Linguistic techniques have been especially helpful to ethnographers. Many of the populations studied by ethnographers earlier in this century had spoken languages only. When an ethnographer arrives in the field and wants to learn a language that has never been written, he has to know the most rapid and efficient means of acquiring that language. His linguistic task may be made easier if a missionary has preceded him and has compiled a dictionary of the language, with some of the rules of sound and grammar included. In this case, the ethnographer has a head start in learning his field language. Otherwise, he must himself undertake to translate the strange cacophony he hears at first into understandable form.

From your own experience you can probably picture the dilemma the ethnographer faces when he arrives in a village where he plans to do fieldwork and hears people speaking an unfamiliar language. For example, you have probably heard radio broadcasts in languages other than your own. When you first tune in the broadcast, you hear what seems to be a garbled stream of sounds with no apparent pattern and no discernible meaning. As you listen longer and more carefully, however, you begin to notice that some of the sounds you are hearing are similar or identical to the sounds of your native language. Others remain totally foreign, and you are hard put to pronounce them. Merely by listening long enough to a broadcast or sample of speech in a foreign language, a trained linguist is able to list many of the sounds he hears. He discovers that some of the sounds have English equivalents while others do not. He can record all sounds using the international phonetic alphabet (IPA), a series of symbols which have been devised after wide experience to describe virtually any sound which occurs in a language.

However, if his knowledge of the language is to advance, the linguist must eventually stop concentrating on sounds alone and try to obtain information about the relationship between sound and meaning in the language. This is usually done by consulting one or more native speakers. The linguist will eventually determine the sounds significant to the language he is learning, and those sound contrasts which serve to differentiate meaning between two utterances which are otherwise very much the same. He will learn how to combine sounds into forms which carry meaning in themselves. And he will discover how minimal meaningful forms—words and their constituents—are combined in larger sequences. In other words, having mastered the sound system of the language, he is ascertaining its rules of grammar.

Simultaneously, he will be amassing a dictionary, a list of things and events which are named in the language. As his work progresses, he will begin to understand more of what is said to him and around him, and his own speech will become more fully comprehensible and more pleasing to native ears. If linguistic study continues long enough, he will also learn some of the subtleties of the language, some of its elegance. If variations in intonation are significant in the language, he will try to master them. He will learn how to avoid misunderstandings, how to vary his speech with different people and in different social situations. He will learn how to use emphasis and gestures as the natives do. In short, he will be acquiring a foreign language much as a child learns his native language; but because the linguist is an adult with specialized training, he learns much more quickly, and in most cases, not as well.

Consider now some of the concepts, definitions, and techniques most basic to descriptive linguistic analysis. You will grasp them more readily if, as you read, you try to apply them either to your native language or to a foreign language that you know. The contributions of descriptive linguistics will be discussed in the context in which they are most useful to most anthropologists, in a field situa-

tion in which a new language is being learned. Once an ethnographer arrives in the field, perhaps the easiest way to start learning the language is to point to things he sees and to ask people to name them. By writing these names down, he is beginning to amass a dictionary. To inscribe these forms, the ethnographer may employ the IPA. As his dictionary grows, some patterns begin to emerge. The ethnographer finds that some forms resemble others. Two names may resemble each other in all but one sound; a single contrast may serve to differentiate their meaning. Linguists call such pairs of words *minimal pairs.* The sounds that differentiate them are known as *phonemes.* As his dictionary grows, the ethnographer hopes eventually to discover all phonemes in the language he is learning. Of course, as he works, he tests his growing understanding and his pronunciation on native speakers.

Phonemes and phones

There is no single language which employs, or even includes, all the sounds designated by the symbols in the IPA. The number of phonetic contrasts that may serve to distinguish meaning is not infinite, but limited to a certain extent by

FIGURE 29 English consonants.

		Bilabial	Labiodental	Dental	Alveolar	Alveopalatal	Velar	Glottal
Stops	voiceless	p			t		k	
	voiced	b			d		g	
Affricates	voiceless					č		
	voiced					ǰ		
Fricatives slit	voiceless		f	θ				h
	voiced		v	ð				
groove	voiceless				s	š		
	voiced				z	ž		
Lateral	voiced				l			
Nasals	voiced	m			n		ŋ	
Semivowels	voiced	w			r	y		

the human articulatory apparatus, the organs of speech. Sounds differ according to the organs involved in their articulation and manner of that articulation. Some of the phonological contrasts which distinguish meaning are very much alike; they differ in only one feature. For example, the only difference between the phonemes /b/ and /p/ in English (conventionally, phonemes are enclosed in slashes) is that /b/ is *voiced* and /p/ is *voiceless*. Voiced sounds are produced when the vocal cords —two bands of elastic tissue enclosed in the larynx, or voice box—vibrate.

All English vowels and many consonants are voiced. These vowels and consonants are produced as the tongue, lips, and other speech organs assume different shapes. The shape of the passage between the larynx and the outside is modified, and thereby the quality of the sound. The English nasal consonant phonemes /m/, /n/, and /ŋ/ (as in "bam," "ban," and "bang") are produced when the breath takes the passage through the nose. There are contrasts between nasalized and non-nasalized vowels in French, Portuguese, and many other languages, but none in English. If the passage involves an opening at one or both sides of the tongue while it is pressed against the upper gums, a lateral is produced. The English lateral phoneme is /l/.

Any very narrow opening can produce friction at different points in the air passage, and sounds known as *fricatives* are then emitted. Variations in the shape of the narrow opening produce differences in the sounds of the fricatives. (See Figure 29 for identification of the fricatives and other English phonemes.) Other sounds, called *stops*, are produced by complete closure of the air passage.

Consonants differ according to their point of articulation and the articulators which meet to produce them. The articulators which produce the English *bilabials*, /p/ and /b/, are the upper and lower lips. *Labiodental* consonants, /f/ and /v/, are produced as the lower lip meets the upper teeth. *Dental* consonants, the initial sounds in thy, /ð/, and thigh, /θ/, are produced as the tip of the tongue meets the upper

teeth. When the tip of the tongue meets the upper gums, several *alveolar* consonants are produced: English /t/, /d/, /s/, /z/, /l/, /n/, and /r/. Five English consonants are known as *alveopalatals* because to produce them the front of the tongue must meet the far front of the palate. Finally, the English *velar* consonants /k/, /g/, and /ŋ/ are produced as the back of the tongue meets the velum or soft palate.

As Figure 29 documents, some English phonemes are very much alike in terms of their articulation: /b/ and /p/, /d/ and /t/, /g/ and /k/, all differ only in that the first member of each pair is voiced, while the other is not. The initial sound of *the*, indicated by the symbol /ð/, differs from /v/ only by point of articulation: /v/ is labiodental, while /ð/ is dental. Other English phonemes, however, are very dissimilar, sharing few or no features. The only similarity between /ŋ/ and /ð/, for example, is that they are both voiced.

Our ethnographer probably hopes that the language he is learning is no more difficult phonologically than his own. However, he may not be so lucky. English has more than thirty phonemes, but the number of phonemes is known to vary from ten to seventy in different languages, with the average between thirty and forty.

If he has a good ear and is linguistically expert, the ethnographer may learn to pronounce native sounds like a native. He will learn whether he is succeeding by asking for and watching native reactions to his speech. On the other hand, there may be some sounds which he will never learn to pronounce as the natives do, and so he will speak with an accent. Yet this will not necessarily be a barrier to communication if he has learned the phonemic system well. Although a Frenchman may always pronounce his English /r/ in the Parisian manner, the fact that he does so consistently means that any English speaker who talks with him for awhile will have no difficulty understanding him. He will recognize that although he is hearing a

Parisian sound, it is being used as an English phoneme. Since the Frenchman never confuses his [r] (sounds are characteristically enclosed in brackets to distinguish them from phonemes) with another English phoneme, he will be understood. However, if the contrast between two English phonemes, for example, /b/ and /v/ or /l/ and /r/, is missing in the foreigner's own language, and if he does not recognize the contrast in English, there will be difficulty in communicating. "Bet" and "vet," "craw" and "claw," will be pronounced in the same way. In other words, linguistic analysis aims to describe the sound contrasts which differentiate meanings in a given language. If the significant contrasts are mastered, minor deviations in pronunciation may be accepted and understood by natives, and the ethnographer may never learn that he has a foreign accent.

Furthermore, it is not just the foreign ethnographer who mispronounces. Even native speakers may emit sloppy speech. Shifting our attention from *phonemics* to *phonetics*, from the study of sounds which are significant within a particular language to the study of human speech sounds in general, we see that phonemes normally incorporate and gloss over a number of phonetic contrasts. In English, /b/ and /v/ are phonemes, occurring in minimal pairs like "bat" and "vat," "jibe" and "jive." They differ only in one distinctive feature: /b/ is voiced, /v/ is voiceless. In many languages, however, the contrast between [b] and [v] does not serve to distinguish meaning, and there is a single phoneme, normally pronounced either [b] or [v]. There can therefore be free variation between [b] and [v] in the pronunciation of this phoneme. In a language where there is no phonemic contrast between [b] and [v], and in which [b] is the normal pronunciation, a linguist may find that occasionally a native speaker will pronounce the phoneme as [v]. Such sloppy pronunciation may bother no one, since the native's

pronunciation does not obscure his meaning.

In a branch of phonetics called *acoustic phonetics*, linguists have at their disposal a machine known as a sound spectrograph, which can actually measure the acoustic properties of human speech. Study of the spectographic records shows that there is wide acoustic variation among native speakers in their pronunciation of certain phonemes. This variation is important in understanding the evolution of language, for, if shifts in pronunciation did not accrue over generations, there could be no sound change in language. Consider, for example, the evolution of a language in which there was originally no phonemic contrast involving [b] and [v]. At one point in time [b] might be the normal pronunciation of the phoneme. Over hundreds of years, however, because of a shift in pronunciation so gradual as to go undetected, [v] might come to replace it. Such long-term shifts in pronunciation can also occur in the absence of phonemic shifts.

Different is the case in which a phonemic contrast originates in a language. How does this happen? In a language in which there is no phonemic contrast between [b] and [v], and in which [b] is the preferred pronunciation, a new word or a series of new words might be coined or adopted from another language. Included could be words containing [v] which formed minimal pairs with older forms containing [b]. These sounds would now be separate phonemes, and the contrast might spread generally throughout the language.

Grammar

Let us return to our hypothetical ethnographer, who by now has mastered the phonemic system of the unwritten language he is trying to learn. In the process, his dictionary has been growing, and he has noticed how sounds are combined to form the names of people, objects, and activities. With a growing record of forms which are meaningful in the language, he is now in a position to concentrate on grammar. His study will be facilitated if he collects, in addition to his dictionary, longer samples of native speech. Working with an informant, he writes down stories, myths, and other oral accounts. By analyzing these texts he learns about the arrangement of forms in the language.

In their description and analysis of the grammar of a language, linguists use the term *morpheme* to refer to minimal forms which convey meaning. Our ethnographer will see that some of the expressions recorded in his dictionary are morphemes. They are forms which carry meaning but which cannot be broken down into smaller units that are meaningful in themselves and also contribute to the meaning of the larger form. For example, the English word "blackberry" contains two morphemes, *black* and *berry*, but *black* is a single morpheme. One can see other meaningful forms in "black"—namely, *lack* and *a*. However, since these constituents do not contribute to the meaning of "black" as *black* contributes to "blackberry," they are not constituent morphemes.

In the case of "blackberry," the constituent morphemes are capable of standing alone. However, this is not the case with several common English morphemes. The word "cats," for example, contains two morphemes, *cat* and *s* (phonemically transcribed /k æ t/ and /s/). "Cat" designates a minimal meaningful form which names a specific referent in the real world. The suffix /s/ indicates plurality. In English, you will find that there are several meaningful forms which never occur in isolation. They are always included in words that contain another morpheme as well. Some other examples that occur as suffixes are the -*es* in dishes and the -/z/ in "cads," also indicating plurality; the -/t/ in "slept," "dreamt," and so forth; and -*ing*. There are also English prefixes which are always bound to another morpheme. *Un-*, *pre-*, and *dis-* are examples.

Note, too, that there are many cases in English in which different sounds have the same meaning. Several suffixes convey the meaning of plurality in English, the /s/ at the ends of "cats," the /z/ at the end of

"cads," the -*es* at the end of "dishes," the -*en* at the end of "oxen" and "brethren." Where such phonologically different forms convey a single meaning, each of the phonetically different forms, or *morphs*, is called an *allomorph* of the same morpheme.

In most cases in English, the occurrence of one allomorph rather than another is phonologically conditioned. When nouns end in voiceless phonemes like /t/ or /p/, a voiceless phoneme forms their plural, -/s/. When the terminal sound of the singular is voiced—/d/ or /b/, for example—a voiced phoneme follows, -/z/, and marks plurality. When the word ends with *ch* (/č/) or *sh* (/š/) as in "church"/ "churches," "knish"/"knishes," the suffix -*es* forms the plural.

The term *zero morph* is used to cover words which do not form their plurals with a suffix. "Sheep" is one such form. In other English words the distinction between singular and plural is marked by a phonetic change within the word: "man" and "men," for example.

Our ethnographer must also learn the patterns whereby morphemes and words are arranged to form phrases and sentences. To what extent is it possible to subdivide these utterances into groups similar to the parts of speech in English and other European languages: nouns, verbs, adjectives, pronouns, adverbs, and so forth? How can similar meanings be conveyed in different ways by varying grammatical structure? Is there, for example, a grammatical difference which parallels the one between the active and passive voice in English? Is it possible to formulate analytical rules to cover all the grammatical sequences permissible in the language?

The study of meaning

Although analysis of phonology, grammar, and vocabulary can proceed separately at certain stages, these systems are obviously interrelated. Phonemes are defined by their ability to differentiate meaning in minimal pairs. Morphemes are minimal units which independently convey meaning in the language. It has therefore been necessary for the ethnographer to pay attention to vocabulary in his analysis of phonology and grammar. If his aim is a grasp of the language which approaches that of the native, however, the ethnographer must also pay attention to the meaning system itself. The verbal forms characteristic of a language presumably reflect something about how native speakers conceptualize the world. Some linguists and anthropologists have argued that variations in the grammatical structure of language produce distinctions in conceptualization, that grammar places constraints on how man perceives the world around him—in short, that grammar may *condition* human thought.

Certain other languages conceptualize and divide up the world in ways which are very different from English. As was indicated in the discussion of kinship terminology, there are cultural differences in native folk taxonomies. The study of folk taxonomy, also called *ethnoscience* or *ethnosemantics*, involves analysis and description of the ways in which cultures customarily categorize the world. It examines the significant contrasts and classifications that various cultures incorporate into their language.

Anthropologists and linguists have described several ethnosemantic domains recognized in language. Some of the most frequently and thoroughly studied domains have been kinship terminology and color terminology. Others include native categorization of disease, including causes, symptoms, and cures (see Frake, 1961); native astronomy (see Goodenough, 1953); and the folk taxonomy (*ethnobotany*) of plant life (see Conklin, 1954). Other studies have examined native classification of animals (*ethnozoology*), firewood, and foods.

The contributions of ethnosemantic analysis to linguistics, and particularly to anthropological linguistics, have been great. In particular, ethnosemantic studies have

	Speaker Included	Speaker Not Included
Hearer Included	5. (dual) 7. (plural)	2. (singular) 8. (dual) 9. (plural)
Hearer Not Included	1. (singular) 4. (dual) 6. (plural)	3. (singular) 10. (dual) 11. (plural)

FIGURE 30 Palaung pronouns.

demonstrated that, like phonology and grammar, meaning, too, can be analyzed systematically. Furthermore, the analysis of a meaning system may proceed independently of phonology or grammar. Consider, for example, Robbins Burling's formal semantic analysis of the domain of personal pronouns in Palaung, a language spoken by a small tribe in Burma. Burling has demonstrated differences between Palaung and English in the way the pronouns of these languages classify people. Palaung has eleven personal pronouns, which can be translated into English as follows (Burling, 1970, pp. 14–15):

1. I
2. you (singular)
3. he, she
4. he or she, and I
5. you (singular) and I
6. they and I
7. you (singular), I, and he, she, or they
8. he or she, and you (singular)
9. they and you (singular)
10. they two
11. they, three or more

There are some obvious differences between Palaung and English in the way in which people are perceived and classified. For example, English has "he" and "she," but the Palaung pronoun (item 3) makes no distinction for sex in the third person singular. Furthermore, Palaung does not lump the second person singular and plural under a single term, as the English "you" does. What are the significant dimensions of contrast involved in the domain of Palaung pronouns? There appear to be three, and they are summarized in Figure 30. First, like English pronouns, Palaung pronouns reflect distinctions in number.

However, in contrast to English, Palaung has three numbers: singular, dual, and plural. Dual, as the term suggests, means that the pronoun refers to two and only two people. Second, like English, which distinguishes between "I" and "we," the first person forms, and all other personal pronouns, Palaung distinguishes between pronouns which include the speaker and those which do not. There is, however, a third dimension of contrast which Palaung shares with many other languages but not with English. Palaung pronouns indicate whether the person spoken to is included or excluded from the remark (see items 6 and 7, for example).

Figure 30 demonstrates that these three dimensions of contrast are sufficient to distinguish the meaning of each Palaung personal pronoun from every other. The meaning of each represents a unique combination of three different components, one from each dimension. Because it isolates the components which are minimally sufficient to distinguish meaning of each item within the domain, a formal semantic analysis such as Burling's is also known as a *componential analysis.*

The same procedure which Burling used in his componential analysis of Palaung pronouns has been used by anthropologists in describing other domains in languages. For example, several componential studies of kinship terminological systems have been published since the 1950s. A formal semantic analysis of the domain of kinship terminology for any culture involves identification of the smallest number of dimensions of contrast and their components which will serve to distinguish the meaning of any kinship term from any other. The number of components, and even of dimensions of contrast, necessary in the analysis of a domain varies widely. Componential analysis provides an orderly approach to this study of meaning. From the point of view of sociocultural anthropology, the contribution has been even greater, for componential analyses have increased our knowledge of the relationship between language and other cultural variables.

It is time to leave our ethnographer, who by now has mastered the phonology and grammar of his field language and is well on his way to understanding its meaning system. Study of the way in which his informants perceive the world is, of course, an important part not only of linguistic but also of ethnographic inquiry. Study of lan-

Elementary school students in Tokyo adopting a second language— English. *(Paolo Koch/Rapho Guillumette)*

guage has therefore merged with ethnographic research.

Evolution and Language

Historical linguistics deals with changes in phonology, grammar, and meaning over time. Historical linguists reconstruct phonology, grammar, and vocabulary of past languages by examining *daughter languages*, contemporary languages or speech communities which, after hundreds or thousands of years of separation and linguistic change, are the diversified descendants of an original speech community called the protolanguage. Historical linguists have also been interested in classifying contemporary languages according to their *genetic relationships*.

In speaking here of genetic relationships of languages we are making an analogy with genetic relationships of people. Of course, languages do not have genes or chromosomes, but they change nevertheless. If it is discovered that several contemporary languages are related, that is, that they are diversified descendants of the same protolanguage, this does not necessarily mean that the people who speak these languages are related genetically. Because language is a nonbodily means of adaptation, people may shed their languages and adopt others independently of genetic change. In the equatorial forest of central Africa, many groups of Pygmy foragers have discarded their ancestral languages and adopted those of their horticultural neighbors, relatively recent arrivals in the forest. Emigrants to the United States have spoken many different languages, but today their descendants speak English as their native tongue. In nation-states, people who are otherwise very different socioculturally may speak a single language. On the other hand, people who are culturally similar over a large area, like the Pygmies, may speak different languages. There is, in other words, no inevitable or permanent bond between

language and other sociocultural patterns or between language and biological characteristics of contemporary and recent human populations.

Historical Linguistics and Other Anthropological Concerns

With these facts in mind, we can now explore some of the ways in which historical linguistics has been useful in other studies. Knowledge of linguistic relationships is often valuable to anthropologists interested in the recent past, in events which have taken place, say, during the past 5,000 years. An ethnographer is usually interested in the relationships between the group he is studying, neighbors who claim a different ethnic or tribal identity, and other human populations. If he finds that some of the group's neighbors speak unrelated languages while other neighboring groups speak closely related languages, he may speculate that the different language families or stocks (groups of genetically related languages) have been spoken in the area for different lengths of time. Many ethnological studies have focused on certain areas of the world which incorporate several human populations claiming separate ethnic identity. Usually, the aim of such ethnological research is to examine sociocultural differences and similarities. It may be that multiple language families are represented in the area. Certain other sociocultural features may be correlated with the distribution of language families. Groups who speak related languages may be more similar to one another in their sociocultural means of adaptation than they are to populations whose speech patterns derive from different traditions.

ADAPTIVE RADIATION Sometimes, an original ancestral population will differentiate into several subgroups which still bear the marks of the original linguistic (protolanguage) and cultural (protoculture) heritage. Natural selection works on variety which is already present in the evolving population. For various reasons, a population grows, and there is linguistic and sociocultural diversification. If there is little or no contact between the dispersing daughter populations, linguistic change in each may proceed independently of the others.

The model of adaptive radiation through sociocultural means among genetically, historically, and linguistically related human populations applies with greatest accuracy to island populations. For example, the populations of all the islands of Polynesia speak closely related languages. In this case, most Polynesians are genetic, as well as linguistic, descendants of an original ancestral population with a distinctive language and culture. When groups of migrants leave their ancestral homeland and settle islands spread out over a vast ocean, their subsequent isolation from one another is more likely than when dispersion takes place on a continent. This does not mean that trade and other forms of contact did not occur among Polynesian Islanders. It only asserts that interethnic contact was probably not as frequent in the Pacific as it was in most continental areas. When trade and contact are developed, the evolution of related populations does not proceed independently. Inventions made in one group may spread to, and prove adaptive in, another.

BORROWING The ethnologist who is studying social and cultural similarities in a specific part of the world may find that certain sociocultural traits and patterns do not reflect linguistic relationships. Such traits may have spread through *diffusion*. Even groups whose members speak unrelated languages may have contact with one another. They may trade, intermarry, or wage war. Ideas, inventions, and other cultural baggage will diffuse among them. Again we see that language and other aspects of culture may vary independently. However, in borrowing as in genetic relationships, historical linguistics makes a contribution to the study of the past.

The historical linguist can, for example, examine the English speech community at different points in time. Many items of vocabulary and even some sounds included in contemporary English dialects come from French. If the historical linguist were unaware of France's influence on England following the Norman Conquest in 1066, he would discover that a long period of important first-hand contact had occurred merely by examining linguistic evidence. However, not only do we have written records documenting the Norman Conquest and subsequent relationship between England and France, we can even compare Old English, which was spoken previously, with Middle English, which evolved thereafter.

However, comparable historical information about nonliterate populations is usually absent. In this case, linguistic evidence alone may reveal contact and borrowing. By considering which forms and meanings have been borrowed, we may even be able to learn a great deal about the nature of the contact. Consider the case of the island of Madagascar. All the people of Madagascar speak related Malagasy languages. Despite the nearness of Africa, the Malagasy languages are members of a widespread language family, the Malayo-Polynesian stock, which also includes the languages of Polynesia, Indonesia, and the Philippines, as well as some languages spoken in Southeast Asia. The language most closely related to the Malagasy languages is spoken in southeastern Borneo, in Indonesia.

The first human settlers began to colonize Madagascar some 2,000 years ago. These were apparently members of a far-ranging population of sea-going traders who participated in an ancient network of commerce linking the Indonesian Islands, India, Arabia, the East African Coast, and Madagascar. As they traded along this route, they met and married East Africans, and their descendants colonized Madagascar. Physically, the Malagasy are generally more like East Africans than contemporary Indonesians, but their languages are as indisputably related to Indonesian as French,

Spanish, and Portuguese are to Latin.

Although the contact between Madagascar and East Africa has continued throughout the history of the island, it is poorly documented. Nevertheless, the Malagasy languages provide extensive clues to its nature. Malagasy words for several species of economically useful plants and animals clearly have been borrowed from languages spoken in East Africa. This suggests that these items reached Madagascar from somewhere in East Africa. Many of the terms used by Malagasy in commercial activities, particularly in the marketplace, have been borrowed from Swahili, a widely spoken language of East Africa which is a member of the Bantu linguistic group. Such evidence suggests a long period of trade between Madagascar and East Africa. Further, it suggests that Swahili-speaking peoples were important in this trade.

COMMON HISTORY   The study of language can, therefore, be of great interest to the sociocultural anthropologist, to the archeologist, and to the biological anthropologist concerned with relationships among comparatively recent human populations, namely those of the past few thousand years. Linguistic evidence can suggest periods of common history involving the ancestors of different speech communities. This common history may have resulted from genetic relationship. A period of common history may also have involved borrowing or contact. Speakers of two languages may at one time have been in actual contact, or each may have been influenced by a third group known to both. Such information is extremely valuable in the study of populations who lack written history.

The Evolution of Language

In the preceding sections, ways in which linguistics contributes to other subdisciplines of anthropology have been stressed.

Here, the evolution of language itself is examined. That language changes form, that it evolves, is implicit in the preceding discussions of historical and comparative linguistics. Over time, a protolanguage spreads, splits, or otherwise segments into subgroups. Distinct daughter languages grow out of a single parent, especially if the subgroups are isolated from one another. Some of these may then segment, and new languages will differentiate. If some people remain in the ancestral homeland, however, their speech patterns will also change over time. It is appropriate, therefore, to consider the evolving speech patterns which occur in the ancestral homeland as a daughter language like the rest.

Though it is often difficult to say why languages have changed, we know a great deal about the ways in which they change, and it is possible to offer some generalizations about their evolution: Of the three subsystems of language discussed earlier, the one that seems to be least resistant to change is vocabulary. In most languages it is fairly easy to coin or borrow new words for new concepts and new things. Innovations in vocabulary will reflect modifications in the daily lives of members of the speech community. That the vocabularies of contemporary human groups are more complex—include more words and recognize a wider range of concepts—than the vocabularies of *Homo erectus* and the Neanderthals cannot be demonstrated, but this would probably be accepted by most anthropologists. Furthermore, it can also be said that languages spoken in more complex societies tend to have larger and more complex vocabularies than those spoken in primitive societies. Note, however, that the larger vocabulary applies to the *language* of the complex society and not to its individual speakers. The average American's vocabulary may be no greater than that of a person chosen at random from a tribal society.

Sound shifts

The sound system of a language appears to be more resistant to change than its vocabulary. This means simply that phonological changes typically take longer to accomplish. Earlier in this chapter, I described the manner in which sound shifts occur. Phonological changes take place over several generations, and many of them are so slight and gradual that they go undetected by each generation of speakers. Though you may never notice subtle changes in your own pronunciation, phonological changes in English are obvious from written documents. Perhaps you have heard Chaucer read aloud. You note differences in pronunciation, in the phonetics of many phonemes which have remained the same. Shakespeare is often difficult for many American high school students because of differences in English grammar, pronunciation, and meaning. When contemporary pronunciation is used, some of Shakespeare's apparent rhymes don't rhyme at all. This, however, merely reflects phonological change. Shakespeare's rhymes did indeed rhyme in his day.

Although shifts in pronunciation take time, historical linguists have noted that sound shifts are regular. If there is a change in a sound in one word, corresponding changes in pronunciation will occur in all words which contain that sound. A new sound and even a new phoneme may also enter a language, but this occurs far less frequently than sound shifts.

Bearing out the generalization that it is easier for vocabulary than for phonology to change, contrast the tremendous number of French loan words in English with the incorporation of only one French phoneme. This is the sound of the z /z/ in the word "azure," and, in some English dialects, of the final g in "garage." The incorporation of this phoneme into English has been gradual, and this is why many Americans say "garage" as though it were spelled *garadge*. Perhaps with the increasing exposure to French of Americans trained in foreign languages, there will be new phonemes introduced into English. There are many Americans, for example, who now pronounce the word "fiancé" with the French nasalized vowel rather than as Good Old American *fee-ant-say*. A new distinctive feature capable of differ-

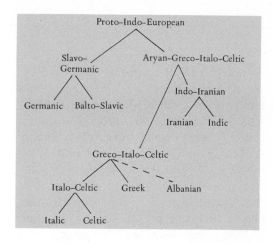

FIGURE 31 The Indo-European language family tree.

entiating vowels—nasalization—could conceivably be incorporated into English.

Because sound shifts are regular rather than capricious, and because phonetic change may proceed independently of phonemic change, it is possible for historical linguists to extend their analyses back in time. As daughter languages differentiate out of a common protolanguage, they change phonologically. The shifts in pronunciation which take place in one may not be the same as those which take place in another. On the other hand, overall phonological change, the sum total of all sound shifts, may occur at a constant rate in languages, particularly in related languages. By comparing the phonologies of several daughter languages, it is possible to work back in time and reconstruct a great deal of the phonological system of the protolanguage.

The comparative method

The comparative method, which involves identifying homologous forms in related languages and then reconstructing the original form, was developed in Europe during the nineteenth century. The bulk of the historical linguistic work carried out during the nineteenth century was concerned with Indo-European languages and their parent language, proto–Indo-European. (See Figure 31.) The Indo-European family is widespread. Its name is derived from India and Europe, the easternmost and westernmost areas in which such languages were spoken prior to European explorations. Proto–Indo-European was probably spoken in northern Europe around 5,000 years ago. Over time, through population growth, dispersions, migrations, and conquests, linguistic differentiation occurred and the present-day distribution of the Indo-European languages was accomplished.

Among the contemporary languages descended from proto–Indo-European are the tongues of Iran and India; Albanian; Greek; Celtic; Italic, including Latin and all the Romance languages; Slavic; Lithuanian; and the Germanic languages, including German, English, Dutch, and Scandinavian. French, a member of the Italic subgroup, and English, a member of the Germanic subgroup, are distantly related languages whose most recent common ancestor is proto–Indo-European itself. English and German, on the other hand, belong equally to the Germanic subgroup and are more closely related. This means that it is easier for an English-speaking student to learn the phonology and grammar of German than of French. On the other hand, because of the long period of common history following the Norman Conquest, there are as many similarities between French and English vocabulary as there are between German and English vocabulary.

Many of the phonemic contrasts, and some of the phonetic contrasts, which exist in modern English can be traced back to proto–Indo-European, and the same is true of French phonology. In other words, there are sound correspondences between English and French, as between any two related languages, which reflect their common ancestry and the regularity of sound shifts in each. Knowledge of the corresponding pronunciations of phonemes in related languages facilitates language learning. For example, there is a regular correspondence between the German phoneme written *z* (as in *zu*) and pronounced /ts/ and the English phoneme /t/ (as in "to"). Consider some pairs in the two languages which have the same or similar meanings and show phonetic correspondence: *zu*, "to"; *zwei*, "two"; *sitz*, "sit"; *zeit*, "time." Similarly, there have been different but regular shifts in the pronunciation of the same phoneme in Spanish and Portuguese, two closely related languages. There is a correspondence between the Spanish sound written *ue* (as in *fuego*, fire), and the Portuguese sound written *o* (as in *fogo*, fire). Some pairs are *fuego*, *fogo*; *puerco*, *porco*; *huerta*, *horta*. When the relationship is more remote, as in the case of English and French, it is more difficult, but still possible, to trace the shifts which have taken place in the daughter languages. Since it is impossible to hear proto–Indo-European spoken, of course, linguists must examine several daughter languages and consider their interrelationships in order to guess about pronunciation of a phoneme in the parent language.

Subgrouping

Languages, like life forms, can be differentiated by degrees of relationship. How is this done? Groups of closely related languages within the same family are called *genera*, or subgroups. As in biological taxonomy, subgrouping reflects differences in recency of common linguistic ancestry. For example, the most recent common ancestor of French and English is proto–Indo-European. German and English have a more recent common ancestor, called proto-Germanic because it has differentiated into all the Germanic languages. The close relationships between the Germanic languages are revealed in phonology and grammar. There are certain innovations which all the Germanic languages share, indicating a period of common history, a time when a proto-Germanic speech community existed apart from other Indo-European languages whose descendants now belong to other linguistic subgroups. *Shared innovations*

1. I	21. dog	41. nose	61. die	81. smoke
2. thou	22. louse	42. mouth	62. kill	82. fire
3. we	23. tree	43. tooth	63. swim	83. ash
4. this	24. seed	44. tongue	64. fly	84. burn
5. that	25. leaf	45. claw	65. walk	85. path
6. who	26. root	46. foot	66. come	86. mountain
7. what	27. bark	47. knee	67. lie	87. red
8. not	28. skin	48. hand	68. sit	88. green
9. all	29. flesh	49. belly	69. stand	89. yellow
10. many	30. blood	50. neck	70. give	90. white
11. one	31. bone	51. breasts	71. say	91. black
12. two	32. grease	52. heart	72. sun	92. night
13. big	33. egg	53. liver	73. moon	93. hot
14. long	34. horn	54. drink	74. star	94. cold
15. small	35. tail	55. eat	75. water	95. full
16. woman	36. feather	56. bite	76. rain	96. new
17. man	37. hair	57. see	77. stone	97. good
18. person	38. head	58. hear	78. sand	98. round
19. fish	39. ear	59. know	79. earth	99. dry
20. bird	40. eye	60. sleep	80. cloud	100. name

in certain related languages indicate a separate connection apart from the common history of the family as a whole.

Lexicostatistics

Traditionally, historical linguistics has relied on phonological and morphological evidence to indicate relationships and degrees of relationship in language. More recently, however, a new technique has received a great deal of attention. It is called *lexicostatistics* because it deals with vocabulary (lexicon) in a statistical, or quantitative, manner. Lexicostatistical analysis is based on the fundamental distinction in any language between *basic vocabulary* and *cultural vocabulary*. The assumption is that while changes in cultural vocabulary may be rapid and unpredictable, changes in basic vocabulary take place more slowly and more regularly. The notion that some lexical domains are more resistant to change than others seems reasonable. Contrast, for example, the difficulty in getting Americans to adopt the Japanese word for the number one with the ease with which they have been taught to use terms like sukiyaki, hari-kari, and other items of nonbasic vocabulary.

The second assumption of lexicostatistics is that the same meanings are basic in all languages, that is, that the same list of basic vocabulary items applies equally well to all languages, present and past. Provided here is a list of one hundred words for the basic vocabulary items in English and other languages.

The third assumption is that changes in basic vocabulary occur at a constant rate and that the rate is the same in all languages. Change is assumed to occur among the items in the 100–word list at a rate of 14 percent per 1,000 years. This means that if we look at a language spoken 1,000 years ago and its contemporary descendant, we can expect to find that 14 percent of the basic vocabulary items have changed and 86 percent have been retained. Change occurs because of borrowing, internal innovation, and for various other reasons.

If we wish to determine how closely related two languages are, we must examine the basic vocabulary of each. We must look for *homeosemantic cognates*, items which are similar both in phonological form and in meaning. This similarity is assumed to reflect development out of a common ancestral form with the same meaning. If two contemporary languages developed from a common ancestral speech community, and if their divergence took place 1,000 years ago, each of the daughter languages is assumed to have been changing independently of the other. In each, because of separate histories, we can expect to find that 14 percent of the basic vocabulary items have changed and that 86 percent have been retained—and also that the changes have not been the same in each language. According to lexicostatistics, these languages are separated by 2,000 years of separate history—1,000 for language A and 1,000 for language B. Lexicostatisticians therefore expect the percentage of shared cognates to be the square of 0.86, or about 74 percent. On the basis of the number of shared cognates, and by using a simple formula, some lexicostatisticians have argued that it is possible to date the divergence of any two related languages.

Although few linguists accept all the assumptions of lexicostatistics uncritically, many have used basic vocabulary lists as a quick means of seeing relationships between languages and of defining the subgroups of those languages. If certain daughter languages share a large number of homeosemantic cognates, a period of separate history, and thus a linguistic subgroup, can be assumed. In a sufficiently large sample of contemporary languages drawn at random, some will show remarkable similarities, others will show less obvious but still perceptible similarities, and still others will hardly be alike at all. More traditional linguistic analysis will be able to refine the results of lexicostatistical comparison by determining sound correspondences between related languages and tracing daughter forms back to original forms. For the sociocultural anthropologist or for the archeologist who has not received extensive training in linguistics, lexicostatistics represents the quickest and easiest way to spot relationships and degrees of relationships in language.

Language has been cited as a major adaptive advantage which differentiates *Homo* and *sapiens* from other genera and species and which has been responsible for the evolutionary success of humans. However, precisely because it is a generic advantage, because all contemporary human populations speak languages, language cannot be viewed as an adaptive advantage that distinguishes one contemporary human population from another. The adaptive status of language in human evolution is like that of the large and complex brain. The large and complex brain has been a specific advantage which contributed to the evolutionary success of humans compared with other genera. Yet, precisely because all contemporary human populations have complex brains and display equivalent potentialities for learning, variable brain complexity is no longer a factor in adaptation of contemporary human populations. Speechless hominids with small and simple brains have long since vanished from the earth; their descendants evolved into *Homo sapiens* and their languages into ancient languages. These earliest of languages were spoken so long ago in the history of the human race as to render their reconstruction impossible. Just as there are no documented differences in brain complexity or intelligence among contemporary human populations, no one has ever been able to demonstrate the absolute superiority of certain languages over others.

Linguistic relativity has been accepted as one of the basic tenets of twentieth-century anthropology and linguistics. All languages are interpreted, according to this view, as instances of specific evolution. They have evolved within a speech community and provide perfectly adequate means of communication for its population. They can communicate all the ideas and information essential to the conduct of daily life. This doctrine of linguistic relativity goes against popular stereotypes. Frenchmen who believe that theirs is the only appropriate language for civilized discourse would reject it. Even non–Frenchmen might argue that French is the best language for diplomats. And there are many Englishmen and Americans who would assert the superiority of their language in commercial negotiations. These claims, however, reflect sociocultural rather than linguistic facts. They reflect events in the history of world politics and economy rather than anything about evolutionary potential of language. In establishing a world empire, Frenchmen spread their culture through the medium of their language, and, since they asserted to the people they conquered that they were engaged in a civilizing mission, they naturally came to equate their language with civilization itself. The widespread use of French as a diplomatic language reflects France's long-term political influence and its geographical position between Britain and other European powers. English became dominant as a commercial language because English commerce was widespread and ultimately flourished in a political and economic empire even larger than France's.

The extent of contemporary use and distribution of languages reflects sociocultural and ecological variables other than intrinsic factors in the language itself. One language spoken in China has more native speakers than English, not because it is a superior language but because the population which speaks it has grown. Reasons for population growth have nothing to do with language, but reflect ecological and sociopolitical factors. English is the native language of Englishmen, North Americans, Australians, New Zealanders, and many South Africans because of vast English colonization and conquest. The success of such colonization and conquest had nothing to do with language. Weapons, ships, and sociopolitical organization played decisive roles.

Between 2,000 and 3,000 years ago, a small population lived in a confined area of West Africa in what are now the nation-states of Nigeria and the Cameroons. Today, the linguistic descendants of this language, proto–Bantu, cover most of central and southern Africa. The reason for the expansion of the Bantu languages has nothing to do with any intrinsic superiority of Bantu as a vehicle of communication. Population growth and territorial expansion of speakers of proto-Bantu appears to have taken place because of an adaptive advantage, early reliance on iron tools and weapons, and cultivation of certain food crops.

Linguistic relativity is well established and its demonstration is clear. Specific languages are not important adaptive advantages of contemporary human populations. It is usually a fairly easy matter for a language to accommodate a new item or a new concept in its vocabulary. Old forms may be combined, a foreign name may be borrowed, or an entirely new form may originate. Languages are flexible systems which are tied neither to culture nor to phenotype, and can occur independently of genetic changes. In many respects the daily lives of rural Englishmen prior to the Industrial Revolution were more similar to those of traditional West Africans than to those of their contemporary descendants. Yet linguistic change in English has proceeded at a relative snail's pace.

Although attempts to make general evolutionary statements about languages have, for the most part, failed, it is still possible to apply some of the principles of evolution discussed in previous chapters to language. There are, however, some important differences between change in language and change in other aspects of culture. Lexicostatistics assumes that there is for all languages a basic vocabulary consisting of the same meanings, and that there is a constant rate of change in this domain. Similarly, although the specific sound shifts and grammatical changes which take place in various languages may be different, the rate of total phonological and morphological change in related languages may turn out to be relatively constant. When attention shifts to changes in sociocultural forms among related human populations who have diverged, we may find that sociocultural change has been much more rapid in some of these groups than in others. Changes in nonbasic, or cultural, vocabulary may reflect such rapid sociocultural change.

All languages change. A common American myth is that pockets of people who speak "pure Elizabethan English" still survive in the mountains of Tennessee. This is like the belief that people are descended from contemporary apes or monkeys. Daughter languages and dialects, wherever they are spoken, are the end results of specific evolutionary sequences. They are collaterals, cousins or sisters, rather than ancestors and descendants. While it may be true that certain archaic forms of speech have been preserved in certain daughter languages and dialects and not in others, other innovations have certainly taken place that distinguish the daughter from the protolanguage. This does not deny that it is possible, through written records, to preserve languages. Latin, Sanskrit and ancient Greek all exist as living fossils inscribed on stone or paper and spoken and understood in special, primarily ritual, contexts. Latin does not live in its ancient form. If Latin is spoken today, it is as French, Spanish, Portuguese, Italian, or Romanian—that is, as one of its many divergent descendants.

Are there other similarities between linguistic change and biological evolution? The phenomenon of adaptive radiation discussed earlier in this chapter occurs linguistically: it has been found that related languages whose speakers have lost contact with one another sometimes change in analogous ways. The same shifts in pronunciation, for example, may take place independently in the two languages. This phenomenon is called *linguistic drift*, and its causes are poorly understood. Because the original evolutionary material is the same—in this case, linguistic rather than genetic—changes may be parallel even though descendant groups are separate and distinct entities.

Despite parallels between the evolution of life and of languages, there are impor-

tant differences. Obviously, in the evolution of life forms, of diverse species, borrowing is not possible after speciation takes place. In language and in culture complete speciation never occurs. Linguistic items, cultural items, and means of adaptation may pass from one speech community to another, from one human population to another. Changes in languages after divergence from a common ancestor may not, therefore, be independent. Like sociocultural means of adaptation, subsequent linguistic evolution may be, and usually is, influenced by contact with others.

Language and Culture

The preceding comments might lead you to the conclusion that there is no ascertainable relationship between language and culture. This is far from the truth. It has merely been stressed that languages themselves are not particularly significant means of adaptation for contemporary human populations. Good examples of the relationship between language and culture are the formal semantic analyses of folk taxonomies which were discussed earlier. The way in which people divide up the world, the contrasts they perceive as significant, should reflect their daily lives and their specific adaptations to their environments. As we have seen in Chapter 7, there is a relationship between kinship terminology and forms of social organization. Language reflects distinctions that are socially important. Some anthropologists have even suggested that general evolutionary statements can be made about the lexical systems of specific languages. Brent Berlin and Paul Kay (1969), for example, have suggested that there is a relationship between color terminology and general evolutionary status. After examining the color terms in more than one hundred languages, they found that although different languages varied in the number of color terms in their vocabularies, there were only eleven basic color terms for all languages. Significantly, the number of basic color terms in a specific language appeared to vary directly with general cultural complexity. Representing one extreme were the languages of New Guinea horticulturists and Australian foragers, which used only two basic terms that translate as *black* and *white* or *dark* and *light*. At the other end of the continuum were languages with all eleven color terms. These were languages of Europe and Asia. Measures of general evolutionary complexity are still relatively crude. However, on the basis of Berlin and Kay's research, anthropologists and linguists should certainly investigate the possibility of other relationships between lexical domains and general cultural complexity.

Sociolinguistics

Also significant to understanding interrelationships between language and other aspects of culture is a field of study to which both anthropologists and linguists have made contributions—sociolinguistics. Sociolinguistics investigates relationships between language and social and cultural differences. Language expresses social and cultural differences, reflects these contrasts, and helps to maintain them. Anthropologists often find that linguistic differences serve as mechanisms which define the boundaries of human groups. As this is true among horticultural populations in New Guinea or in the tropical forest of South America, it is also true in complex nation-states. Speech patterns in a modern nation-state vary from class to class, region to region, and ethnic group to ethnic group, as well as among people with different occupations, and socially defined milieux at different educational levels. Sociolinguistics studies the role of language in demarcating socially significant groups and linguistic variation in different social contexts.

The relationship between language and sociopolitical organization is particularly clear in certain stratified societies in which different speech forms are used for discourse depending on the relative social status of the parties to the conversation. Frenchmen regularly employ two forms of the second person pronoun you: *tu*, which is always singular, and *vous*, which may be singular or plural. In France the use of *tu* signals familiarity. It is used for dis-

course within the family, among close friends, and lately among French people of college age or younger. *Vous* is less intimate and is used in all other contexts. In colonial areas, however, Frenchmen often used the familiar form to address their employees, servants, and any member of the native population. Natives, on the other hand, were expected to use the formal pronoun when addressing members of the colonial elite.

In the archaic state known as Imerina, which developed in the highlands of Madagascar during the eighteenth century, different terms were used in addressing the king and referring to his actions. For example, when a commoner wanted to say that the king walked, he did not use the common term but a special one which could be applied only to the sovereign. Sociopolitical structure influenced vocabulary in Madagascar in still another way. Personal names, including those of sovereigns in Madagascar, were usually compounds of several common words. A king, therefore, might bear a name which could be translated as "the sweet lord who conquered the seven hills." Upon his death, it was the practice in some areas of Madagascar to place taboos on further use of the words which had been included in the king's name. Thus royal deaths often forced Malagasy to coin new terms for things already in their language.

A more extreme example comes from Javanese, one of the native languages of Indonesia. Three socioeconomic classes exist in Javanese society: aristocrats, townsmen, and rural cultivators. Different levels of discourse in the Javanese language parallel these class divisions. Different words are used, for example, to state the same meaning depending on the speaker's stratum and the social situation. There are three basic levels of discourse, involving meanings which can be expressed in three different ways, by a triad of spoken forms. The most basic level, the discourse of peasants, is learned in the home by every Javanese child no matter what his social position. If he is a member of the middle or upper stratum, however, he will eventually be taught one or two of the other forms of speech so that he can converse more elegantly.

In addition to a stratified lexicon, Javanese may also vary their speech by including certain honorifics, special terms and expressions which slightly elevate the level of their speech. Upper-class Javanese, for example, employ high-level honorifics when they want to be especially elegant. When an upper-stratum Javanese converses with a rural cultivator, he usually

SUMMARY

The research interests of anthropological linguists, like those of other anthropologists, encompass both past and present human populations and changes over time. Descriptive linguistics examines speech communities at specific points in time, generally the present, while historical linguistics studies linguistic change. In addition to these two traditional subdivisions, new fields of anthropological linguistic study—meaning systems, relationships between language and culture, research on linguistic universals, and sociolinguistics—are attracting considerable attention.

Some of the techniques employed by descriptive linguists to describe and analyze the phonology, grammar, and lexicon of specific languages are also used by historical linguists. Knowledge of principles and techniques of both descriptive and historical linguistics is useful to other anthropologists for several reasons. Knowledge of basic linguistic techniques will aid the ethnographer in learning his field language. For the ethnologist, archeologist, or biological anthropologist interested in relationships between nonliterate populations of the present and recent past, historical linguistic information is often very useful.

For example, similarities and differences in other aspects of culture are often associated with linguistic similarities and differences. Linguistic clues can suggest past contact between now distinct populations. Two populations may also speak different languages that are descended from an original protolanguage. Thus historical linguistics may reveal information that will help to explain differences and similarities in cultural patterns and to unravel past relationships for which no written records exist.

Linguists have developed terms, concepts, and techniques useful in the analysis of different aspects of language. Scientific description of a language commonly involves analysis of its sound system—determination of the minimal contrasts in sound that serve to distinguish meaning within that language. Linguists also analyze grammar, identifying minimal forms that carry meaning in themselves, the arrangement of these forms into larger utterances, and the variability in forms and arrangements that convey the same or different meaning.

Recently, anthropological linguists have devoted considerable attention to meaning systems of different languages. An area of study known as ethnoscience, or ethnose-

Sources and Suggested Readings

BERLIN, B.
  1970   A Universalist-Evolutionary Approach in Ethnographic Semantics. In *Current Directions in Anthropology: A Special Issue*, vol. 3 (3), part 2, ed. A.

Fisher, pp. 3–17. Washington, D.C.: American Anthropological Association. Argues for the possibility of a comparative evolutionary approach to the study of meaning.

adopts the lowest level of discourse. Owing to the structure of their language, Javanese can define, through linguistic usage, their perception of any social situation.

Sociolinguistic differentiation is found, with varying degrees of elaboration, in all stratified societies and in all states. Ethnosemantic research promises to increase our knowledge of relationships between language and other aspects of culture; further work in sociolinguistics should increase our knowledge of ways in which culture operates on language—that is, how people use language to distinguish status and to define social situations.

mantics, attempts to determine for specific cultures native taxonomies of the world. One technique developed by ethnoscientists is componential analysis, a method of identifying dimensions of contrast which intersect to define specific concepts within folk domains and to distinguish these concepts (unique meanings) from others.

An increasingly popular field of study known as sociolinguistics also explores interrelationships involving language, society, and culture. Linguistic habits serve in many contexts to demarcate groups and social relationships. In many stratified societies, for example, linguistic usage varies with class or ethnic status.

Application of evolutionary principles to language is more difficult than in the case of other sociocultural phenomena. Only a few linguists and anthropologists have demonstrated plausible links between linguistic phenomena and general evolutionary status of human populations. When languages are compared, a position of linguistic relativity seems best: each language should be viewed as an instance of specific evolution, a human communication system as adequate as any other for enabling people to exchange essential information.

Despite difficulty in applying evolutionary principles to the study of language, we know that languages change, and we also know a great deal about how they change. Vocabularies, for example, appear to change more easily and rapidly than grammars and sound systems. Within vocabulary, however, there appears to be a basic vocabulary which is most resistant to change. On the assumption of such a unit rests a technique known as lexicostatistics—a means of evaluating degrees of interrelationship between closely related languages. Using this and other techniques, historical linguists have studied linguistic divergence, the gradual development of separate languages out of ancestral speech communities. Genetic relationships between languages do not necessarily reflect genetic relationships between their speakers, since languages and speech habits can be adopted or shed independently of phenotypical or genetic changes. However, certain kinds of linguistic similarities, if not evidence for common genetic ancestry, certainly indicate a period of common history, and therefore may explain some other differences and similarities of interest to anthropologists.

BERLIN, B., and KAY, P.
  1969   *Basic Color Terms: Their Universality and Evolution.* Berkeley: University of California Press. Partial correlation between number of basic color terms recognized and general evolutionary status of cultures.

BURLING, R.
  1970   *Man's Many Voices: Language in Its*

Cultural Context. New York: Holt, Rinehart and Winston. Role of language in social life, and the cultural context of variations in grammar, phonology, and meaning.

CHOMSKY, N.

1957 *Syntactic Structures.* The Hague: Mouton. A revolution in linguistics toward the construction of transformational grammars was prompted by this technical book.

CONKLIN, H. C.

1954 *The Relation of Hanunóo Culture to the Plant World.* Unpublished Ph.D. dissertation. Yale University. Detailed study of classification of plant life by the Hanunóo, a group of Philippino horticulturalists; great influence on students of ethnoscience and componential analysis of folk domains. Available only on microfilm.

1955 Hanunóo Color Categories. *Southwestern Journal of Anthropology* 11: 339–344. Names for colors in the Hanunóo language differ markedly from American terms; some of the contrasts treated by the Hanunóo as significant in their color classification are indicated.

FRAKE, C. O.

1961 The Diagnosis of Disease among the Subanun of Mindanao. *American Anthropologist* 63: 113–132. Ethnodiagnosis; how members of Philippino tribe classify and treat their illnesses.

GARDNER, R. A., and GARDNER, B.

1969 Teaching Sign Language to a Chimpanzee. *Science* 165:664–672. Washoe learns to communicate.

GLEASON, H. A.

1961 *An Introduction to Descriptive Linguistics.* Rev. ed. New York: Holt, Rinehart and Winston. Good, though now dated, introductory linguistics textbook.

GOODALL, J. VAN LAWICK

1968 A Preliminary Report on Expressive Movements and Communication in Gombe Stream Chimpanzees. In *Pri-*

mates: Studies in Adaptation and Variability, ed. P. C. Jay, pp. 313–374. New York: Holt, Rinehart and Winston. Technical report on field study of chimpanzee communication.

GOODENOUGH, W. H.

1953 *Native Astronomy in the Central Carolines.* Philadelphia: University of Pennsylvania. Field study of ethnoastronomy; how a group of islanders in Micronesia classify the planets and stars.

GRACE, G. W.

1966 Austronesian Lexicostatistical Classification: A Review Article. *Oceanic Linguistics* 5: 13–31. Assessment of family tree relationships among languages of the widespread Malayo-Polynesian stock.

GREENBERG, J. H.

1957 *Essays in Linguistics.* Chicago: University of Chicago Press. Collection of some of Greenberg's early essays.

1968 *Anthropological Linguistics: An Introduction.* New York: Random House. Introductory treatment of phonology, grammar, meaning, and linguistic universals.

1972 Linguistic Evidence Regarding Bantu Origins. *Journal of African History* 13: 189–216. Recent conclusions about area of origin of the proto-Bantu speech community.

GUDSCHINSKY, S. C.

1967 *How to Learn an Unwritten Language.* New York: Holt, Rinehart and Winston. Brief manual applies techniques of linguistic science to learning a foreign language; intended for college students.

GUMPERZ, J. J., and FERGUSON, C. A., eds.

1960 *Linguistic Diversity in South Asia.* Bloomington: Indiana University Press. Examination of languages of India and other areas of southeast Asia by major authority on sociolinguistics.

HALL, R. A., JR.

1960 *Linguistics and Your Language.* 2nd ed. Garden City, N.Y.: Doubleday. Entertaining paperback which explodes some myths about correctness in language taught to students by generations of English teachers.

HOCKETT, C. F.

1958   *A Course in Modern Linguistics.* New York: Macmillan. Comprehensive introduction to anthropological linguistics.

HOIJER, H.

1954   The Sapir-Whorf Hypothesis. In *Language in Culture*, no. 79, ed. H. Hoijer, pp. 92–104. Washington, D.C.: American Anthropological Association. Extent to which language, particularly grammar, determines patterns of thought in different cultures.

HYMES, D. H.

1960   Lexicostatistics So Far. *Current Anthropology* 1: 3–44. Review of studies of glottochronology and other lexicostatistical techniques as of 1960.

HYMES, D. H., ed.

1964   *Language in Culture and Society: A Reader in Linguistics and Anthropology.* New York: Harper and Row.

LANGACKER, R. W.

1968   *Language and Its Structure: Some Fundamental Linguistic Concepts.* New York: Harcourt, Brace and World. Technical treatment of some fundamental linguistic concepts.

LEHMANN, W. P.

1962   *Historical Linguistics: An Introduction.* New York: Holt, Rinehart and Winston. Introduction to language families and other aspects of historical linguistics.

1972   *Descriptive Linguistics: An Introduction.* New York: Random House. Many of the new approaches to linguistics developed during the 1960s.

LOUNSBURY, F.

1964   A Formal Account of Crow- and Omaha-Type Kinship Terminologies. In *Explorations in Cultural Anthropology: Essays in Honor of George Peter Murdock*, ed. W. H. Goodenough, pp. 351–387. New York: McGraw-Hill. An anthropological linguist proposes rules to generate certain classifications of kinsmen.

LYONS, J.

1968   *Theoretical Linguistics.* London: Cambridge University Press. Technical treatment of linguistic theory.

METZGER, D., and WILLIAMS, G. E.

1966   Some Procedures and Results in the Study of Native Categories: Tzeltal "Firewood." *American Anthropologist* 68: 389–407. How the Tzeltal Indians classify words they use for fuel.

SAHLINS, M. D.

1958   *Social Stratification in Polynesia.* Seattle: University of Washington Press. Similarities and differences in social and political complexity of Polynesian societies.

SAPIR, E.

1911   The History and Varieties of Human Speech. *The Popular Science Monthly* 79: 45–67. Early linguist proposes role of language in conditioning thought.

STURTEVANT, W. C.

1964   Studies in Ethnoscience. In *Transcultural Studies in Cognition*, ed. A. K. Romney and R. G. D'Andrade. *American Anthropologist* (special publication) 66, no. 3, part 2; pp. 99–131. Comprehensive review article summarizes results and prospects of anthropological studies of native classification systems.

SWADESH, M.

1951   Diffusional Cumulation and Archaic Residue as Historical Explanation. *Southwestern Journal of Anthropology* 7: 1–21. Originator of glottochronology introduces his subject.

VERIN, P., KOTTAK, C. P., and GORLIN, P.

1969   The Glottochronology of Malagasy Speech Communities. *Oceanic Linguistics* 8: 26–83. Study of languages and dialects of Madagascar; includes a computer program for glottochronological comparison and tables giving various estimates of divergence time for between 1 and 99 shared cognates on the 100-word list.

The End of the Primitive
World and the Contemporary
Relevance of Anthropology

12. Culture and Personality

Anthropology and psychology intersect in the study of culture and personality. Psychologists have concerned themselves primarily with variations in individual behavior in a given society, most commonly their own country. Anthropologists, on the other hand, have attempted to view personality in comparative perspective. Intensive fieldwork on child rearing, personality formation, and other aspects of enculturation has established generalized interrelationships between cultural and psychological variables. Personality types associated with sex and age, and, in more heterogeneous societies, with classes, subcultures, and ethnic groups, have been investigated. Culture and personality researchers have also attempted to abstract basic or modal personality types which override status differences and apply, to some extent at least, to all members of a given culture.

To understand fully the nature and implications of culture and personality research, it is necessary to define personality and understand its relationship to culture. According to anthropologist Victor Barnouw, "personality is a more or less enduring organization of focus within the individual associated with a complex of fairly consistent attitudes, values, and modes of perception which account in part for the individual's consistency of behavior [1973, p. 10]." Anthropologist Anthony F. C. Wallace has defined personality as "those ways of behavior or techniques of solving problems which have a high probability of use by one individual [1970, p. 7]."

Wallace introduces the term *mazeway*, which includes the entire set of cognitive maps, of positive and negative goals, that an individual maintains at a given time. Its relationship to the individual parallels that of culture to population. Personality covers the same phenomena, but on a higher level of abstraction whereby parts of individual mazeways are examined and classified. As every culture is unique, every individual's mazeway has its own peculiarities, is the sum total of that individual's experiences. Comparison of mazeways and personalities of individuals from different social groups, abstracted from their behavior, from conversations with them, from various test results, and from discussions of dreams, allows the anthropologist to abstract personality types associated with these groups and to formulate a modal personality type for the society as a whole. Deviations of specific individuals can then be evaluated.

What is the relationship between such research and cultural anthropology in general? Culture and personality studies do not take a topical approach to specific institutions such as kinship, marriage, economics, politics, religion, and social stratification. Rather, culture and personality studies emphasize individuals as representatives of their culture and also as individuals. Certain psychological variables, such as levels of anxiety, aggression, goals of achievement, motivations, conservatism, receptivity to change, degree of cooperation, and individualism, are examined. Studies often include speculations about the inner attitudes of individuals, abstracted from their verbal and nonverbal behavior, and attempt to determine how widely these psychological attributes are shared. Ethnographic fieldwork more usually focuses on actual behavior and its outward results, on analyses of production, distribution, consumption, interpersonal behavior, household organization, marriage patterns, and other relationships between individuals and between groups.

Early Contributions to Culture and Personality Research

Many psychologists agree that the early years of life are crucial in personality formation. Accordingly, anthropologists have paid special attention to child rearing in non-Western cultures, often with the goal of contrasting modes of enculturation in such areas with those of the contemporary Western world. Recently, more ambitious scientific aims, including statistical generalization about relationships between child training and other aspects of culture, have been undertaken.

Margaret Mead: child training and sex roles

Margaret Mead, one of the leading anthropologists of this century, is perhaps best known for her comparative studies of culture and personality in the South Sea Islands. One of her earlier works, *Coming of Age in Samoa* (1949, orig. 1928), involved a nine-month study of adolescent Samoan girls. Her goal was to compare Samoan adolescence with the stressful adolescence characteristic of American youth. Mead's hypothesis was that the psychological changes associated with puberty here were not inevitable but were culturally conditioned. She found, as anticipated, that Samoan adolescence was a relatively easy period; sexual frustrations imposed in American society were absent. Other studies conducted subsequently in the Pacific, and employing psychological instruments unavailable to Mead in 1925, suggest that sexual freedom does not always guarantee the absence of frustrations and anxieties in adult life.

Like other early culture and personality researchers, Mead relied heavily on her own impressions of the feelings and emotions of Samoan girls. Although she reported several cases of deviant individuals, Mead was more interested in the *typical* adolescent experience. She eschewed use of statistical data, so that the ratio of normal to deviant behavior cannot be established. In commenting on her method of culture and personality research, Mead stated that "the student of the more intangible and psychological aspects of human behavior is forced to illuminate rather than demonstrate a thesis [1949, p. 169]." Different approaches to culture and personality research, including a more "scientific" one, are discussed later.

Growing Up in New Guinea (1930) is Mead's examination of enculturation (which she called education) among the Manus of the Admiralty Islands north of New Guinea. She found both similarities and differences between the personalities of Manus and Americans, which she attributed to patterns of enculturation. She found that the Manus possessed a kind of "Protestant ethic"; they valued hard work and respected property and financial success. Children were allowed considerable independence from parental supervision and were enculturated as much or more by their age peers as by their parents. Individualism and independence were emphasized, and deference to elders was not stressed. Mead found that Manus children, though alert, lacked imagination. She attributed this to lack of parental interest and supervision. The Manus economy was based on trading and fishing, and such a personality type has been reported for other foraging societies.

Sex and Temperament in Three Primitive Societies (1950, orig. 1935) does not focus on enculturation, but is a comparative study based on Mead's fieldwork among three different groups in New Guinea. According to Mead, Arapesh men and women act much as Americans expect women to act, in a mild, parental, responsive way; Mundugumor men and women, on the other hand, act as she believed we expect men to act, fiercely and aggressively. Finally, Tchambuli males suggested the American female stereotype—were catty, wore curls, and went shopping—while women were energetic and managerial and placed less emphasis on personal adornment than the men (p. 170).

Ruth Benedict: cultures as individuals

Though her principal interest was not in child rearing, Ruth Benedict's widely read *Patterns of Culture* influenced much subsequent research on child-training practices. Unlike Mead's work, *Patterns of Culture* drew on published materials rather than personal field experiences. Benedict contrasted what she perceived as broadly different cultural orientations among the Dobu of the Pacific, the Kwakiutl of the Northwest Coast of North America, and the Zuñi of the American Southwest. Her description of the Zuñi and the Kwakiutl have proved the most provocative, and I

shall examine these people as Benedict characterized them. The Kwakiutl, whose potlatch system was described in Chapter 9, are atypical foragers. They inhabit a nonmarginal and relatively propitious environment and possess tribal rather than band organization. The Zuñi, like the Hopi whom Benedict also includes in her description, are one of the Pueblo groups of the American Southwest. They were irrigation agriculturalists but lacked state organization.

Benedict saw entire cultures as integrated by one or two dominant psychological themes, and she proposed that cultures, in this case the Zuñi and the Kwakiutl, might be labeled in terms of these psychological attributes. *Dionysian* describes the psychological character of the Kwakiutl and most other American Indian cultures, and *Apollonian* describes the Zuñi and other Pueblo groups. Benedict took these labels from the study of Greek drama *The Birth of Tragedy* by the German philosopher Friedrich Nietzsche. She portrayed the Kwakiutl as constantly striving to escape the ordinary limitations of existence, to achieve excess, which would allow them to break into another order of experience. Given these strivings, Dionysians valued drunkenness, the use of drugs, fasting and self-torture, and frenzy and other forms of religious intoxication. The Apollonian Zuñi, on the other hand, were described as noncompetitive and retiring, gentle and peace-loving. Benedict found Dionysian traits, including strife and factionalism, painful ceremonials, and disruptive psychological states, to be absent among them. She described instead their preference for the middle of the road and their distrust of drunkenness and other forms of excess.

The type of approach used by Benedict in her study of culture has been termed *configurationalism*. In Benedict's view, cultures were integrated wholes; each was uniquely different from each other, and no cross-cultural comparison was possible.

She represents perhaps the most extreme of the cultural relativists, those who assert that particular cultures are ineffable jewels, comprehensible only in their own terms and therefore not comparable to any others. However, Benedict's descriptions of populations of the Northwest Coast and the Pueblos have been disputed by several authorities. They point out that she ignored more cooperative and amiable aspects of Kwakiutl life, while at the same time overlooking evidence of factionalism, strife, suicide, painful whipping ceremonies, and actual incidences of alcoholism among the Zuñi, Hopi, and other Pueblo peoples. Others have very aptly criticized Benedict for her "shreds and patches" characterization of most American Indians. In exempting only the Pueblos from the Dionysian category she ignored considerable cultural variation in the Americas. In ironic contrast to what the title of her work purports, only the Kwakiutl and Zuñi were treated as integral wholes. The behavior of other groups could be ripped from its cultural fabric and used to bolster the Dionysian stereotype.

Nevertheless, Benedict's use of individual psychologistic labels to characterize whole cultures contributed to subsequent culture and personality studies. In her work as in others, child-rearing practices were found to be very influential in the formation of individual personality and national character.

National character

Studies of national character enjoyed considerable popularity in the United States during World War II and through the early 1950s. Few national character studies have been published since 1960, however, probably in part because of difficulties in abstracting basic personality types from nations whose populations number several million. Those conducted by anthropologists Ruth Benedict, Margaret Mead, and Geoffrey Gorer used only a small number of informants to generalize about shared personality traits of entire nations. During World War II, several anthropologists involved in the war effort attempted to provide clues to the personality structure and patterns of customary response of the Japanese people. Naturally, due to the war, these were studies of culture at a distance. Some techniques used were interviewing Japanese living in the United States or other areas outside their homeland, viewing Japanese films, and reading Japanese books, magazines, and historical works.

Since their aim was to describe *common* behavior patterns and personality traits, the anthropologists engaged in national character research often ignored significant variation in personality and behavior. They relied on the assumption that each individual samples, to an extent at least, group-wide patterns. Examination of individuals could therefore contribute to the composite pattern insofar as such differences attributable to special status and peculiarity of experience were taken into account.

Some conflicting notions of culture have emerged in the debate over the value of national character studies: Should culture be viewed as a more or less autonomous force which influences individual personality and behavior patterns? Or is description of a culture derived from the observation of the behavior of numerous individuals, with the variations in socioeconomic status and differences in life experiences? The national character researchers never satisfactorily drew a sample which could encapsulate the entire range of variation in a complex nation, nor does it seem that such a goal will ever be attainable.

The influence of Freud is also apparent in many national character studies. The most famous example involves a proposed relationship between severe early toilet training and a compulsive Japanese personality preoccupied with ritual, order, and cleanliness. According to Geoffrey Gorer (1943), toilet training and the compulsion it engendered led to aggressive feelings which expressed themselves in warfare. Other anthropologists concurred with Gorer. Weston LaBarre (1945), for example, found the Japanese to be the most compulsive people in the world and linked this to sphincter control. In *The Chrysanthemum and the Sword* (1946), Ruth Benedict also accepted the toilet-training hypothesis. Subsequent research on Japanese both in Japan and elsewhere questions this compulsive stereotype. In fact, many researchers have found that toilet training is less of a preoccupation among Japanese than among Americans.

Under the auspices of a program known as Columbia University Research in Contemporary Culture, Gorer and Rickman produced *The People of Great Russia* (1949), a study of Russian national character. Gorer subsequently defended a much vilified hypothesis proposed in this book linking certain aspects of Russian national character and events in recent Russian history to the restrictive swaddling of Russian infants. He associated an alleged manic-depressive Russian personality structure with alternate swaddling (constraint) and unswaddling (freedom); and he attributed a host of events in Russian history, including the Russian Revolution and the confessions of intellectuals at Stalinist purge trials, to the guilt and anger fomented by such treatment. Among the criticisms leveled against the swaddling hypothesis is Harris' (1968, p. 455), which points out that the Stalinist confessors may not even have been swaddled. It is clear that extreme anger and guilt and revolutions have appeared in countries where swaddling is absent. Obviously, better explanations than infant training must be found for major historical events.

Often when anthropologists attempt to describe typical personality structures of human groups, what they really do is offer personal impressions. Objective fieldwork is put aside and canons of cultural relativism seem somehow to dissipate. It is difficult to believe that Ralph Linton, himself a major contributor to the culture and personality school, would write in a professional report that "the Betsimisaraka are stupid and lazy, and insolent unless kept in check. . . . The Tsimahety are moderately straightforward and courageous, and are courteous to whites, but indifferent. . . . The Sakalava are by far the bravest of the Madagascar tribes, and are also fairly intelligent [1927, pp. 296–297]." If it is this difficult to maintain scholarly objectivity in ethnographic research in a strange land, how much more difficult it is to balance a description of enemy nations. Thus we can see one of the basic flaws in national character studies.

Basic personality structure

The idea of *basic personality structure*, an earlier, though in many respects considerably more sophisticated approach, was first proposed in 1936 by the psychoanalyst Abram Kardiner. He conducted a series of culture and personality seminars, in which participating anthropologists gave reports, generally on their own ethnographic fieldwork, and Kardiner provided psychoanalytic interpretations, which were then discussed by the seminar.

Kardiner's first anthology of the seminar results, *The Individual and His Society* (1939), includes Ralph Linton's description of the Malagasy Tanala, the Betsileo, and the Marquesas Islanders. Unfortunately, Linton's research among the Tanala involved only about two months of intensive fieldwork, and his knowledge of the Betsileo was even more limited. Linton had visited the Marquesas as an archeologist and had no training or special interest in psychology during his stay there. Many errors and dubious impressions of Linton's are indicated in my fuller discussion of Tanala and Betsileo.

Kardiner's later anthology, *The Psychological Frontiers of Society* (1945), drew on ethnographic reports by James West, who had studied a community in the American Midwest, which he called Plainville; by Cora DuBois, who had conducted lengthy and exemplary culture and personality research in the Dutch East Indies; and again by Linton, whose report on the Comanche involved ethnographic reconstruction rather than firsthand fieldwork. DuBois' information, later published in *The People of Alor* (1944), had been collected most carefully and was very useful. Setting out to do a cultural-psychological study of the Alorese, she gathered Rorschach tests, children's drawings, and eight very detailed life histories. Her materials were independently analyzed by DuBois, Kardiner, and other psychologists, and their conclusions about the basic Alorese personality were similar. Kardiner found one of the major ingredients of Alorese personality to be apathy, which, in Freudian fashion, he linked to maternal neglect. DuBois felt, on the other hand, that disease might explain it.

Kardiner's work is dominated by a theoretical framework which seems to me more useful than those of other early contributors to culture and personality study. He asserted that there is a basic personality structure which typifies the members of a given society. This structure functions within a series of *cultural institutions*, patterned ways of doing things found in different cultures. Kardiner divides such institutions into two categories: primary and secondary. *Primary institutions* are those which create basic and inescapable problems of adaptation. They may include patterns of family organization, feeding, weaning, child care, sexual training and taboos, and subsistence patterns; and although they vary from one culture to another, they operate with sufficient uniformity in a given culture to develop certain similar psychological traits in all members of the society. Kardiner argued that in adapting to primary institutions, an individual acquires his personality or ego structure. Since the primary patterns are similar throughout the society, personality traits will be shared.

A culture's *secondary institutions* arise as individuals strive to cope with the primary institutions. Conceptualization of

Adapting to primary institutions: Through their relationship to their father, a Zulu warrior, these children will acquire their ego structures. *(Keystone Press Agency)*

gods, for example, may be a reflection of ego structure modeled after a primary institution—the child's relationship to his parents. While secondary institutions also vary from society to society, Kardiner felt that they would often include aspects of religion, rituals, folk tales, and other aspects of ideology.

Although Kardiner, like other students of culture and personality, argued for a form of childhood determinism, his theoretical framework could accommodate limited comparative studies and not only described cultures and personalities, but also incorporated a theory of change. On the basis of Linton's reports on Tanala and Betsileo culture, Kardiner attempted to link change in certain aspects of basic personality structure and secondary institutions to the economic change from dry rice to wet rice cultivation.

BASIC PERSONALITY OF TANALA AND BETSILEO
The Tanala, literally "people of the forest," inhabit a forested escarpment immediately to the east of the Betsileo. The Tanala are tribal horticulturalists who base their subsistence on cultivation of nonirrigated rice and several other crops. The Betsileo use artificial irrigation systems to cultivate wet rice. Linton correctly perceived a close linguistic relationship between the Tanala and

Betsileo. Noting, too, certain similarities in their cultures and their close proximity, he argued that they were closely related. The Betsileo had formerly been horticulturalists like the Tanala, and but for subsistence their cultures were similar. Linton claimed that the Betsileo had forsaken dry rice horticulture for irrigated rice agriculture. Therefore, deduced Kardiner, one must attribute differences in their basic personality structures and secondary institutions to the subsistence shift.

On the basis of my own fieldwork, I find several factual errors in Linton's account. Foremost among them is the lack of evidence that the Betsileo were ever horticulturalists. All evidence I have examined suggests that they shifted gradually from pastoralism to agriculture. Despite the incorrect observation on the part of Linton and Kardiner, however, it is true that the major contrast between the two is one of subsistence and that they come from the same ancestral population. A comparison in terms of basic personality structure and secondary institutions is therefore appropriate and may illuminate some of the psychological correlates of subsistence contrasts.

Kardiner found the Tanala primary institutions described by Linton to be similar to our own in the general character of family organization, the supreme position of the father in the family, and the nature of childhood discipline. While these similarities to American culture are debatable, the differences are clear; they include polygamy, the privileged position of the oldest son, the relatively low and immobile status of younger siblings, differences in the nature of the prestige system, and differences in the basic economy. To each of the primary institutions Kardiner attributes elements of ego structure (basic personality structure) and secondary institutions. For example, the values associated with the patriarchal family (primary institution) allowed the father to discipline his children at will, especially his sons; to exploit them by laying first claim to their labor; to frustrate their subsistence needs by controlling access to land and overseeing distribution of food to children still residing in the parental household. Various personality traits developed in response to patriarchal family organization, including repression of hatred for the father and patterns of submission to elders. These basic personality traits were then expressed in secondary institutions, such as the belief that ghosts caused illness, ancestor worship and the cult of patrilineal ancestors, and other patterns of behavior demonstrating loyalty to the dead.

A second example involves the primary institution of sibling inequality, which leads to hatred of siblings as a basic personality trait and to fear of magic as a secondary institution. Kardiner notes that to discourage the use of magic against siblings, the Tanala taboo the use of magic against agnates. Kardiner also derives the personality trait of repression of aggression from sibling inequality and links it to the secondary institutions of homosexuality and blood brotherhood (a form of ritual kinship which links two males, a male and a female, or two females as kinspeople with attendant solidarity and incest taboos).

Kardiner then contrasts Betsileo and Tanala cultures and basic personality structures, attributing differences to a change in one of the primary institutions—subsistence. According to Linton and Kardiner, the shift to irrigation resulted in several contrasts between Betsileo and Tanala, including perfection of new uses of labor to ensure water supply for irrigation, change in village descent group structure from one named descent group to many, and a difference in the basis of village social relations. When ties of kinship and marriage no longer linked villagers, they became bound by common interests and mutual antagonisms. Civil rather than familial religious sanctions incorporated within lineage organization were used to check intravillage antagonisms. Village exogamy became more typical among the Betsileo, and personal ownership of land replaced communal rights to corporate estates. The significance of patrilineal ties gradually declined. A stratum of slaves grew up in Betsileo society. The basis of social and political unity shifted from family organization to tribal associations of allied descent groups and finally to a kingdom, and new types of class interests and conflicts were engendered. The contrast obviously involves a difference between tribal and state organizations, and Kardiner indicates that in the new stratified structure different personality types—for examples, slaves and nobles—developed.

Despite these institutional changes, many of the basic patterns of child training remained essentially the same. Emphasis on early sphincter control, with toilet training beginning between two and three months and completed by six months, and certain sexual taboos persisted. The role of the father changed; since the Betsileo father, according to Kardiner, had less to dispense than the Tanala father, there was a limit to what sons could gain through submission. As private property replaced communal land, conflict among brothers increased and was extended to neighbors and more distant relatives. Hostility was openly expressed in adult life rather than being repressed. New loyalties were forged to kings and nobles. Given these changes, Betsileo personality placed a high emphasis on individual enterprise, skill, cunning, treachery, aggression, plunder, and subjugation of others. Political institutions partially checked these tendencies.

Kardiner's general impression of Betsileo compared with Tanala is unfavorable. He sees wet rice cultivation as resulting in a host of new needs and new anxieties and a great increase in insecurity among the Betsileo. He states that certain contrasts in Betsileo secondary institutions, including greater emphasis on malevolent magic and severe forms of spirit possession, had their origins in the anxiety caused by the alteration in basic personality structure. Though he was dealing with a contrast of social and economic types rather than with an actual change, Kardiner made the interesting and probably valid generalization that once a basic personality structure is established, any change in primary institutions will lead to personality changes, but these changes will move only in the direction of the already established psychic constellations. In other words, personality does not change randomly but by modification of the evolutionary material at hand. This recalls evolutionary principles that were discussed earlier.

Although factual errors in Linton's reports mar Kardiner's interpretation, Kardiner nonetheless produced a valuable comparative study of two related cultures. He attempted to place his psychological analysis within an evolutionary framework, linking personality changes to economic change and, more generally, to changes in basic institutions. Kardiner also warned students of culture and personality that diversity of personality types in a given culture increases with general social and political complexity, and he pointed to some of the anxieties associated with social stratification, private property, warfare, and state organization. Linton described Betsileo anal training as more severe than it is, and unduly emphasized conflict among brothers. My own ethnographic inquiry suggests that cooperation in Betsileo agriculture and ceremonial is extremely important and that the role of the Betsileo father who, as benefactor and respected figure, administers estates of corporate descent groups, is actually more like the role described by Linton for the Tanala father.

Since the 1950s many anthropologists have used statistical comparison of different cultures to test propositions such as Kardiner's about relationships between primary institutions and basic personality types. These have verified certain relationships between subsistence practices and attributes of culture and personality.

Cross-cultural and Comparative Studies

Beginning in the 1950s, culture and personality studies have tended to employ data from several different societies instead of just two. Scholars like John and Beatrice Whiting have attempted to improve the quality of data on child training in different societies and to generalize about personality variables on a cross-cultural basis.

Limited comparison: concern for improvements of techniques

In a project conducted in the early 1960s, six research teams used similar techniques to investigate aspects of child training in six different societies (see B. B. Whiting, 1963). The researchers worked among the Gusii of East Africa, in a New England community, in a village in northern India that was inhabited by a land-owning caste, in a peasant community in Okinawa, in a lower-caste Indian ward of a Mexican community, and in a Philippine neighborhood. Their emphasis was on comparability of

A mother and her children in a Guatemalan village. Interaction between mother and child has been the subject of comparative studies. *(Max Hunn/Frederic Lewis)*

field methods and data rather than on similarities, differences, or relationships between the societies chosen for study. Prior to the fieldwork, the time range of which was between six and fourteen months, John Whiting and his associates prepared a field guide to be used by all the field teams.

In each community the researchers studied between fifty and one hundred families, concentrating on the interaction between mothers and young children. Their field techniques included interviews and actual observation of behavior. The researchers paid particular attention to patterns of nurturance and succorance, degree of self-reliance, stress on achievement, degrees of responsibility, dominance, obedience, aggression, and sociability. The six societies were rated on the basis of psychological tones of child rearing; for example, mothers in some societies were found to be more affectionate than those in others.

On the basis of the comparative data, Beatrice Whiting noted greater frequency of homicide, assault, and disputes in the northern Indian village and among the East Africans. She suggested a relationship between these patterns and the fact that husbands and wives did not eat, sleep, or work together on a regular basis. In the other four communities, married couples had greater contact. As Victor Barnouw (1973) has suggested, however, both the East Africans and the northern Indians lived in societies where militarism, including raiding, was an established part of cultural adaptation, and historical rather than child-training variables might better explain assault, homicide, and disputes. When dealing with data from a single society, or a small number of haphazardly chosen societies, it is often difficult to discover cause and effect relationships. As we shall see, comparative studies on a larger scale contribute more to our understanding of causation in the field of culture and personality.

Limited areal comparison: value systems

In 1961 Florence Kluckholn and Fred Strodtbeck published *Variations in Value Orientation*, which was based on coordinated fieldwork among five groups in the American Southwest: Texans, Mormons, Spanish Americans, Navajo, and Zuñi. Researchers were not principally concerned with child training but with adult value systems. A questionnaire consisting of twenty-two items was administered to between twenty and twenty-five people, males and females, in each of the five communities. Questions were intended to measure differences in value orientations related to five central aspects of world view: human nature, man's relationship to nature, time orientation, activity orientation, and modality of human relationships. The researchers predicted the ratings for each community before conducting the study, and their predictions were generally borne out. Texans were characterized as individualistic, future time oriented, mastering nature, and active. Spanish Americans valued individualism, with more emphasis on present time orientation, subjugation to nature, passivity, and lineality in their relationships with others. Statistical analysis of the responses demonstrated that differences in values were significant not only from one community or ethnic group to another, but within any one community.

Anthropologist John Whiting (1970) and his associates carried out a subsequent study of three of these southwestern groups, in an attempt to link child training to the inculcation of value systems. They linked family organization to such values as tolerance or intolerance of aggression and discovered that Zuñi, whose family organization is extended, tolerate less aggression on the part of children toward peers than groups with nuclear family organization such as Texans. Extended family organization, they felt, was associated with conformity, while nuclear family organization was found in societies which placed greater value on individualism and independence and allowed greater aggression. Some comparative studies relating such family and personality variables to economy are discussed in the next section.

Limited areal comparison: personality

In the early 1960s Walter Goldschmidt organized a research project to investigate cultural and ecological variation among four groups in East Africa: the Hehe, Kamba, Pokot, and Sebei. All four groups have mixed economies combining pastoral and agricultural communities. Anthropologist Robert Edgerton, a participant in this project, gathered comparable, quantifiable information in eight of these communities, two for each group, one pastoral and one agricultural. Field instruments included eighty-five questions, ten Rorschach plates, and twenty-two color slides. A sample of at least thirty married persons of each sex was drawn for each community, and a total of 505 people were interviewed.

Statistical analysis of their responses revealed basic personality configurations which differentiate the four tribes (Edgerton, 1965). The Kamba, for example, were characterized by extreme male dominance, fear of poverty, and restrained emotions. Hehe responses suggested that they were impulsively aggressive, concerned with formal authority, profoundly mistrusting, and secretive. Other constellations marked the Pokot and the Sebei.

There were also similarities reflecting closeness of linguistic relationship. The Pokot and Sebei speak closely related languages of the Kalenjin group, while the Hehe and the Kamba speak more distantly related languages of the Bantu group. Edgerton found that the Bantu speakers were more concerned with sorcery and witchcraft and valued land over cattle. The Kalenjin speakers valued sons and daughters; the Bantus preferred sons. The Bantu groups respected rich men, the Kalenjins, prophets.

Edgerton also investigated the roles of

sex and acculturation in differentiating value systems and personality. Contrary to expectation, he found differences in responses of males and females to be insignificant. Furthermore, he could find no significant relationship between degree of contract with European culture and patterns of responses.

Ecological differences, however, did produce different constellations. The eight communities could be placed on a continuum from pastoral to agricultural. Edgerton found that the cultivators consulted with sorcerers and with one another, while the pastoralists acted more individually. The farmers valued hard work; the herders did not. The cultivators were more hostile toward, and suspicious of, their fellows than the herders. In terms of personality, the responses showed the farmers to be more indirect, given to fantasy, abstract, and anxious, and also less able to deal with their emotions and control their impulses. The herder's personality, on the other hand, was more direct, open, and bound to reality, with more effective control over emotions.

Edgerton's study is important for several reasons. His description is based on comparable, quantifiable data, collected according to definite and objective standards. Analysis of these data makes it possible to evaluate the relative contributions to overall personality of distinctive cultural traditions, historical relationships, sex, exposure to acculturation, and ecology. If personality differences reflect ecological differences in East Africa, can we generalize that similar ecology-personality interrelationships are important on a world-wide scale? Several anthropologists have argued in the affirmative.

World-wide comparisons

Irvin Child and especially John Whiting have been major contributors to cross-cultural generalizations about culture and personality, particularly about child rearing. In 1953 Whiting and Child published their *Child Training and Personality*, a cross-cultural study of attitudes toward illness. Since Whiting's influence on cross-cultural studies has been profound, his theoretical assumptions will be briefly described. Whiting has been influenced by Freudian theory as well as behavioristic psychology, in which stress is on individual, learned behavior patterns rather than instinctive drives. He has also been influenced by Clark Hull, whose learning theory approach in psychology was compatible with anthropology's traditional emphasis on culture as learned behavior. Whiting and his associates have attempted to translate certain Freudian concepts into observable categories of learned behavior and, in so doing, to apply learning theory to cross-cultural data.

The theoretical framework of Whiting's cross-cultural studies bears a noteworthy resemblance to Abram Kardiner's scheme. Whiting and Child (1953) argued that child-training practices originate in different cultural maintenance systems. Like Kardiner's primary institutions, these maintenance systems include the economic, social, and political organizations of society, especially patterns of nourishment, shelter, and protection. Similar maintenance systems produce the same kinds of child-rearing practices and subsequently adult personality types (Kardiner's basic personality structures but on a cross-cultural basis). Such personality configurations then lead to similar ideological projective systems (Kardiner's secondary institutions).

As Naroll (1970) has pointed out, many of the explanations of cultural variables provided by Whiting and his associates are *psychogenic* explanations, so called because they regard cultural variables as delayed reactions to earlier experiences, most notably those of childhood. At times, however, Whiting has offered *biogenic* explanations, linking cultural variables to physiological, genetic, climatic, dietary, or pathological causes. An example is the link between the tropics, protein malnutrition, and circumcision (Whiting, 1964).

Some scholars have related child-training practices to different levels of sociocultural evolution in human populations. For example, Barry, Bacon, and Child (1959) attempted to link child rearing to subsistence economy on a cross-cultural basis. They found that populations with large accumulations of food resources (generally herders and cultivators) usually stressed responsibility and obedience in their child-rearing patterns, while foragers and other populations with little or no food accumulation emphasized achievement, competition, self-reliance, and independence. They did not, like Edgerton in his East Africa research, differentiate personalities of cultivators from those of herders.

Yehudi Cohen (1961) has linked readiness to gratify the infant's demands for food to patterns of adult sharing, and suggests that such infant gratification and sharing will be found among foragers, where sharing has survival value. John Fisher attributes sharing among foragers to the irregularity of the food supply.

Cross-cultural studies of interrelationships between cultural and psychological variables have not been limited to child training. For example, comparative statistical studies of alcoholism, crime, internal warfare, frustration and aggression, suicide and witchcraft, have been published. Whiting and Child (1953) suggest that witchcraft accusations are more frequent in societies with a variety of stressful childtraining practices. Robert LeVine (1962), on the other hand, links witchcraft to polygyny.

Sex roles in cross-cultural perspective

While Edgerton found the personalities of East African males and females to be similar, other cross-cultural studies have suggested differences in sex roles. Barry, Bacon, and Child (1957) report a significant statistical tendency for female enculturation to stress nurturing, obedience, and responsibility, while male enculturation generally emphasizes achievement and self-reliance. The extent to which this cross-cultural generalization reflects the predominance of males in anthropology, however, has yet to be determined.

A number of interpretations balancing psychogenic against sociological explanations have been offered for some of the customary observances which differentiate males and females in society. Many cultures taboo contact of males with menstruating women. Frank Young and Albert Bacdayan (1965) have interpreted menstrual taboos as an institutionalized form of discrimination against women arising in populations where males dominate and are tightly organized. William Stephens (1961), on the other hand, has tried to explain menstrual taboos as a manifestation of castration anxieties. The problem with the latter explanation is that it does not tell us why castration anxieties arise to begin with, or, if they are universal, why menstrual taboos are not.

Some of the more interesting, if often very intricate, comparative statistical studies of sex roles are concerned with initiation ceremonies. Judith Brown (1963) found that female initiation rites generally occur in societies with uxorilocal postmarital residence, where they serve to mark the transition from girl to woman. Brown argued that in societies with virilocal postmarital residence, such ceremonies are unnecessary and therefore absent, since adulthood is marked when a girl leaves home to join her husband. Brown further argues that female initiation rites are found in societies in which women make major contributions to subsistence, for example, among cultivators and foragers.

In his book *Initiation Ceremonies* (1965), Frank Young approaches ceremonials differently. Considering not only initiation ceremonies, but also parenthood rites among women, he argues that such rites serve to dramatize female sex roles and to strengthen female solidarity.

Even more has been written about male initiation ceremonies. Frank Young (1962) argues that the ceremonies function again principally to dramatize and reinforce the social solidarity of males. Furthermore, he specified the conditions under which such rites occur—in intermediate societies where resources are varied and scattered and most efficiently exploited by cooperating groups of males.

The most intricate approach to male initiation rites emerges in a series of articles by John Whiting and various associates. Whiting believed that male initiation ceremonies would be found in societies with prolonged postpartum sexual taboos (restrictions on intercourse between husband and wife for a year or more after the birth of a child) and prolonged mother-infant sleeping arrangements that excluded the husband. Whiting, Kluckholn, and Anthony (1958) argued that such sleeping arrangements would promote extreme dependence of boys on their mothers. A boy would feel hostile to his father when, the taboo period over, the father displaced him from the mother's bed. Furthermore, fathers would resent their sons for separating them from their wives. Male initiation ceremonies, in which adolescent males are often separated from women and subjected to exposure, tests of endurance, or circumcision, would sever emotional dependency on the mother as puberty approached, quell any incestuous desires of boy for mother, dissipate the boy's rivalry toward his father, and allow the father to express his hostility toward his sons. The hypothesis was validated by cross-cultural data. Whiting and his associates chose fifty-six societies representing forty-five of the sixty cultural areas in Murdock's World Ethnographic Sample (1957). They found that 80 percent of the cases corresponded with the prediction—that is, initiation ceremonies, prolonged postpartum taboo, and mother-infant sleeping arrangements occurred together. On the basis of more detailed examination and discussion of the data, they were also able to offer convincing explanations for the exceptions.

Subsequently, Whiting (cf. Burton and Whiting, 1961; Whiting, 1964) revised his rationale and focused on circumcision, linking it, through an intricate chain of statistical correlations, to climate and diet. Because it illustrates so well the often intricate stages between cause and effect in cross-cultural studies, let us examine this series of correlations in greater detail.

PROTEIN DEFICIENCY, CROSS-SEX IDENTIFICATION, AND CIRCUMCISION In certain parts of the tropics, low protein diets are provided by cultivation of root crops and fruits, and cultivation is more important than hunting, fishing, or herding. Young children are in such areas especially susceptible to kwashiorkor, a condition caused by lack of protein. If a mother becomes pregnant while still nursing an infant, the quality of her milk may decline, and the child may be in danger of protein malnutrition. Certain populations, including many in tropical South America, attack this problem through abortion, and there are professional abortionists in such societies.

In many parts of Africa and in the islands of the Pacific, however, the problem is solved by tabooing sexual relations between wife and husband for a year or more after childbirth, and sometimes until the child is weaned. Often, the child sleeps in the mother's bed while the postpartum taboo is in effect, and the father sleeps in a separate bed or room or outside the maternal household altogether. Whiting (1964) found that sleeping practices are also associated with climate. Husband and wife normally sleep in the same bed when winter temperature falls below fifty degrees but apart when winter climate is hot and humid. However, presumably because it is cooler to sleep with an infant than with a husband, in tropical areas women often sleep with their babies.

Given the postpartum taboo and the prolonged mother-child sleeping arrangement, Whiting suggests that several consequences follow. Since the father is deprived of sexual access to his wife, he is likely to try to become polygynous. After all, a man may have sexual relations with his other wife or wives while one wife is still nursing and therefore tabooed. Whiting found that in many polygynous societies men in fact never sleep in the same bed with their wives, and thus they do not necessarily feel hostility toward their sons.

He subsequently argued that a strong cross-sex identification may be produced in the male infant from sleeping with his mother. Furthermore, the mother may derive sexual gratification from her son's proximity at a time when she is deprived of sexual attentions from her husband. Polygyny is commonly found in societies with virilocal postmarital residence patterns, since males bring their wives to their own village rather than moving themselves. Virilocal residence demands more solidarity and cooperation and strong masculine identification in sons. Yet sons, having slept with their mothers, develop strong identifications with the opposite sex. To establish male sex identification in sons and to divert incestuous feelings between mothers and sons as puberty approaches, such societies often have severe male initiation rites of which the most common is circumcision. Thus climate leads to circumcision.

Cooperation, Competition, Individualism, and Social Types

Peasant society and the image of limited good

George Foster (1965) has described a general cognitive orientation that he believes to be characteristic of all "classic" peasant societies—presumably, communities that farm and are included within a nation-state. Rather than relying on quantitative data from ethnographic samples, Foster discusses evidence from several peasant societies in different world areas to confirm the existence of a dominant theme of peasant orientation, or world view, which he calls the "image of limited good."

Foster argues that this cognitive orientation was never verbalized. However, he felt that such an unconscious structure did exist and served to explain a great deal about similarities in peasant behavior in different areas.

According to Foster, the image of limited good views all desired goods as finite in quantity. These would include land, wealth, health, love and friendship, manliness and honor, respect and status, power and influence, safety and security. Because all goods within the social, economic, and natural worlds are regarded as scarce, peasants believe that one member of a community can only profit by taking more than his rightful share of goods from the common pool and therefore depriving others. To the image of limited good Foster links several of what he regards as general attributes of peasant societies: emphasis on luck, fatalism, quarreling within and between families, stress on individualism, difficulties in cooperating; lack of emphasis on achievement, hard work, or thrift; and disposal of wealth in ritual expenses rather than capital accumulation. Foster pictures peasant communities as consisting of individualistic, atomized persons and households who never cooperate for the welfare of the community but only to satisfy reciprocal obligations.

When certain individuals improve their position over others, through increased wealth, for example, peasant ideology deals with these improvements in several ways. Differential wealth may be allowed, Foster suggests, if it comes from outside the community, thus not dipping into the finite pool of good. Individuals may prosper by external wage work, by favors from external patrons, or by sheer luck, and still leave the community's supply of good intact. If, however, wealth differentials reflect activity within the community, certain informal and unorganized forces of community opinion come into play as mechanisms of leveling differences. Individuals are forced to undertake ceremonial obligations, expenses that take away their wealth and leave them with prestige, which is not regarded as dangerous. Or they may become targets of community censure, character assassination, gossip, backbiting, envy, ostracism, and sometimes physical violence.

Given these sanctions, individuals who prosper try to hide their good fortune. Their dress, homes, and diet reflect the general standards. People who suffer ill fortune and fall below the community norm are also distrusted, for they are thought to be envious and potentially dangerous to all above them.

Although Foster's image of limited good is intriguing, it may be questioned. He finds his best evidence for such a cognitive orientation among peasants in Latin America and Europe. Peasants in other parts of the world, notably in African states, are often considerably less individualistic. If there is competition among the Betsileo, for example, it is normally expressed in rivalries between descent groups rather than individuals or families. Foster finds love and friendship, like wealth, to be conceived as finite, and links widespread sibling rivalry in peasant societies to competition for mother's love. Scholars who stress the role of child training in the formation of adult personalities might question whether sibling rivalry is confined to peasant societies. Older children the world over are weaned to make way for younger siblings, thus precipitating much hostility. Rivalry for parental affection is well known in the United States and is basic to Freudian theory. The relationship of Betsileo siblings, as Linton and Kardiner pointed out, has a hostile component, but we might also link this to rivalries over inheritance.

It seems to me that Foster's image of limited good is most characteristic given certain cultural traditions. Many Latin American communities share with Europeans an emphasis on nuclear family organization. Surely ideology will differ if other social units, like corporate descent groups, are important. An image of limited good, as Foster himself points out, is also a response to the typical structural and economic position of peasants within the larger, national societies that include them. As Foster states, often good *is* lim-ited by outsiders. Among the externally imposed limitations to peasant mobility are prior land ownership patterns and lack of access to adequate medical attention, government services and benefits, and the national power hierarchy. In concluding his article Foster suggests—and there is considerable ethnographic evidence to support him—that where access to wealth, power, and influence is more open, the image of the limited good declines.

The Protestant ethic and the spirit of capitalism

Consider now an argument for change from a peasant mentality operating on the principle of limited good to a personality structure valuing hard work, thrift, and capital accumulation. This rational, entrepreneurial type has been immortalized by sociologist Max Weber in his famous work *The Protestant Ethic and the Spirit of Capitalism* (1958). This controversial but influential book examines some of the differences between industrial capitalism in Europe and elsewhere, that is, in economies which stress the pursuit of profit. Weber argued that capitalism involving rational industrial organization attuned to a regular market demanded an entirely new personality type, and he linked this personality type to values inculcated by the ascetic Protestantism promulgated by Luther, Calvin, and other early Protestant leaders.

Weber noted that European Protestants tended to be more successful financially than European Catholics, and he attributed their relative success to the difference in religion. He characterized Catholics as more traditional, more concerned with happiness and security than Protestants, whose faith substituted other-worldly concerns for enjoyment of this life. Modern industrial capitalism, according to Weber, demanded that traditional attitudes, such as those typically expressed by European peasants, be replaced by others, more compatible with profit seeking and capital accumulation. (In an illustration of traditionalism, which recalls Foster's limited good, Weber described the case of a wealthy farmer who, in an attempt to increase the productivity of his hired workers, raised their piece rates, only to find that rather than working more to earn more, they actually decreased productivity to maintain their previous earnings.) Early Protestantism, according to Weber, provided a different ethos, one which valued hard work, an ascetic life, and profit seeking.

Associated with early Protestantism were notions that man's success on earth was a barometer of divine favor. In some versions of Protestantism, individuals could gain divine favor through a life of good works. Other Protestant sects stressed predestination, the doctrine that only a few mortals had been selected by God for eternal life, and that no one could change his fate. However, material success, achieved through hard work, could serve to indicate that an individual was one of the elect; and therefore, success, and its companion hard work, were valued because of their role in convincing individuals of their salvation.

English Puritanism continued the earlier Calvinist thrust in emphasizing hard work and asceticism. Puritanism stressed constant activity involving physical or mental labor, discouraged leisure and enjoyment of this life, called waste of time the deadliest sin, and placed no value on meditation. Labor came to be considered man's duty as ordained by God. This Protestantism valued the simplicity and asceticism of the middle-class home and condemned ostentation as a form of worldly enjoyment. The fruits of success, a sign of faith or preelection, could only be offered to the church or reinvested; otherwise, hoarded wealth might lead to temptation. Weber also attributes to early Protestantism a character of self-righteousness and a sober legality, consonant with the notion that a man could expand his profit-making activity as long as he kept in mind the common good as well as his own and did not engage in injurious, illegal, avaricious, or dishonest activity.

According to Weber, the change in the European world view which followed the Reformation resulted in modern, rational, industrial capitalism. Weber indicates that the transition from traditionalism to rational capitalism was blocked at times by social and psychological barriers, similar to the negative sanctions against improvement which Foster has described for peasant communities. The struggle to exceed the limits set by need, the attitude which seeks profits rationally and systematically, engendered mistrust, hatred, and moral indignation. Weber reports that successful Protestant innovators were men of unusually strong character, possessing definite and highly developed ethical qualities. Because of these attributes they could command the absolute confidence of their customers and workmen, which was essential to their success. Furthermore, Weber argues that rational organization of capitalist enterprise depended on separation of business from the household, its nexus in peasant societies. Again Protestant doctrines made such disassociation possible. Protestantism emphasized individualism. Persons, not families, were predestined to salvation, and an individual's good works could reveal his grace. His family, more important in Foster's peasant society, was a secondary matter for Weber's Protestant.

Controversy surrounds Weber's thesis. He dismisses economic forces, historical events, and political structures as causes of Western capitalism, but other scholars have simply demonstrated their importance. In the 1970s people of many religions and world views are successful capitalists, and the Protestant ethic and the spirit of capitalism as Weber described them survive most obviously in the books of Ayn Rand. There are ample signs that Protestant asceticism has been replaced by a broad tolerance for the enjoyment of this life. The need for hard and constant work has been replaced by the weekend football

Salmon fishing by American Indians in Oregon, who depend on their catches for profit as well as subsistence. *(Brown Brothers)*

syndrome. Some of our Protestant politicians mouth the value of hard work to people on welfare, while counting themselves among our major sports fans.

In fact, traditional Protestant emphasis on honesty and hard work often seems antithetical to modern capitalism maneuverings. Regardless of how much it contributed to the development of Western capitalism, however, the Protestant ethic did exist. Its individualistic focus was very compatible with the severance of ties to land and kinsmen which accompanied the Industrial Revolution. Might such an ethic exist in nonindustrial areas, as an example of convergent evolution? In the case that follows, I argue that it does.

The spirit of fishermen Foster's image of limited good cautions peasants against producing beyond their needs. Weber's Protestant ethic demands that they do so. To produce profits, however, one must dispense with certain social and ceremonial obligations, which would otherwise limit his accumulation of capital. The relationship between independent, achievement-oriented personalities and foraging economies has already been mentioned. Thus we might expect individualistic personality types to be found most characteristically at different ends of the evolutionary continuum, among foragers and industrialists.

Arembepe is a village of some 800 people located near Salvador, capital of Bahia state in northeastern Brazil. Most Arembepeiros derive their income directly or indirectly from fishing in the Atlantic Ocean. However, Arembepe is not an isolated foraging community, but is tied to the Brazilian nation economically, politically, and socially. Arembepeiros sell their fish to marketers from outside their village, often to the detriment of their own subsistence needs. Some people in Arembepe farm small plots in addition to fishing. Although they do not live off the land, they are similar in their behavior and ideology to peasants in nearby communities, and their economic and political ties to the Brazilian nation are also similar. Since they share cultural and structural features with peasants, we might expect to find some of the principles of Foster's image of limited good among them—and we do. On the other hand, since they are fishermen, we can also expect them to be independent and achievement-oriented. Arembepeiros have no corporate descent groups, nor are social units larger than the household, which is generally inhabited by a nuclear family. Their social organization is individualistic and atomistic, though not to the extent that Foster leads us to expect in a peasant community.

Despite its inclusion within a stratified nation-state, Arembepe is a relatively homogeneous community socially and economically. All Arembepeiros belong to the national lower class. While differences in wealth and status exist within Arembepe society, these are infinitesimal compared with the economic variations that exist in Brazilian society as a whole. For reasons that will be discussed in Chapter 13, achieved economic status is far more significant than ascribed status in Arembepe. Individuals have a relatively equal chance to ascend the local ladder of success, and social and economic advance often reflects success in the local fishing industry. Sailboats normally fish with crews of four or five men, one of whom is the captain. Often captains are full or half owners of these boats. In general, the Arembepe fishing fleet can be divided into four groups: (1) ordinary fishermen; (2) successful young captains; (3) older captains who once belonged to the second group; and (4) the least successful captains who fish more irregularly, primarily because of alcoholism.

On the matter of what determines success in fishing, measured in terms of total annual catch, there are different opinions. Ordinary fishermen, the first group, argue that captains must have good eyesight to espy distant landmarks that mark profitable fishing spots. They cite inadequacies in their own eyesight to justify their not becoming captains. Similarly, captains in the third group blame their declining catches on their failing eyesight, which prevents

them from fishing as effectively as in the past. Members of group four, the least successful group of captains, also cite good eyesight as the major requirement for a captain, and say that all captains have it. Ordinary fishermen explain differential success of fishing boats in terms of better eyesight of their captains and also luck. Older, but once successful, captains explain differential catches in terms of captains' eyesight. The fourth group of captains, however, generally attribute differential success to luck, refusing to admit that some captains are better than others.

The most successful, and generally the youngest, captains, those in group two, have a still different rationale for their success. They link it to factors which recall Weber's Protestant ethic. They cite their hard and constant work and sobriety, rarely mentioning luck or eyesight. My own analysis of determinants of success in fishing corresponds strikingly with this explanation. I found systematic differences in their behavior compared with less successful fishermen. First, because they are generally in their twenties and early thirties, they enjoy good health, which permits their boats to go out more regularly than the others. Thus they attract hard-working crew members because they are dependable, are able to remain at sea longer, and can tolerate more work and weather conditions that are often unpleasant. Second, like Weber's Protestant entrepreneurs, they take calculated risks. Unlike other captains, they sometimes travel to further fishing zones during the winter, when there is always the danger of a sudden storm and rough seas. They experiment more, seeking new fishing zones. Often their risks pay off in terms of larger catches. Third, although unlike Weber's Protestants they are not teetotalers, they drink only on festive occasions, and they prefer beer to the crude sugar cane rum that ordinary fishermen and less successful captains consume. Because it is more expensive, beer is a status symbol. It is also less intoxicating than rum. Hence, young captains can drink more without getting drunk, and they miss no fishing days because of drunkenness. Fourth, they command better crew allegiance (and attract better crew members). Fifth, they are respected within the community. They become officers of the local fishermen's society; other people are aware of their success and eager to join their crews.

Like Weber's Protestant entrepreneurs, they constantly strive to use profits derived from fishing to produce additional profits —by purchasing plots of land and livestock, by planting coconut trees, or by investing in new technology to increase their fishing productivity.

In contrast to the ideal peasant described by Foster, Arembepeiros do not rely on land, which is an easily limitable resource. Their subsistence comes from the sea, a more open frontier in which the assignment of property rights poses more difficulties. Hard work there does pay off. Furthermore, the high rate of inflation which plagues Brazil has also selected for reinvestment. With constant devaluation, hoarding would be disastrous.

As in the United States, kinship in Arembepe is relatively narrow. Only parents, siblings, "niblings" (nieces and nephews), aunts, uncles, and first cousins are important relatives. However, Arembepeiros do not normally restrict their kinship ties to the extent that we do, nor as severely as did Weber's Protestant capitalist. Since fishing demands hard work and youthful vigor, even the most successful fishermen know that their productivity will eventually decline. While they attempt to anticipate their declining years by building up alternative sources of income on the land, in the absence of a pension or social security system they can never be totally sure that they will not have to depend on their kinsmen at some time in the future. Community opinion forces them to share a part of their present wealth with their kinsmen.

Arembepeiros do not appear to think of good as limited. No doubt this reflects their combination of an open economy and articulation with an external economy. However, social mechanisms similar to those that Foster has described for the classic peasant community do operate in Arembepe to ensure that individuals do not stray too far from what is considered appropriate behavior. Consider the case of Laurentino, Arembepe-born son of a migrant from the Brazilian interior. Like his father, Laurentino has never been a fisherman but runs two stores in the village. Laurentino spent several years outside of Arembepe, and when he returned to the community he opened one of his stores. Arembepeiros say that during his absence he made a pact with the devil, and they attribute his initial commercial success in Arembepe to this pact. His store prospered; he bought four fishing boats; and he took over his father's store when the latter died.

Since his return, the social gap between Laurentino and other Arembepeiros has steadily widened. Villagers fear his devil, which, on the basis of his early success, they believe is powerful. They speak of nightly devil worship sessions in his house and of a demon kept in a cage somewhere in his store. They distrust him because, unlike other local storekeepers, he does not extend credit. Laurentino has played a major role in cultivating social distance, perhaps in an attempt to free himself from the obligations of kinship that all other Arembepeiros assume. He finds it amusing that other villagers think of him as a witch. Flaunting Catholic doctrine, he bought birth control pills for his wife and demanded that she take them. When she did become pregnant, he let it be known that he would not have his child baptized.

He has suffered as a result of his unconventional behavior. Villagers avoid his stores because they fear him and he does not extend credit. No longer able to find men willing to serve as captains of his sailboats, he had to destroy all four of them. Not only is he the most isolated man in the community, but his efforts to increase his wealth have been blocked by community opinion. Obviously, it is possible to prosper in Arembepe, but only within the limits set by community opinion.

Detailed analysis of Arembepe illustrates that several different ideological themes can coexist in a single, relatively homogeneous community. Explanatory frameworks and other aspects of cognitive orientation reflect reference group. Yet the ideology of sharing with less fortunate kinsmen overrides differences in outlook among village subgroups and, as we shall see in the following chapter, has social and economic implications. This analysis sug-

SUMMARY

Anthropologists have placed psychological findings in comparative perspective through culture and personality research. In contrast to traditional ethnography, which is principally interested in observed behavior and its results, the culture and personality approach is an attempt to explore the inner attributes of individuals and to determine personality types characteristic of different statuses and different cultures.

Early students of culture and personality often relied on personal impressions in gathering field data. Assuming that within any culture individuals share some personality traits, anthropologists also undertook studies of basic personality structure and national character. National character studies, popular during World War II, have been criticized for various reasons, including their frequently impressionistic basis, their overemphasis on childhood determinism, and their lack of range. A similar, but theoretically more sophisticated approach was developed by Abram Kardiner, a psychoanalyst, in association with anthropologists including Ralph Linton, James West, and Cora DuBois. Kardiner proposed that a culture's basic personality structure represents the end result of individual adaptations to certain primary institutions, including family organization and subsistence economy. The basic personality structure then influenced secondary institutions, including aspects of religion and ideology. Religious conceptions might be modeled after a man's relationship to his parents, for example. Statistically oriented anthropologists John Whiting and Irvin Child later applied a framework similar to Kardiner's to cross-cultural relationships between culture and personality variables.

The quality of culture and personality generalizations improved as research teams undertook problem-oriented fieldwork, using objective techniques for gathering

Sources and Suggested Readings

BARNOUW, V.
  1973 *Culture and Personality*. Rev. ed. Homewood, Ill.: Dorsey Press. Most readable and complete introduction to the field.

BARRY, H., BACON, M. K., and CHILD, I. L.
  1957 A Cross-Cultural Survey of Some Sex Differences in Socialization. *Journal of Abnormal and Social Psychology* 55: 327–332. Data in this article suggest some generality for American sex roles.

  1959 Relation of Child Training to Subsistence Economy. *American Anthropologist* 61: 51–63. Describes similarities in child training and personality among herders and cultivators who are contrasted with foragers.

BENEDICT, R.
  1946 *The Chrysanthemum and the Sword*. Boston: Houghton Mifflin. Descrip-

gests that despite their demonstrated value, statistical cross-cultural studies of relationships between personality variables and cultural, social, and economic variables must be supplemented with intensive analysis of particular cases in order to clarify influences of culture on personality.

Internal variation within a cultural unit or cross-cultural type may turn out to be as significant, and as explicable, as variation between types.

data on child training and other aspects of personality formation. Limited comparisons of value systems and personality configurations have been conducted in certain world areas, and ecological, cultural, historical, and other correlates of personality structure have been specified. In world-wide studies using statistical techniques and quantitative data, anthropologists have demonstrated relationships between personality variables, on the one hand, and social evolutionary type and economy, on the other. Male initiation ceremonies, for example, have been associated with polygyny, virilocal postmarital residence, temperature, and diet. Female initiation ceremonies have been linked to uxorilocal postmarital residence and importance of female labor in subsistence. Rationales for such relationships have been offered in terms of child rearing, dependency relationships, and cross-sex identifications.

Other social scientists have taken a non-statistical approach, arguing for relationships between personality and economy. George Foster found an "image of limited good" to be part of the cognitive orientation of "classic" peasant societies. Max Weber attributed the emergence of industrial capitalism to rationality, asceticism, emphasis on hard and constant work, and profit seeking, all of which he believed to be associated with Protestantism.

A case study of a Brazilian fishing community demonstrates that differences in explanatory frameworks and other aspects of cognition may reflect reference group even in a relatively homogeneous community. Nevertheless, all members of the Brazilian community partook in a general ideology of sharing. Both individual studies of personality and cognition and larger, comparative studies promise to increase our understanding of the determinants and effects of psychological and cognitive variation.

tion of national character based on the study of Japanese culture from a distance.

1959   (orig. 1934). *Patterns of Culture.* New York: New American Library. Popular handbook of configurationalism; examines Kwakiutl of Northwest Coast of North America, Melanesians of Dobu, and Zuñi of the American Southwest.

BROWN, J. K.
1963   A Cross-Cultural Study of Female Initiation Rites. *American Anthropologist* 65: 837–853. Relates female puberty rites to uxorilocal residence and major female role in subsistence economy.

BURTON, R. V., and WHITING, J. W. M.
1961   The Absent Father and Cross-sex Identity. *Merrill-Palmer Quarterly of Behavior and Development* 7: 85–95.

Psychological rationale, minus the Oedipus complex, for association between male initiation ceremonies, postpartum taboos, and prolonged mother-infant sleeping practices.

COHEN, Y.
1961   Food and Its Vicissitudes: A Cross-Cultural Study of Sharing and Non-Sharing. In *Social Structure and Personality: A Casebook*, ed. Y. Cohen. New York: Holt, Rinehart and Winston, pp. 312–350. Surveys gratification of infant demands for food; other articles in book also bear examining.

DRIVER, H. E.
1969   Girls' Puberty Rites and Matrilocal Residence. *American Anthropologist* 71: 905–908. Disputes Brown's argument for relationship between female initiation ceremonies and uxorilocal residence, on basis of North American Indian data.

DUBOIS, C.
1944   *The People of Alor: A Social Psychological Study of an East Indian Island.* Minneapolis: University of Minnesota Press. Best of the early field studies of basic personality structure.

EDGERTON, R.
1965   "Cultural" versus "Ecological" Factors in the Expression of Values, Attitudes and Personality Characteristics. *American Anthropologist* 67: 442–447. Analysis of quantitative data on culture and personality variables among four neighboring East African societies.

FOSTER, G. M.
1965   Peasant Society and the Image of Limited Good. *American Anthropologist* 67: 293–315. Nonquantitative approach to cognitive orientation of peasants; influential and controversial article.

GORER, G.
1943   Themes in Japanese Culture. *Transactions of the New York Academy of Sciences* (Series II) 5: 106–124. Compulsive Japanese national character attributed to early and severe toilet training.

GORER, G., and RICKMAN, J.
1949   *The People of Great Russia.* London: Cresset. Russian national character, including the swaddling hypothesis.

HARRIS, M.
1968   *The Rise of Anthropological Theory.* New York: Crowell. Chapters 15–17 contain lively evaluations of culture and personality research.

HSU, F. L. K., ed.
1961   *Psychological Anthropology.* Cambridge, Mass.: Schenkman. Basic reader, in which Hsu discusses why he prefers term "psychological anthropology" to "culture and personality."

KARDINER, A., ed.
1939   *The Individual and His Society.* New York: Columbia University Press. Framework of primary and secondary institutions and basic personality structure; uses Linton's incomplete accounts of Tanala, Betsileo, and Marquesas Islanders.

1945   *The Psychological Frontiers of Society.* New York: Columbia University Press. Reports by DuBois, Linton, and West on Alor, Comanche, and Plainville, U.S.A., respectively, and Kardiner's psychocultural analysis of each.

KLUCKHOLN, F., and STRODTBECK, F.
1961   *Variations in Value Orientations.* Evanston, Ill.: Row, Peterson. Statistical evaluation of values among five ethnic groups in the modern American Southwest.

LABARRE, W.
1945   Some Observations on Character Structure in the Orient: The Japanese. *Psychiatry* 8: 326–342. Another attempt to link Japanese compulsion and anal training.

LEVINE, R. A.
1962   Witchcraft and Co-Wife Proximity in Southwestern Kenya. *Ethnology* 1: 39–45. Attributes witchcraft accusation to hostility engendered when co-wives live under the same roof.

LINTON, R.
1927   Report on Work of Field Museum Expedition in Madagascar. *American Anthropologist* 29: 292–307. Unusual combination of field data and character assassination of certain Malagasy peoples.

MEAD, M.
1930   *Growing Up in New Guinea.* New York: Blue Ribbon. Enculturation among the Manus, with suggestions for American education.

1939   *From the South Seas.* New York: Morrow. *New Guinea, Samoa,* and *Sex and Temperament* in one volume.

1949   (orig. 1928). *Coming of Age in Samoa.* New York: New American Library. Popular report of Mead's first fieldwork, a study of female adolescents in a Polynesian society.

1950   (orig. 1935). *Sex and Temperament in Three Primitive Societies.* New York: New American Library. Mead has called this examination of sex roles in three New Guinea societies her most misunderstood book.

MURDOCK, G. P.

1957   World Ethnographic Sample. *American Anthropologist* 59: 664–687. Test a hypothesis yourself! Includes coded data for 565 cultures on fifteen variables, including aspects of economy and social and political organization.

MURDOCK, G. P., and WHITE, D.

1969   Standard Cross-Cultural Sample. *Ethnology* 8: 329–369. Quantified data on 186 well-reported cultures.

NAROLL, R.

1970   What Have We Learned from Cross-Cultural Surveys? *American Anthropologist* 72: 1227–1288. Survey of statistical cross-cultural studies of culture and personality and other areas of anthropology.

STEPHENS, W. N.

1961   A Cross-Cultural Study of Menstrual Taboos. *Genetic Psychology Monographs* 64: 385–416. Relates menstrual taboos to castration anxieties of males.

1962   *The Oedipus Complex: Cross-Cultural Evidence.* New York: The Free Press. Evaluation, through cross-cultural data, of the universality of Freud's most celebrated syndrome.

WALLACE, A. F. C.

1970   *Culture and Personality.* 2nd ed. New York: Random House. More specialized and theoretical than Barnouw, but highly original demarcation of the field and theory of psychological anthropology.

WEBER, M.

1958   (orig. 1920). *The Protestant Ethic and the Spirit of Capitalism.* New York: Scribner's. Controversial explanation of rational industrial capitalism in terms of religious tenets of Protestantism.

WHITING, B. B., ed.

1963   *Six Cultures. Studies of Child Rearing.* New York: Wiley. Case studies including data gathered on comparable techniques of child training in Okinawa, India, New England, East Africa, Mexico, and the Philippines.

WHITING, J. W. M.

1964   The Effects of Climate on Certain Cultural Practices. In *Explorations in Cultural Anthropology: Essays in Honor of George Peter Murdock*, ed. W. Goodenough, pp. 175–195. New York: McGraw-Hill. Intricate chain of statistical associations leading from tropical climate to circumcision.

WHITING, J. W. M., CHASDI, E. H., ANTONOVSKY, H. F., and AYRES, B. C.

1970   (orig. 1966). The Learning of Values. In *People of Rimrock: A Study of Values in Five Cultures*, ed. E. Z. Vogt and E. M. Albert, pp. 83–125. New York: Atheneum. Values in the American Southwest.

WHITING, J. W. M., and CHILD, I.

1953   *Child Training and Personality: A Cross-Cultural Study.* New Haven: Yale University Press. Influential comparative statistical study of relationships between child-training practices and conceptions of illness.

WHITING, J. W. M., KLUCKHOLN, R., and ANTHONY, A.

1958   The Function of Male Initiation Ceremonies at Puberty. In *Readings in Social Psychology*, 3rd ed., ed. E. E. Maccoby, T. M. Newcomb, and E. L. Hartley. New York: Holt, Rinehart and Winston. First statement of relationship between initiation ceremonies, postpartum taboo, and prolonged mother-infant sleeping, using Oedipal feelings as a rationale.

YOUNG, F.

1962   The Function of Male Initiation Ceremonies: A Cross Cultural Test of an Alternative Hypothesis. *American Journal of Sociology* 67: 379–396. Critique of Whiting, Kluckholn, and Anthony, 1958.

1965   *Initiation Ceremonies: A Cross-Cultural Study of Status Dramatization.* Indianapolis: Bobbs-Merrill. Basic book examining *rites de passage* of males and females in cross-cultural perspective.

YOUNG, F., and BACDAYAN, A. A.

1965   Menstrual Taboos and Social Rigidity. *Ethnology* 4: 225–240. Male chauvinism in intermediate societies.

13. The Anthropology of Complex Societies

Although many anthropologists still prefer fieldwork in small communities where they can get to know most of their informants personally, they no longer study primarily primitive society. One of the principal reasons for this is that there are simply not too many primitive societies left. Some 10,000 years ago food production began to absorb and replace foraging adaptations in environments where they had reigned supreme. Technologically advanced adaptations have a way of replacing simpler ones. Thus today, if an anthropologist wishes to study an isolated primitive society, he must journey to the highlands of New Guinea or to the tropical forests of South America. In faraway Madagascar one finds motels run by AGIP, a hotel chain based in Italy. In Australia sheep owned by speakers of English graze where totemic ceremonies once were held.

Metropole-Satellite Relationships

The advent of food production was the beginning of the end for the forager. The origin of archaic states in different parts of the Old and New Worlds signaled the disappearance of tribal society. As Europeans took to ships, developing a trade-oriented, mercantile strategy of adaptation, archaic civilizations and tribal populations alike were gradually brought under European control. The Industrial Revolution brought people everywhere into a growing world economy based on capitalism. In the early years of exploration European ships landed on foreign shores and engaged in reciprocal trade—albeit characterized by negative reciprocity, with people strange to them. With colonization, however, exchange became a facsimile of redistribution, with colonial populations, *satellites*, providing goods and services for a European center, the *metropole*. Typically, there was more siphoning than redistribution in this form of exchange. Rarely did natives in colonial areas get back what they had given up. Nor, in a multiethnic society, was the relationship between European superordinates and native subordinates phrased in the same terms as, for example, that between king and subjects in archaic states, or between chief and his kinsmen of lower rank in chiefdoms.

As the Industrial Revolution spread in Europe and North America, raw materials from the colonies were transported on European ships to manufacturing areas in the metropole. Finished products were largely consumed in the metropole. However, some of these manufactured goods were sold in colonial areas, at prices which reflected the cost of transportation and manufacture, plus a margin of profit. England, France, Spain, Portugal, and other European nations all became metropolitan centers of empires, managed by colonial administrations. Colonial officials, who were true economic men and wanted to avoid duplication of effort and products in their different colonies, were overseers of territorially dispersed empires as chiefs and their advisers had been overseers of different areas of their chiefdoms. They encouraged economic specialization. Thus there was a colonial gold coast, an ivory coast, a slave coast, an area that exported spices, and another, in Brazil, that exported chiefly a certain kind of wood.

In the colonies of the New World, plantation economies based on the cultivation of a single crop (*monocrop production*) developed during the seventeenth, eighteenth, and nineteenth centuries. Europeans established plantation colonies in other world areas—for example, in the Indian Ocean—but the New World plantations bear responsibility for the largest forced migration of human beings in world history. To the lowlands of the West Indies and Latin America, generally areas where native population densities had been low, European slave ships brought Africans, whose labor built the lowland economies of the New World. The plantation monocrops differed from century to century and from area to area. In Brazil's early colonial history, its major export crop was sugar; subsequently, it became coffee. Cotton, of course, was the principal plantation crop in the southern United States.

The metropolitan interests of each empire planned and promoted productive diversity in its colonies, possessions, and trade areas, so that there were, in each empire, specialized sources of sugar, slaves, spices, and coffee. Throughout the period of European colonization in the New World, the influence of different metropolitan powers waxed and waned; empires contracted and expanded. There was, however, always more than one metropole.

During the nineteenth century, plantation economies based on slave labor became, in many parts of the world, monocrop economies based on free but poorly paid labor. In the twentieth century, many former colonies gained their political independence. However, economic control of an underdeveloped nation does not generally end with its political independence. The specialization promoted under European colonialism remains the basis for much of the poverty in the world today. Former colonies remain economic satellites of metropolitan powers. They continue to provide raw materials, crops, and other produce intended for consumption in these nations. In many cases the items exported are the same ones that flowed from satellite to metropole under colonialism, and the same system of distribution still prevails. In addition underdeveloped areas in different parts of the world often have the same item to sell. This is because each was formerly a specialized appendage of a metropolitan empire. Brazil provided sugar to its metropole, Portugal, while islands in the West Indies grew sugar for Britain and France. As long as underdeveloped nations continue to specialize in traditional cash crops and raw materials, the economic situation of, say, a cacao worker in Brazil will be affected by what happens to the cacao crop in Ghana.

Today there are new metropoles: Japan, Taiwan, and Israel; the Soviet Union, China, and other members of the "Communist" bloc. Some, of course, wield greater political and economic power than others. The economic policies of the United States, for example, can affect the economies of Western Europe. It is in the context of such economic colonialism that isolated, primitive societies have become few and far between. There has been a breakdown of isolation as metropolitan powers have sought, and still seek, new markets and new possessions. Contemporary metropolitan-satellite relationships represent merely the latest example of the general evolutionary tendency toward replacing or otherwise modifying previous adaptive means. The means whereby the United States maintains its range of control include legal agreements with other governments, designed to protect American interests; one of the world's most technologically sophisticated means of gathering information; a mobile and widely dispersed military apparatus with an extensive arsenal of weapons; and social and political relationships which function to protect the interests of the metropole in its many satellites. Of course, each of the other metropoles duplicates these means, though usually on a smaller scale.

Although the isolated ways of life which represent its traditional concern are disappearing, the subject matter open to anthropology is, in fact, expanding. This book has been oriented around a major interest which unifies the different subdisciplines of anthropology—the study of evolution. Recall that the definition of environment employed here has never been limited to the immediate natural surroundings. Alterations in the wider environments of contemporary human populations—that is, in their relationships with foreigners—represent changes to which formerly isolated populations must adapt. Although the process of metropolitan incorporation is proceeding today on a larger scale and more rapidly than ever before, it is not new. It began on a large scale with the European voyages of discovery and grew during the period of colonialism in the New World. But there were empires in ancient civilizations, too. Capitals of archaic states served as metropoles to economically and ecologically specialized satellites, and in this way also changed the wider environments to which many tribal populations had to adapt.

Since the 1940s many anthropologists have become interested in the changes which accompany or follow contact between industrial and nonindustrial populations. Published results of research concerned with "social change," "cultural change," "socioeconomic change," or "acculturation" are now abundant. Several larger questions have guided specific studies. What kinds of social, cultural, and economic changes have accompanied sustained contact between metropolitan nations and satellite areas? Have satellite populations been able to survive their incorporation within larger systems through changes in their sociocultural means of adaptation? Have sociocultural changes been major or minor? Have some populations been able to adapt more easily or rapidly than others? Answers to these questions, documented with specific cases, will surely become more abundant in future years.

In short, because complex societies are expanding, anthropologists are studying problems in these societies and problems associated with their expansion. The study of peasants, rural inhabitants of archaic states, is flourishing. Archaic states are complex societies, but they, like band and tribal societies, have been incorporated into metropoles. Many archaic states have become *satellite states*—weakly industrial or nonindustrial, internally stratified, economically specialized appendages of metropolitan nations. In addition, some stratified societies—for example, in Latin America—that were originally founded as satellites have become satellite states. Some of the results of anthropological studies of populations that live in satellite states will be presented here.

The remainder of this chapter is intended to give you some idea of the research problems and field methods which have recently engaged anthropologists working in peasant communities and cities. I will not present here an exhaustive summary of recent anthropological research, but rather confine the discussion to the two areas of the world I know best: Latin America and Africa. The list of readings at the end of this chapter includes mention of similar studies done in other parts of the world.

The Study of Contemporary Peasantries

Community studies: variation within complex societies

Ethnographers working among foragers, tribesmen, and peasants usually survey several communities before choosing one for intensive fieldwork. After they have made a long-term study of everyday life, usually lasting at least a year, ethnographers describe and treat this community as representative of the larger society. Any anthropologist will recognize, however, that even in the most homogeneous and egalitarian society, there are differences between communities. An occasional ethnographic report will take account of such variations, relating them perhaps to differences in physical or social environments. However, in complex societies variation is not so easily explained. Obviously, ño single community can serve as a microcosm for an entire nation with its many regional, ecological, class, ethnic, and subcultural contrasts.

Two pioneering examples of anthropological research in complex societies were carried out in Latin America. In the early 1950s Julian Steward (1956) and several of his students did research in Puerto Rico, involving coordinated study of several areas with different economies and historical backgrounds. Charles Wagley (cf. Wagley, ed., 1952) directed graduate students in communities in northern Brazil, sampling different economic and ecological conditions. These community studies employed traditional anthropological techniques of participant observation, firsthand observation of behavior, formal and informal interviewing and other questioning, gathering of genealogical information, and census taking.

In their published reports, the ethnographers also viewed these communities historically. Comparison produced a picture of regional ecological and economic variation in northern Brazil: the Amazon community (Wagley, 1964) with its early twentieth-century rubber boom and subsequent decline; the plantation economy (Harry W. Hutchinson, 1957); the interior community settled originally by gold miners (Marvin Harris, 1956); the subsistence-oriented community of pastoralists and horticulturalists in the backlands (Ben Zimmerman, 1952). None of these communities provided a microcosmic view of Brazilian society, but together studies of all revealed a great deal about historical and contemporary variation in Brazilian society. Subsequent work by Wagley (1971), Harris (1964), and their students has increased still further our knowledge of Brazilian society. Through these and other community studies, anthropologists have learned a considerable amount about peasant life in different world areas.

Peasant communities in Latin America

The anthropologist Eric Wolf has written extensively about peasantries. In a 1955 article he drew a distinction between two types of peasant communities in Latin America, the "closed, corporate peasant community" and the "open, non-corporate peasant community." Another anthropologist who has written extensively on Latin America, Charles Wagley (1968), drew a similar distinction between Indian and mestizo communities there. Both were pointing to a difference between Indian communities located in the highlands (Wolf's closed, corporate type) and non-Indian communities located in the lowlands (Wolf's open type). Closed, corporate peasant communities are found in the highlands of Mexico, Guatemala, Ecuador, Peru, Bolivia, and, to a lesser extent, Colombia.

The highlands of Latin America were

generally areas of high population density and sophisticated political development, chiefdoms and states, prior to the arrival in the New World of the *conquistadores*. The highlands of Mexico had seen the growth of the Aztec state, and the Incas had extended a major empire from a site in the Peruvian highlands. With the arrival of European diseases, aboriginal populations declined considerably. However, Indian influence has remained significant in the highlands, and in each of the countries where closed, corporate peasant communities are found, a large percentage of the national population is Indian.

In the Latin American lowlands where horticultural and foraging strategies of adaptation and tribal forms of sociopolitical organization were characteristic, on the other hand, aboriginal population densities were very much lower. Here foreign diseases, slave raids, and warfare with Europeans proved more devastating, and in some cases completely eliminated populations. It is in the lowlands of these peasant nations, and in nonhighland areas like Brazil, that the Indian population is smallest and that their cultural contribution is least marked. Here, too, the open community is the characteristic rural settlement.

Wagley has used the term "mestizo" to describe the communities of the lowlands because their populations generally represent mixtures of Europeans, Indians, and/or Africans. In Brazil and other Latin American nations with plantation economies, large numbers of slaves were imported from Africa during the seventeenth, eighteenth, and nineteenth centuries. These Africans left their mark, both phenotypically and culturally, on the Latin American lowlands, as they did on the British West Indies and the United States. In Brazil the populations of most peasant communities represent a wide array of phenotypes—a result of the intermingling of Europeans, Africans, and Indians.

THE HIGHLAND PEASANT COMMUNITY To understand life in the peasant community of highland Latin America, consider its de-

Production for subsistence rather than profit orients this closed community in the highlands of Guatemala. *(Max Hunn/Frederic Lewis)*

scription. It is *corporate*. Like descent groups in many parts of the world, it has an estate, which usually consists of land. In general, closed, corporate communities are located in marginal lands in the Latin American highlands, areas which the European invaders and their descendants could not profitably exploit for cultivating plantation crops. In Peru and Guatemala, as in other nations which include both highlands and lowlands, plantation economies developed in the lowlands. In the closed, corporate community of the highlands, peasants use their estate to grow the crops which make up their daily diet. Production for subsistence rather than for profit is characteristic here.

Highland communities are also *closed*. In other words, status as a member of a community is usually ascribed at birth and cannot be shifted. For further isolation, endogamy is emphasized; most marriages take place between members of the community. All members of a community have access to its estate.

Corporate economically and closed socially, highland communities maintain a feeling of solidarity and distinctiveness from other, similar communities. In some areas of Latin America, people in neighboring communities speak different dialects and sometimes even different languages. Intercommunity linguistic differentiation is especially obvious in some highland areas of Mexico and Guatemala. Communities are also distinguished by differences in costume. In a marketplace, it is possible to identify rather precisely a person's home by his dress. Finally, although the Indians who live in these communities are all Roman Catholics, each community has its own patron saint. In the course of the year fiestas are held to honor each particular saint. Thus the saint of the closed, corporate peasant community serves a function analogous to that of the totem in corporate descent groups. It is an emblem of internal solidarity and a ritual marker of social differentiation.

THE LOWLAND PEASANT COMMUNITY There are several differences between lowland and highland communities. First, inhabitants of a lowland community do not typically farm a joint estate. If the economy is based on plant cultivation, individuals and nuclear families own or control the land which they farm. Second, the lowland community is not closed. Membership in a particular community is not determined at birth and it may be shifted. Finally, there is no cultural preference for endogamy. Depending on the community, marriages can involve people from inside or outside the community, and there may be an even split. If the latter situation prevails, we speak of the community as an *agamous unit*; it has no marriage rule.

Because the lowland community is not corporate, we would expect none of the features of community solidarity and distinctiveness characteristic of the highlands —and we don't find them. Like neighboring communities, Arembepe, an open peasant community in Brazil, has a patron saint. Each year, in February, a festival is held in his honor. However, the typical lowland festival is less of a blowout than the highland fiesta, and its functions are different. The patron saint is not an important means of identifying communities in the lowlands. Most of the people who live in Arembepe, for example, were unable to identify the patron saints of villages located only a few miles away.

Peasants in lowland areas work and produce for profit as well as subsistence, cul-

Salvador, a Brazilian coastal city, where fishermen sell their fish for cash rather than subsistence. *(Green/Frederic Lewis)*

tivating cash crops which they sell in regional markets or to marketers who come to the community from the outside. Wolf estimated that between half and two-thirds of what is produced in open communities is sold for cash. This does not mean that people eat better; it merely means that they can buy more than highland Indians, that they are more dependent on the outside world. In fact, I found that among the marine fishermen of Arembepe, people would often sell their fish to buy manioc flour and sugar, which are high in calories but lower in protein and most other nutrients than fish. Peasants also use cash profits to purchase clothing, household items, and other goods manufactured outside the community.

All inhabitants of the lowland community speak the national language—Portuguese in Brazil, Spanish in other Latin American countries. Because lowland peasants speak the national language, they are better able to participate in national life. Politicians come to the community to woo voters, and people who know how to write their names may vote in national elections. Some lowland peasants avidly follow national events. In Brazil, lotteries, soccer, and the Miss Universe contest are national pastimes. Lowland peasants also celebrate national holidays.

In short, the inhabitants of the open peasant community feel less attached to the community and more attached to the nation than do peasants in the highlands. Yet it would be wrong to suppose that the Indian populations of closed communities are totally isolated from their nation-states and from the world economy; and it would be equally erroneous to suppose that life in open communities is necessarily better, happier, or more fulfilling. People in open communities are often just as poor as those in the highlands. They may eat as poorly; they are just as illiterate; their health conditions are as bad; and their life expectancies are equally short. Furthermore, the impediments to progress are frequently just as great in both lowlands and highlands. Some of these impediments will now be examined.

Poverty in highland Latin America: the cargo system

In the absence of a permanent political structure like that found in chiefdoms and states, redistribution of wealth among local groups in primitive societies may be accomplished through such mechanisms as the ceremonial feast (see Chapters 9 and 10). There is ceremonial feasting in highland Latin America. It operates within the context of a political and religious hierarchy characteristic of each highland community—the *cargo system*. (This term derives from the Spanish *cargo*, meaning "charge" or burden.) Males in highland communities move up in the cargo system by undertaking more and more onerous burdens to gain the respect of other members of their community. Young men enter the cargo system by undertaking menial burdens, for example, running errands for older men. As they grow older, however, they hold political offices in the community; they are the highland equivalents of sheriffs, councilmen, mayors, or community leaders. Associated with each political office are religious burdens. Highland communities celebrate several saints' days throughout the year, often culminating in a large fiesta designed to honor the patron saint of the community. As individuals move up in the political hierarchy, they are expected to contribute more and more of their time and wealth to these religious celebrations. In return for conformity, they are awarded prestige by other members of their community.

Several anthropologists who have studied highland communities have pointed out that the burdens associated with office and with religious celebrations act as a *leveling mechanism* in terms of intracommunity wealth differences. The amount of time and wealth invested by an Indian in organizing fiestas is great, and among community members it is the wealthiest individuals who are chosen to fill the most important offices and perform the major cargos. In his book *Patterns of Race in the Americas* (1964), Marvin Harris describes some of the expenses which devolve on the fiesta organizer. He must dispense considerable quantities of food and liquor. Additional expenses involve special church services, candles, costumes for dancers and players, musicians' fees, fireworks, and bulls and bullfighters. Harris also points out that since fiesta organizers are also expected to serve on the village council, they are required to be away from their fields during most of the year. Thus they give in time as much as or more than they give in money.

The cargo system recalls another, inter-community, leveling device: the potlatch. However, although the institutions are similar, their effects are quite different. Closed, corporate peasant communities exist within satellite states, within stratified, multiethnic nations where Indians are usually members of the lowest stratum. Such nations also include mestizos. The principal difference between Indians and mestizos is not genetic but cultural. Indians are people who live in Indian communities, speak Indian languages, wear Indian costumes, and take part in the cargo system. Mestizos are individuals who are not members of closed, corporate peasant communities, who speak the national language, who wear modern dress, and who are either members of, or have strong ties with, the national elite. They do not participate in the cargo system; but indirectly they benefit from it.

The cargo system helps to maintain inequalities in wealth and social status between Indians and mestizos; it reinforces systems of stratification in which Indians are socioeconomic subordinates. To understand this, recall the economy of the highland community. Indians expend most of their productive energy in growing crops for subsistence rather than for profit. Since they sell little, they also buy little. However, fiestas require large expenditures of cash on goods produced outside the community. Here mestizos profit, since they are generally the storekeepers and merchants who supply nonfood items consumed during the fiesta.

There is still another way in which mestizos profit from the cargo system. Nations with highlands generally also include lowland zones, often areas of plantation or cash crop economies. Highland Indians are a source of cheap labor for these plantations. How, in view of the solidarity of the closed, corporate peasant community, do plantation owners get the Indians to leave their homes to work for wages? The cargo system provides an answer. Recruiters from the lowlands regularly travel through highland communities seeking out Indians who have assumed some of the most onerous cargoes that year. Since these often leave the Indian with a great deal of prestige but destitute, former *cargueros* are often willing to sign labor contracts or accept loans from mestizos. They can only get the cash to repay these loans by selling their labor on the national market. The cargo system, then, functions to provide cheap labor for the national economy and to maintain the status quo.

Thus in the satellite states of highland Latin America, there are institutions which are similar in form to those in tribal society. However, rather than functioning to maintain a nonstratified society by leveling out temporary fluctuations in wealth and subsistence resources between communities, these institutions preserve a stratified society by transferring wealth and labor from the lower-stratum Indians to the upper-stratum mestizos.

Why then do Indians continue to take part in the cargo system? In many parts of highland Latin America, Indians are extremely reluctant to assume religious and civil burdens. Ruth Bunzel (1952), in her study of a highland community in Guatemala, describes cases of Indians so reluctant to fill the offices to which other members of their community have elected them that they literally have to be dragged in to office. Members of the community often apply pressure on one another to assume cargos. Indians who have themselves assumed cargos are not eager to excuse others from the same cultural obligations. Church and government officials, too, compel compliance. (For a more extensive discussion of the cargo system, see Harris, *Patterns of Race in the Americas*.)

Poverty in lowland Latin America: kinship in Brazil

In the rural mestizo community of lowland Latin America, the kinship system serves functions analogous to those of the cargo system in the highlands. Like the cargo system, it levels out wealth differences between members of a subordinate stratum. It also provides cheap labor for the national economy, and it preserves social and economic stratification within the satellite state.

The following analysis of kinship is based on my own fieldwork in Brazil. It applies to Brazil's most underdeveloped area—the northeast, a region where a plantation economy based on sugar flourished from the seventeenth to the nineteenth century. Whether or not kinship also serves the same leveling function in other parts of lowland Latin America may be determined by future ethnographic fieldwork.

Arembepe is an open community with a population of about 800 people, most of whom derive their livelihoods from fishing on the Atlantic Ocean. The community is mestizo; but because this was an aboriginal region of low population density, the Indian contribution has not been great. Most of the people of Arembepe are mixed descendants of Europeans and slaves brought from Africa to work on the sugar plantations.

For lower-class Brazilians, the functions of kinship in impeding vertical mobility and limiting social and economic advancement overshadow its adaptive functions. All the people who live in Arembepe are members of the Brazilian lower class. However, there are no completely homogeneous human societies. In all societies there are, at least, differences in social position related to age, sex, and personality. This is true in Arembepe, where adult males are able to increase their wealth and social

position within the community through hard and constant work. While there are no class divisions in Arembepe, there are differences in wealth.

Certain aspects of Brazilian social structure impede the economic advancement of lower-class Brazilians. Most obvious are obligations associated with kinship. Men who through hard work have become more successful within the community are expected to share their wealth with a larger number of people. First of all, a man must share his wealth with his close kinsmen. As he becomes more successful, earns more from the sale of his fish, he can provide his family with a better diet. This means that more of his children survive than do those in poorer households. The people of Arembepe do not practice birth control, so their families are often large. Furthermore, as a man's wealth increases, he is more likely to have other relatives move in with him—or at least ask him for doles. He finds himself supporting his widowed mother, a few aunts and uncles, and some cousins perhaps.

Obligations associated with marriage also drain wealth from the enterprising man. In Brazil the union with most prestige is that which has been sanctified by both church and state. The poorer couples in Arembepe are generally involved in common law unions. Upwardly mobile young men may add to their reputations by having civil and religious ceremonies when they marry. If they do this, however, they undertake obligations to affinals which do not exist with the common law union. There is no socially recognized obligation to share wealth with the wife's relatives if a union is only common law. On the other hand, a formal bond creates such obligations. Since there is no divorce in Brazil, these obligations are for life.

Finally, as wealth increases, a man will accumulate more fictive kinsmen, godchildren and coparents (*compadres*). A couple asks a man and a woman to stand as godparents at the baptism of their child. The two couples become coparents to each other, and the child has godparents. Two of the wealthiest men in Arembepe each had more than one hundred godchildren. By agreeing to become a godparent a Brazilian assumes a special obligation to share with both his godchild and his coparents.

The ways in which kinship acts to level wealth differences and impede individual vertical mobility among the lower classes should be clear by now. The harder a man works, the more successful he becomes within the community, but the greater the number of dependents he must support. If he wishes to spend his life within the community, he must fulfill his obligations to relatives in the socially prescribed way. One further observation should be made. People who are successful in fishing usually also buy or create estates on the land, generally coconut groves. You might think, then, that if a man worked very hard at accumulating an estate, his children would benefit. This is not the case. Inheritance is equal among all children in Brazil. As a man's wealth grows, the number of his children also grows, and the estate is severely fragmented when he dies. His children cannot rely on their inheritance to give them a head start in life. Their success must again be based on individual hard work.

In the upper class, kinship has different functions. Upper-class Brazilians usually consider as relatives a far larger number of individuals than do lower-class Brazilians. Yet the extended kindred system of the upper class does not serve to drain wealth. A member of the upper class is not expected to support his kinsmen; however, if he is in a position to help a kinsman get a job, this he certainly must do.

As long as there is poverty in Brazil, the obligations associated with kinship in the lower class will continue to exist. There is no social security system to protect peasants when they grow old. People are forced to share with their kinsmen because they may have to rely on them when they themselves grow old and are unable to work. The lower class, then, keeps its members, and Brazilian society retains its highly stratified form.

Urban Anthropology

Topical fields called "rural sociology" and "urban anthropology" suggest that interests and techniques of anthropology and sociology are converging. Often, when anthropologists return to New Guinea, Madagascar, or other tribal and peasant areas, they discover that the cultural adaptations they once observed have been altered by contact with modern life. Many anthropologists have specifically set out to investigate examples of recent social and cultural change. Others, drawing on prior first-hand experience with tribal groups, have followed their informants into cities, seeking to understand urban migration and how the migrant adapts to city life. Still others have set out explicitly to examine aspects of the urban situation of migrants without prior study of their subjects' backgrounds.

Today, the United States provides an especially popular arena for urban anthropological research. To understand why, consider that research problems and theoretical concerns of American anthropology, like other academic disciplines, reflect a larger context of issues, events, and movements in American society. Tax dollars that funded anthropological research during the early and middle 1960s were later diverted toward the war in Southeast Asia or toward more "practical" problems. Increasing interest in the United States also reflects growing awareness by anthropologists and by society in general of minority problems and grievances. American minority problems and movements have directed anthropologists to certain areas of research —the study of poverty and class and subcultural variation. The war on poverty, for example, bred anthropological studies of poverty in the United States and cross-culturally. The cross-cultural study of the poor remains a major concern of contemporary anthropology.

In his book *Five Families* (1959), anthropologist Oscar Lewis coined the phrase "subculture of poverty," which he often shortened to "culture of poverty," to refer to a subculture of Western society with its own structure, rationale, and history. Lewis listed seventy economic, social, and psychological traits characteristic of this culture. Economically, the poverty culture is marked by a constant struggle for survival; reduced family income reflecting unemployment and underemployment; low wages; unskilled and unspecialized occupations; frequent change of jobs; low purchasing power; reliance on child labor; the absence of food reserves in the home; a pattern of spending money freely when there is a little on hand; little saving; and frequent pawning. Some of the social and psychological attributes include crowded living quarters; lack of privacy; gregariousness; a high incidence of alcoholism; frequent use of physical violence; corporal punishment for children; wife beating; early initiation into sex; free or consensual marital unions; marital instability; a relatively high incidence of abandonment by family heads; a trend toward mother-centered households; a much greater knowledge of matrilateral relatives; the predominance of the nuclear family; a strong predisposition to authoritarianism; and a great emphasis on family solidarity, as the ideal.

Among the psychological traits which Lewis viewed as particularly important are a feeling of marginality, of not belonging to something; critical attitudes toward the institutions of society and toward government and political figures; and, in general, a feeling of insecurity and desperation. However, the culture of poverty also includes cultural and psychological traits which are compensatory and rewarding—a capacity for spontaneity and adventure, enjoyment of the sensual, and the indulgence of impulse.

In various works Lewis asserted that to an extent the culture of poverty transcends regional, rural-urban, and national differences. The existence of a subculture of poverty in different nations represents convergent evolution; the traits recur as common adaptations to common problems. Lewis linked the appearance and persistence of the subculture of poverty to certain historical conditions: a cash economy of wage labor and production for profit; a consistently high rate of unemployment and underemployment for unskilled labor; low wages; and the failure of society to provide social, political, and economic organization for the poor. Furthermore, the subculture of poverty, according to Lewis, depends on the existence of a set of values in the dominant class which stresses the accumulation of wealth and property, allows for the possibility of upward social and economic mobility, stresses thrift as an idea, and views low economic status as the result of personal inferiority. The values of subculture of poverty members represent their attempts to cope with feelings of hopelessness and despair.

Although poverty exists in different nations, Lewis denied that it inevitably produces the subculture of poverty. Rather, it is most often found in Western nations, notably in those of Latin America and, to a lesser extent, in the contemporary United States. Specifically, Lewis asserted that the subculture of poverty is a manifestation of the early, free enterprise stage of capitalism, and it is also endemic in certain colonial contexts, particularly in Latin America.

There are several reasons why poverty does not always breed the subculture of poverty. Lewis asserted that when the poor become class conscious, when they become active in trade organizations, or when they adopt an internationalist outlook on the world, they remove themselves from the culture of poverty—although they may still be desperately poor. Lewis believed that the culture of poverty does not exist in such socialist countries as postrevolutionary Cuba. He visited Cuba both before and after Castro's revolution. In postrevolution-

ary Cuba, he found slums where the people did not complain about the government or talk in a fatalistic manner, where they showed some hope for the future. Slum life now seemed to be highly organized, with block committees, education committees, and political party committees. The people had a sense of power and importance. They had been armed and given a revolutionary doctrine which glorified the lower class as the hope of humanity.

In addition to fieldwork among Mexicans and Puerto Ricans, Lewis conducted earlier ethnographic fieldwork in India, where he found the culture of poverty to be absent. His Indian experience convinced Lewis (cf. 1968) that there was no direct relationship between poverty and the culture of poverty. In Indian villages he observed greater poverty than in the slums of Mexico City and San Juan. However, he found that the Indian caste system contributed a sense of identity and organization which was lacking in Latin American nations, for all the Indian castes were highly organized. Caste organization transcends communities and villages. Lewis reported that sometimes members of the sweeper caste representing as many as sixty villages met to decide how they were going to modify the system of ceremonial obligations. Lewis attributed the absence of the culture of poverty in India not only

to the organization and therefore the power of its castes, but also to the fact that India remained a civilization in the sense that all people were incorporated into a single social system—even members of the lowest castes felt that they were still Hindus.

Lewis argued that the culture of poverty in Western nations developed in the context of real poverty as well as the lack of such a feeling of belonging. The subculture of poverty appeared in Europe and the New World with the breakdown of old feudal structures and the migration of people from rural zones to cities. In this process the poor had no organization and therefore no power. Lewis also linked the subculture of poverty to the bilateral kinship systems of European and New World cultures, stating that the prior existence of descent group organization would also impede its development. In areas where social organization includes corporate descent groups, specifically in India and Africa, Lewis predicted that the subculture of poverty would fail to appear, even though poverty was great. Lewis saw something positive in the nature of descent group organization, the feeling that one corporate body continues to exist though individuals come and go. This gives a sense of the past and of the future even to the desperately poor. As we shall see, through descent and other social mechanisms, African town dwellers usually maintain village ties. Most Latin American rural populations, on the other hand, made the transition from a tribal to a peasant society far earlier than did Africans. And, as the earlier discussion of Brazilian kinship confirms, descent groups and other forms of social and political solidarity are of diminished importance among the poor in Latin America.

Linking the subculture of poverty primarily to the early stages of capitalism and to colonialism, Lewis located its most typical expressions in Latin America. He found the culture of poverty to be considerably less prevalent in the contemporary United States, and he calculated that while between 40 to 50 million Americans live in poverty, only about 8 million of them exhibit the cultural and psychological traits of the culture of poverty. The American welfare apparatus, he suggested, had successfully eliminated many of the conditions which produce the culture of poverty. Nevertheless, it might be characteristic of certain American ethnic minorities, including poor blacks and urban Indians, Mexican Americans and Puerto Ricans, and possibly some poor whites. At the time of his death in 1970, Lewis was planning research among poor white and black families in Chicago's slums, to determine the presence or absence of the subculture of poverty.

When Lewis announced in 1968 that he would begin his work among American whites and blacks, it was with a sense of trepidation that reflects the controversy surrounding this somewhat touchy area. Former Nixon adviser and Harvard professor Patrick Moynihan, for example, in his book *The Negro Family* (1965) and elsewhere, argues for the existence of a self-perpetuating subculture of poverty among American blacks. Moynihan views this subculture as consisting of distinctive norms and values which are transmitted through enculturation and which do not simply represent responses to situations of extreme poverty. This view echoes Lewis, who believed that, because it was a real culture, it would be more difficult to eradicate the subculture of poverty than the

objective conditions of poverty. Lewis's research among Puerto Ricans convinced him that by the age of six, children in the slums of Manhattan's East Side had already psychologically constructed a model of what life is, an internalization of the subculture of poverty. Therefore, he believed that it would take more than one generation to eliminate a well-established culture of poverty and to create basic changes in the attitudes of the poor.

The views of Lewis and Moynihan have been criticized by Charles Valentine (1968) and by several others. Valentine has proposed that there are no significant differences between the cultural norms of the poor and the more affluent in America. The poor are merely unable to live up to the dominant norms of the society because of the severe social and economic disadvantages to which they are exposed. Valentine admits, however, that the poor may have some specific alternative values which enable them to adapt to the necessities of their situation. Seymour Parker and Robert Kleiner (1970) have suggested that the poor hold two sets of values and attitudes simultaneously, one shared with the larger society and the second developed in response to the objective conditions of poverty. The latter help poor people to make necessary psychological adjustments and preserve their sanity.

In *Tally's Corner* (1967) Elliot Liebouw describes the results of extended participant observation of street corner behavior in a Washington ghetto. Liebouw's research convinced him that poor blacks do internalize many of the dominant values of the larger society, but, because their hopes are often frustrated, which contributes to deep feelings of failure, they also develop alternative values. Seymour Parker (1973) suggests that middle-class social scientists often focus on only a narrow range of the attitudes and values of poor people, for example, those which Lewis makes diagnostic of the subculture of poverty, while ignoring the wider attitudinal

A street scene in a ghetto of Washington, D.C.
(*Morton Broffman/Nancy Palmer*)

context, which is shared with the larger society. In attempting to reconcile the opposing views about the relationship between culture and poverty, Parker suggests, reasonably, that ongoing social behavior results from both enculturation and the constraints imposed by the objective situation. Parker suggests that the crucial questions for future research involve the relative contributions of enculturation patterns and situational constraints to the perpetuation of poverty in the United States.

Ethnographic research in the United States

Research concerned with poverty, urban life, ethnicity, and subculture in the contemporary United States is of general theoretical interest because of its use in cross-cultural study. Practically, however, such research is booming because travel to field sites in the United States is considerably cheaper than travel to Australia or South

Africa, and because the National Science Foundation and other government agencies have been instructed to give priority to relevant and applied, rather than to basic, research. Research on culture and poverty exemplifies merely one recent trend.

Urban anthropological research in the United States can be traced to earlier ethnographic studies of towns, neighborhoods, or ethnic enclaves within cities. Using community study techniques, Carl Withers (writing as James West, 1945) studied a decaying town in the American Midwest. Sociologists Robert and Helen Lynd (1929) applied ethnographic techniques to their study of Middletown, another midwestern community.

A traditionally wholistic anthropological description can be provided more easily for a small midwestern town than for a major city. Thus, like Oscar Lewis in his early Mexican research, other anthropologists have chosen urban neighborhoods, slums, and ethnic enclaves as research sites for community study. In his study of a neighborhood in Boston, William Foote Whyte (1943), for example, demonstrated through ethnographic description of the cohesive behavior of gangs of Italian American youths that there was a high degree of social organization in an urban slum. Whyte's study was important because it countered what he saw as a tendency of other researchers to concentrate on poverty and reform to the exclusion of the ongoing social life of slum dwellers. Herbert Gans (1962) restudied Whyte's neighborhood two decades later and documented a remarkable cultural persistence. These are only a few of the many recent studies of American life that sample subcultural, ethnic, and class-related variation.

Anthropological methods in studying cities

In the United States and elsewhere, a major problem confronts anthropologists who want to work in cities, among industrial and industrializing populations: How are field methods and procedures which were originally developed to describe and analyze small, isolated communities to be elaborated or altered to deal with apparently more complex, less obviously structured situations?

Robert Redfield has been prominent—although certainly not alone—among anthropologists in indicating contrasts between rural communities whose social relations are on a face-to-face basis, and larger, socioeconomically heterogeneous urban populations where impersonality characterizes many aspects of everyday social life. Commenting on community, town, and urban research in Britain, Ronald Frankenberg (1966) indicates that researchers have tried to apply many of the same methods in their studies of large towns and segments of urban populations that have been used in small rural communities. In Britain, as in the United States, anthropological studies span a continuum ranging from rural communities supported by subsistence farming, through towns with mixed economies, to great urban centers such as London.

Redfield described only some of the characteristic differences between rural and urban communities. Anthropologist Aidan Southall (1959) suggests that role texture changes along a rural-urban continuum. Roles that are combined in the same individuals and institutions in rural settings are differentiated and attached to specific individuals and institutions in cities. Southall suggests that at the rural end of the role continuum, status is often ascribed and determines how people will behave when they meet. In cities, on the other hand, status is often achieved and determines whether they will ever meet at all.

In *The Folk Culture of Yucatan* (1941) Redfield argued that culture change could be studied along a rural-urban continuum, and he described certain differences in values and social relations in four settings spanning that continuum. He compared an isolated Maya-speaking Indian community, a rural peasant village, a small provincial city, and a large capital. Redfield suggested that similar studies could be conducted elsewhere in the world. Several recent studies in Africa have been influenced

by Redfield's view that cities are centers through which cultural innovations are introduced into tribal areas. Kenneth Little (1971), for example, writes of the diffusion of values and behavior patterns from city to countryside, stating that the farmer-villager may become urbanized as urban culture is incorporated into the ideational and behavioral patterns of the rural resident.

Pointing out that scholars in Africa have concentrated particularly on contrasts between tribal and urban life and on diffusion of urban patterns to tribal areas, J. Clyde Mitchell and other students of African urbanization have argued that major unsolved research problems require intensive study of urban social systems. Mitchell (1966), for example, suggests that anthropologists should recognize the distinction between *historical* and *situational* change. The former refers to actual changes in social systems, while the latter describes variations in behavior of individuals in different situations—rural and urban, for example. Rural and urban systems exist side by side in Africa and other world areas, and Aidan Southall (1961) points out that we must carefully distinguish between the rapidity of changes within a system or a situation and within individual behavior. Southall suggests that changes in behavior patterns from a rural to an urban set of objectives are as rapid as the migrant's journey to the town. Discussing migration of Puerto Ricans from San Juan to New York, Oscar Lewis (1968) made essentially the same observation when he asserted that people from San Juan, just by taking an airplane, skipped several stages in their evolution in modern society.

Mitchell argues that the migrant does not bring his rural institutions with him to town, for urban and rural institutions are parts of different social systems and the individual may move back and forth from one to the other. Continuing this reasoning, Mitchell suggests that it is a mistake to view urban institutions as variants of rural institutions. Rather urban people develop new institutions to meet their specific needs. These differ from rural institutions which meet similar needs in the tribal situation. Mitchell advocates a situational approach in order better to understand life in cities.

Mitchell is right in suggesting that there are problems and cultural adaptive responses, in the form of institutions and behavior patterns, specific to cities. However, it would be fallacious to assume that the enculturative experiences of home do not affect the adjustment of individuals to urban situations and that social forms developed in rural settings do not influence adaptation to city life. Lewis made exactly this point when he argued that descent groups and other forms of tribal organization provide migrants to African cities with adaptive mechanisms which many Latin American peasants lack. Some examples are given in the discussion of structural relationships in cities.

Since urban research has been especially prominent in recent anthropological studies of Africa, some of the methods of research and its results may profitably be examined.

AFRICAN CITIES While at present less than 10 percent of the total population of sub-Saharan Africa lives in cities of 100,000 or more people, African cities may be growing faster than those of other continents. Scholars frequently distinguish between two types of African city. Southall (1961), for example, argues that type A cities, found in Tanzania, Uganda, the Sudan, and throughout Equatorial and West Africa, are old, established centers. Very large towns existed in some of these areas long before European commercial expansion into Africa. Many such towns originated as administrative centers in pre-European states. Generally supported by traditional economic pursuits, urban populations in these areas tend to be ethnically homogeneous, and their rate of increase is slower than

that in the towns of type B. Southall classifies in the latter group the newer African towns whose rapid population increase is based on industrial and commercial development. Many of them originated with European expansion in Africa during the latter half of the nineteenth century. Most type B towns have resulted from African involvement in colonialism and the international economy. Located mainly in South Africa, Rhodesia, Zambia, Kenya, and the Congo, these towns tend to be ethnically heterogeneous.

Both types of city share common features of urban life, including high settlement density, geographical mobility, social heterogeneity, demographic disproportions (in type B cities especially, there is a preponderance of young people over old and of men over women, reflecting demands and opportunities of the cash labor market), economic differentiation, and concentration of political power and administrative apparatus. Despite these similarities, which define both types as true cities, patterns of social life differ. W. R. Bascom (1955) has asserted that in the long-established cities of the Nigerian Yoruba, kinship remained the principal factor in, and primary determinant of, behavior in every aspect of life. Each lineage group, or its larger subdivisions, resided together. Some additional contrasts involving determinants of social relations in different African cities are considered next.

METHODS OF STUDYING AFRICAN CITIES AND TOWNS J. Clyde Mitchell (1966) points out that urban anthropological studies in Africa have relied on two strategies of data collection: the social survey and, more traditionally, intensive qualitative research. In the first instance, anthropologists have often been forced, in the absence of sufficient archival and statistical material, to employ survey techniques to acquire quantitative data on urban social characteristics. Another reason for anthropological surveys that Mitchell mentions is what he regards as a rather prevalent belief among anthropologists that because urban data are much more complicated than tribal data, quantitative approaches are essential. Mitchell disagrees with this assumption and argues that social surveys should be combined with intensive qualitative research on cultural patterns and social institutions in African towns. Furthermore, he suggests that fruitful hypotheses will arise more frequently from qualitative than from quantitative research. He does not see that urban data are more complicated than rural data. Although the social situations may be more varied for the town dweller than for the tribesman, Mitchell suggests that the townsman's behavior itself in a given situation is probably not more complicated. Reviewing the literature of African urban studies, Mitchell suggests that three broad types of relationships may be investigated qualitatively in African towns: structural relationships, categorical relationships, and personal or egocentric relationships. Since similar qualitative methods are being employed in anthropological studies in cities outside of Africa, let us consider these methods in greater detail.

ANALYSIS OF STRUCTURAL RELATIONSHIPS
Mitchell argues that several types of urban institution and relationships within the urban social structure represent areas for fruitful investigation by anthropologists. Among the African urban institutions that have been studied anthropologically are voluntary associations, burial societies, social clubs, courts, and marital relationships. Mitchell suggests that anthropologists should pay more attention to work relationships.

Voluntary associations have been investigated by several anthropologists. Kenneth Little (1965) and Michael Banton (1957) have suggested that voluntary associations in West African towns are adaptive institutions which help a newly arrived migrant to understand urban norms of behavior and to construct, through membership in such organizations, a network of supportive relationships for himself. There are several sorts of voluntary associations in Africa. There are, for example, secular social clubs whose members have Western educations, sometimes at universities and

colleges. There are religious organizations associated with Christianity and with other religions. Some associations concern themselves with their members' occupational or commercial activities, others sponsor various forms of entertainment.

Anthropologists have also investigated ethnic associations, which build for the rural migrant a kind of bridge between one social system and another. Frequently called "tribal" associations, ethnic associations are common both in West and East Africa. Associations like that of the Luo in Kampala, Uganda, studied by David Parkin (1969), are segmented first into subtribes or regions, and these are internally segmented into clan groups. Similarly, in Nigeria, voluntary associations of the Ibo and other groups are segmented, with extended families or lineages organized into clan associations; the clan associations unite in district associations and the latter combine to form the total ethnic association (cf. Banton, 1957). The Ugandan Luo association concerns itself with urban problems which directly affect the individual, providing economic as well as moral support, including transportation of the destitute to the rural area. In Nigeria, although most members of a given ethnic association are illiterate day laborers, the membership inevitably includes doctors, lawyers, and other professionals. The ideology of the association is that of a gigantic kinship group; members are expected to address one another as brothers and sisters. As in an extended family, richer people are obligated to help the less fortunate. When their own members are involved in a dispute, voluntary associations often assume arbitration functions characteristic of courts. Such associations control their membership through the financial help they offer, and their ultimate sanction is expulsion, usually an unhappy fate for a migrant in an ethnically heterogeneous city.

Parkin has suggested that the groups that form such ethnic associations are al-

ways decentralized tribes whose rural social systems are based on descent group
organization with a segmentary model.
Parkin suggests that because migrants from
centralized tribes are already familiar with
political and economic specialization and
with socioeconomic stratification, they have
little need to reorganize themselves for
urban life. As in the countryside, their
problems and mutual aid networks will involve informal networks of kin and others,
for example, neighbors, affines, trade
partners.

Other types of association play analogous roles in allowing individuals to adapt
to city life. Trade associations, for example, help their members to acquire and
save capital; occupational societies often
guarantee members that their burial expenses will be paid.

The existence of voluntary associations
as means of adaptation to urban life is not
confined to Africa. Paul Doughty (1970),
for example, has investigated associations
of urban migrants in a region of Lima, Peru,
and notes that these organizations serve a
variety of important functions for the individual and the nation. Doughty documents ways in which they help to mitigate
the stress of social and cultural changes
on the migrant.

ANALYSIS OF CATEGORICAL RELATIONSHIPS
By "categorical relationship" Mitchell refers to a process through which superficial
relationships between people come to be
regulated. He points out that in a variety
of urban scenes, town dwellers tend to
categorize people on the basis of some vis-
ible characteristic and to organize their behavior uniformly toward all people who
display this characteristic. Examples include relationships between Europeans
and Africans, in which members of each
reference group often treat the other in a
stereotyped way; relationships between
tribes in ethnically heterogeneous cities;
relationships between classes or members
of occupational groups; and relationships
between the sexes and different age groups.

ANALYSIS OF PERSONAL RELATIONSHIPS: NET-
WORK ANALYSIS Organizing field data
gathered during community studies in Nor-
way and London, John Barnes (1954) and
Elizabeth Bott (1957) developed the concept of social network analysis, a technique
which Philip Mayer (1964) believes may
eventually play the role in urban studies
that the genealogy has played in analysis
of tribal life. Barnes and Bott distinguished
two broadly different types of social network: the contained, small-mesh, close-
knit network characteristic of the rural
community, and the dispersed, large-mesh,
loose-knit network characteristic of urban
society. Network analysis is a form of egocentric analysis; it focuses on specific individuals and determines their patterns of
association with others. In the small-mesh,
close-knit network, many of ego's friends,
neighbors, and relatives know one another;
in the large-mesh, loose-knit network, this
is not so. With more closely knit networks,
Bott argues, it is easier to reach agreement
on norms, and because of tight association,
people exert consistent and final pressure
on network members to conform to those
norms.

Several scholars have investigated the
networks of personal links which individuals in African towns build up around
themselves. Explicitly attempting to adapt
network analysis to urban anthropology
in Africa, Philip Mayer (1961) reported
differences in the social networks of two
groups of Xhosa migrants to the town of
East London, Republic of South Africa.
One group of Xhosa, called the "Red People" by Mayer, insist on remaining typically pagan and illiterate. The other group,
the "School Migrants," modify their behavior in Western directions more easily.
The Red People encapsulate themselves in
tight-meshed, close-knit networks of personal relationships. East London lies so
close to the rural Xhosa homeland that most
migrants, if they choose, can make brief
visits home during their prolonged stays in
town. The personal networks of the Red
People extend into the rural areas. Their

strong ties with home protect them from being tied into town-based social relationships and also reinforce their rural orientation. The loose-knit networks of the School Migrants, on the other hand, enable them to participate in urban social activity while simultaneously maintaining close relationships with their rural kinsmen. A. L. Epstein (1961) has applied network analysis to the study of norm and value communication among urban Africans.

OTHER UNITS OF ANALYSIS IN URBAN ANTHROPOLOGY Interest in urban life has forced anthropologists to innovate in selecting analytic techniques and units of study. It has been found, for example, that a series of specifically anthropological field techniques may be used in conjunction with quantitative, survey techniques in analyzing city life. Mitchell and several others have demonstrated that anthropologists can profitably examine urban associations, structural relationships, categorical relationships, and varying individual networks. Anthropologists Victor Turner (1957), Max Gluckman (1958, orig. 1940, 1942), Ronald Frankenberg (1966), and others have stressed the additional value of analysis of unusual events in complex societies. Aspects of urban life may, for example, be perceived and studied at large gatherings, including ceremonials, political events, and plays.

Oscar Lewis was responsible for still other innovations in the anthropological study of urban life. Lewis' concept of the subculture of poverty was developed after he had conducted traditional ethnographic fieldwork in India and Mexico. His earliest Mexican research (see Lewis, 1951) involved a peasant community, Tepotzlan, which had originally been studied by Robert Redfield (1930). Lewis' general interest in cultural and social variation in Mexican society led him from rural to urban research. In his earliest work in Mexico City (see Lewis, 1958), he continued to rely on community study techniques in his research on a slum neighborhood. Eventually, his urban research led him away from traditional anthropological wholism and toward the study of personal experience. In *Five Families* (1959), whose Mexican title means "The Anthropology of Poverty," Lewis described a day in the lives of each of five families. In his well-known book *The Children of Sanchez* (1961), he focused even more sharply on individual experience, using information provided by members of a single Mexican family. Here Lewis added a novelistic dimension by having the same events described by different family members. His next book, *Pedro Martinez* (1964), viewed changes in Mexican society principally through the eyes of a Mexican peasant.

By the time Lewis began the research which culminated in *La Vida* (1966), the culture of poverty had become his major research objective. To determine whether this culture existed among other Hispanic populations, he shifted his study of the poor from Mexicans to Puerto Ricans in San Juan and New York City. *La Vida* combines an autobiographical technique, with the characters narrating their own lives, and objective description. Lewis started this work by interviewing one hundred families from four suburbs of San Juan. After the general survey, he selected ten extended families for more concentrated study. For the first time, he included a child's narrative as evidence, and he found that at age seven the lower-class Hispanic child had a well-developed notion of the culture of poverty.

Lewis' techniques of urban anthropological research have been severely criticized. Other scholars have pointed out that his concentration on specific families and individuals inevitably required him to ignore considerable variation, and they fault him for often skimping on his own anthropological analysis in favor of informants' accounts. Some critics have characterized his books as literature rather than anthropology. None of his critics can deny, however, the uniqueness, sympathy, and value of his accounts of poverty as actually experienced by the poor.

SUMMARY

Continuing metropolitan dominance of satellite areas threatens the existence of populations that sociocultural anthropologists have traditionally studied. The effects of this domination on underdeveloped nations has expanded the range of problems amenable to anthropological investigation. The study of contemporary peasantries has grown enormously, as have investigations of other areas within sociocultural anthropology: urban anthropology, applied anthropology, and studies of acculturation.

This chapter has concentrated on variations in peasant societies in Latin America and Africa. Anthropologists have pointed to the existence of two basic types of rural peasant communities in Latin America: the closed, corporate (generally Indian) peasant community of the highlands and the open, non-corporate (generally mestizo) community of the lowlands. Highland and lowland communities include some sociocultural institutions that are formally similar to those which were described previously for tribal societies. Yet, comparing similar forms—for example, ceremonial, kinship, and marriage forms in states and nonstates—we find that functions may be very different. The role of the cargo systems of highland Latin America in leveling wealth differentials within communities and maintaining poverty among the national lower class has

been contrasted with the adaptive, inter-community leveling associated with blowouts in tribal societies. Similarly, the functions of the kinship system in lowland Latin America in impeding individual vertical mobility and maintaining poverty there have been contrasted with adaptive functions of kinship and marriage in band and tribal organization.

Poverty, however, is not confined to rural areas of the Third World. It extends to the slums of San Juan, Mexico City, New York City, and a thousand other cities. Oscar Lewis, perhaps best-known among anthropologists who have studied urban poverty, created great controversy because of his popularization of the "subculture of poverty," a set of behavioral and ideological traits which he believed characterized the poor in certain areas of the world. Lewis believed that through enculturation the subculture of poverty became self-perpetuating, and that it would be more difficult to eradicate than poverty itself. However, he also asserted that poverty did not always breed the culture of poverty. The fatalism associated with the culture of poverty would not be found among poor people whose history or social organization provided a sense of belonging to some larger, more enduring unit. For example, Lewis discovered no culture of poverty in

Sources and Suggested Readings

BANTON, M.
   1957   *West African City. A Study in Tribal Life in Freetown.* London: Oxford University Press. Role of voluntary associations in adaptation to urban life.

BARNES, J. A.
   1954   Class and Committees in a Norwegian Island Parish. *Human Relations* 7: 39–58. Pioneering use of network analysis.

BASCOM, W.
   1955   Urbanization among the Yoruba. *American Journal of Sociology* 60:

446–455. The role of lineage and kinship among urban Nigerian Yoruba.

BOTT, E.
   1957   *Family and Social Network.* London: Tavistock. Applies network analysis to family relations in London.

BUNZEL, R.
   1952   *Chichicastenango: A Guatemalan Village.* New York: J. J. Augustin. Field study of a "closed, corporate peasant community"; includes a discussion of the highland cargo system.

BURLING, R.
   1965   *Hill Farms and Padi Fields: Life in*

India. He suggested that here caste solidarity and a feeling of historic participation in Hindu civilization impeded the formation of the culture of poverty. Similarly, solidarity associated with corporate descent group organization would combat the culture of poverty in African cities. And in revolutionary Cuba he found it replaced by a feeling of active participation by the poor in a new social order.

Criticism of Lewis points to research which shows that although America's poor share many values with the national majority, their deprivations prevent them from actualizing these values. Some scholars have asserted that in adapting to poverty, the poor develop alternative values which help them preserve their sanity. It may be that social scientists have concentrated too exclusively on a narrow range of the values of the poor, while ignoring a much larger set of values shared with the larger society.

Although ethnographic techniques have been employed in research in the United States for several decades, anthropological research in American cities is currently booming. In the United States and elsewhere, anthropologists encounter difficulties in applying their traditional field methods to urban situations. In Africa, for example, where statistical data on social characteristics of cities is usually lacking, many anthropologists have employed social surveys as means of gathering quantitative data. Yet more traditional, qualitative techniques have also been used successfully in studies of urban life. Anthropologists have studied structural relationships in cities, examining, for example, the role of voluntary associations in enabling migrants from rural zones to adapt to urban life. Anthropologists have also studied patterns of interaction of individuals and groups in cities, noting that social encounters are often regulated by categorical perceptions, in which members of one group treat any member of another in a stereotyped way. Based on work principally in Western Europe and Africa, anthropologists have developed social network analysis as a tool for urban research. They have found that there are characteristic differences in the social networks, the web of personal ties, of townsmen and rural dwellers.

Anthropologists have used still other methods in urban studies. Social events have been described and analyzed. Oscar Lewis has combined intimate field study with tape recordings of his informants' life histories and observation of their daily lives in several enlightening studies of urban poverty and its cultural manifestations.

Mainland Southeast Asia. Englewood Cliffs, N.J.: Prentice-Hall. Peasant societies of Southeast Asia viewed historically and anthropologically; paperback.

COHEN, A.
1969   *Custom and Politics in Urban Africa.* London: Routledge and Kegan Paul. A major contribution to the anthropology of urban life in Africa.

DALTON, G., ed.
1967   *Tribal and Peasant Economies: Readings in Economic Anthropology.* Garden City, N.Y.: The Natural History Press. Includes several excellent articles.

1971   *Economic Development and Social Change: The Modernization of Village Communities.* Garden City, N.Y.: The Natural History Press. Articles on development and culture change in several Third World countries.

DAVIDSON, B.
1966   *African Kingdoms.* New York: Time-Life Books. Beautifully illustrated volume on African history, including indigenous states; discussion of early European impact on African societies.

The End of the Primitive World and the Contemporary Relevance of Anthropology

DOUGHTY, P.
1970   Behind the Back of the City: "Provincial" Life in Lima, Peru. In *Peasants in Cities: Readings in the Anthropology of Urbanization*, ed. W. Mangin, pp. 30–46. Boston: Houghton Mifflin. Discusses role of voluntary associations in adaptation to urban life in Peru.

EPSTEIN, A. L.
1961   The Network and Urban Social Organization. *Rhodes-Livingstone Journal* 29: 29–62. The social network as a means of information dispersal in African cities.

FRANK, A. G.
1969   *Capitalism and Underdevelopment in Latin America: Historical Studies of Chile and Brazil*. New York: Modern Reader Paperbacks. Metropole-satellite relationships with reference to Latin American underdevelopment.

FRANKENBERG, R.
1966   British Community Studies: Problems in Synthesis. In *The Social Anthropology of Complex Societies*, ed. M. Banton, pp. 123–154. London: Tavistock. Problems in adapting anthropological field techniques to life in cities and other areas of complex society.

GANS, H.
1962   *The Urban Villagers*. New York: The Free Press. Re-examination of Whyte's (1943) Italian-American community in Boston.

GLUCKMAN, M.
1958   (orig. 1940, 1942). *Analysis of a Social Situation in Modern Zululand*. Manchester, England: Manchester University Press. Analysis of a bridge opening as a key to modern Zulu life in South Africa.

HARRIS, M.
1956   *Town and Country in Brazil*. New York: Columbia University Press. Field study of urban ethos in a former gold-mining town in the Brazilian interior.

1964   *Patterns of Race in the Americas*. New York: Walker. Determinants of different patterns of race and ethnic relations in North and South America.

HEATH, D. B., and ADAMS, R. N., eds.
1965   *Contemporary Cultures and Societies of Latin America*. New York: Random House. Most complete anthology of anthropological research in Latin America.

HUTCHINSON, H. W.
1957   *Village and Plantation Life in Northeastern Brazil*. Seattle: University of Washington Press. Ethnographic and historical study of a sugar plantation town in Bahia, Brazil.

JORGENSEN, J. G.
1972   *The Sun Dance Religion: Power for the Powerless*. Chicago: University of Chicago Press. An American Indian religious movement as an adaptation to political and economic events in the larger society.

JORGENSEN, J. G., ed.
1972   *Reservation Indian Society Today: Studies of Economics, Politics, Kinship and Households*. Berkeley: University of California Press. Series of articles examining the plight of native Americans in a variety of reservation settings.

KOTTAK, C. P.
1967   Kinship and Class in Brazil. *Ethnology* 4: 427–443. Lower-class kinship and relationship between kinship and class.

LEWIS, O.
1951   *Life in a Mexican Village; Tepotzlan Restudied*. Urbana: University of Illinois Press. Re-examination, with surprisingly different results, of a peasant community first studied by Robert Redfield in 1930.

1958   The Culture of the *Vecindad* in Mexico City: Two Case Studies. *Actas de XXXIII Congreso Internacional de Americanistas*, San Jose, 20–27 julio, pp. 387–402. Anthropological research in an urban neighborhood.

1959   *Five Families*. New York: Basic Books. A day in the life of each of five Mexican families.

1961   *The Children of Sanchez*. New York: Random House. Family life as perceived by five members of the Sanchez family in a Mexico City slum.

1964   *Pedro Martinez: A Mexican Peasant and His Family*. New York: Random House. A peasant views the Mexican revolution.

1966   *La Vida: A Puerto Rican Family in the Culture of Poverty—San Juan and New York*. New York: Random House. Controversial study of Puerto Rican family life.

1968   Poverty, Bourgeoisie, Revolution, translated by R. U. Ballesta. From a conversation between O. Lewis, K. S. Karol, and C. Fuentes which appeared in *Mundo Nuevo*, no. 11. May, 1967. Courtesy of Dr. Nan Pendrell. Informal discussion of some of the characteristics of the culture of poverty and reasons why it is not a national universal.

LIEBOUW, E.
1967   *Tally's Corner*. Boston: Little, Brown. Field study of a Washington, D.C., ghetto.

LITTLE, K.
1965   *West African Urbanization: A Study of Voluntary Associations in Social Change*. Cambridge, England: Cambridge University Press. Role of voluntary associations in adaptation to urban life.

1971   Some Aspects of African Urbanization South of the Sahara. Reading, Mass.: Addison-Wesley, McCaleb Modules in Anthropology. Review article.

LYND, R., and LYND, H.
1929   *Middletown*. New York: Columbia University Press. Early sociological-ethnographic study of a Midwest community.

MANGIN, W., ed.
1970   *Peasants in Cities: Readings in the Anthropology of Urbanization*. Boston: Houghton Mifflin. Articles on urban life in several countries; reprints and originals.

MAYER, P.
1961   *Townsmen or Tribesmen: Conservatism and the Process of Urbanization in a South African City*. Capetown, South Africa: Oxford University Press. Network analysis of migrants to East London, South Africa.

1962   Migrancy and the Study of Africans in Towns. *American Anthropologist* 64: 576–592. Techniques of studying labor migration to African cities.

1964   Labour Migrancy and the Social Network. *Problems of Transition: Proceedings of the Social Sciences Research Conference*, ed. J. F. Holleman et al., held in the University of Natal, Durban, South Africa, July, 1962, pp. 21–34. Pietermaritzburg, South Africa, Natal University Press. Argues that social network analysis will do for urban studies what the genealogical method has done for traditional ethnography.

MINER, H.
1953   *The Primitive City of Timbucktoo*.

Princeton: Princeton University Press. Field study of a small city in the West African interior.

MITCHELL, J. C.
1957   *The Kalela Dance. Aspects of Social Relationships among Urban Africans in Northern Rhodesia*. Rhodes-Livingstone Paper no. 27. Manchester, England: Manchester University Press. Analysis of urban life through field study of a dance association.

1966   Theoretical Orientations in African Urban Studies. In *The Social Anthropology of Complex Societies*, ed. M. Banton, pp. 37–68. London: Tavistock. Comprehensive review of techniques of urban anthropological study in Africa.

MOYNIHAN, D. P.
1965   *The Negro Family: The Case for National Action*. Washington, D.C.: U.S. Government Printing Office. The much maligned Moynihan report, linking family organization and other attributes of some members of the American black population to a subculture of poverty.

PARKER, S., ed.
1973   Poverty and Culture. In *To See Ourselves: Anthropology and Modern Social Issues*, gen. ed. T. Weaver. Glenview, Ill.: Scott, Foresman. Articles on poverty and the culture of poverty and Parker's prefatory comments and concluding synthesis.

PARKER, S., and KLEINER, R.
1970   The Culture of Poverty: an Adjustive Dimension. *American Anthropologist* 72: 516–527. Cultural values and mental illness among Philadelphia blacks.

PARKIN, D.
1969   *Neighbours and Nationals in an African City Ward*. London: Routledge and Kegan Paul. Analysis of ethnic associations among the Luo of Kampala, Uganda.

PETRAS, J., and ZEITLIN, M., eds.
1968   *Latin America: Reform or Revolution? A Reader*. Greenwich, Conn.: Fawcett. Class and class conflict, development and politics in Latin America.

POTTER, J. M., DIAZ, M. N., and FOSTER, G. M., eds.
1967   *Peasant Society: A Reader*. Boston: Little, Brown. Peasant society in many world areas.

REDFIELD, R.

1930   *Tepotzlan: A Mexican Village.* Chicago: University of Chicago Press. The peasant community later restudied by Oscar Lewis.

1941   *The Folk Culture of Yucatan.* Chicago: University of Chicago Press. The rural-urban continuum as exemplified in four Yucatecan communities.

1953   *The Primitive World and Its Transformations.* Ithaca, N.Y.: Cornell University Press. Growth of heterogeneity from homogeneous folk societies.

1956   *The Little Community.* Chicago: University of Chicago Press. Good introduction to community study techniques in traditional ethnography.

SERVICE, E. R.

1968   War and Our Contemporary Ancestors. In *War: The Anthropology of Armed Conflict and Aggression,* ed. M. H. Fried, M. Harris, and R. F. Murphy, pp. 160–167. Garden City, N.Y.: The Natural History Press. Brilliant delineation of problems in extrapolating past conditions from contemporary primitive populations in the wake of European disruption of native life in many world areas.

SOUTHALL, A.

1959   An Operational Theory of Role. *Human Relations* 12: 17–34. Variations in role structure along the rural-urban continuum.

1961   Introductory Summary. In *Social Change in Modern Africa,* ed. A. Southall, pp. 1–46. London: Oxford University Press. Good introduction to social change and urban anthropology in Africa; includes a classification of African towns.

SOUTHALL, A., and GUTKIND, P.

1957   *Townsmen in the Making.* Kampala, Uganda: East African Institute of Social Research. Early urban anthropological field research in Africa.

STEWARD, J. H.

1956   *People of Puerto Rico.* Urbana: University of Illinois Press. Pioneering research by anthropological field team of variation in a complex society.

TUMIN, M. M., ed.

1969   *Comparative Perspectives on Race Relations.* Boston: Little, Brown. Anthology of studies of race and ethnic relations in several world areas.

TURNER, V. W.

1957   *Schism and Continuity in an African Society.* Manchester, England: Manchester University Press. Analysis of social drama as a tool for anthropological study of complex societies.

VALENTINE, C.

1968   *Culture and Poverty.* Chicago: Uni-

versity of Chicago Press. Controversial critique of the culture of
poverty.

WAGLEY, C. W.

1964   (orig. 1953). *Amazon Town: A Study
of Man in the Tropics.* New York:
Knopf. Best Brazilian community
study; an ethnography of the boom
and bust of rubber in the Amazon
region.

1968   *The Latin American Tradition.* New
York: Columbia University Press.
Collected essays on unity and diver-
sity in Latin American culture.

1971   *An Introduction to Brazil.* Rev. ed.
New York: Columbia University
Press. Introduction to history, society,
and culture of Latin America's
largest nation.

WAGLEY, C. W., ed.

1952   *Race and Class in Rural Brazil.* Paris:
UNESCO. Studies by Wagley and his
students of social stratification and
race relations in four areas of Brazil.

WAGLEY, C., and HARRIS, M.

1958   *Minorities in the New World: Six
Case Studies.* New York: Columbia
University Press. Qualitative descriptions of native Americans in Brazil
and Mexico, Afro-Americans in Mar-
tinique and the United States, and
Euro-Americans (French Canadians
and Jews) in the United States.

WEST, J.

1945   *Plainville, U.S.A.* New York: Columbia University Press. A rural community in the American Midwest
during World War II.

WHYTE, W. F.

1943   *Street Corner Society.* Chicago: University of Chicago Press. Field study
of a Boston neighborhood of Italian
Americans, with emphasis on the
social organization of youths.

WOLF, E. R.

1955   Types of Latin American Peasantry.
American Anthropologist 57: 452–
471. Classic article defining closed,
corporate and open, noncorporate as
basic types of peasant communities in
Latin America.

1966   *Peasants.* Englewood Cliffs, N.J.:
Prentice-Hall. Best introduction to
cross-cultural study of peasants.

1969   *Peasant Wars of the Twentieth Century.* New York: Harper and Row.
An anthropologist examines revolutionary movements in Mexico, Russia,
China, Vietnam, Algeria, and Cuba.

ZIMMERMAN, B.

1952   Race Relations in the Arid Sertão.
In *Race and Class in Rural Brazil*, ed.
C. Wagley, pp. 82–115. Paris:
UNESCO. Race relations in the Bra-
zilian backlands.

14. Uses and Abuses of Anthropology

Many anthropologists would agree with Kathleen Gough (1973) that anthropology is rooted in the Enlightenment's humanistic vision of a science of man which could liberate us and improve human welfare by expanding human knowledge. Anthropologists show justifiable pride in the contributions of their discipline toward reducing ethnocentrism by instilling appreciation for cultural diversity, and in questioning racist attitudes and the validity of race as a scientific concept. Presumably this broadening, educational function affects the knowledge, values, and attitudes of those exposed to anthropology, but now we must ask what role has anthropology to play with respect to contemporary practical and political questions? What are the ethical components of the anthropologist's involvement in practical and political matters?

Ralph Piddington (1960) has divided attitudes toward the appropriate role of the anthropologist in practical affairs into three schools of thought. The first, characteristic of many contemporary anthropologists, is an ivory tower conception, which maintains that anthropologists should remain aloof from practical matters and should devote themselves to research, publication, and teaching.

The second group, which includes a large number of social scientists in addition to anthropologists, represents what Piddington calls the "schizoid interpretation" of the role of the social scientist. According to this viewpoint, the anthropologist may appropriately employ concepts and methods of his discipline in collecting facts related to conduct of a given policy. He may then report his findings to the client who has commissioned his study. However, the anthropologist should play no role in formulating or criticizing policy and should refrain from advocating decisions which would only reflect the anthropologist's personal value judgment. According to this view, value judgments and scientific investigation should be kept strictly separate, although the social scientist has a right to express his own values when not engaged in professional work. This notion of the role of the practical anthropologist is exemplified by Bronislaw Malinowski and several other anthropologists considered below.

The third point of view maintains that since the anthropologist is the person who is most aware of the human problems involved in carrying out policies, he is entirely correct in advocating certain policies. Furthermore, he should supply facts needed to accomplish only those policies which he approves.

Kathleen Gough, Gerald Berreman, and many other anthropologists (cf. Weaver, ed., 1973) hold opinions characteristic of the third group. Gough suggests that no one is more qualified to propose and evaluate guidelines for human society than those who study it. She argues that anthropologists, as scientists, have the responsibility to present their knowledge and the inferences they can draw from such knowledge as clearly, thoughtfully, and responsibly as possible. She laments the fact that many anthropologists have been unwilling to do this, stating that "it is as though the more we study the world's cultures, the less capable we feel of making judgments as citizens [1973, p. 158]." Berreman (1973, p. 55) similarly stresses the anthropologist's responsibility to actively combat widespread ignorance on the part of politicians and policy makers about comparatively simple aspects of social existence which have been described, analyzed, understood, and amply demonstrated by anthropologists. Those adhering to the third viewpoint thus reject both the ivory tower and schizoid interpretations of the anthropologist's role. Not only do they feel it is their duty to propose and advocate guidelines for society, they feel their professional responsibility is to communicate as widely and effectively as possible the findings of their research.

Piddington finds the third view attractive; however, he questions its effectiveness, since anthropologists do not normally occupy important policy-making positions, and since many administrators have a low opinion of social scientists. It seems to me, however, that anthropologists can increase their effectiveness in several ways. By drawing on their knowledge, awareness, and opinions of contemporary social and political problems, they can express themselves collectively through the American Anthropological Association. It would appear, too, that anthropologists have a duty to popularize findings which relate to current issues through wider publication in nonprofessional journals. Finally, more anthropologists can follow the example of those of their colleagues whose knowledge of and concern for human problems has been expressed through participation in contemporary social and political movement.

Perhaps we should add a fourth group to Piddington's classification. It would include anthropologists who concern themselves with practical matters, not on behalf of government or other clients, but because of their own research goals. Two approaches to applied anthropology, the research and development approach and the action anthropology approach (both discussed below), exemplify attempts by anthropologists to introduce changes, not in the context of government policy, but by helping the people they study and by advancing their own research goals.

Practical and Applied Anthropology

James A. Clifton defines *applied anthropology* as "the use of anthropological findings, concepts and methods to accomplish a desired end [1970, p. viii]." He traces the application of anthropological knowledge to practical problems from the mid–nineteenth-century debate in England over slavery, and discusses the roles of anthropologists on different sides of the question. Applied anthropology, as Clifton has defined it, played a role in European colonialism in Africa and other areas. In 1929, for example, in a memorandum to the International African Institute, an organization of scholars interested in Africa and based in Britain, Bronislaw Malinowski advocated a new branch of anthropology and called it "practical anthropology." Chiding his colleagues for their antiquarian emphasis on singular, quaint, and exotic institutions and customs rather than description of behavior and process in social life, Malinowski argued that anthropology should begin to study "the changing Native" and the impact of Westernization on traditional African societies, especially the diffusion of European culture into "savage" communities.

Malinowski, clearly representing Piddington's second group, argued that the anthropologist could serve the "practical man," that is, the administrator or missionary, by investigating such matters as law, economics, and other customs and institutions. He pointed out that the constitution of the International African Institute eliminated all political issues and considerations from its activities. Even had this not been the case, however, Malinowski believed that anthropologists could easily avoid politics by concentrating exclusively on facts and processes. He asserted that decisions about how to apply the results of anthropological investigations should be left to statesmen and journalists. According to Malinowski, the anthropologist should be free to pursue his "impartial cold-blooded passion for sheer accuracy."

Jacques Maquet (1964) and others have pointed to direct and indirect associations between anthropologists and colonial administrations, and many Africans feel that anthropologists and their findings were tools of colonial regimes. Malinowski's statements to the International African Institute indicate that he saw nothing wrong with this role. As examples of ways in which the anthropologist could help the "practical man," Malinowski advocated training of cadets (trainees) in the British colonial service in the languages and cultures of Africa. The anthropologist working in Africa could also help the colonial regime by studying such matters as land tenure and determining traditional land use patterns and the indispensable minimum of land to be reserved for native groups in the face of European land claims.

Although he argued for a separation of anthropology and politics, Malinowski's expression of his own political values in these statements to the International African Institute cannot be ignored. He did not question the legitimacy of the colonial regime or the role of the anthropologist in bolstering it by helping it function smoothly. He cautioned against too rapid attempts to undo or subvert traditional African value systems with external moral codes on the grounds that "black bolshevism" would inevitably result. His assumption that rebellion against colonial authority is to be avoided certainly bears witness to Malinowski's own value judgments and political biases.

Despite the fact that his comments represent perhaps an extreme view of the appropriateness of collaboration between anthropologists and officials of their own government, Malinowski's conception of the practical role of anthropology in colonial regimes is certainly not unique. The Rhodes-Livingstone Institute of Central African Studies, located in Zambia, was created to study the impact of European culture on traditional African societies and began research activities in 1938. Godfrey Wilson (1940), who participated in its research, felt that the fact that the Institute was responsible neither to any government nor for any government policies guaranteed intellectual freedom to its anthropologists. Wilson partially adopts the schizoid view, on the one hand asserting that the social scientist cannot judge good and evil, but only objective social fact and its implications, while at the same time suggesting the potential value of general sociological understanding in inspiring governmental actions.

Both during and after the period of European colonialism, anthropologists have played a variety of applied roles. In addition to advising administrators, anthropologists have actually held positions in colonial regimes. They have served as community development advisers, working as researchers, cultural interpreters, and intermediaries between natives and communities and government officials; they have worked in mental hospitals, public health programs, and educational programs; and, as we shall see below, they have undertaken research roles on behalf of the military.

Although the formal colonial structure of the United States has never been as well developed as in England, France, and other European nations, anthropologists have held government positions in American trust territories, and they have acted as consultants for American government programs abroad. In almost all these cases, anthropologists involved in administration or technical assistance programs have willingly or unwillingly adopted the schizoid view of the social scientist's role.

Like the development of national character studies (discussed in Chapter 12), an association of practical anthropology and government responded to American involvement in World War II. In 1943, reflecting the war effort in the Pacific, the United States Office of Naval Intelligence, jointly with the Military Government Section of Naval Operations, contracted with Yale University for a research program on Micronesia, under an anthropologist's direction. The relationship between anthropology and government continued in the Trust Territory of Micronesia even after control passed from the Navy to the Interior Department in 1951. In this project six anthropologists, a staff anthropologist assigned to the Political Affairs Department, and five district anthropologists under his direction were employed to gain information useful to administrators. Like Malinowski's colonial anthropologists, the Americans were to have no say in determining or implementing policies, nor were they charged with control or enforcement. Theoretically freed of administrative responsibilities, they were to become experts on Micronesian attitudes and behavior, and they were to devise and recommend techniques to accomplish objectives decided upon by the administration. The staff anthropologist was to organize and conduct

research and to maintain professional relationships with other anthropologists interested in Micronesian research. All the anthropologists were expected to confine themselves to sociological analyses of means and results rather than concern themselves with objectives. On the basis of their familiarity with village life, they were expected to assess prospects for success of specific programs and to evaluate results. As intermediaries between the Micronesians and the American government, they were expected to serve as vehicles of communication. For example, they were to interpret American legal norms and educational standards for natives, and to indicate problems and cultural incompatibilities to the administrators (cf. Barnett, 1956).

Despite the limitations placed on them by certain types of government sponsorship and by policies over which they have no control, many anthropologists have attempted to use the findings, concepts, and methods of their discipline for some purpose which they regard as worthy. Undoubtedly the anthropologists who participated in the Micronesian project were motivated by their humanitarian concern over problems inflicted by Japanese occupation and other effects of war on these island societies.

Other anthropologists have intervened in the lives of their subjects in order to bring about what they regard as beneficial economic and social changes. In some cases such intervention has been sponsored by the United States government, and in some of these cases one may entertain considerable doubt about the long-range benefits of these programs. In other cases anthropologists have been able to devise their own intervention programs.

Research and development:
the Vicos project

One of the best examples of independent anthropological intervention is found in the *research and development approach* to applied anthropology. In 1952 Cornell University, jointly with the Peruvian Institute of Indigenous Affairs, initiated an experimental five-year program of induced social and economic change (Holmberg, 1958, 1965). The project focused on the transformation of Vicos, one of Peru's most unproductive and highly dependent manor (or *hacienda*) systems, into a productive, self-governing community, adapted to the realities of surviving in the modern Peruvian state. This intervention in the social and economic life of Vicos reflected a humanitarian awareness on the part of anthropologist Allen Holmberg that peasants, who represent more than half the world's population, often live in underdeveloped countries with natural and social conditions which deny them effective participation in modern life.

The manor of Vicos spanned some 40,000 acres with a population of about 1,700 monolingual Quecha-speaking Indians and was located between 9,000 and 20,000 feet above sea level. Since colonial times, the inhabitants of Vicos, like many other Peruvian Indians, had been bound to the land as serfs, or peons. Title to Vicos, a public manor, was held by a Public Benefit Charity Society, which rented it out to the highest bidder at public auctions for periods ranging from five to ten years. When the industrial firm which was running Vicos on a ten-year lease went bankrupt in 1952 after five years, Cornell was able to sublease the manor and utilize its serfs for the remaining five years.

Part of any Peruvian *hacienda*, usually the most fertile bottom lands, is reserved for commercial exploitation by the renter. Rental of a manor, always by an outsider who is a mestizo, also entitles him to the labor of the manor's serfs for a certain number of days each week. In return for their work, the renter is, in theory but often not in practice, legally bound to provide them with sufficient marginal land to support their households. Representing the renter locally is a mestizo administrator; under him, depending on the size of the estate, are one or more foremen, also mestizos, whose job is to mobilize Indian labor. Indian straw bosses organize the work of the serfs.

The phrase "research and development approach" to anthropology reflects the fact that Holmberg and his colleagues wanted to change the conditions just discussed, and to study the nature and results of their intervention. The major goal of Cornell's acquisition of Vicos was devolution of power to members of the community, in an attempt to promote the production and distribution of greater wealth, the introduction of new and modern skills, the encouragement of general health and well-being, the enlargement of the local status and role structure, and the formation of a modern system of education through schools and other media. Holmberg believed that every Vicosino should have, if he so desired, the right and the opportunity to take part in decisions affecting his community, to enhance his own knowledge, health, esteem, and talents, and to preserve the dignity of his private life. Holmberg described the Cornell personnel as using their own power to share power to the point that they no longer held power.

The changes that they promoted were guided by two principles. First, they assumed that people would be most likely to accept innovations in areas where they felt greatest deprivation. Second, they believed that an integrated or contextual approach to change is usually better than a piecemeal approach. The anthropologists formulated about 130 specific lines of research and development. Each line was matched to a specific developmental goal such as the development of community leadership, the diversification of agriculture, the improvement of educational opportunities, and the reduction of social distance between Indians and mestizos.

In the last case, in order to test the hypothesis that prejudice will be reduced by conditions of social equality, one of the research and development projects involved scheduling social events to draw mestizos from neighboring communities into Vicos and then conducting the event in such a way as to break down the traditional system of mestizo-Indian segregation. Their hypothesis was confirmed in more equal social relations between Vicosinos and mestizos by the time the project ended.

In contrast to the old system, in which profits from the renter's commercial land were removed from the community, Cornell's profits were reinvested in the community to improve agricultural productivity, to construct health and educational facilities, and to increase the Indians' skills. Simultaneously, new agricultural techniques were introduced and adopted by the Indians for use in their own fields.

There are several indications of the success of the Vicos project. In 1958 the Peruvian Institute of Indigenous Affairs began conducting five similar experiments in other areas of the country. Attached to each of these were Peruvian anthropologists, many of whom had participated in the Vicos project. In addition to the specific hypotheses that were tested in the field, the Vicos project is of scientific interest for several reasons. It demonstrates that significant social, political, and economic change can be produced quickly using this model of intervention. Furthermore, apropos of the image of limited good and other notions about peasant conservatism, Vicos suggests that under favorable conditions, attitudes and behavior patterns can be changed very rapidly indeed.

In addition, events in the late fifties, as Cornell's lease ran out, suggest that obstacles to changes in peasant attitudes and behavior do not lie primarily in peasant world view but in forces external to the community. Vicos has been called an "experiment in revolution in microcosm." How did vested interests view this experiment? During the project, Peruvian media gave considerable favorable publicity to Vicos. However, the power elite in this area of Peru—which consisted of mestizos, businessmen, landed families, political figures, and so on—paid little attention to the Vicos experiment, believing that any benefits would eventually return to future renters,

members of the mestizo elite. With the end of the Cornell project, the Vicosinos applied for the right to buy the estate themselves. Hearing of this, vested interests resisted and attacked with a variety of legal maneuvers. Because of its own elitist ties, the Peruvian government avoided action in favor of the Vicosinos, while paying lip service to their cause. Finally, through the intervention of the Institute of Indigenous Affairs and certain American government officials in Peru, an agreement was reached between the Public Benefit Charity Society and the Vicos community for direct sale at a price and on terms that the Vicosinos could realistically afford. The community actually became economically independent in July 1962, and since that time Cornell's role has involved research, consultation, and advice (Holmberg, 1965).

As Holmberg points out, the major lesson of Vicos is that a suppressed population of peasants, once freed from external exploitation and given encouragement, technical assistance, and learning, *can* succeed by their own efforts and become productive citizens of their nation. Although the achievements of Cornell and the Vicosinos have been impressive, we cannot forget that the Vicosinos represent only 1,700 people among several million Peruvian Indians bound to such manor systems. Experiments modeled after Vicos are going on in other areas of Peru, but while change in Vicos was rapid, change throughout the Peruvian nation requires massive governmental action. If we view Vicos as a revolution in microcosm, then the intensity of the opposition of vested interests to freedom there, when seen on a national scale must be viewed as an enormous opposition to major social and economic change.

Action anthropology: the Fox project

A less ambitious example of intervention by anthropologists to promote community change began in 1948 among the Fox Indians living in the town of Tama in central Iowa. Under the direction of Sol Tax, six anthropology graduate students from the University of Chicago went to central Iowa as part of a field-training program involving research on processes of acculturation, adjustment, and community organization. However, for a variety of reasons, the students eventually asked Tax if they could help their study population try to solve some of its problems. Tax accepted their proposal, and coined the term "participant interference" to describe this new role of the anthropological researcher (Tax, 1958). The anthropological techniques exemplified by the Fox project were also called *action anthropology* by those involved.

As with the research and development approach in the Vicos project, action anthropology fully involves residents of the community in directing change. In contrast to Vicos, however, the Fox anthropologists had absolutely no power; they were not estate lords, nor were they affiliated with the Bureau of Indian Affairs, a government agency. Their approach to change was considerably vaguer than in the case of Peru, and all evidence indicates that the effects of participant interference were considerably less pervasive. The action anthropologists assumed that new behavior should entail neither loss of Fox identity nor violation of Fox moral beliefs. The objective of their action was to free the Indians to make only those changes that they wished and that simultaneously appeared to be in their interests. The anthropologists intended to inspire changes which, while not conflicting with Fox values, would enable the community to sustain itself.

Correctly perceiving the genesis of the Fox problem to lie in their relationships with white society, the action anthropologists attempted to increase both Fox self-confidence and understanding of the Fox by whites. To instill self-confidence, their first target was education. They introduced adult education courses in civics, examining historic relationships between Indians and whites, including the nature of certain treaties. Following from their assumption that people most readily accept changes which they understand, perceive as relevant, and play a part in planning, education was a necessary initial target. They

eventually instituted a scholarship program to train young Indians for professional careers and tried to help the Fox develop a cooperative project to design and produce Indian crafts.

Action anthropology as undertaken among the Fox represents what Art Gallaher (1973) has described as the clinical rather than the utopic model of intervention. The Vicos project also represents the former, although it includes some utopic elements. Utopic intervention, which guides many technical assistance programs, assumes that intervention is necessary to gain the acceptance of change, and that results are best achieved by doing things for people rather than involving them in the action. Utopic intervention is more concerned with ends than means.

With a clinical model of intervention, people are actively involved in promoting change; ends are often vague and the outsiders are more concerned with means than ends. The Fox researchers attempted, through discussion with the Fox, to suggest genuine alternatives which the Fox could freely choose; they attempted to impose as few restrictions as possible and never made decisions for the Fox. The anthropologists acted merely as catalysts, helping the Fox develop and clarify goals, and, in the process of doing so, promoting compromises among conflicting ends and values within the Fox community. The objectives of the action anthropologists tended to be open-ended goals like growth of understanding and clarification of values (cf. Gearing, Netting, and Peattie, 1960).

Economic Development and Technical Assistance Programs

Anthropologists have traditionally studied people directly at the local level. This aspect of the ethnographic method places anthropologists in a unique position to see what effects national and international development and aid programs have on the populations they are supposed to help.

Community research by anthropologists often reveals severe inadequacies in the yardsticks which economists and political scientists use to measure economic development and a nation's economic health. Measures like per capita income and gross national product tell us nothing about the distribution of wealth. Although these measures may reveal an increase in overall wealth, since the first is an average and the second a total, what may really be happening is that the rich are getting richer and the poor poorer.

What is to be the role of the anthropologist in a position to evaluate results of economic development schemes? Several agencies of the United States government and private foundations are encouraging and funding basic research on aspects of economic development. Yet, in addition to doing basic research on development, many anthropologists have chosen the alternative of actually participating in such programs. In the cases of the Vicos and the Fox projects just described, anthropologists were free to formulate intervention strategies. However, when they hire themselves out to clients such as the United States government, other governments, or private foundations, their capacity for criticism and direction of policy is severely limited.

In an insightful essay written in 1956, Robert Manners suggests that attempts by the United States and the United Nations to introduce fundamental change in underdeveloped countries through technical assistance, health education, and other programs have involved even more anthropologists than were used by the British and others in their colonial activities. What are the implications of such heavy involvement of anthropologists in these and similar programs? There are notable similarities in the roles of such practical anthropologists and their colonial office prototypes. Both have been expected to instruct government agents in means of introducing change with the least diffi-culty. According to anthropologist Charles Erasmus (1954), the anthropologist's role in studying patterns of resistance and acceptance in the face of attempts to bring about technical change is to indicate the implications of cultural patterns for the successful and economical operation of such programs.

In practice, the anthropologist helps administrators to make wise decisions in the context of a broad policy over which he normally has no control and which determines larger social and cultural consequences. Laura Thompson (1965), a prominent contributor to the literature of applied anthropology, suggests that the role of the applied anthropologist is scrupulously to refrain from making decisions, leaving that function to the client. The applied anthropologist appropriately provides the client with decision-making tools, relevant information including the probable consequences of alternative courses of action. Piddington's schizoid view of the role of the social scientist reemerges here. Thompson states that the applied anthropologist must assiduously avoid commitment to values other than those of the scientific method, formulating specific action alternatives in a value-neutral framework. Richard Schaedel (1964) suggests the dilemma of the hired action anthropologist even more clearly, stating that however much one feels that a series of measures being carried out in a host country may do more harm than good, once the policy has been set, and once the anthropologist has participated in the program, he is no longer free to criticize it.

Thus, severe ethical dilemmas may trouble many anthropologists who become involved in action anthropology for clients. The anthropologist's traditional appreciation of cultural diversity may be offended by the fact that efforts to extend benefits of industrialization and technological advances entail profound cultural modifications, often including some deleterious effects of Westernization. Or perhaps the action anthropologist will find that his most serious dilemma is his association with American interests that may not, in the long run, coincide with the best interests of the people he is trying to change. For more than two decades, American aid has not necessarily been channeled where need and suffering are most intense, but in accordance with priorities of the Cold War. Manners (1956) points out that in President Truman's inaugural address in January 1949, he launched the Point Four program of technical assistance with the assertion that one of the major aims of technical assistance was to create conditions propitious to the overseas investment of American capital.

The applied anthropologist may also be troubled by the common tendency of Western powers to bolster feudal and reactionary regimes through their aid programs rather than to help the progressive forces opposing these regimes. The realization of the disproportionate amount of American foreign aid destined for military dictatorships has begun to trouble a number of our legislators during the past few years. Manners (1956) suggests that when aid is channeled through political and administrative agencies within the underdeveloped country, officials are often reluctant to interfere with existing political arrangements and social conditions. Thus, the United States lends moral and financial support to the groups in power. As a result, most of the changes that are financed with American aid function to maintain and even strengthen the status quo. If they did not, Manners suggests, they would undoubtedly be resisted by the controlling elements.

Action anthropologists may find that people are reluctant to accept innovations not because of an unreasonably conservative attitude, but because of their relationship with vested interest groups. Vicos demonstrates the intensity of resistance of elites to land reforms. Many of the sharecroppers and tenants who populate underdeveloped nations have learned from bitter experience that if they raise their incomes, their taxes and rents will also be raised. Ignoring for a moment the major impediment to radical change, that is, vested interest groups, Charles Erasmus

(1954) and others have suggested that changes will be most readily received if there is clear and immediate proof of their effectiveness and desirability. These changes usually achieve a more rapid and widespread acceptance than those with only long-range benefits which cannot be immediately recognized. He suggests that the cultivation of high yield varieties of certain crops may be accepted readily, although they may ultimately be abandoned because people prefer the taste of their old crops, or because they do not prove to be especially well-adapted to natural conditions in the area.

The Brazilian sisal scheme

Even anthropologists may fail to predict the long-range results of a major change promoted by a program of planned development. Consider now a change which took place rapidly because of perceived immediate benefits and was widely believed to have helped an underdeveloped population, but which, in fact, has had a negative effect on this population. This case occurred in Brazil, in a fairly arid area of the northeastern interior called in Portuguese the *sertão*. Until the mid-twentieth century, the economy of the sertão was based on cultivation of corn, beans, manioc, and other subsistence crops. The sertão was also a grazing region for herds of cattle, sheep, and goats. During most years the peasants were able to derive a living from their plots; however, on an average of once every eleven years, major droughts came to the Brazilian northeast, drastically reducing yields and forcing people from the interior to migrate to the coast in search of nonexistent jobs. As part of a scheme to develop the northeast and to dampen the effects of drought, the Brazilian government began encouraging peasants in the sertão to plant sisal, a plant naturally adapted to arid areas.

Peasants began to plant sisal on a large scale. Sisal is a cash crop—no part of it can be eaten. Furthermore, the sisal grown in the sertão is exported, most of it to the United States where the fiber is used in binding and baling, especially of animal fodder. To ready sisal for export, preparation in the field is necessary. Thus, there arose throughout the sertão local centers with decorticating machines, devices which strip water and other residue from the sisal leaf, leaving only the salable fiber. Decorticating machines are expensive; small-scale sisal cultivators cannot afford them and must rely on machines owned by members of the local elite.

The decorticating operation involves a small team of workers with a marked division of labor. Two jobs are especially arduous, both done by adult men. One is that of disfiberer—the man who feeds the sisal leaf into the machine—a demanding and dangerous job because the machine exerts a strong pull with the possibility of getting one's fingers caught in the press. The other is that of residue man, who shovels the residue which collects under the machine onto a heap at some distance from the press and brings new leaves to the disfiberer.

Anthropologist Daniel Gross (1971) set out to study the effects of the introduction of sisal on the lives of the people of the sertão. He observed that most peasants who have begun to grow sisal have turned over most of their land to this cash crop and have completely abandoned subsistence agriculture. Furthermore, since it takes four years for sisal to mature, after planting the peasant must seek wage work, often as a member of a decorticating team, to sustain him until he can harvest his own crop. When he does harvest, he often finds that the price of sisal on the world market is less than when he originally planted. Moreover, once sisal has been planted in a plot, it is virtually impossible to revert the soil to food crops. The land and the population of the sertão were hooked on sisal.

How did the new strategy of adaptation based on cash cropping affect the population? Gross was fortunate to have the collaboration of a professional nutritionist, Dr. Barbara Underwood, in his field study (1971). They were interested in the effects of a sisal economy on nutrition. The nutritional requirements of a human population are specific to the ecological adaptation of that population. In order to subsist, the calories expended in daily activity must be replaced by calories in the daily diet. To determine if there is balance of energy consumed and energy expended, the caloric content of the daily diet and the cost in calories of work must be determined. Gross was able to calculate the energy expended in two of the jobs on the sisal decorticating team: disfiberer and residue man. Observing one disfiberer and one residue man over an extended period of time, he was able to show that the disfiberer expended an average of 4,397 calories per day and the residue man an average of 3,642 daily calories.

Gross then examined the diets of the households headed by each man. The earnings of the disfiberer were the equivalent of $3.65 U.S. per week; those of the residue man were $3.24 U.S. per week. The household of the disfiberer included only himself and his wife, while the residue man had a pregnant wife and four children aged three, five, six, and eight. By spending most of his income on food, the disfiberer was producing at least 7,145 calories a day for himself and his wife, ample to supply his own daily needs of 4,397 calories and to leave his wife a comfortable allotment of 2,748 calories.

However, the situation of the residue man is less favorable. With more than 95 percent of his meager income going for food, he was only able to provide himself, his wife, and his four children with 9,392 calories per day. Of this, he consumed 3,642 calories, sufficient to enable him to go on working; his wife consumed 2,150 calories. His children, on the other hand, were clearly being nutritionally deprived. Figure 32 compares the minimum daily

	Calories			
Age of Child	Minimum Daily Requirement	Actual Daily Allotment	Percentage of Standard Body Weight	
8 (M)	2,100	1,112	62%	
6 (F)	1,700	900	70	
5 (M)	1,700	900	85	
3 (M)	1,300	688	90	

Adapted from Gross and Underwood, 1971, p. 733.

FIGURE 32 Malnutrition among children of a Brazilian sisal residue man.

requirement in calories for his children with their actual daily caloric intake.

Long-term malnutrition has physical and psychological results which are still incompletely understood. Clearly though, sustained malnutrition will be revealed in body weight. As Figure 32 shows, average weight of malnourished children will be inferior to that of their better nourished peers. The longer the malnutrition continues, the greater will be the disparity between the nutritionally deprived and those with a normal diet. The oldest children, who have been malnourished longest, compare least favorably with the standard body weight.

Although the children of sisal workers were being undernourished to enable their fathers to continue to work for wages which could not feed them, Gross and Underwood suspected that the children of members of the local economic elite, businessmen and owners of decorticating machines, were faring better. They found that malnourishment was much less severe among these children. Finally, Gross and Underwood thought that the nutritional condition of poor sisal workers today might actually be considerably worse than those of subsistence cultivators before the introduction of sisal. To confirm this, they compared the body weights of people in the older generation, who had grown up prior to the conversion to sisal, with those of the generation which had grown up following the shift. When compared to a standard scale of body weights, they found that the weights of the older generation were actually closer to the norm than was true for the post-sisal generation.

The conclusions of this pioneering collaboration between an anthropologist and a nutritionist are extremely important for understanding problems which beset most people in the world today. An irreversible shift from a subsistence economy to a cash economy devised as part of an economic development scheme led to an improvement neither in diet nor in leisure time for the mass of the population. Rather, it produced a situation in which, in concrete caloric terms, the rich got richer and the poor got poorer. This is certainly not an isolated example of the effects of economic development programs and of shifts from subsistence to cash production.

Fortunately, Gross undertook his study as an independent researcher rather than as an adviser to any client organization. The publication of his findings was therefore unhampered by any reluctance to criticize a program or policy he helped to execute. Through studies such as that of Gross and Underwood, anthropologists will be able to evaluate the effects, in terms of basic biological variables affecting human populations, of economic development programs.

Conditions for development

Not all contemporary governments are equally committed to improving the lot of their people. Moreover, even if such aims exist, interference by major powers often prevents their realization. This commitment is lacking, or exists in an extremely rudimentary form, in many satellite states and highly stratified societies, like Brazil, in which the class structure has a caste-like rigidity, in which mobility from the lower into the middle class is very difficult, and in which it is equally hard to raise the living standards of the lower class as a whole. Such societies have a long history of powerful private interest groups who have control over the government, who run it for their own aims. On the other hand, one may also find some satellite states in which the government views itself as an agent of the people, in which, for various reasons, private economic interest groups have developed to a lesser extent. To illustrate the difference, two Third World nations—Brazil and Madagascar—will be briefly compared.

IMPEDIMENTS TO DEVELOPMENT   Brazil was founded as a colony of Portugal during the sixteenth century. Certain European migrants to Brazil received land grants from the Portuguese crown. Their estates grew into a plantation economy, based first on sugar, and later, in different parts of Brazil, on a variety of crops and other export products. The crown continued its land grant policy until the nineteenth century. By this time, the Brazilian upper class was composed mainly of descendants of recipients of land grants. Some stayed close to the ancestral estate; others moved to the cities, where they became involved in business, for example, in activities related to export. Rural landed families entered local and state politics and came to control the government as well as the economy.

In Brazil the relationship between the state and members of the lower class has always been very tenuous. In Arembepe, the marine fishing village I studied, people rarely see a government official in their community. They receive little from the state in the form of benefits, and they give little to the state in the form of taxes and labor. Their social structure consists of a small network of kinsmen, friends, neighbors, affinals, and fictive kinsmen. Since they do not belong to descent groups, since membership in open peasant communities fluctuates, and since the nation

shows little interest in their problems, they have little loyalty to social groups— not to descent group, community, or state. Mechanisms within Brazilian social structure and economy act to maintain the lower class and to supply the controllers of Brazilian resources with a cheap labor supply. When, in the past, federal administrations have seriously concerned themselves with problems of most Brazilians, they have been ousted by military takeovers supported by the United States and other foreign powers. The status quo is being protected through half-hearted and ineffective attempts at change, and by development programs like the sisal scheme which actually increase the socioeconomic marginality of the Brazilian poor.

DEVELOPMENT AND DESCENT GROUP ORGANIZATION   As in many areas of continental Africa, archaic states grew up in Madagascar prior to its conquest by the French in 1896 and the satellite state status which it has subsequently occupied. Furthermore, as in many parts of Africa, the people of Madagascar were organized into descent groups even before the origin of the state. The major native state of Madagascar, that of the Merina, never attempted to destroy descent group organization. Rather it incorporated descent groups into its structure, making members of important commoner descent groups advisers to the king, giving them considerable authority in government. The Merina state, which in the nineteenth century ruled over two-thirds of the island's territory, made provisions for the people it ruled. It required that they work for the state; it collected taxes; and it forced labor in public works projects. In return it redistributed some of what it had collected to peasants in need. It also granted them relative safety against war and slave raids, and it allowed them to cultivate their rice fields in peace. It supplied and maintained the water works necessary for rice cultivation, and it opened to ambitious peasant boys the chance of becoming, through hard work and study, state bureaucrats.

Thus, historically, among the Merina

there have been strong relationships between the individual, the descent group, and the state. Local communities, in which residence is usually based on descent, have also been more solidary in Madagascar than in Brazil. Madagascar gained its political independence from France in 1960. Although its economic dependence on France and other Western European nations was still strong when I did research there in 1966–1967, the Malagasy government appeared to be committed to a form of socialist development. Economic development schemes were increasing the ability of the Malagasy to feed themselves; they emphasized more productive cultivation of rice, a subsistence crop, rather than any cash crop. Furthermore, at the local level, representatives of important and populous descent groups and long established communities were elected to represent the interests of peasants in the National Assembly.

In a sense, the corporate descent group appears to be preadapted to socialist national development. In Madagascar, members of local descent groups have customarily pooled their economic resources to educate their especially intelligent members. Once educated, these men and women gain responsible and economically secure positions in the national economy and polity. They share the advantages of their new positions with their kinsmen, for example, by giving room and board to rural cousins while they attend school and by helping them to find jobs.

The Malagasy government appeared to be committed to meaningful economic development, perhaps because its officials are of the peasantry or have strong personal ties to the peasantry. This has never been the case in Brazil, where the controllers and the lower class have different origins and no strong connections of kinship, descent, or marriage. Furthermore, the case of Madagascar and other African societies with descent group organization contradicts an assumption which many economists and sociologists seem to make. These instances show that it is not inevitable that as nations become more and more tied to the world cash economy, aboriginal forms of social organization will break down into nuclear family organization with concomitant impersonality and alienation. There is every indication that descent groups, with their traditional communalism and corporate solidarity, have important roles to play in meaningful economic development. Some of their effects on social life in African cities have already been mentioned in the discussion of the culture of poverty in Chapter 13.

The underdeveloped talk back

In a provocative critique which echoes the thoughts of many of our colleagues in the Third World, Mexican anthropologist Guillermo Batalla (1966) presents "an anguished analysis" of six "conservative and essentially ethnocentric assumptions" that he believes underlie much of the applied anthropology in Latin America. Batalla criticizes many North American anthropologists for their total failure to exercise the sociological imagination (cf. Mills, 1959), that is, to see the relationship between the troubles of people and the political circumstances which nurture and perpetuate them. His characterization of applied anthropology as conservative reflects the tendency of certain anthropologists to stress a gradualist approach to change and to favor suppression of overt conflict under any circumstances and at any cost. The result, he claims, is an applied anthropology which favors, intentionally or unintentionally, maintenance of the status quo.

The first expression of conservative thought in applied anthropology that Batalla discusses is the heavy psychological emphasis of many studies, assertions that applied anthropology should investigate and deal with attitudes and beliefs about such matters as health and nutrition rather than with the basic material causes of poor health and malnutrition. A second component is what he sees as the almost axio-

Women in a Mexican village await the arrival of a doctor. Some anthropological studies stress related attitudes and beliefs rather than basic material causes of poor health. *(Arnold Weichert/D.P.I.)*

matic affirmation that the main function of the anthropologist is to avoid rapid changes because of the resulting maladjustments and conflicts that often lead to social and cultural disorganization. Because of this attitude, the anthropologist promotes only small and partial reforms and condemns alterations of the basic institutional structures of a society. Third, he laments what he regards as a misuse of the anthropological doctrine of cultural relativism among certain applied anthropologists, who feel disinclined to interfere in existing social situations because of the inappropriateness of judging or guiding. He suggests that such opinions should be rejected in favor of greater anthropological attention to the study of history, which provides patterns and laws of change which can be used in formulating development programs.

Fourth, Batalla faults the multiple causation theory, which, because it assumes that there are countless small and diverse causes of any social event, cannot isolate as targets for attack major social and economic inequities. Fifth, he criticizes applied anthropologists for viewing communities as isolated units. As has been shown previously, changes within communities are

accepted or opposed in a larger context. Batalla suggests that applied anthropologists pay greater attention to regional, national, and international frameworks of communities. Finally, he faults applied anthropologists for assuming that diffusion, usually of skills from the United States to the underdeveloped nation, is the only, or the only significant, process involved in change.

Batalla certainly does not argue that all applied anthropology in Latin America has suffered from these faults. Many aspects of the Vicos project, for example, can stand up to his criticisms. However, I personally see a great deal of validity in his arguments. More important, many social scientists in the Third World would agree, and are increasingly critical of American anthropology, not only because of static theory, but because of connections between certain anthropologists and agencies of the United States government.

Anthropologists and Government

Remarks by anthropologist Ward Goodenough to the Society for Applied Anthropology in 1962 present striking parallels to Malinowski's comments to the International African Institute in 1929, and exemplify some of the theoretical assumptions that Batalla has criticized. According to Goodenough, much of the government's need for research "has to do with some form of intelligence gathering that calls for the behavioral scientist's professional skills in data collection and interpretation [1965, p. 173]." Like Malinowski, Goodenough allots only an advisory role to the anthropologist. He states that after government officials have decided on the classes of phenomena they must consider in developing a policy, they may ask behavioral scientists what is known about these phenomena. Goodenough himself prepared a manual for agents of social and economic development (cf. Goodenough, 1963) in which he discussed human considerations affecting the course of development. Goodenough mentions the role of the anthropologist as "trouble shooter" in community development projects to determine what is going wrong and why.

In addition to the usefulness of the ethnographic skills of anthropologists to officials of the United States Agency for International Development and the Peace Corps, Goodenough suggests that "the Army is another potential market," since "the successful conduct of modern guerilla warfare obviously requires both extensive and intensive ethnographic intelligence." He further suggests that ethnographic skills are vital "if one is to enlist people's cooperation in economic development or in guerilla warfare, and if one is to assess reliably the way in which people are likely to respond to changed conditions in the future [1962, pp. 174–175]."

How is the anthropologist to serve the government? In 1962 Goodenough perceived a shortage of anthropologists. To remedy this, he suggested establishment of special programs to train people to do competent ethnography. These people would have some knowledge of the cultural and psychological aspects of social process, but would not be academic scholars. In a phrase which recalls Malinowski, he suggests a master's degree program in "practical ethnography."

Instruction would involve the "kind of ethnography that has the greatest utility for people engaged in overseas action programs that require the cooperation of local populations in order to succeed." Assuming positions that Batalla has criticized, Goodenough regards the community as a self-contained unit and advocates study of the psychological manifestations of social problems rather than the problems themselves. Thus, "what is vital is not the material state of affairs that characterizes a community as a *more-or-less self-contained system* [my italics], but the ideas and values of the people in the community." Goodenough suggests that what AID officials want is a "dictionary" and a "grammar" of social conduct. That is, they desire "good accounts of the local codes of manners and etiquette, the kinds of roles that people can play in dealing with one another, and the acts and avoidances symbolic of these roles [Goodenough, 1962, pp. 175–176]."

Like Malinowski (1929), Goodenough suggests that the association of anthropology and government will have the potential to improve the scientific rigor of anthropology. Thus, "if we are effectively to fill our government's need for our ethnographic skills by developing training programs in practical ethnography, we are again challenged to develop methods of descriptive ethnography capable of producing the kind of ethnographic intelligence that is practically more needed." As to the specifics of the association between anthropology and government, Goodenough suggests that "at present, it is impossible to say what requests, if any, for our ethnographic services may emerge from government agencies, but there are straws in the wind suggesting that we may be called upon. If this should happen, how are we to respond [1962, pp. 175–176]?"

Project Camelot

Project Camelot was the outgrowth of

United States Army concern over revolutions in Cuba and Yemen, insurgency movements in the Congo and Vietnam, and guerrilla warfare elsewhere. As conceived by the army in 1963, the project was intended to measure and forecast the causes of such movements for social change. In addition, it was to find ways of eliminating these causes and/or coping with them if they did occur. Project Camelot was to take three to four years, was funded at $4 to $6 million, and was to involve social science research carried out by the Special Operations Research Organization. Latin America was the first area chosen for study, but there were plans to include countries in Asia, Africa, and Europe.

In a recruiting letter sent to scholars all over the world in late 1964, the aims of the project were defined as a study to "make it possible to predict and influence politically significant aspects of social change in the developing nations of the world." This would include devising procedures for "assessing the potential for internal war within national societies" and "identify-[ing] with increased degrees of confidence those actions which a government might take to relieve conditions which are assessed as giving rise to a potential for internal war." The letter also stated that "the U.S. Army has an important mission in the positive and constructive aspects of nation-building in less developed countries as well as a responsibility to assist friendly governments in dealing with active insurgency problems [Horowitz, 1965, p. 4]." Such army activities were described as "insurgency prophylaxis."

A well-known Latin American area specialist, a sociologist, was recruited to direct the project. An anthropologist who ultimately became involved was primarily responsible for the blow-up which followed widespread discovery of the project's existence and aims. In the early days of Camelot, he had asked to be officially connected with the project. Although never given a regular Camelot appointment, he

was commissioned to prepare a report on the possible cooperation of scholars in Chile. Presenting himself as a Camelot official, he interviewed the Vice-Chancellor and a professor of a Chilean university. During the interview, the professor, who had received from an outraged Norwegian sociologist a copy of the 1964 recruitment letter, confronted the anthropologist with his knowledge of the aims of the project, its army sponsorship, and its military implications. When the true nature of the project was revealed, the specter of American military intervention in the internal affairs of Chile was debated in the Chilean Senate, decried in the Chilean press, and ultimately provoked a debate in the American Senate and academic community. The Johnson administration canceled Project Camelot in July 1965.

Senator William Fulbright recognized the conservative implications of the army's research goals and stated his objection to Project Camelot's "reactionary, backward-looking policy opposed to change. Implicit in Camelot, as in the concept of 'counter-insurgency,' is an assumption that revolutionary movements are dangerous to the interests of the United States and that the United States must be prepared to assist, if not actually to participate in, measures to repress them [quoted in Horowitz, 1965, p. 3]." On the day that the project was canceled, a congressional committee was told by the Special Operations Research Organization that the project had taken its name from King Arthur's domain because "it connotes the right sort of things—development of a stable society with peace and justice for all [quoted in Horowitz, 1965, p. 3]."

Although the project died, Camelot's repercussions still haunt anthropologists. Batalla's critique of conservative thought in applied anthropology, published a year after the revelation of Camelot, echoes Fulbright's concern with the assumption that order and stability should be promoted by the United States. In more practical ways, the revelation of Camelot and of other associations of anthropologists with agencies of the United States government has hampered legitimate anthropological research by creating suspicion of American anthropologists as possible agents of their government. In the Camelot instance, the Chilean press and academic community expressed outrage at scholars being recruited for spying missions. The *New York Times* noted the harm done to legitimate anthropological research in the wake of Camelot; it cited the difficulty anthropologists face in providing acceptable evidence that they are not involved in clandestine research, when it is known that the CIA is engaged in funding established agencies and in creating new illicit ones (cf. Sahlins, 1967). In 1965 Professor Ralph Beals was named by the American Anthropological Association to chair a committee on research problems and ethics, necessitated by the Camelot controversy.

The Camelot social scientists undoubtedly believed that their participation in the project would accomplish some worthy goals, for example, education of the more progressive elements of the military. However, in the final analysis, social scientists who sell their skills to powerful clients do not, as the discussion of applied anthropology demonstrates, make final policy, nor do they determine the ultimate uses of the information they collect.

Other government sponsored research

Normally anthropologists design their own research projects and apply for funding to such nonmilitary government agencies as the National Science Foundation and the National Institutes of Health, or to private foundations such as the Social Science Research Council. In violation of the usual procedure, the Camelot social scientists were recruited by the military to participate in a preestablished research plan. Sponsorship by an American military agency, aside from the ethical considerations discussed below, is often perceived as a threat in less-powerful nations, where people are familiar with examples of American intervention.

Gerald Berreman (1973a) decries involve-

ment of social scientists in clandestine research, their acceptance of military funding, and covers adopted by intelligence agents who claim that they are anthropologists engaged in standard ethnographic research. He points out that the people who are most affected by such activities are the scholars who regard their work as the legitimate and sympathetic pursuit of knowledge, who attempt to contribute to international understanding, and who believe that the results of their research should be open to all rather than classified for exclusive government use. As a specialist in South Asia, Berreman experienced first-hand the damaging results of collaboration between anthropologists and the United States military.

In the summer of 1968 American scholarship in India was jeopardized by the disclosure that the University of California Himalayan Borders Project was to be financed for three years at almost $300,000 by the United States Department of Defense. The immediate result was that Indian officials delayed all applications for permits to conduct anthropological research and examined them closely. After considerable outrage by Indian scholars and in the Indian press, the Indian government decreed that no further social science projects supported by United States government funds would be approved. Individual scholars with other sources of support would, however, be allowed into India if their proposals were approved by the Indian government.

Governments of other nations appear to be wise in their suspicion of United States military sponsorship. In testimony to the Senate Foreign Relations Committee, the Director of Defense Research and Engineering of the Department of Defense stated, "We are interested only in those so-called cultural and social factors that have clear relationship to defense activities [quoted in Berreman, 1973a, p. 153]."

Additional damage has been done to the academic freedom of legitimate researchers by the more recent revelation of involvement of a large number of American anthropologists and other social scientists in army-sponsored research on counterinsurgency in northern Thailand. In the wake of Camelot, India, and Thailand, anthropologists have recently begun to concern themselves more intensely with their ethical responsibilities not only toward their colleagues, but toward the public, and, most importantly, the people they study.

Ethics and Anthropology

In 1967 the American Anthropological Association adopted a Statement of Problems of Anthropological Research and Ethics. A Committee on Ethics appointed in 1968 published a draft version of a Code of Ethics in the association's newsletter in April 1969 and proposed the election of a standing committee on ethics in anthropology. In 1970 a draft of a code prepared by the standing committee became a focus of debate but was eventually adopted. Examination of this code, entitled "AAA: Principles of Professional Responsibility," reveals fundamental differences between the attitude of a majority of contemporary anthropologists and the viewpoint which holds that the anthropologist's ethical and value judgments should be totally distinct from his scientific work.

The preamble to the code suggests that anthropologists should avoid research which can potentially damage either the people studied or the scholarly community. The code covers six areas of the anthropologist's professional responsibility: to those studied, to the public, to the discipline, to students, to sponsors, and to governments, one's own and those of host countries.

1. RESPONSIBILITY TO THOSE STUDIED The anthropologist's paramount responsibility in research is to those whom he studies.

He must do everything he can to protect their physical, psychological, and social welfare, and to honor their dignity and privacy. If interests conflict, these people come first. The rights, interests, and sensitivities of those studied must be protected. Specifically, the anthropologist should make known to his informants the aims and the anticipated consequences of his investigation; he should insure that informants preserve their anonymity in all forms of data collection. Individual informants should not be exploited 'for personal gain. The anthropologist must anticipate and take steps to avoid potentially damaging effects of the publication of his research results. In accordance with the association's official disapproval of clandestine or secret research, no reports should be provided to sponsors that are not also available to the general public.

2. RESPONSIBILITY TO THE PUBLIC The anthropologist owes a commitment to candor and to truth in the dissemination of his research results and in the statement of his opinion as a student of man. The anthropologist should make no secret communications, nor should he knowingly falsify his findings. As people who devote their professional lives to understanding man, anthropologists bear a positive responsibility to speak out publicly, both individually and collectively, on what they know and what they believe as a result of their professional expertise. They bear a professional responsibility to contribute to an "adequate definition of reality," upon which public opinion and public policy may be based. In public discourse the anthropologist should be honest about his qualifications and aware of the limitations of his discipline's expertise.

3. RESPONSIBILITY TO HIS DISCIPLINE The anthropologist bears responsibility for the good reputation of his discipline and of its practitioners. He should undertake no secret research or any research whose results cannot be freely derived and publicly reported. He should avoid even the

appearance of engaging in clandestine research by totally and freely disclosing the objectives and sponsorship of all research. He should attempt to maintain a level of rapport and integrity in the field such that his behavior will not jeopardize future research there.

4. RESPONSIBILITY TO STUDENTS The anthropologist should be fair, candid, non-exploitative, and committed to the welfare and academic progress of his students. He should make them aware of the ethical problems of research.

5. RESPONSIBILITY TO SPONSORS The anthropologist should be honest about his qualifications, capabilities, and aims. He should be especially careful not to promise or to imply acceptance of conditions in violation of his professional ethics and competing commitments. He must require of the sponsor full disclosure of the sources of funds, personnel, and aims of the institution and the research project, and the disposition of the research results. He must retain the right to make all ethical decisions in the research. He must enter into no secret agreement with a sponsor regarding the results or reports.

6. RESPONSIBILITY TO ONE'S OWN AND TO HOST GOVERNMENTS The anthropologist should be candid and honest. He should demand assurance that he will not be required to compromise his professional responsibilities and ethics as a condition of his permission to pursue the research. Specifically, he should engage in no secret research, should write no secret reports, nor agree to debriefings of any kind.

The authors of the code stress that this statement of principles of professional responsibility is not designed to punish anthropologists but to provide guidelines. However, there is provision for censure of unprofessional conduct. When the actions of an anthropologist jeopardize the people studied, professional colleagues, students, or others, or if the anthropologist other-

wise betrays professional commitments, his colleagues may legitimately inquire into the propriety of those actions and take such measures as lie within the legitimate powers of their Association, as the members deem appropriate.

The Continuance of Diversity

Anthropology teaches us that populations respond to environmental changes through modification of the evolutionary material at hand. Adaptive responses of human populations can be more flexible than in the case of other biological populations because the principal adaptive means are sociocultural. However, the sociocultural forms of the past always influence subsequent adaptation, producing continued diversity and imparting a certain uniqueness to adaptive responses of specific human populations. Anthropology focuses attention on similarities and differences among human populations in their sociocultural means of adaptation. Because evolution through natural selection must always accommodate itself to and proceed on the basis of the material at hand, populations with different traditions and different adaptive means have reacted to, and will continue to react to, metropolitan incorporation differently. Because of this, among human populations who manage to survive and to adapt successfully to events of the twentieth century, the diversity that has intrigued students of anthropology since its inception may be expected to endure. Let us hope that adaptive divergence will continue to provide a major obstacle to what some social scientists see as a bland convergence of the future and that free and open anthropological investigation of human diversity will be decreasingly imperiled by the actions of a few. With our knowledge and with awareness of our professional responsibilities, let us work to keep anthropology the most humanistic of all disciplines.

SUMMARY

Among anthropologists there are different opinions regarding the relationship between the anthropologist's personal values and his scientific research and application of its findings. Some adopt an ivory tower position, maintaining that the anthropologist should confine himself to teaching, research, and publication, while avoiding practical and political issues. Others believe that the anthropologist may appropriately offer his techniques and findings for practical tasks; however, he should strictly separate his personal values from his endeavors in research or in applied anthropology. According to this second view, an anthropologist may work for governments, colonial administrations, and other clients; however, his role is not to set or to influence policy, but to determine how policies, once set, can be carried out effectively or to investigate reasons for acceptance or rejection of changes inspired by policy makers. A third group argues that the anthropologist, because of his discipline's familiarity with many aspects of the human condition, and especially of human problems in underdeveloped areas, should actively seek to influence government positions and policies and should participate only in those projects of which he approves.

Anthropologists traditionally have been interested in social and cultural change, and many such changes have accompanied the incorporation of formerly primitive populations into modern nations and metropole-satellite webs. In addition to the three views mentioned above, a fourth group, including many applied anthropologists, have used techniques and findings of anthropology to introduce changes on their own, rather than for a client, and to study the nature and effects of such changes.

Allen Holmberg and colleagues were instrumental in introducing beneficial economic and social changes in Vicos, Peru, formerly a rented manor on which impoverished Indians lived as serfs. Over the course of the five-year period during which Cornell University rented Vicos, project personnel introduced several economic and social changes along specific lines of development with predetermined goals. Holmberg characterized the Vicos project as a "research and development approach" to the study of change because directions of development had been hypothesized in the early stages of the project, and because not only could the nature and effects of the changes be studied as research problems, but deviations away from the hypothesized developments as well.

Graduate students from the University of Chicago followed the techniques of "action anthropology" among Fox Indians in central Iowa. This approach to applied anthropology was guided by what anthropologist Sol Tax calls "participant interference." The students attempted to help the Fox formulate their own goals for change aimed at improving Fox material conditions, self-esteem, and the image of them held by white Iowans. Since they wielded no power, the action anthropologists confined their efforts to the rather vague objectives of improving the economic and social position of the Fox in the larger society and of getting the Fox to help themselves.

In European colonial regimes, in American experiments in colonialism, and in development and technical assistance programs sponsored by the United States, the United Nations, and others, anthropologists have been hired to apply their skills in projects aimed at economic and cultural change. The anthropologist who is so employed often faces both practical and ethical problems reflecting his subordination to the larger goals of the client, his inability to set or to influence policy, and the difficulty in criticizing programs in which he has participated.

Some anthropologists, however, have made independent investigations of the results of economic development schemes. Daniel Gross, for example, studied changes that accompanied a shift from subsistence farming to cultivation of a cash crop in the interior of northeastern Brazil. Gross found that material conditions of most people affected by the change had actually worsened. His research demonstrates some of the unfortunate and unforeseen consequences which often accompany development schemes, particularly those aimed at replacing subsistence economies with economies that must rely on the vagaries of the world cash economy.

For historical, political, and economic reasons, not all governments are committed to the improvement of the material conditions of the lower classes of their countries. Social forms of the past, including the nature of the relationship between elites and masses, affect the potentiality and course of economic development.

Many of our colleagues in Third World nations criticize North American anthropologists for a conservative bias in the research problems they choose to investigate and in their approaches to economic development and social change. They point to a tendency on the part of anthropologists to stress gradual change and to fear social disorganization, which therefore leads them to sanction only minor changes rather than the major institutional ones often necessary to rapid material improvement.

Perhaps as a result of the traditional field methods of their discipline, many anthropologists have viewed communities as isolated units, ignoring the ties these communities have with region, nation, and world. They have been criticized for such views, since many of the major impediments to development lie in such exogenous relationships.

Anthropologists have shown this conservative bias in areas beyond research and publications. Some have participated in projects actually designed to combat rapid social changes and sponsored by the United States Army and Department of Defense. Not surprisingly, revelation of this participation has imperiled access to certain countries by the majority of independent anthropologists who desire only to conduct free and open research. Worse still, by their participation in research sponsored by certain government agencies, anthropologists have collected data which potentially or actually damage the people they have studied.

In recognizing the dangers of such participation, the American Anthropological Association has recently issued a statement of professional conduct, indicating the responsibilities of anthropologists to informants, universities, colleagues, students, sponsors, and governments. The Association has also committed itself to action against breaches of professional ethics.

Greater attention to professional responsibilities ensures, hopefully, that anthropologists may continue a free and open study of human diversity and that anthropology remains the most humanistic of all the sciences.

Sources and Suggested Readings

AMERICAN ANTHROPOLOGICAL ASSOCIATION
 Newsletter. Published ten months a year; best source of news and controversy affecting anthropologists.

BARNETT, H. G.
 1956 *Anthropology in Administration.* New York: Harper and Row. Uses of anthropology in administration, including Micronesia.

BATALLA, G. B.
 1966 Conservative Thought in Applied Anthropology: A Critique. *Human Organization* 25: 89–92. A Latin American colleague views North American anthropologists.

BERREMAN, G. D.
 1973a (orig. 1969). Academic Colonialism: Not So Innocent Abroad. In *To See Ourselves: Anthropology and Modern Social Issues,* gen. ed. T. Weaver, pp. 152–156. Glenview, Ill.: Scott, Foresman. Repercussions of U.S. Defense Department support of anthropological research in India.

 1973b Foreword to O. C. Stewart, The Need to Popularize Basic Concepts. In *To See Ourselves: Anthropology and Modern Social Issues,* gen. ed. T. Weaver, pp. 55–57. Glenview, Ill.: Scott, Foresman. Need for anthropologists to make the concepts and findings of their discipline more widely known.

CLIFTON, J. A., ed.
 1970 *Applied Anthropology: Readings in the Uses of the Science of Man.* Boston: Houghton Mifflin. Best available reader on applied and "practical" anthropology. Includes several of the articles discussed in this chapter.

ERASMUS, C.
 1954 An Anthropologist Views Technical Assistance. *Scientific Monthly (Science)* 78: 147–158. Some reasons for acceptance of or resistance to externally induced technical change.

 1961 *Man Takes Control.* Minneapolis: University of Minnesota Press. Role of economic motivation in change.

FOSTER, G. M.
 1962 *Traditional Cultures and the Impact of Technical Change.* New York: Harper and Row. A standard textbook in applied anthropology.

 1969 *Applied Anthropology.* Boston: Little, Brown. Updated expansion of his 1962 book.

GALLAHER, A.
 1973 Introduction and Conclusion to Intervention: Changing the System. In *To See Ourselves: Anthropology and Modern Social Issues,* gen. ed. T. Weaver, pp. 436–437, 475–478. Glenview, Ill.: Scott, Foresman. Comments on current problems in applied anthropology.

GEARING, F., NETTING, R. M., and PEATTIE, L. R.
 1960 *Documentary History of the Fox Project.* Chicago: Department of Anthropology, University of Chicago. The first experiment in action anthropology.

GOODENOUGH, W.
 1962 The Growing Demand for Behavioral Science in Government: Its Implications for Anthropology. *Human Organization* 21: 172–176 (also in Clifton, ed., 1970). How ethnographers can modify their field methods to meet needs of the American government.

 1963 *Cooperation in Change.* New York: Russell Sage Foundation. Manual for technical assistance workers and the anthropologists who help them.

GOUGH, K.
 1973 (orig. 1968). World Revolution and the Science of Man. In *To See Ourselves: Anthropology and Modern Social Issues,* gen. ed. T. Weaver, pp. 156–165. Glenview, Ill.: Scott, Foresman. The role and responsibilities of the anthropologist in the context of contemporary colonialism and imperialism.

GROSS, D.
 1971 The Great Sisal Scheme. *Natural History,* March, pp. 49–55. Failures of an economic development scheme in northeastern Brazil.

GROSS, D., and UNDERWOOD, B.
 1971 Technological Change and Caloric Costs: Sisal Agriculture in Northeastern Brazil. *American Anthropologist* 73: 725–740. More technical presentation of anthropological and nutritional data included in Gross, 1971.

HOLMBERG, A.
1958   The Research and Development Approach to the Study of Change. *Human Organization* 17: 12–16 (also in Clifton, ed., 1970). Strategy of an applied anthropology project in Vicos, Peru.

1965   The Changing Values and Institutions of Vicos in the Context of National Development. *American Behavioral Scientist* 8: 3–8. Results of the Vicos project (also in Clifton, ed., 1970).

HOROWITZ, I. L.
1965   The Life and Death of Project Camelot. *Trans-action* December (also in T. Weaver, gen. ed., 1973, pp. 138–148). History of Project Camelot and some of its implications.

MALINOWSKI, B.
1929   Practical Anthropology. *Africa* 2: 23–38. Anthropology for cadets in the British colonial administration (also in Clifton, ed., 1970).

MANNERS, R.
1956   Functionalism, Realpolitik and Anthropology in Underdeveloped Areas. *America Indigena* 16 (also in T. Weaver, gen. ed., 1973, pp. 113–126). Some of the political and ethical problems that beset "practical anthropologists."

MAQUET, J.
1964   Objectivity in Anthropology. *Current Anthropology* 5: 47–55 (also in Clifton, ed., 1970). Formal and informal connections between anthropologists and colonial administrations in Africa.

MEAD, M., ed.
1955   *Cultural Patterns and Technical Change.* New York: New American Library. Changes in nutrition and medical and maternal care in underdeveloped countries.

MILLS, C. W.
1959   *The Sociological Imagination.* New York: Oxford University Press. Brilliant debunking of the myth of a value-free social science.

PIDDINGTON, R.
1960   Action Anthropology. *Journal of the Polynesian Society* 69: 199–213 (also in Clifton, ed., 1970). Three contrasting conceptions of the role of the values of the social scientist in his work.

SAHLINS, M. D.
1967   The Established Order: Do Not Fold, Spindle or Mutilate. In *The Rise and Fall of Project Camelot: Studies in the Relationship between Social Science and Practical Politics*, ed. I. L. Horowitz. Cambridge, Mass.: M.I.T. Press (also in T. Weaver, gen. ed., 1973, pp. 148–152). Sahlins, an anthropologist, is one of several scholars who discuss Camelot's implications for their disciplines in this book.

SCHAEDEL, R. P.
1964   Anthropology in AID Overseas Missions: Its Practical and Theoretical Potential. *Human Organization* 23: 190–192 (also in Clifton, ed., 1970). Anthropology's practical value in overseas development programs.

SPICER, E. H.
1952   *Human Problems in Technological Change.* New York: Russell Sage Foundation. Includes case studies of agricultural development schemes.

TAX, S.
1958   The Fox Project. *Human Organization* 17: 17–19 (also in Clifton, ed., 1970). Some results of action anthropology and participant interference.

THOMPSON, L.
1965   Is Applied Anthropology Helping to Develop a Science of Man? *Human Organization* 24: 277–287. Draws distinction between "engineering" and "clinical" approaches to technological and culture change, and discusses examples of the latter.

WEAVER, T., gen. ed.
1973   *To See Ourselves: Anthropology and Modern Social Issues.* Glenview, Ill.: Scott, Foresman. Timely anthology of articles on the social responsibility of the anthropologist, anthropology and the Third World, race and racism, poverty and culture, education, violence, environment, intervention, and anthropology in the contemporary United States.

WILSON, G.
1940   Anthropology as a Public Service. *Africa* 13: 43–60. The inception and research of the Rhodes-Livingstone Institute of Central African Studies.

Glossary

acculturation Changes in behavior patterns involving continuous first-hand contact between one or more cultures.

achieved status Position that an individual occupies through his own efforts, abilities, and achievements; for example, role of the big man.

action anthropology Variety of applied anthropology, exemplified by the Fox project, in which anthropologists help people to formulate their own goals for and directions of change.

adaptation Process whereby a population establishes means of existing and surviving in a specific environment.

adaptive radiation Development of an array of diverse types out of a relatively homogeneous ancestral population as a result of population increase and adaptation to a variety of different environments.

affinal, affine A relative by marriage, an in-law.

agamy Absence of a rule regarding marriage, or a tendency toward either endogamy or exogamy.

agnates Members of the same patrilineal descent group.

agriculture Nonindustrial system of plant cultivation characterized by intensive use of land and human labor.

ahimsa Hindu doctrine prohibiting the consumption of zebu cattle.

ambilineal Principle of descent which does not automatically exclude from descent group membership either the children of sons or daughters. Descent group membership is achieved rather than ascribed.

ambilocal Nonunilocal postmarital residence pattern in which couples may reside with either the wife's or the husband's group.

analogies Phenotypical similarities caused by natural selective forces operating in similar environments.

animatism Concept of the supernatural as a domain of raw, impersonal power that influences man but can be controlled. According to Marett, the most rudimentary form of religion.

animism Belief in spiritual beings, souls or doubles. According to Tylor, the most primitive form of religion.

apical ancestor Common ancestor of all members of a given descent group. Called "apical" because the ancestor stands at the apex of his common genealogy.

applied anthropology Use of anthropological findings, techniques, or methods to accomplish some worthy purpose.

ascribed status Position occupied by an individual involuntarily; for example, sex, age.

Australopithecus africanus Applied to the first "Homo africanus" skull, that of a juvenile, analyzed by Raymond Dart in 1925. Species has given common name to this stage of human evolution—the Australopithecines.

Aztec Late postclassic empire extended from Tenochtitlan in the Valley of Mexico.

band Basic social unit in many foraging populations. Normally includes one hundred or fewer people, all related by kinship and marriage.

Bantu Group of closely related languages spoken over a large area of central, eastern, and southern Africa.

basic personality structure Abram Kardiner's term to refer to the constellation of personality traits shared by all members of a given society.

basic vocabulary Notion fundamental to lexicostatistics. As distinguished from cultural vocabulary, it is the area of lexicon which is most resistant to change.

bifurcate collateral System of kinship classification on the parental generation employing separate terms for M, F, MB, MZ, FB, and FZ.

bifurcate merging System of kinship classification on the parental generation whereby M and MZ are called by the same term, F and FB are called by the same term, and MB and FZ are called by different terms.

big man Figure often found among tribal horticulturalists and pastoralists. The big man occupies no office but creates his own reputation through entrepreneurial expertise and generosity to others. Neither his wealth nor his position passes to his heirs.

bilateral kinship calculation Kinship ties which are calculated equally through kinsmen of both sexes, that is, through mother and father, sister and brother, daughter and son, and so on.

hiogenic explanation Links cultural variables to physiological, genetic, climatic, dietary, or pathological causes; Raoul Naroll's term.

blood feud Feud between families in a nonstate society.

blowout Tribal adaptive distribution of resources, usually in ceremonial context.

bride price See *progeny price.*

bridewealth See *progeny price.*

call systems Systems of communication among nonhuman primates composed of a limited number of acoustically distinct sounds which vary in intensity and duration. Tied to specific environmental stimuli.

cargo systems A series of obligations associated with the political and religious hierarchies of Latin American communities, generally in the highlands.

caste system Stratified groups in which membership is ascribed at birth and lifelong.

catastrophism Doctrine that extinct life forms met their end through catastrophic events. Often combined with creationism.

ceremonial fund Investment of scarce resources within a ceremonial or ritual context.

chiefdom Form of sociopolitical organization based on food production, usually agriculture or intensive horticulture, in which kinship remains important and generosity is associated with political office. Often a transitional form between tribal society and state.

chromosomes Long, threadlike structures contained in the nucleus of each cell of a living being and normally occurring in homologous pairs. Human cells generally contain twenty-three pairs, or forty-six chromosomes.

circulating connubium Variant of generalized exchange in which several descent groups are arranged in a closed circle, such that women of descent group A always marry men of B, women of B always marry men of C, and so through N, the number of descent groups in the circle.

city Population of 10,000 or more concentrated in a small, continuous, compact area. Characterized by intense internal social differentiation based on variations in wealth, economic specialization, and power.

civilization Variety of state with writing, exact, practical sciences, full-time artists, and sophisticated art styles.

civitas Term used by anthropologist Lewis Henry Morgan to describe the basis for personal relations in state-organized societies. Opposed to *societas.*

clinical model of intervention Intervention in which people are actively involved in planning a change which affects them; outsiders promoting change are more concerned with means than ends, which are usually vague.

closed, corporate peasant community Generally Indian, located in the highlands of Latin America. Corporate in sharing an estate and closed by birth and through endogamy.

collateral relative A relative who is neither a lineal nor an affinal relative.

common history That which results when two or more populations are divergent descendants of a common ancestral population; also occurs with borrowing or contact.

compadre Co-parent: the godparents of a child and the child's parents become co-parents.

comparative method Historical linguistic technique. Reconstructs protolanguages by comparing their divergent descendants; for example, proto–Indo-European from French, English, and the other contemporary Indo-European languages.

componential analysis Technique important in the study of meaning systems of different languages. Examines certain domains in the folk taxonomies of different speech communities and attempts to identify dimensions of contrast and their components.

configurationalism School of anthropology which viewed cultures as integrated by spirits, characters, or psychological themes. Ruth Benedict was most prominent member.

conspecifics Members of the same species.

contagious magic Belief that whatever is done to a material object will affect the person who was once in contact with that object. Based on what Frazer called the law of contagion.

convergence Development of similar structural traits or behavior patterns among distantly related populations, because of adaptation to similar environments and natural selective forces.

conversion Exchange of items from different spheres of a multicentric economy.

conveyance Exchange of items from the same sphere of a multicentric economy.

corporate groups Groups that exist in perpetuity and manage a common estate. Includes some descent groups and modern industrial corporations.

creationism Doctrine of divine creation. Opposed to transformism.

crime Act which is prohibited by law.

cross cousins Children of siblings of the opposite sex.

Crow kinship terminology Manner of classifying kinsmen on ego's own generation, usually associated with matrilineal descent group organization.

cultural vocabulary Portion of the vocabulary of any speech community that is least resistant to change. Contrasted with basic vocabulary.

culture Behavior patterns acquired by humans as members of society. Technology, language, patterns of group organization, and ideology are aspects of culture.

culture of poverty See *subculture of poverty*.

daughter languages Different languages that have developed out of the same parent language; for example, German and English are daughter languages of proto-Germanic.

demonstrated descent Basis for lineage membership. Members of the same lineage demonstrate their descent from their common apical ancestor by citing the actual or accepted descendants in each generation from the ancestor through the present.

descent group Social unit found among horticultural, pastoral, and agricultural populations. All members of a descent group maintain that they are descendants of the founder of that group and share access to the group's territory and estate.

descriptive kinship terminology Manner of classifying kinsmen on ego's own generation whereby there is a separate kin term for each biological kin type.

descriptive linguistics Subdivision of linguistics that deals with languages at a single point in time.

developmental type Category based on convergent evolution and environmental similarity. Includes human populations located in geographically different but ecologically similar environments who have evolved in analogous fashion. Associated with Julian Steward.

differential access Access to strategic and other socially valued resources; basic attribute of chiefdoms and states. Superordinates enjoy favored or unimpeded access to such resources, while subordinates have their access limited by the former.

diffusion Process whereby aspects of culture pass from one group to another.

dominant Gene which is phenotypically expressed in heterozygous form.

double unilineal descent Within a given society operation of both a patrilineal and a matrilineal rule of descent. Contrasts with bilateral descent in that an individual is related to his father's father and not to his father's mother; to his mother's mother, but not to his mother's father.

economizing The allocation of scarce means to alternative ends. Often given as the subject matter of economics.

economy A population's system of production, distribution, and consumption of material resources.

education Process whereby formal knowledge is acquired. Normally proceeds within a school and is most commonly associated with state organization.

ego Latin for *I*. In kinship charts, point at which you enter an egocentric genealogy.

enculturation Process whereby an individual learns, through experience, observation, and instruction, his population's culture.

endogamy Marriage of individuals within the same social group.

environment Surroundings to which a human population adapts, including physical, biotal, and social components.

Eskimo kinship terminology Manner of classification of kinsmen on ego's own generation whereby cousins are distinguished from brother and sister. Associated with nuclear family organization.

ethnosemantics See *ethnoscience*.

ethnocentrism Universal human tendency to interpret and evaluate foreign beliefs and practices in terms of one's own cultural tradition.

ethnoscience The study of classification systems of populations. Often used as a synonym for ethnosemantics.

evolution Change in form over generations. According to Charles Darwin, descent with modification; in anthropology, change in form of man as a biological organism or change in form of his adaptations to the environment.

exogamy Cultural rule which requires members of a group to marry outside of that group.

extended family household Group that may include siblings and their spouses and children (a *collateral* household) or three generations of kinsmen and their spouses. Larger than the nuclear family that resides together in the same household.

family of orientation Nuclear family in which one grows up.

family of procreation Nuclear family established when one marries and has children.

Fertile Crescent Crescent-shaped area running from the Nile River valley in Egypt, along the eastern shores of the Mediterranean, down through the alluvial plain formed by the Tigris and Euphrates rivers in Mesopotamia, and to the Persian Gulf. Location of early civilizations based on agriculture.

folk taxonomy The division of aspects of life into categories; specific to members of a particular culture; for example, the American and Brazilian systems of racial classification.

foraging Hunting and gathering.

fraternal polyandry Marriage of a group of brothers to the same woman or women.

functionalism School of sociocultural anthropology associated with Bronislaw Malinowski and A. R. Radcliffe-Brown, both of whom eschewed speculation about origins and advocated study of psychological and social functions of institutionalized behavior in human societies.

functional alternative Social form which serves the same function as another social form.

functional explanation Explanation that relates a specific practice to other aspects of behavior in the society being examined. When aspects of human behavior are functionally interrelated, if one of them changes, the others will also change.

gene Position on a chromosome, often called a genetic locus or place.

general evolution Study of formal changes, biological and sociocultural, in the genus *Homo*, abstracted from a variety of times, places, and specific populations.

generalized exchange Prescriptive marriage system in which women of descent group B always marry men from descent group A, while men of descent group B always marry women from descent group C.

general-purpose money. Currency which functions as a means of exchange, a standard of value, and a means of payment. Opposed to special-purpose money.

generational kinship terminology System of classification of kinsmen on the parental generation whereby there are only two kin terms, one designating M, MZ, and FZ, the other designating F, FB, and MB.

genetic explanation Demonstration that the presence of a similar item or behavior pattern in two or more populations reflects inheritance from a common ancestral culture. An homology.

genetic relationship in language Developed from a common ancestral language. Describes the relationship between the languages rather than the speakers of the languages.

genitor Biological father of a child.

genotype Genetic composition of an organism as programmed by genes and chromosomes.

Great Tradition Art, music, literature, and other aspects of elite culture. Contrasts to folk art and is characteristic of civilization.

hacienda Estate or manor in highland Latin America.

Hawaiian kinship terminology Manner of classifying kinsmen on ego's own generation whereby brothers and male cousins are called by one term and sisters and female cousins are called by another.

heterozygous Hybrid; processing two unlike alleles of a given gene.

history The ongoing process whereby individuals live and die, migrate in and out of populations or social systems. May proceed without evolution.

historical explanation Demonstration that a social institution or cultural practice exists among two or more different populations because they share a period of common history or have been exposed to common sources of information. Includes diffusion.

historical linguistics Subdivision of linguistics which studies languages over time.

homeostasis Equilibrium, or stable relationship, between population and environment.

homeostat Mechanism which operates to maintain equilibrium.

Hominidae Zoological family which includes fossil and living humans of at least two genera, *Ramapithecus* and *Homo.*

Hominoidea Zoological superfamily which includes fossil and contemporary apes and humans. Composed of three contemporary families: Hylobatidae, Pongidae, and Hominidae.

Homo erectus Second of the stages of human evolution. Occurred between ca. 750,000 and 300,000 B.P.

homologies Similarities present among related species or populations because of inheritance from a common ancestor.

Homo sapiens Neanderthalensis Third of the stages of human evolution. Occurred between ca. 100,000 and 37,000 B.P. The rugged, extreme, classic Neanderthals lived in western Europe during the height of the fourth glacial period; their fossils were among the earliest discovered. For this reason differences rather than similarities between them and modern man were emphasized.

Homo sapiens Sapiens Second of the subspecies of *Homo sapiens,* appeared ca. 37,000 B.P. Includes all contemporary humans.

horizontal groups Social divisions in a complex society which extend across the entire population of that society and are not regionally limited.

horticulture Nonindustrial system of plant cultivation in which plots are fallowed for varying lengths of time.

hydraulic systems Systems of water management, including irrigation, drainage, and flood control. Often associated with agricultural societies in arid and riverine environments.

hypodescent Descent rule, characteristic of the United States and certain other stratified societies, which always associates offspring of mixed marriages with the parent of the subordinate group.

imitative magic Belief that the magician can produce a desired effect by imitating it. Based on what Frazer called the law of similarity.

incest Act of mating with or marrying a close relative.

intermediate societies Populations whose strategies of adaptation involve horticulture, pastoralism, agriculture, or some combination of these. Includes tribal societies and archaic states.

Iroquois kinship terminology Manner of classifying kinsmen on ego's own generation whereby the same term designates parallel cousins and siblings, and a different term is used for cross cousins.

kaiko Pig festival among Maring of New Guinea.

latent function Underlying function served by some behavior pattern in a society.

leveling mechanism Sociocultural form which acts to even out wealth differences within a social unit.

levirate Custom whereby a widow marries the brother of her deceased husband.

lexicon Vocabulary.

lexicostatistics Historical linguistic technique for evaluating degree of relationship between languages on the basis of quantitative comparison of their basic vocabularies.

lineage Descent group based on demonstrated descent.

lineal kinship terminology Manner of classifying kinsmen on the parental generation whereby there are four terms, one for M, one for F, one for FB and MB, and one for MZ and FZ.

lineal relative Any of ego's ancestors or descendants on the direct line of descent which leads to or from ego.

linguistic relativity Anthropological and linguistic doctrine which states that each language should be regarded as an instance of specific evolution.

maize Indian corn. A major domesticate of the New World.

mana Sacred force associated with Polynesian nobility, causing their persons to be taboo.

manifest function Reasons that people in a society give for a custom.

manioc Cassava, a tuber, abundant in South American tropical forests. Along with maize and white potatoes, it became one of the three major caloric staples of the aboriginal New World.

market principle One of three principles orienting exchange in different societies; identified by Karl Polanyi. Exchanges take place by purchase and sale, often involving social unequals, and are governed by the law of supply and demand. The market principle is dominant in the industrial West.

marriage Socially recognized relationship between a socially recognized male (the husband) and a socially recognized female (the wife) such that children born of their union are socially accepted as their offspring.

matrifocal Families or households that are headed by a woman *(mater),* with no permanently resident husband-father.

matrilateral cross cousin marriage Variant of generalized exchange in which men marry their mother's brother's daughter, and women marry their father's sister's son.

Maya Civilization which arose in the tropical lowlands of Mexico and Guatemala. Flourished in classic form between ca. 300 and 900 A.D.

mazeway Stands to the individual as culture does to the population; includes the entire set of cognitive maps, and of positive and negative goals that an individual maintains at a given time. Coined by Anthony F. C. Wallace.

Mesolithic The Middle Stone Age, transitional period between the Paleolithic and the Neolithic. Characteristic tool type was the microlith, small stone tool used for arrowheads, fish hooks, and sickles.

metropole Used by André Gunder Frank to refer to manufacturing and power centers of the world. In the past, these were capitals and ports of colonial nations. A city may serve as a metropole for the surrounding countryside, or a region may serve as a metropole for satellite regions.

Mexico, Valley of Highland area where Mexico City now stands. The site of Teotihuacan, great urban center of the Mesoamerican classic, and Tenochtitlan, capital of the Aztec Empire.

minimal pair Used by descriptive linguists to describe two phonologically similar words whose different meanings are conveyed by a single phonological contrast, for example, "pit" and "bit."

moiety One of two descent groups in a given population. Usually intermarries.

monocrop production Economies based on the cultivation of a single crop, which is specialized usually for sale.

monolatry Primary worship of a single deity.

monotheism Exclusive worship of a single, eternal, omniscient, omnipotent, and omnipresent deity.

morpheme Minimal meaningful form in a language.

multicentric economy Exchange system organized into spheres of exchange.

multilinear evolution Study of evolution of human society "along its many lines" through examination of specific evolutionary sequences. Associated with Julian Steward.

national character Constellation of personality attributes shared by all inhabitants of a nation.

natural selection Doctrine that nature—the sum total of natural forces associated with a specific environment—selects the forms most fit to survive and reproduce in that environment, and thus perpetuates those forms. Charles Darwin's major contribution to evolutionary theory.

Neolithic The New Stone Age, characterized by the grinding and polishing of stone tools.

network analysis Method of egocentric analysis. Social relationships are plotted for specific individuals and constitute their social networks. Networks are then compared for linking and overlapping.

Nilotes Populations including the Nuer, Dinka, and others which inhabit the upper Nile region of eastern Africa.

nonunilinear See *ambilineal.*

nuclear family Coresident group consisting of a married couple and their children. Also called elementary family or biological family.

office Permanent political status.

Omaha kinship terminology Manner of classifying kinsmen on ego's own generation; usually associated with patrilineal descent organization.

open peasant community Located in the lowlands of Latin America; populations represent admixtures of Indians, Europeans, and Africans. Noncorporate; members do not generally farm a joint estate. Not closed; flexibility in admitting new members.

Paleolithic Old Stone Age, traditionally divided into Lower (early), Middle, and Upper.

parallelism The development of traits or behavior patterns among related species or population because of adaption to similar natural selective forces and environments.

parallel cousins Children of siblings of the same sex.

participant interference Coined by Sol Tax to refer to the role of action anthropologists among the Fox Indians.

participant observation Common ethnographic technique, ethnographer participates in some of the events that he is observing and describing in an attempt to improve his rapport with his informants.

pastoral nomadism One of two variants of pastoralism. The entire population moves seasonally with its herds.

pastoralism Food-producing strategy of adaptation based on care of herds of domesticated animals.

pater Socially recognized father of a child, but not necessarily the genitor.

patrilateral parallel cousin marriage Marriage of the children of brothers.

peasant Rural inhabitant of archaic state.

personality Behavior or problem-solving techniques which have a high probability of use by one individual; thus defined by Anthony F. C. Wallace.

phenotype Outward appearance and behavior of an organism. Opposed to genotype.

phone Any speech sound.

phoneme Minimal sound contrasts that serve to distinguish meaning, as in minimal pairs. One of several categories within the phonemic system specific to any language.

phonology Study of the sound system of a language.

plural marriage Marriage involving more than two spouses.

polyandry Variety of plural marriage in which there is more than one husband.

Polynesia Large group of islands in the Pacific Ocean; included in a triangle with Hawaii to the north, Easter Island to the east, and New Zealand to the southwest.

polygamy Any marriage involving more than two spouses.

polygyny Marital relationship involving multiple wives.

Postclassic Period of empires and increasing militarism; in Sumeria began ca. 2500 B.C.; in Middle America, ca. 900 A.D.

pot irrigation Simple irrigation technique that led to early appearance of village farming communities in the Valley of Oaxaca and other highlands areas of Middle America. A high water table permitted early cultivators to dig holes, dip in pots, and pour water on their cultivated plants.

potlatch A festive event among certain Indians in which a sponsor, assisted by other members of his community, gave away or destroyed wealth items in return for prestige. Blowout.

practical anthropology Coined by Bronislaw Malinowski to refer to the use of anthropological findings and skills by colonial administrators and other "practical men."

primitive Populations with band or tribal organization.

primogeniture Inheritance rule which makes oldest child (usually oldest son) the only heir.

progeny price A gift from the groom and his kinsmen to the wife and her kinsmen prior to marriage. Legitimizes children born to the woman as members of the husband's descent group.

Protestant ethic World view associated with early ascetic Protestantism, which values hard and constant work as a sign of salvation. Concept developed by Max Weber.

psychogenic explanation Cultural variables viewed as delayed reactions to earlier experiences, most notably those of childhood; Raoul Naroll's explanation.

quipu Mnemonic device used for calculations in the central Andes.

recessive Gene which is phenotypically suppressed in heterozygous form.

reciprocity One of three principles of exchange identified by Karl Polanyi; governs exchange among social equals. The most characteristic mode of exchange in relatively egalitarian societies. Eventually grades into the market principle.

redistribution One of three principles of exchange identified by Karl Polanyi. Major exchange mode of chiefdoms, many archaic states and states with managed economies.

religion Human behavior involving belief and ritual and concerned with supernatural beings and forces.

rent fund Term used by anthropologist Eric Wolf to describe scarce resources which a subordinate is required to render to a superordinate.

replacement fund Term used by Eric Wolf to describe scarce resources which people invest in technology and other items essential to production and everyday ilfe.

research and development Approach to applied anthropology, as exemplified by the Vicos project; anthropologists learns from changes that they are promoting and test hypotheses about change against change as it actually occurs.

revitalization movements Movements which occur especially in times of rapid social change, in which religious leaders emerge and undertake to alter or revitalize a society.

rites of passage Culturally defined activities associated with the transition from one stage of life to another.

rural-urban continuum Used by Robert Redfield to describe progressive change in certain attitudes and features of social organization as people move from rural to urban communities.

satellite Subsidiary of metropole; may be fully political or principally economic; provides raw materials for consumption and manufacture in metropolitan center; usually economically and ecologically specialized to meet the needs of the metropole.

satellite states Weakly industrial or nonindustrial, internally stratified, economically specialized nations that are appendages of metropolitan nations.

schizoid view Attitude toward the role of the anthropologist set forth by Ralph Piddington; states that anthropologists may offer their skills to clients, but must scrupulously refrain from trying to set or influence policy.

segmentary lineage system Sociopolitical organization based on descent, usually patrilineal, in which individuals belong to multiple descent segments which form at different genealogical levels and function in different contexts.

serial monogamy Marriage of a given individual to several spouses, but not at the same time.

slash and burn Form of extensive horticulture in which the forest cover of a plot is cut down and burned prior to planting to allow the ashes to fertilize the soil.

social fund Investment of scarce resources to assist kinsmen, fictive kinsmen, affinals, or neighbors.

societas Term used by Lewis Henry Morgan to describe societies organized on the basis of kinship, marriage, and kinship-related institutions. Opposed to *civitas*.

sociolinguistics The study of variation in linguistic usage in different social contexts. Increasingly important area of anthropology and linguistics.

sororate Custom whereby a widower marries the sister of his deceased wife.

special-purpose money Currency which serves only one or two of the three functions associated with a general-purpose money.

species Population which consists of organisms capable of interbreeding and producing fertile and viable offspring who are themselves capable of producing fertile and viable offspring.

specific evolution Studies of formal changes in relationships over time between specific human populations and their environments.

speech community Total number of speakers of a given language or dialect.

spheres of exchange Exchangeable goods are organized into separate categories, and items within a given category are normally exchanged only for items within that category. Constitutes a multicentric economy.

state Form of sociopolitical organization whose principal function is preservation of general order and the order of socioeconomic stratification.

status A position in a social structure.

steppe Plain with few or no trees.

steward A representative of a chief.

stipulated descent Basis for clan membership. Clan members claim that they are descended from the same apical ancestor, but they do not trace the genealogical links between themselves and that ancestor.

strategic resources Resources necessary to sustain life, for example, food and water.

stratum One of two or more duosexual, multi-age groups which contrast in social status and economic prerogatives, including access to strategic resources.

subculture of poverty Coined by Oscar Lewis to describe a constellation of seventy social and psychological traits characteristic of the poor in many nations. Often shortened to "culture of poverty."

subgroups Those languages within a taxonomy

of related languages that are most closely related.

subsistence fund Term used by Eric Wolf to describe the fact that most people have to work to eat—to replace the calories they expend in everyday activities.

Sumeria Civilization which developed in southern Mesopotamia.

sumptuary goods Items whose consumption is specific to the life styles of chiefs, kings, and other members of the elite.

Tenochtitlan Capital of the Aztec Empire; located in the Valley of Mexico.

Teotihuacan Classic urban center in the Valley of Mexico with a population between 50,000 and 100,000; was the capital of a major Middle American empire.

totems Stipulated ancestors of human groups. Generally plants or animals; more rarely, inanimate objects.

transformism Doctrine that species have arisen gradually from other species over time. Same as evolution.

transhumance One of two variants of pastoralism; part of the population moves seasonally with the herds, while the rest remain in home villages.

tribe Form of sociopolitical organization generally based on horticulture or pastoralism, more rarely on foraging or agriculture. Socioeconomic stratification and centralized rule are absent in tribes, and there is no means of enforcing political decisions.

troop Basic unit of social organization among nonhuman primates.

tropics Zone bounded by the Tropic of Cancer to the north and the Tropic of Capricorn to the south. Extends for twenty degrees on each side of the equator.

unlineal Type of descent and descent group, either patrilineal or matrilineal. Children of descent group members of one sex are automatically included as descent group members, while children of members of the opposite sex are excluded.

unilineal evolution Doctrine claiming that ideally there are certain set stages through which all human societies must pass—for example, savagery, barbarism, and civilization.

utopic model of intervention Assumes that intervention is necessary to gain the acceptance of change and that results are best achieved by involving them; concerned with ends rather than means.

vertical groups Social divisions of complex societies which are limited to certain regions or settlements. Descent groups.

voiced Sound produced by vibration of the vocal cords; includes all vowels and many consonants.

voiceless Sound produced with no vibration of the vocal cords; includes many English consonants.

Index

ABOUT THE AUTHOR

CONRAD PHILLIP KOTTAK is Associate Professor of Anthropology at the University of Michigan, where he has taught since 1968. He received his Ph.D. from Columbia University in 1966. Between 1966 and 1967 he conducted fieldwork among the Betsileo of Madagascar. In 1973 he undertook ethnographic research on the social effects of modernization in northeastern Brazil. Author of the forthcoming *Ecology and Social Organization in Central Madagascar* and a coauthor, with Kent Flannery and Roy Rappaport, of *Matter, Energy, and Information: An Introduction to Ecological Anthropology*, Professor Kottak has contributed articles to journals including *Ethnology, American Anthropologist*, and *Comparative Studies in Society and History*. He is a Fellow of both the American Anthropological Association and the Royal Anthropological Institute of Great Britain and Ireland.

A NOTE ON THE TYPE

The text of this book was set in Palatino, a type face designed by the noted German typographer Hermann Zapf. Named after Giovanbattista Palatino, a writing master of Renaissance Italy, Palatino was the first of Zapf's type faces to be introduced to America. The first designs for the face were made in 1948, and the fonts for the complete face were issued between 1950 and 1952. Like all Zapf-designed type faces, Palatino is beautifully balanced and exceedingly readable.

Composed by Cherry Hill Composition, Pennsauken, New Jersey
Printed and bound by Halliday Lithograph Corp., West Hanover, Mass.